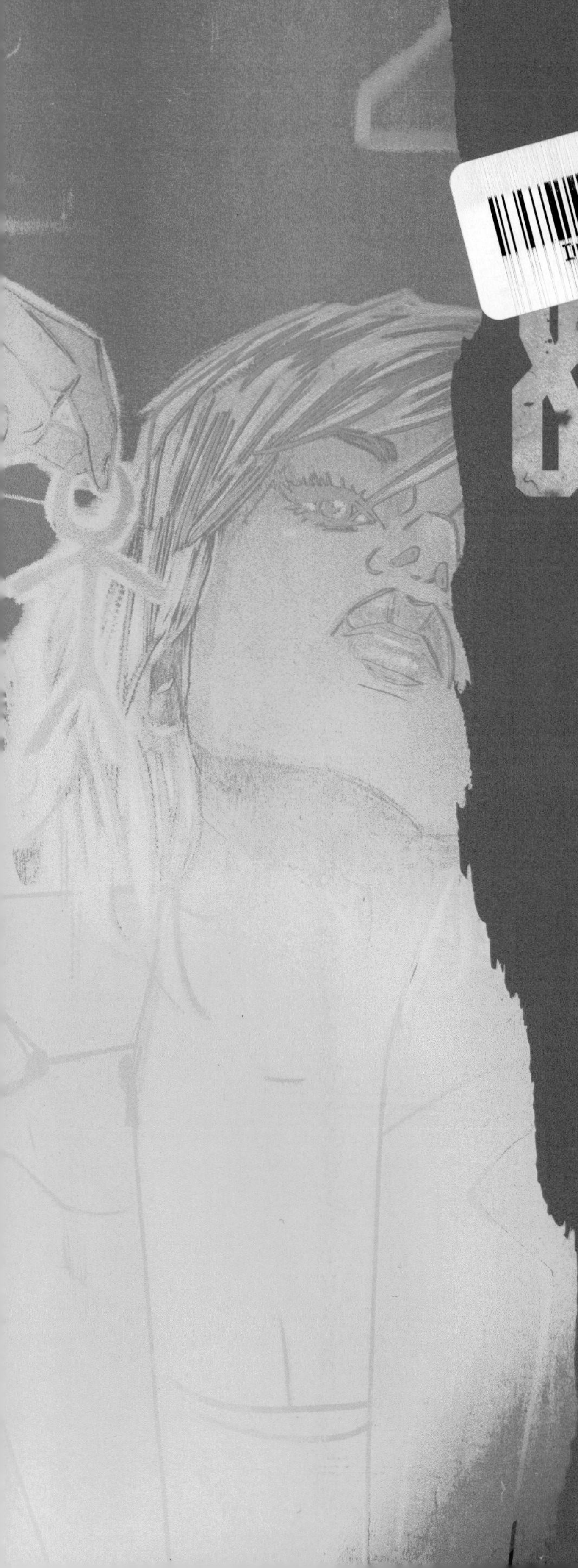

SLASH & BURN

SI SPENCER
Writer

MAX DUNBAR
Penciller

ANDE PARKS
Inker

NICK FILARDI
Colorist

TRAVIS LANHAM
Letterer

TULA LOTAY
Cover Art and
Original Series Covers

SLASH & BURN
created by
SI SPENCER, MAX DUNBAR
& ANDE PARKS

JAMIE S. RICH Editor – Original Series
MOLLY MAHAN Assistant Editor – Original Series
JEB WOODARD Group Editor – Collected Editions
SCOTT NYBAKKEN Editor – Collected Edition
STEVE COOK Design Director – Books
DAMIAN RYLAND Publication Design

SHELLY BOND VP & Executive Editor – Vertigo

DIANE NELSON President
DAN DIDIO AND JIM LEE Co-Publishers
GEOFF JOHNS Chief Creative Officer
AMIT DESAI Senior VP – Marketing & Global Franchise Management
NAIRI GARDINER Senior VP – Finance
SAM ADES VP – Digital Marketing
BOBBIE CHASE VP – Talent Development
MARK CHIARELLO Senior VP – Art, Design & Collected Editions
JOHN CUNNINGHAM VP – Content Strategy
ANNE DEPIES VP – Strategy Planning & Reporting
DON FALLETTI VP – Manufacturing Operations
LAWRENCE GANEM VP – Editorial Administration & Talent Relations
ALISON GILL Senior VP – Manufacturing & Operations
HANK KANALZ Senior VP – Editorial Strategy & Administration
JAY KOGAN VP – Legal Affairs
DEREK MADDALENA Senior VP – Sales & Business Development
JACK MAHAN VP – Business Affairs
DAN MIRON VP – Sales Planning & Trade Development
NICK NAPOLITANO VP – Manufacturing Administration
CAROL ROEDER VP – Marketing
EDDIE SCANNELL VP – Mass Account & Digital Sales
COURTNEY SIMMONS Senior VP – Publicity & Communications
JIM (SKI) SOKOLOWSKI VP – Comic Book Specialty & Newsstand Sales
SANDY YI Senior VP – Global Franchise Management

Logo design by TOM MULLER

SLASH & BURN

DC Comics
2900 West Alameda Avenue
Burbank, CA 91505
Printed in the USA. First Printing.
ISBN: 978-1-4012-6277-8

Library of Congress Cataloging-in-Publication Data is available.

PEFC Certified
Printed on paper from
sustainably managed
forests and controlled
sources
PEFC
PEFC/29-31-75   www.pefc.org

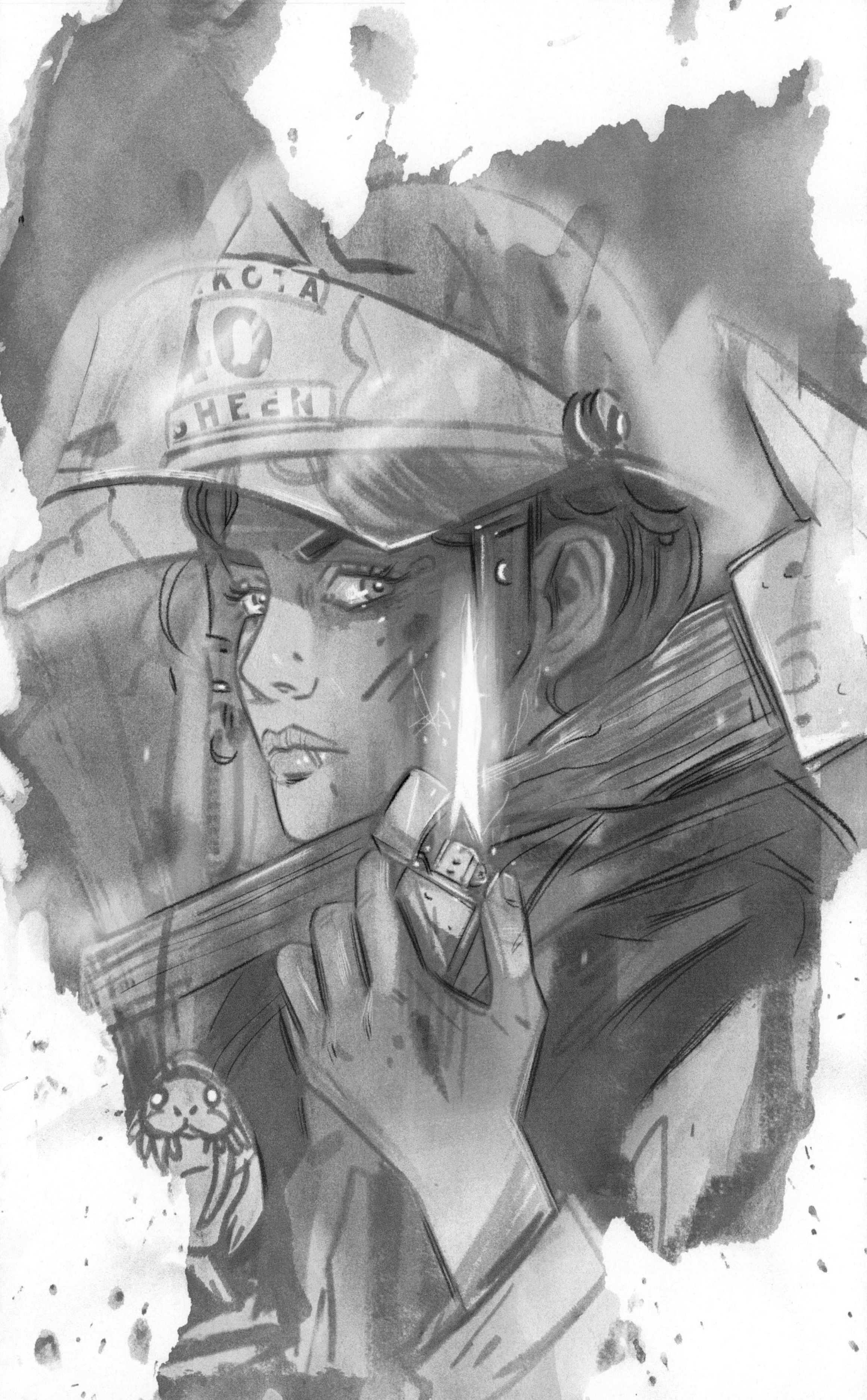

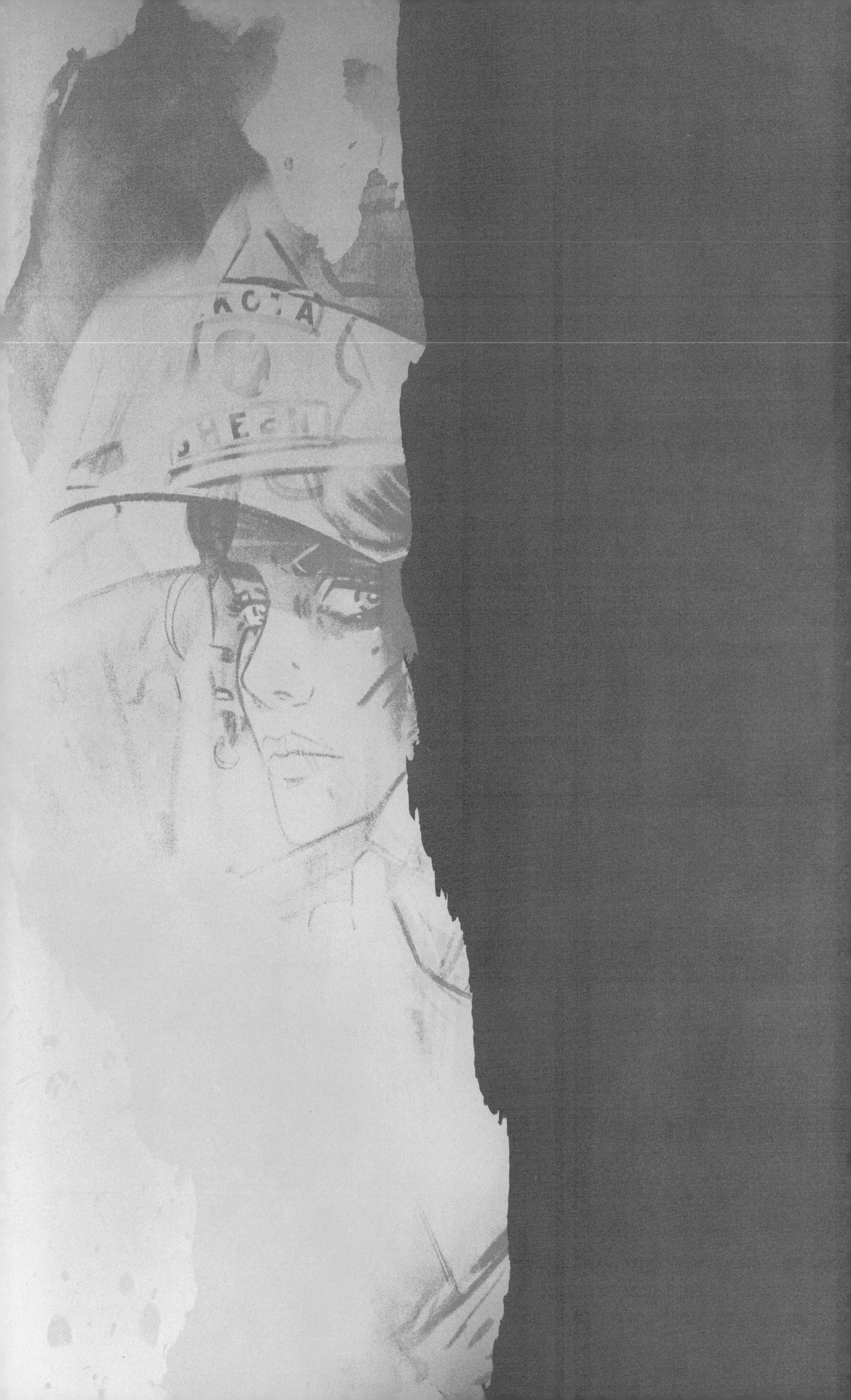

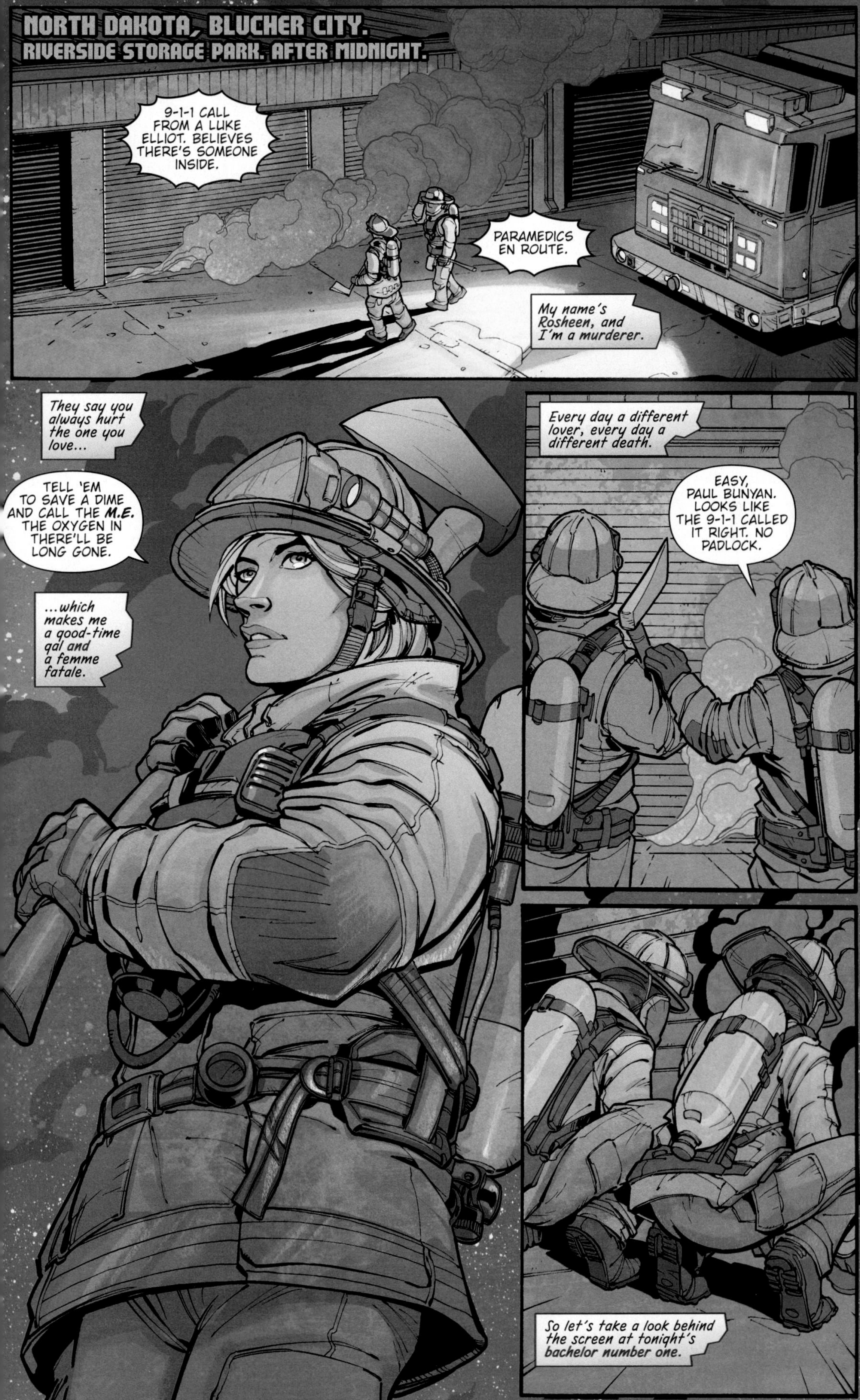
NORTH DAKOTA, BLUCHER CITY.
RIVERSIDE STORAGE PARK. AFTER MIDNIGHT.
9-1-1 CALL FROM A LUKE ELLIOT. BELIEVES THERE'S SOMEONE INSIDE.
PARAMEDICS EN ROUTE.
My name's Rosheen, and I'm a murderer.
They say you always hurt the one you love...
TELL 'EM TO SAVE A DIME AND CALL THE M.E. THE OXYGEN IN THERE'LL BE LONG GONE.
...which makes me a good-time gal and a femme fatale.
Every day a different lover, every day a different death.
EASY, PAUL BUNYAN. LOOKS LIKE THE 9-1-1 CALLED IT RIGHT. NO PADLOCK.
So let's take a look behind the screen at tonight's bachelor number one.

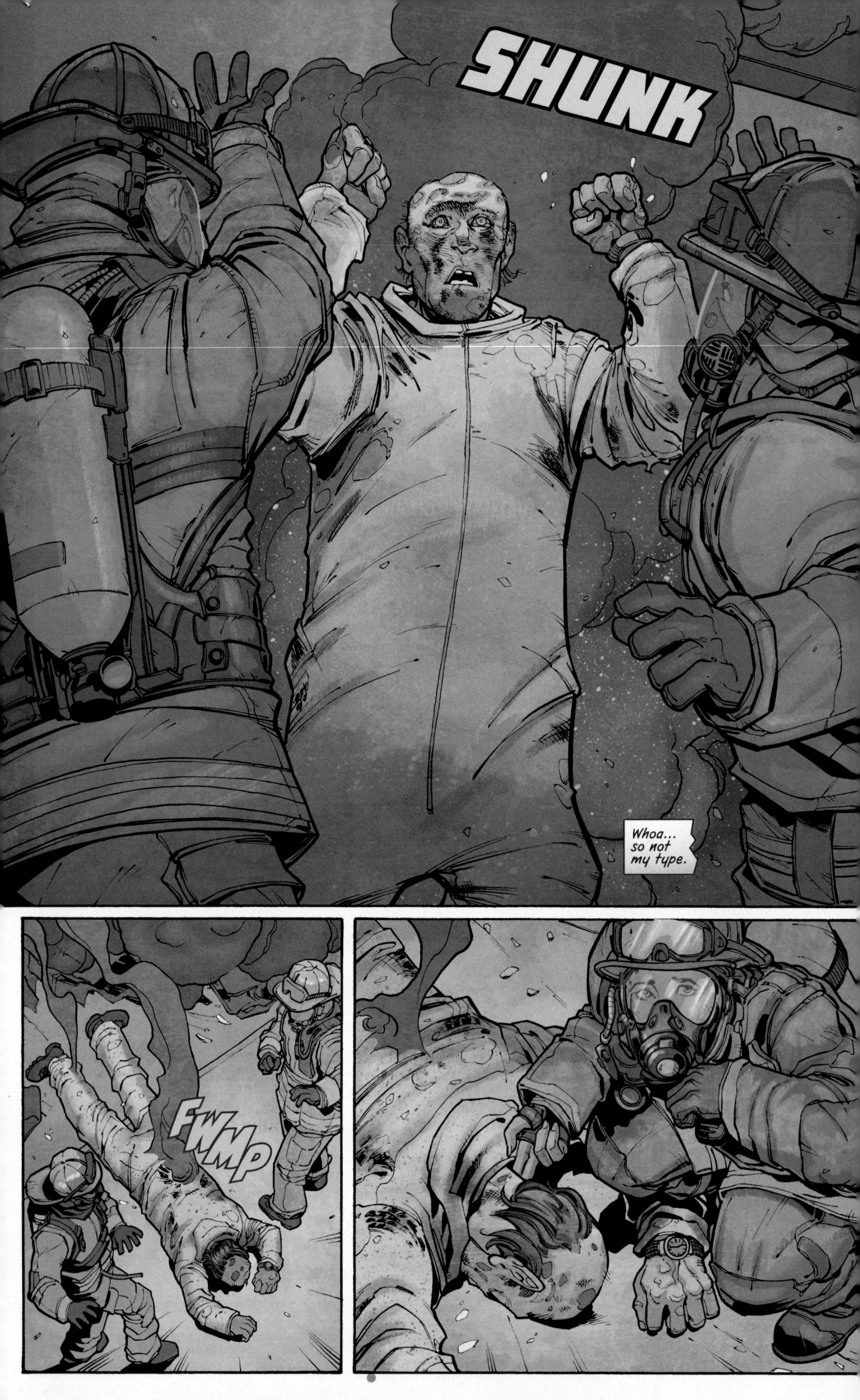
SHUNK
Whoa... so not my type.
FWMP

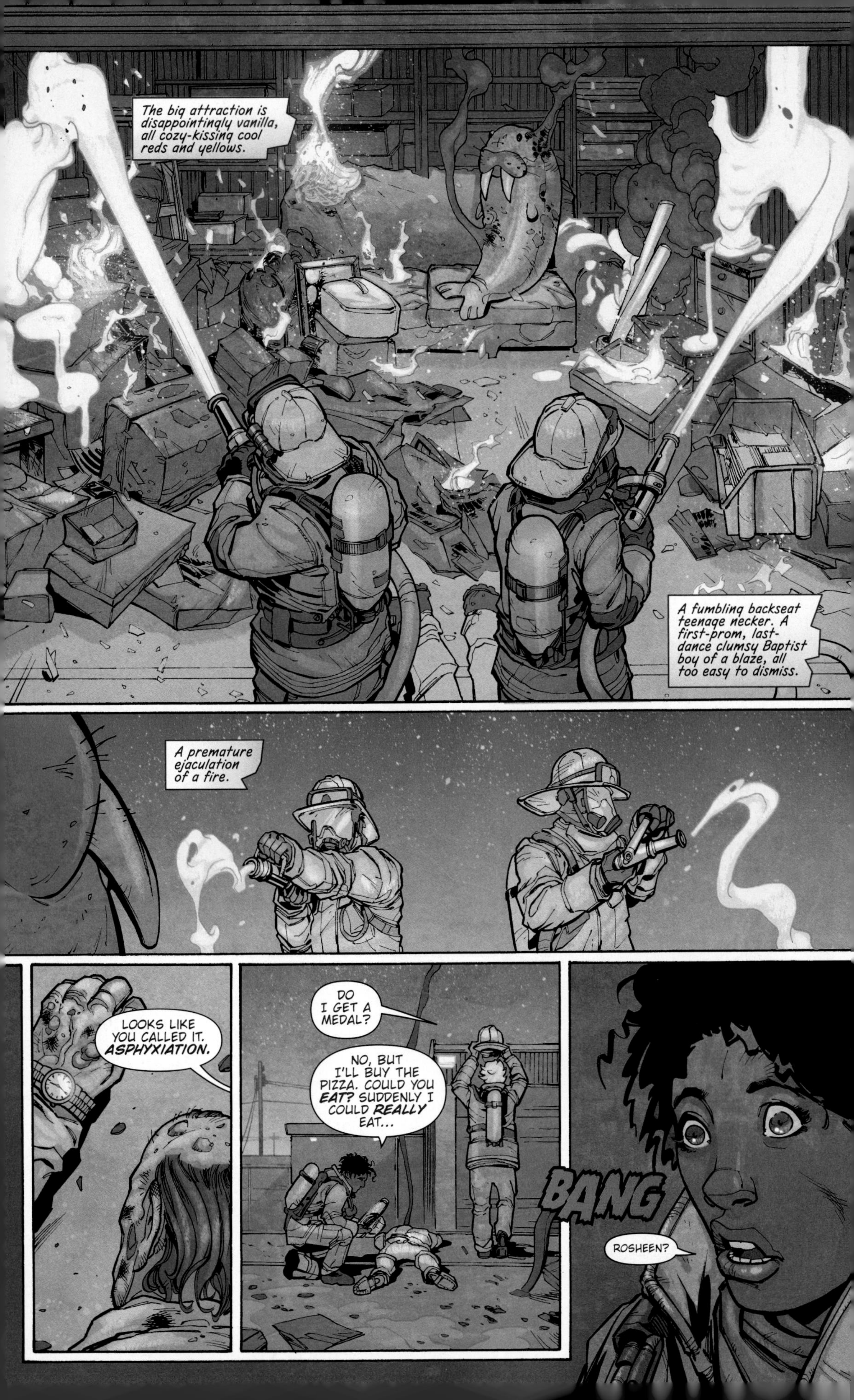
The big attraction is disappointingly vanilla, all cozy-kissing cool reds and yellows.
A fumbling backseat teenage necker. A first-prom, last-dance clumsy Baptist boy of a blaze, all too easy to dismiss.
A premature ejaculation of a fire.
LOOKS LIKE YOU CALLED IT. ASPHYXIATION.
DO I GET A MEDAL?
NO, BUT I'LL BUY THE PIZZA. COULD YOU EAT? SUDDENLY I COULD REALLY EAT...
BANG
ROSHEEN?

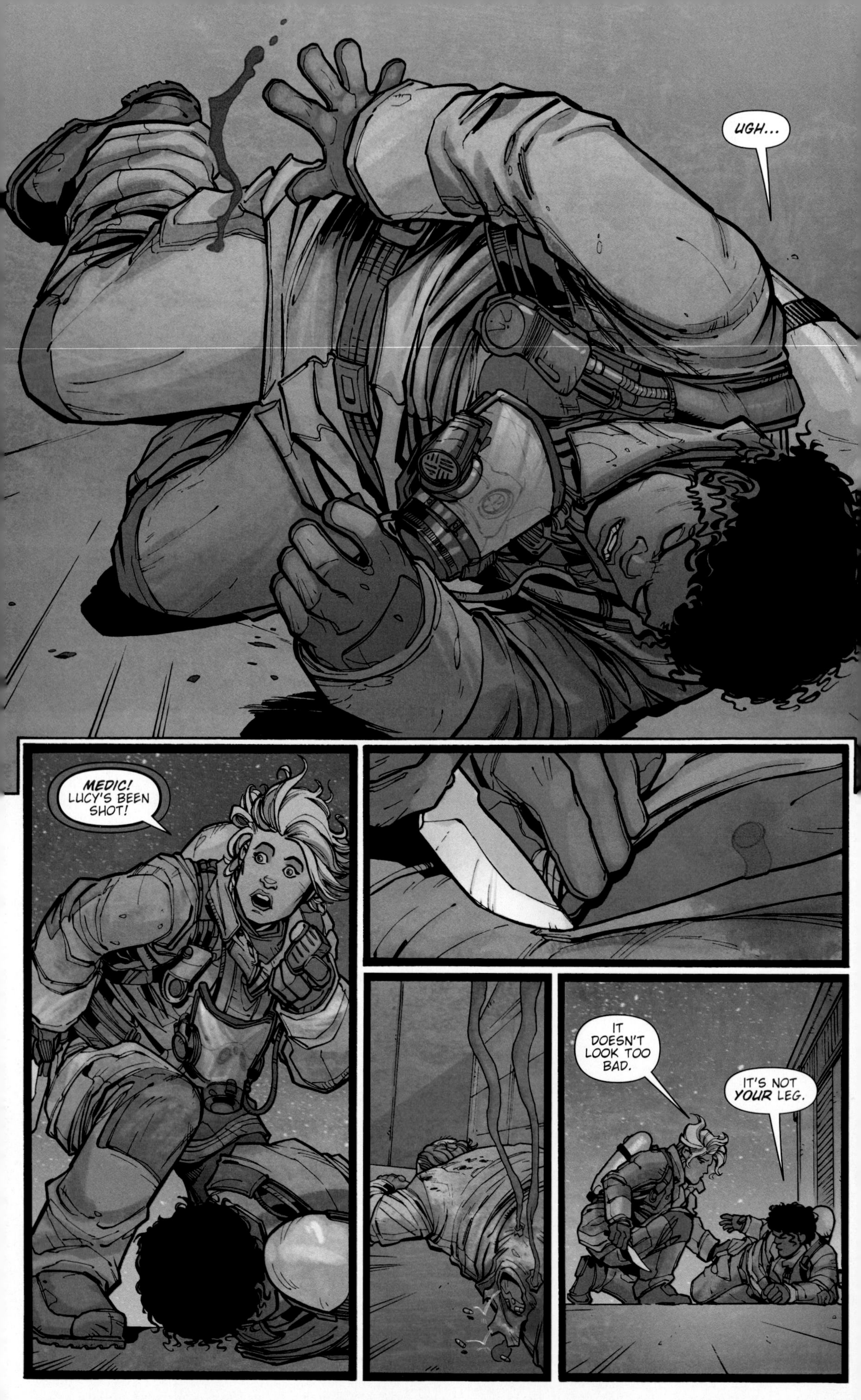
UGH...
MEDIC! LUCY'S BEEN SHOT!
IT DOESN'T LOOK TOO BAD.
IT'S NOT YOUR LEG.

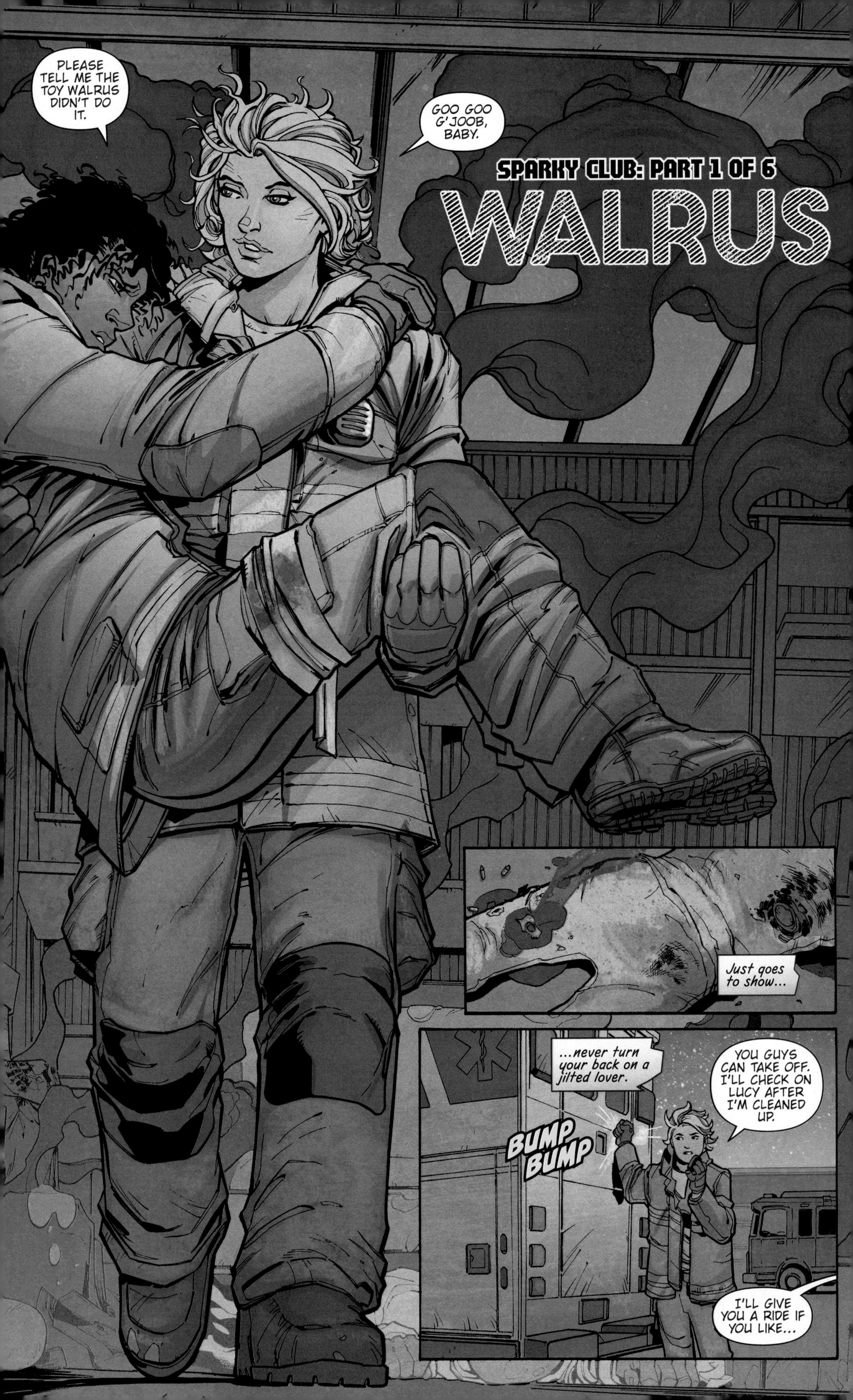
PLEASE TELL ME THE TOY WALRUS DIDN'T DO IT.
GOO GOO G'JOOB, BABY.
SPARKY CLUB: PART 1 OF 6
WALRUS
Just goes to show...
...never turn your back on a jilted lover.
BUMP BUMP
YOU GUYS CAN TAKE OFF. I'LL CHECK ON LUCY AFTER I'M CLEANED UP.
I'LL GIVE YOU A RIDE IF YOU LIKE...

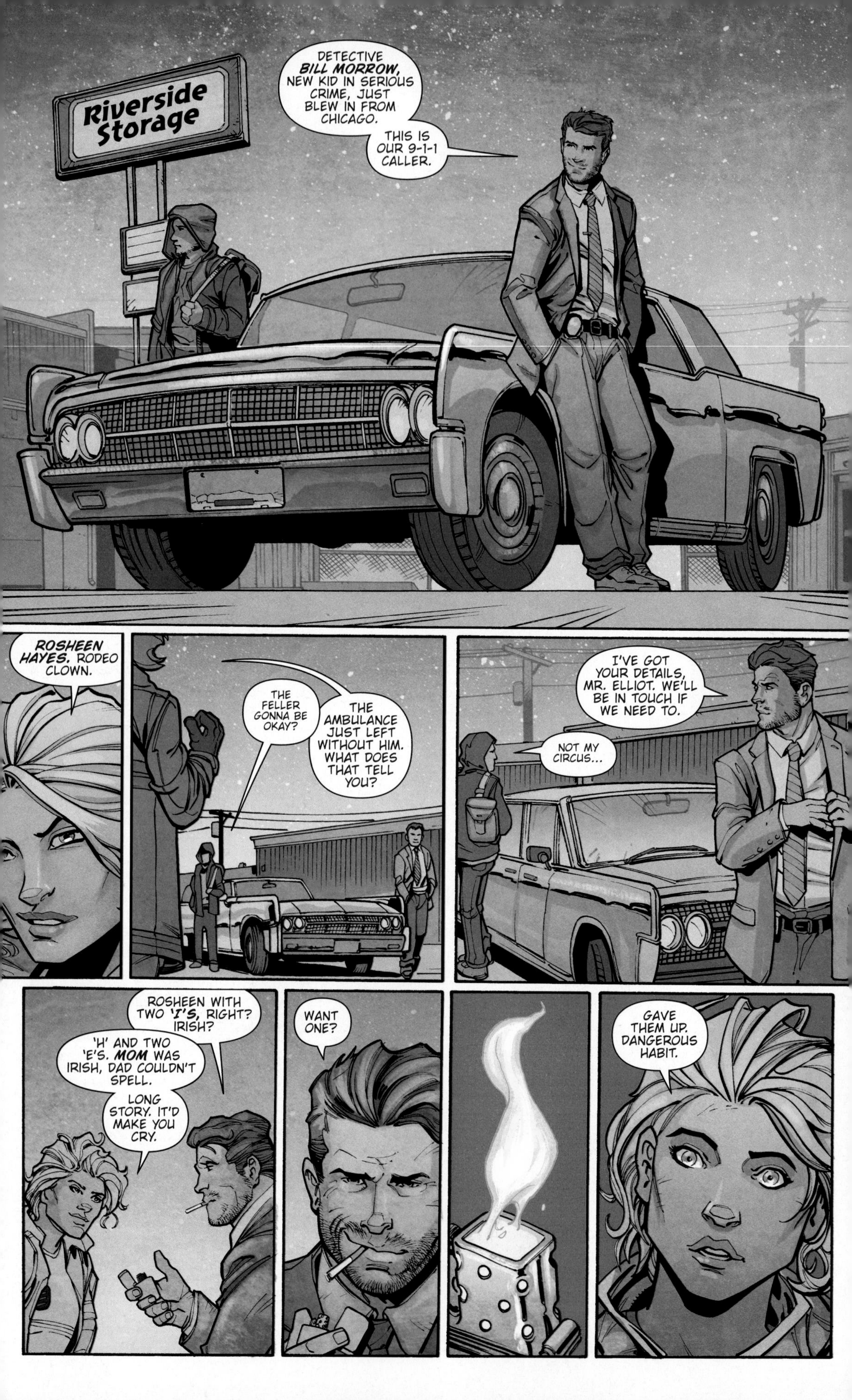
Riverside Storage
DETECTIVE BILL MORROW, NEW KID IN SERIOUS CRIME, JUST BLEW IN FROM CHICAGO.
THIS IS OUR 9-1-1 CALLER.
ROSHEEN HAYES. RODEO CLOWN.
THE FELLER GONNA BE OKAY?
THE AMBULANCE JUST LEFT WITHOUT HIM. WHAT DOES THAT TELL YOU?
I'VE GOT YOUR DETAILS, MR. ELLIOT. WE'LL BE IN TOUCH IF WE NEED TO.
NOT MY CIRCUS...
ROSHEEN WITH TWO 'I'S, RIGHT? IRISH?
'H' AND TWO 'E'S. MOM WAS IRISH, DAD COULDN'T SPELL.
LONG STORY. IT'D MAKE YOU CRY.
WANT ONE?
GAVE THEM UP. DANGEROUS HABIT.

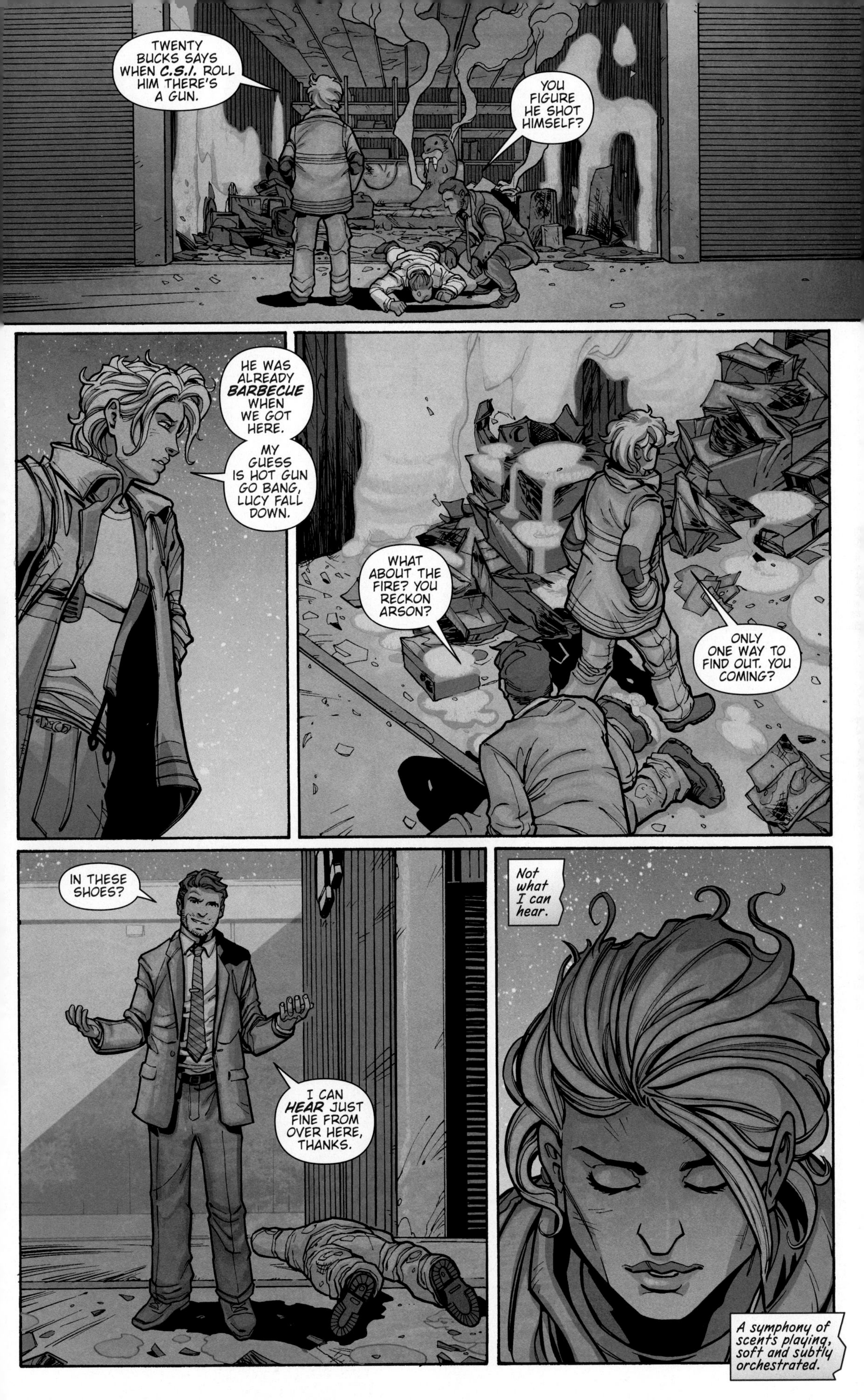
TWENTY BUCKS SAYS WHEN C.S.I. ROLL HIM THERE'S A GUN.
YOU FIGURE HE SHOT HIMSELF?
HE WAS ALREADY BARBECUE WHEN WE GOT HERE.
MY GUESS IS HOT GUN GO BANG, LUCY FALL DOWN.
WHAT ABOUT THE FIRE? YOU RECKON ARSON?
ONLY ONE WAY TO FIND OUT. YOU COMING?
IN THESE SHOES?
I CAN HEAR JUST FINE FROM OVER HERE, THANKS.
Not what I can hear.
A symphony of scents playing, soft and subtly orchestrated.

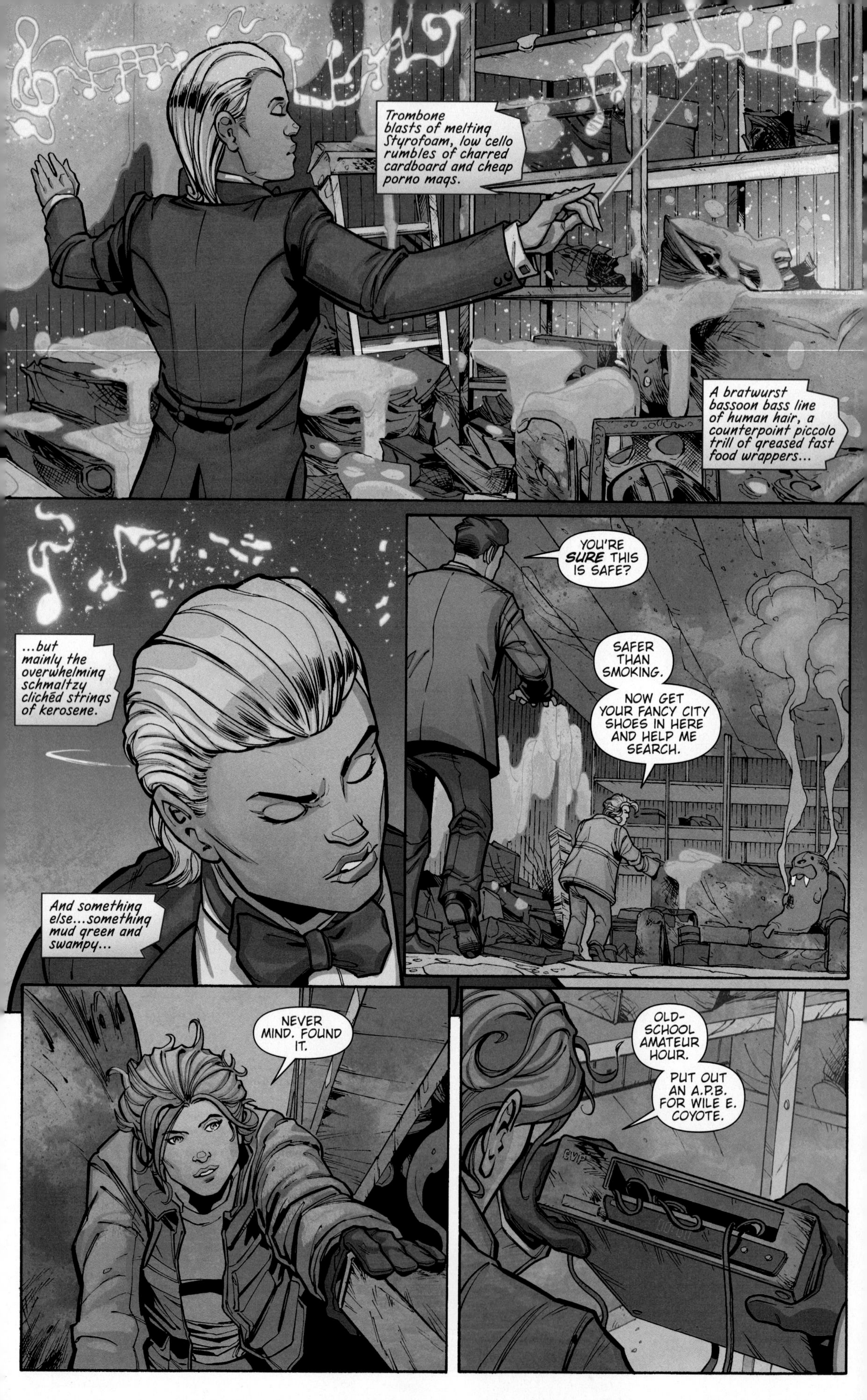
Trombone blasts of melting Styrofoam, low cello rumbles of charred cardboard and cheap porno mags.
A bratwurst bassoon bass line of human hair, a counterpoint piccolo trill of greased fast food wrappers...
...but mainly the overwhelming schmaltzy clichéd strings of kerosene.
And something else...something mud green and swampy...
YOU'RE SURE THIS IS SAFE?
SAFER THAN SMOKING.
NOW GET YOUR FANCY CITY SHOES IN HERE AND HELP ME SEARCH.
NEVER MIND. FOUND IT.
OLD-SCHOOL AMATEUR HOUR.
PUT OUT AN A.P.B. FOR WILE E. COYOTE.

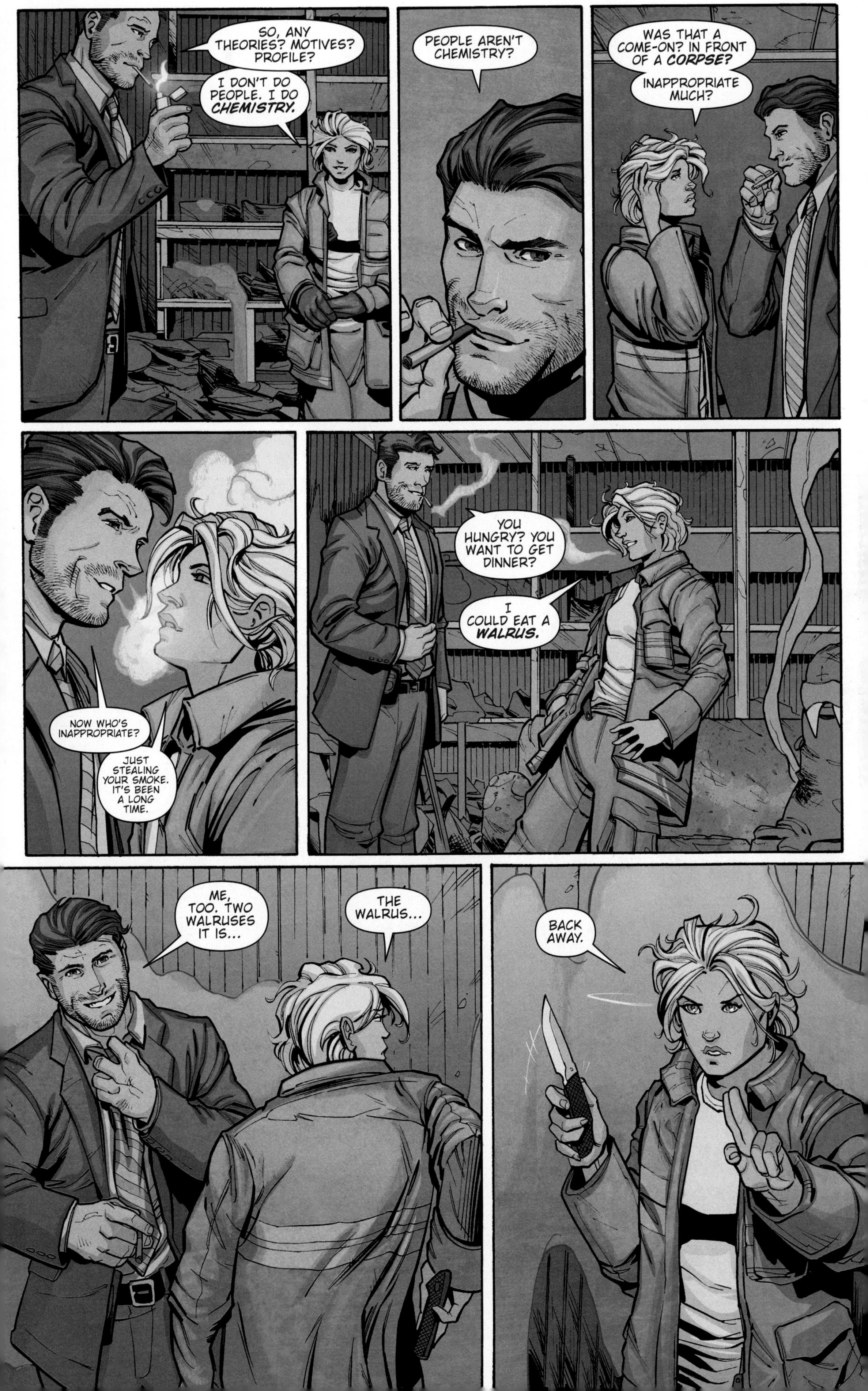
SO, ANY THEORIES? MOTIVES? PROFILE?
I DON'T DO PEOPLE. I DO CHEMISTRY.
PEOPLE AREN'T CHEMISTRY?
WAS THAT A COME-ON? IN FRONT OF A CORPSE?
INAPPROPRIATE MUCH?
NOW WHO'S INAPPROPRIATE?
JUST STEALING YOUR SMOKE. IT'S BEEN A LONG TIME.
YOU HUNGRY? YOU WANT TO GET DINNER?
I COULD EAT A WALRUS.
ME, TOO. TWO WALRUSES IT IS...
THE WALRUS...
BACK AWAY.

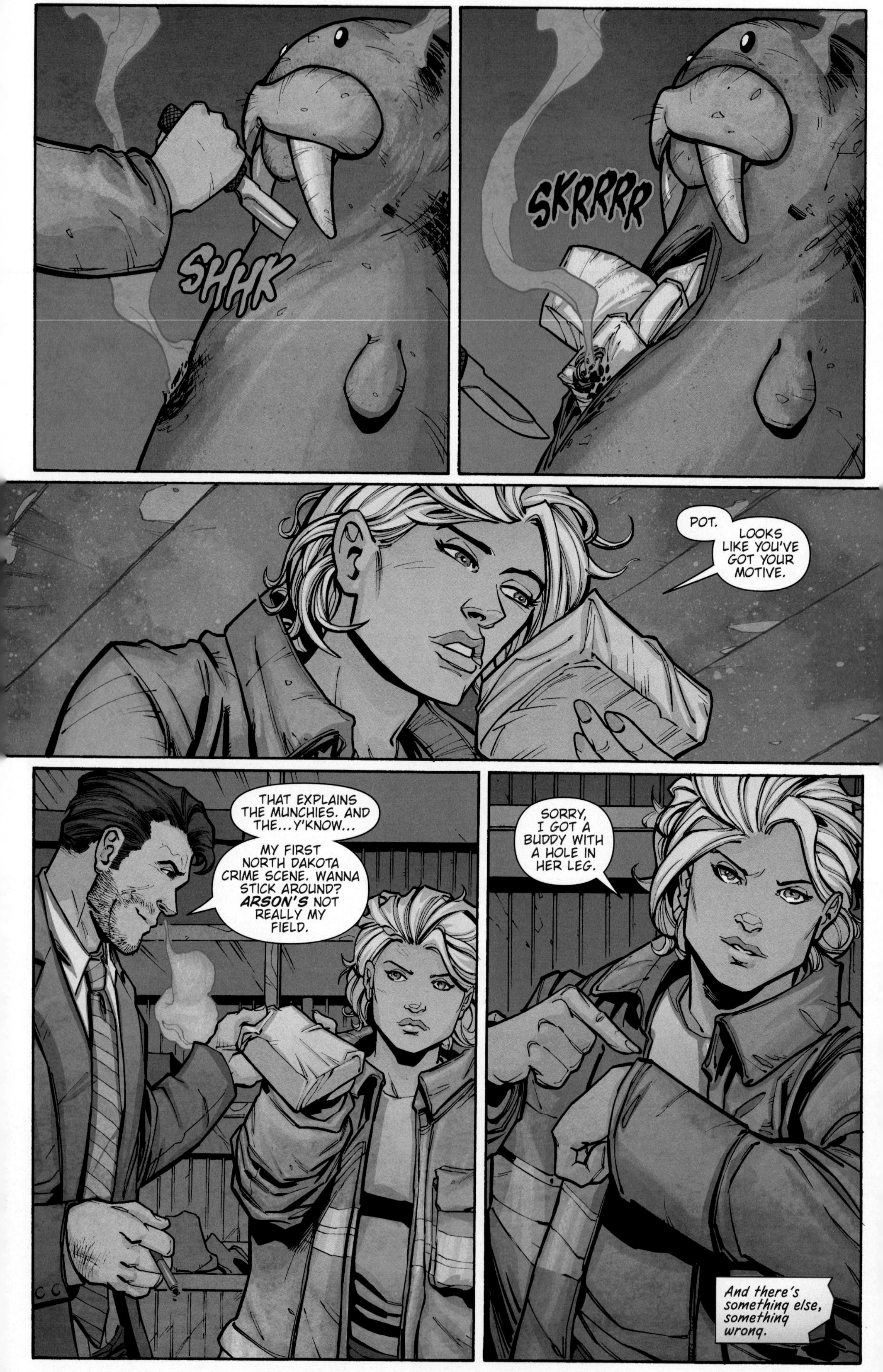
SHHK
SKRRRR
POT.
LOOKS LIKE YOU'VE GOT YOUR MOTIVE.
THAT EXPLAINS THE MUNCHIES. AND THE...Y'KNOW...
MY FIRST NORTH DAKOTA CRIME SCENE. WANNA STICK AROUND? ARSON'S NOT REALLY MY FIELD.
SORRY, I GOT A BUDDY WITH A HOLE IN HER LEG.
And there's something else, something wrong.

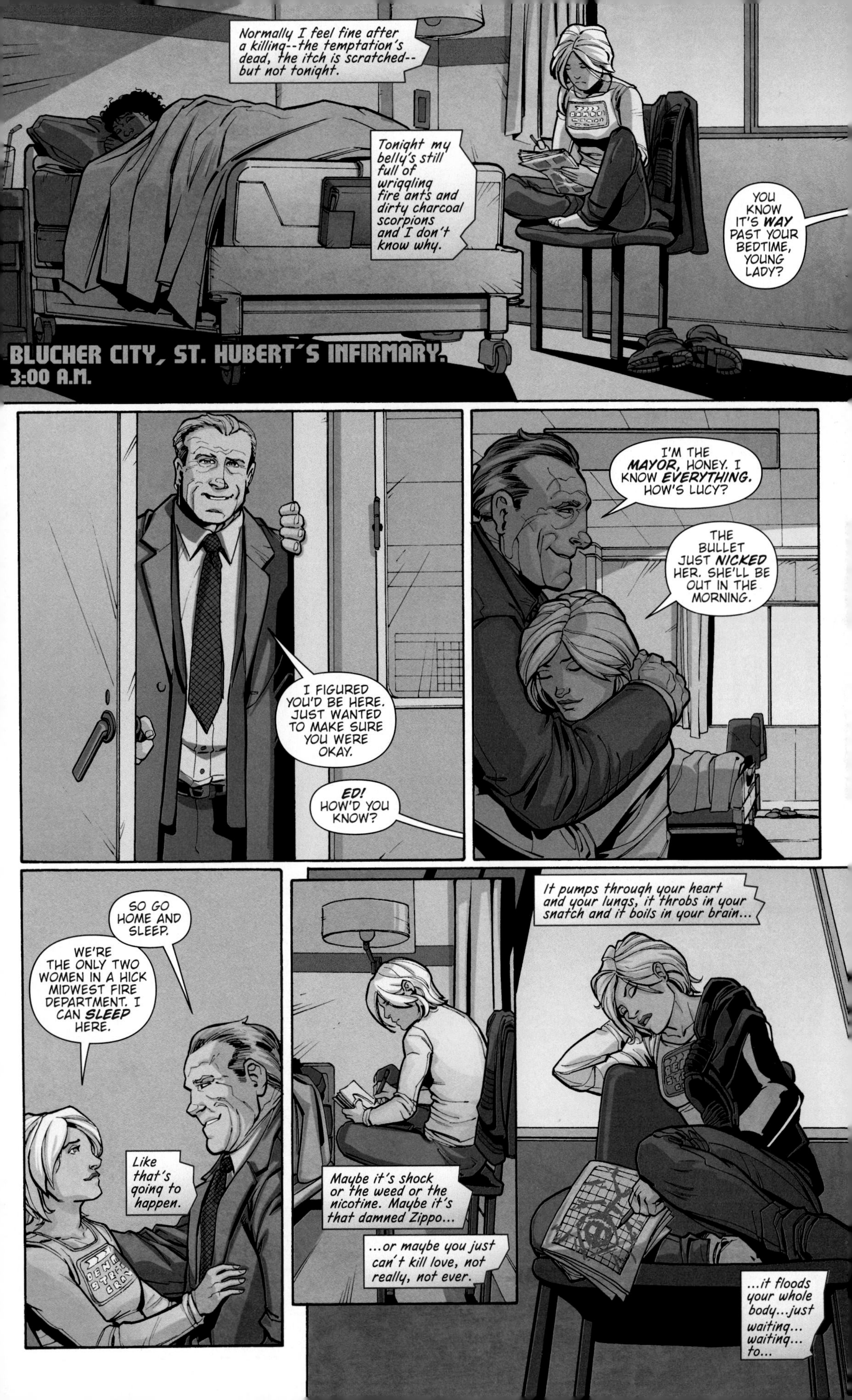
Normally I feel fine after a killing--the temptation's dead, the itch is scratched--but not tonight.
Tonight my belly's still full of wriggling fire ants and dirty charcoal scorpions and I don't know why.
BLUCHER CITY, ST. HUBERT´S INFIRMARY. 3:00 A.M.
YOU KNOW IT'S WAY PAST YOUR BEDTIME, YOUNG LADY?
I FIGURED YOU'D BE HERE. JUST WANTED TO MAKE SURE YOU WERE OKAY.
ED! HOW'D YOU KNOW?
I'M THE MAYOR, HONEY. I KNOW EVERYTHING. HOW'S LUCY?
THE BULLET JUST NICKED HER. SHE'LL BE OUT IN THE MORNING.
SO GO HOME AND SLEEP.
WE'RE THE ONLY TWO WOMEN IN A HICK MIDWEST FIRE DEPARTMENT. I CAN SLEEP HERE.
Like that's going to happen.
Maybe it's shock or the weed or the nicotine. Maybe it's that damned Zippo...
...or maybe you just can't kill love, not really, not ever.
It pumps through your heart and your lungs, it throbs in your snatch and it boils in your brain...
...it floods your whole body...just waiting... waiting... to...

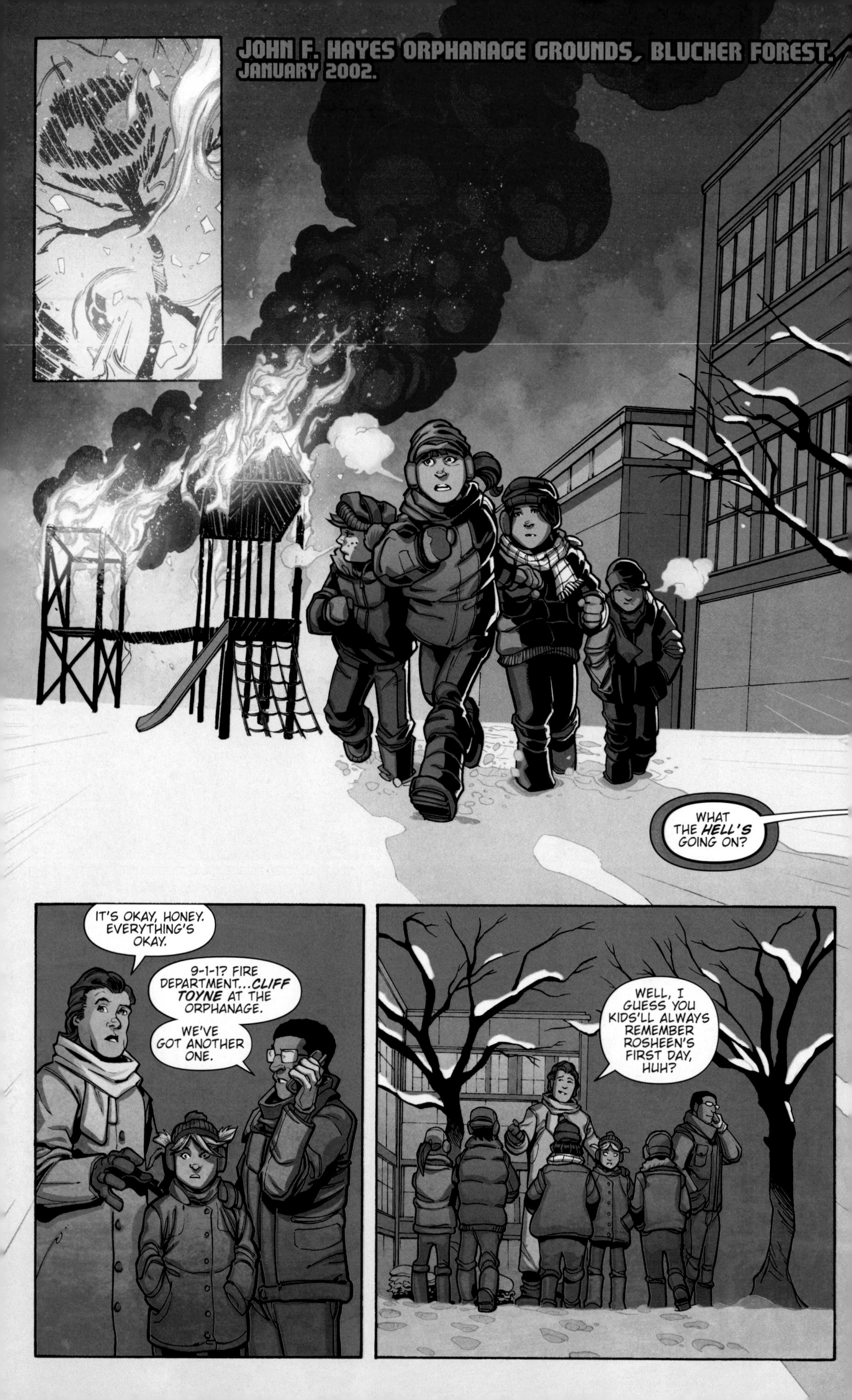
JOHN F. HAYES ORPHANAGE GROUNDS, BLUCHER FOREST. JANUARY 2002.
WHAT THE HELL'S GOING ON?
IT'S OKAY, HONEY. EVERYTHING'S OKAY.
9-1-1? FIRE DEPARTMENT... CLIFF TOYNE AT THE ORPHANAGE.
WE'VE GOT ANOTHER ONE.
WELL, I GUESS YOU KIDS'LL ALWAYS REMEMBER ROSHEEN'S FIRST DAY, HUH?

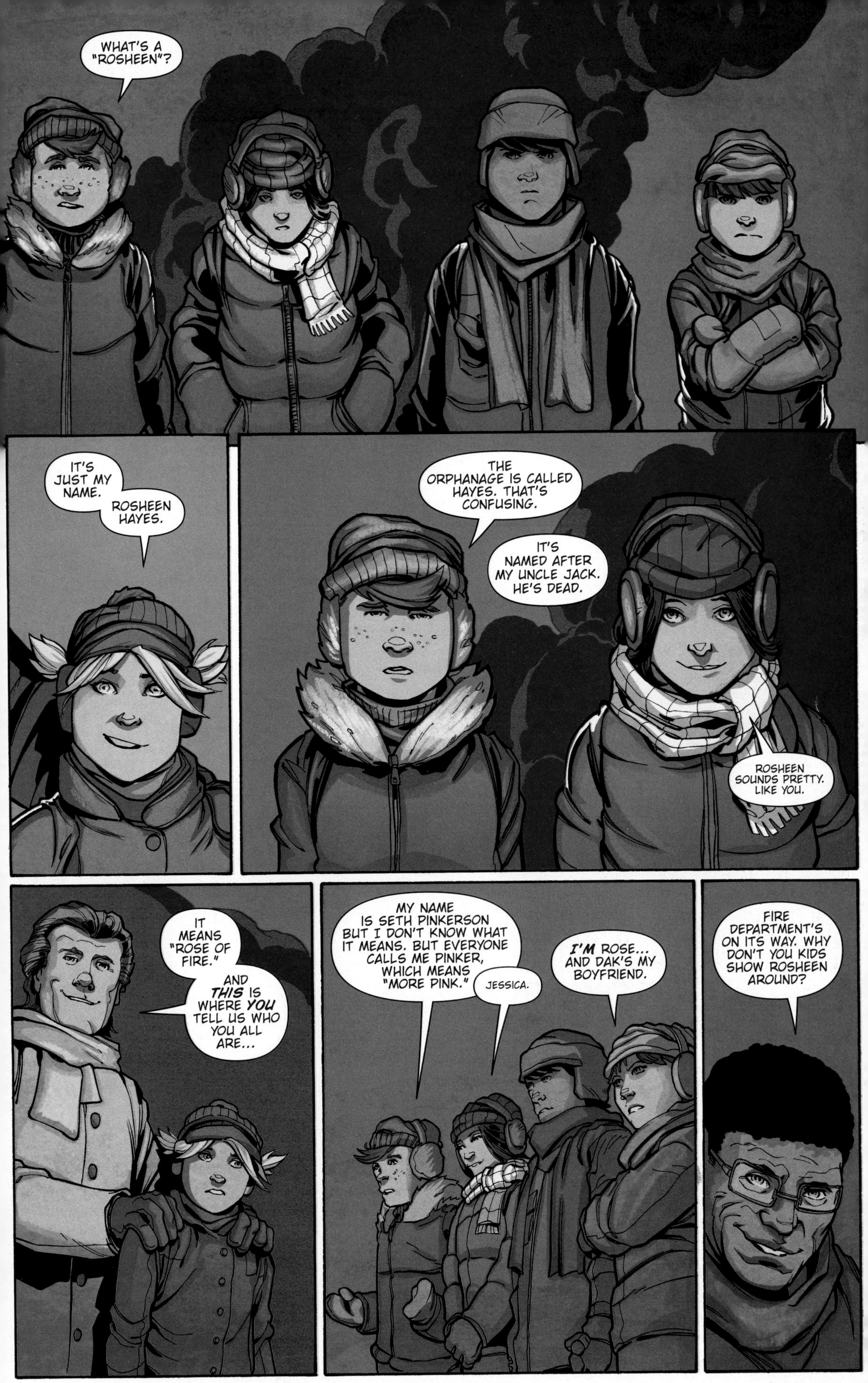

WHAT'S A "ROSHEEN"?
IT'S JUST MY NAME.
ROSHEEN HAYES.
THE ORPHANAGE IS CALLED HAYES. THAT'S CONFUSING.
IT'S NAMED AFTER MY UNCLE JACK. HE'S DEAD.
ROSHEEN SOUNDS PRETTY. LIKE YOU.
IT MEANS "ROSE OF FIRE."
AND *THIS* IS WHERE *YOU* TELL US WHO YOU ALL ARE...
MY NAME IS SETH PINKERSON BUT I DON'T KNOW WHAT IT MEANS. BUT EVERYONE CALLS ME PINKER, WHICH MEANS "MORE PINK."
JESSICA.
I'M ROSE... AND DAK'S MY BOYFRIEND.
FIRE DEPARTMENT'S ON ITS WAY. WHY DON'T YOU KIDS SHOW ROSHEEN AROUND?

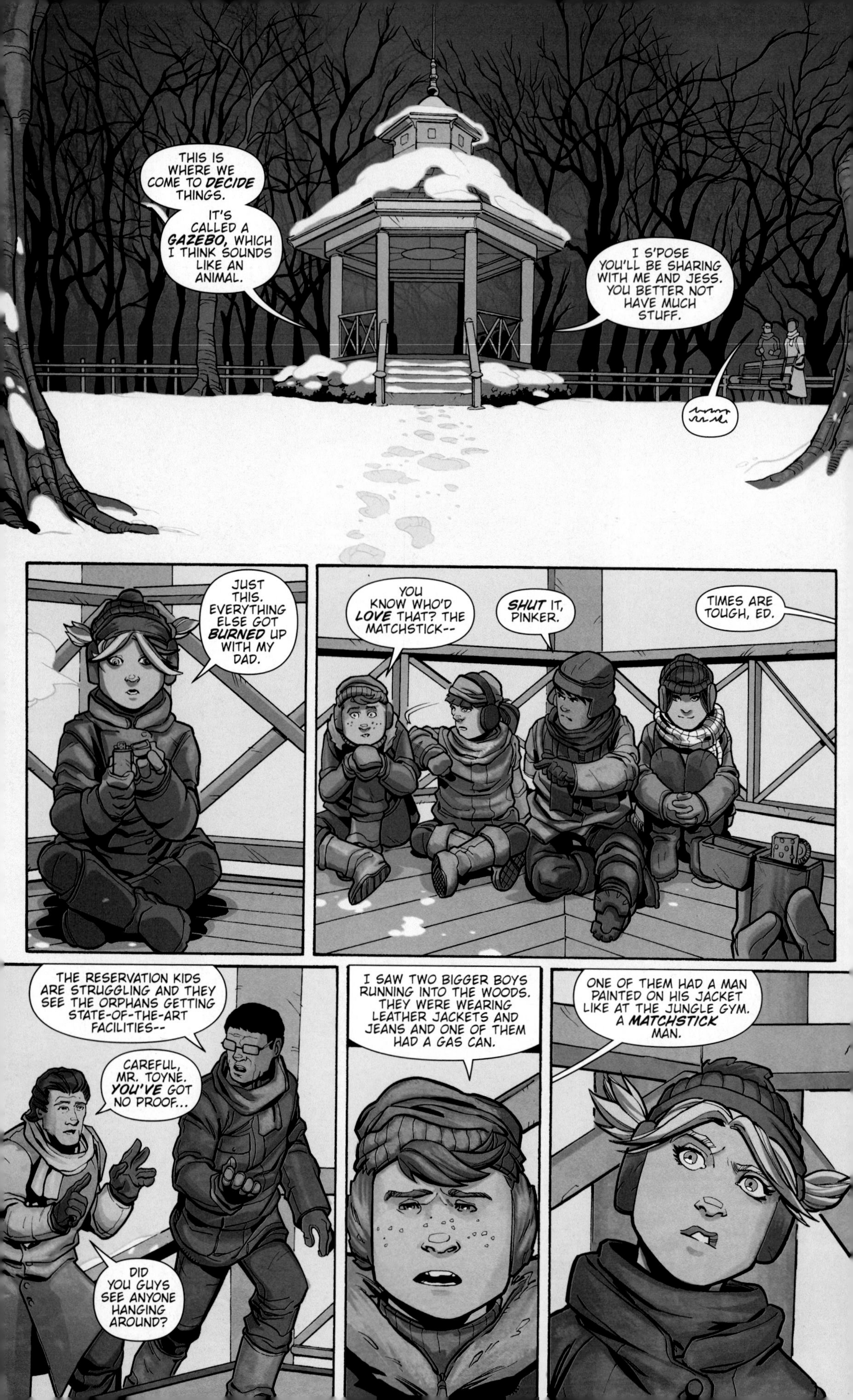
THIS IS WHERE WE COME TO DECIDE THINGS.
IT'S CALLED A GAZEBO, WHICH I THINK SOUNDS LIKE AN ANIMAL.
I S'POSE YOU'LL BE SHARING WITH ME AND JESS. YOU BETTER NOT HAVE MUCH STUFF.
JUST THIS. EVERYTHING ELSE GOT BURNED UP WITH MY DAD.
YOU KNOW WHO'D LOVE THAT? THE MATCHSTICK--
SHUT IT, PINKER.
TIMES ARE TOUGH, ED.
THE RESERVATION KIDS ARE STRUGGLING AND THEY SEE THE ORPHANS GETTING STATE-OF-THE-ART FACILITIES--
CAREFUL, MR. TOYNE. YOU'VE GOT NO PROOF...
DID YOU GUYS SEE ANYONE HANGING AROUND?
I SAW TWO BIGGER BOYS RUNNING INTO THE WOODS. THEY WERE WEARING LEATHER JACKETS AND JEANS AND ONE OF THEM HAD A GAS CAN.
ONE OF THEM HAD A MAN PAINTED ON HIS JACKET LIKE AT THE JUNGLE GYM. A MATCHSTICK MAN.

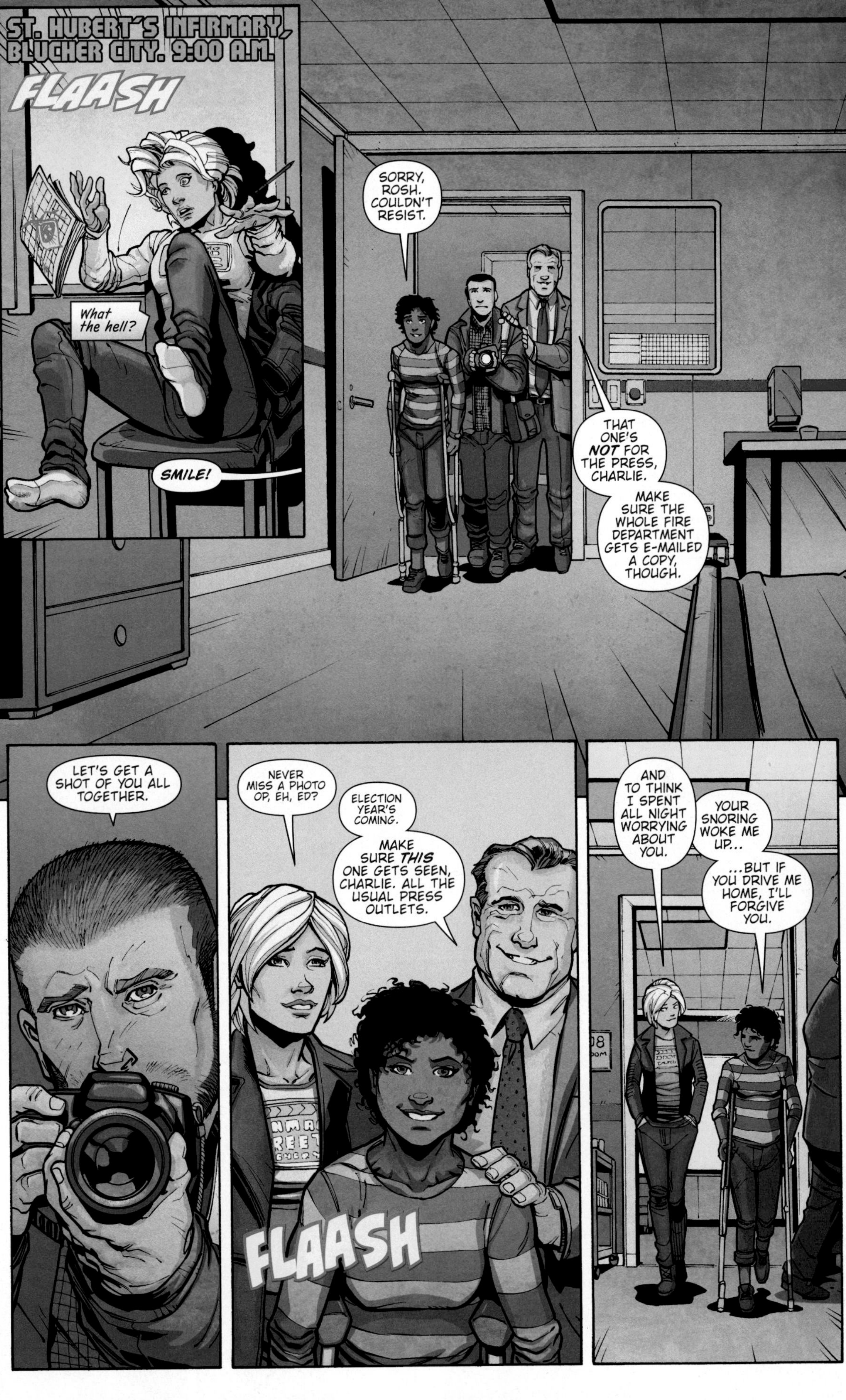

ST. HUBERT'S INFIRMARY, BLUCHER CITY. 9:00 A.M.
FLAASH
What the hell?
SMILE!
SORRY, ROSH. COULDN'T RESIST.
THAT ONE'S NOT FOR THE PRESS, CHARLIE.
MAKE SURE THE WHOLE FIRE DEPARTMENT GETS E-MAILED A COPY, THOUGH.
LET'S GET A SHOT OF YOU ALL TOGETHER.
NEVER MISS A PHOTO OP, EH, ED?
ELECTION YEAR'S COMING.
MAKE SURE THIS ONE GETS SEEN, CHARLIE. ALL THE USUAL PRESS OUTLETS.
FLAASH
AND TO THINK I SPENT ALL NIGHT WORRYING ABOUT YOU.
YOUR SNORING WOKE ME UP...
...BUT IF YOU DRIVE ME HOME, I'LL FORGIVE YOU.

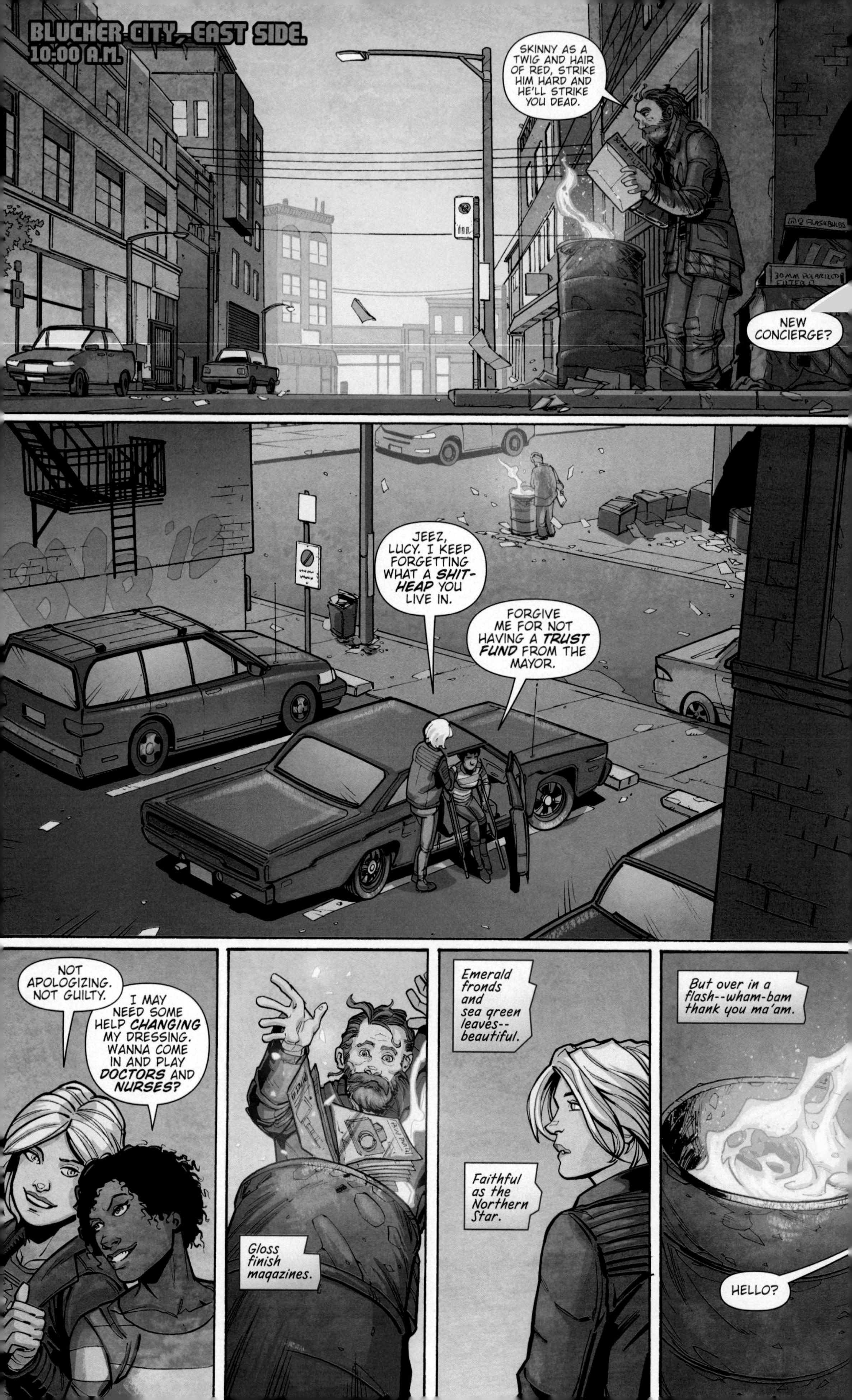
BLUCHER CITY, EAST SIDE.
10:00 A.M.
SKINNY AS A TWIG AND HAIR OF RED, STRIKE HIM HARD AND HE'LL STRIKE YOU DEAD.
NEW CONCIERGE?
JEEZ, LUCY. I KEEP FORGETTING WHAT A SHIT-HEAP YOU LIVE IN.
FORGIVE ME FOR NOT HAVING A TRUST FUND FROM THE MAYOR.
NOT APOLOGIZING. NOT GUILTY.
I MAY NEED SOME HELP CHANGING MY DRESSING. WANNA COME IN AND PLAY DOCTORS AND NURSES?
Gloss finish magazines.
Emerald fronds and sea green leaves--beautiful.
Faithful as the Northern Star.
But over in a flash--wham-bam thank you ma'am.
HELLO?

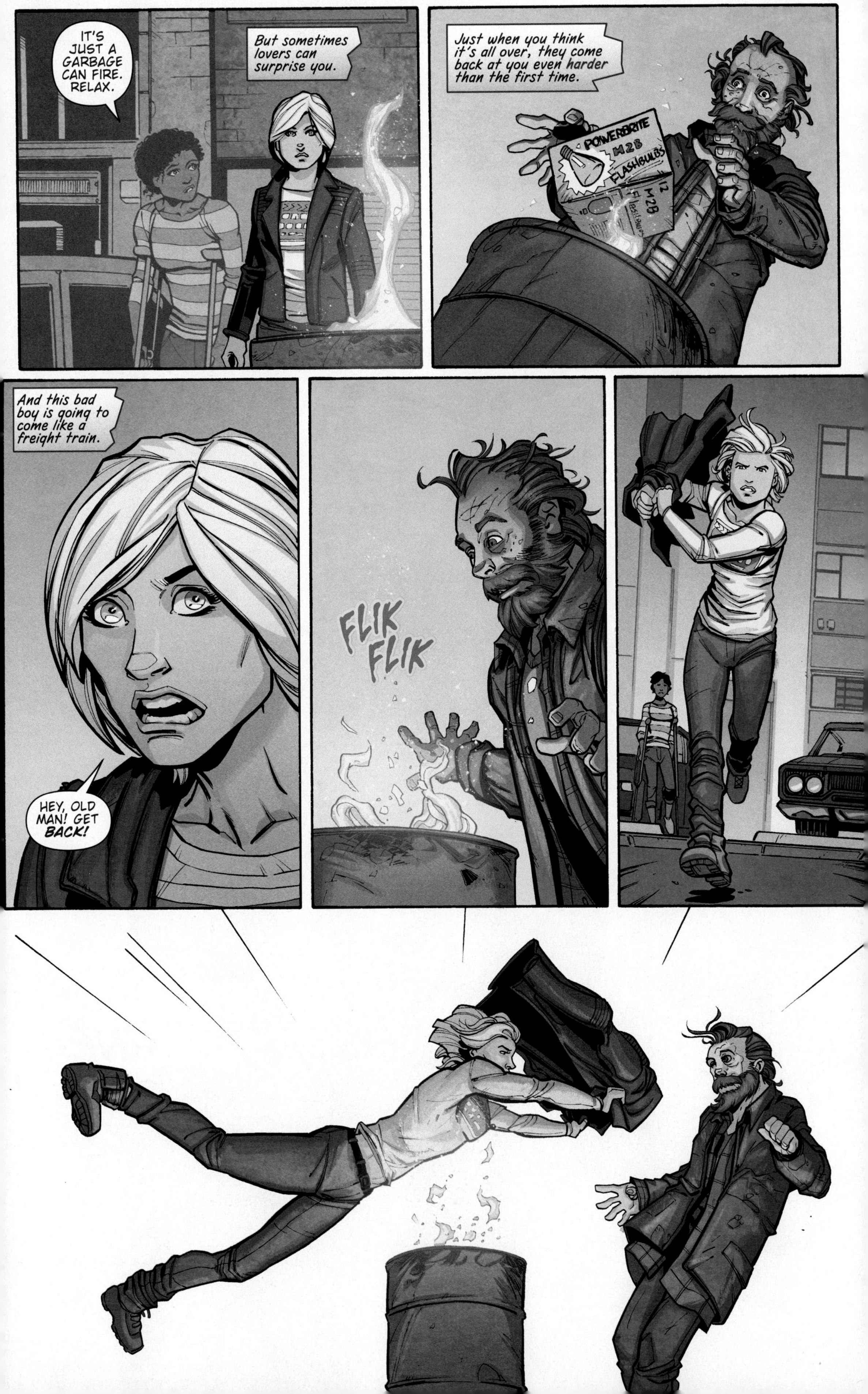
IT'S JUST A GARBAGE CAN FIRE. RELAX.
But sometimes lovers can surprise you.
Just when you think it's all over, they come back at you even harder than the first time.
POWERBRITE M2B FLASHBULBS
And this bad boy is going to come like a freight train.
HEY, OLD MAN! GET BACK!
FLIK FLIK

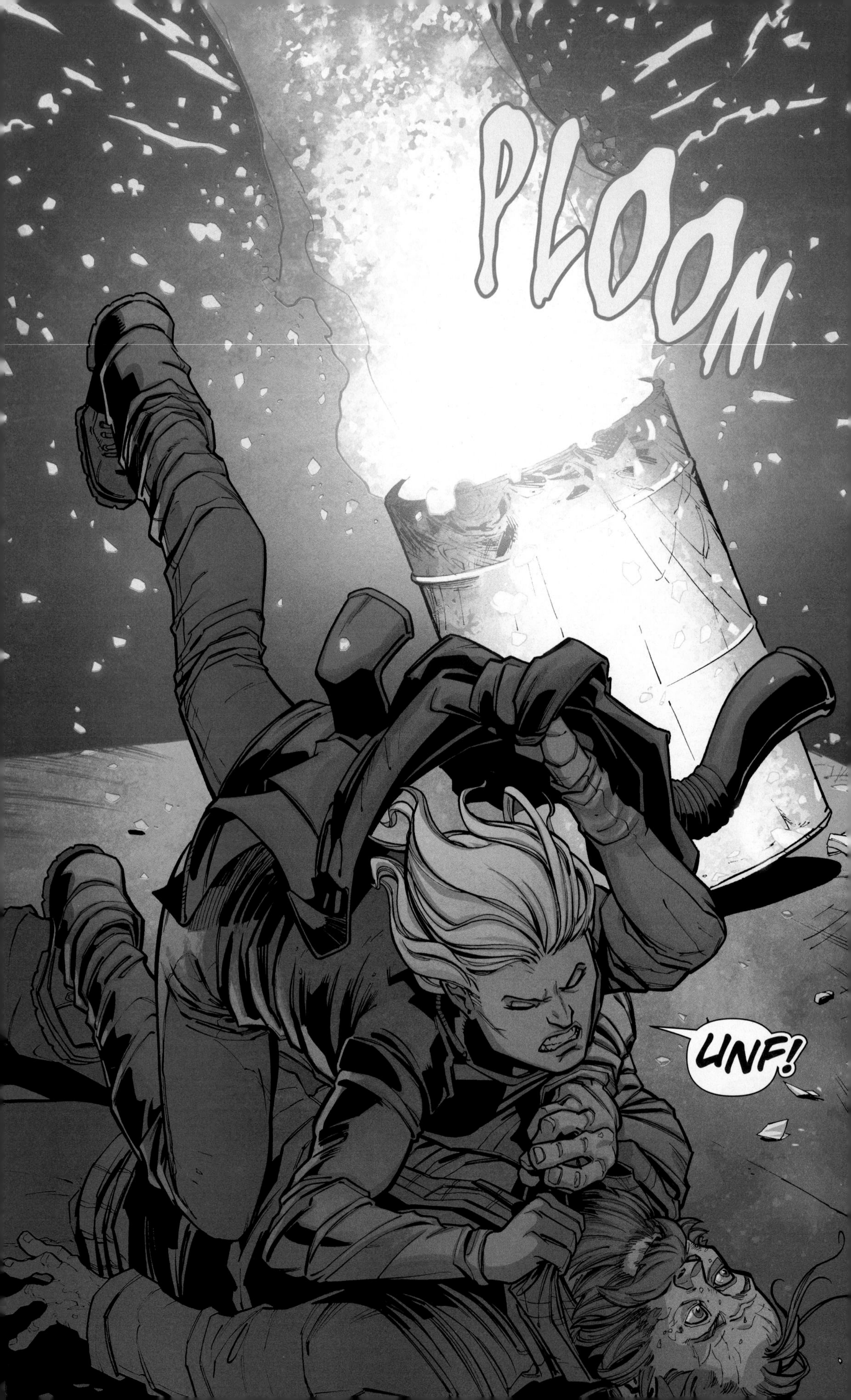
PLOOM
UNF!

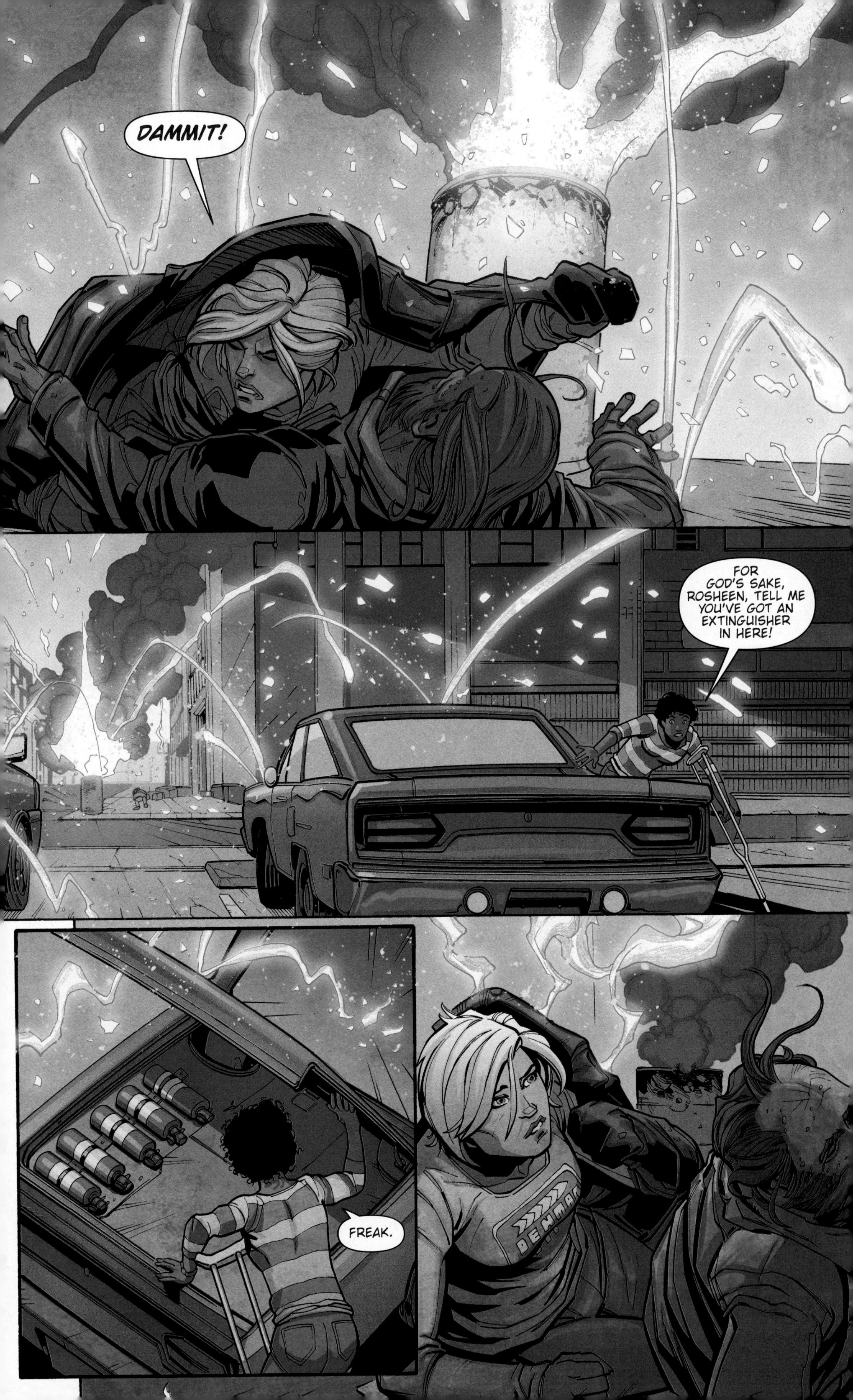
DAMMIT!
FOR GOD'S SAKE, ROSHEEN, TELL ME YOU'VE GOT AN EXTINGUISHER IN HERE!
FREAK.

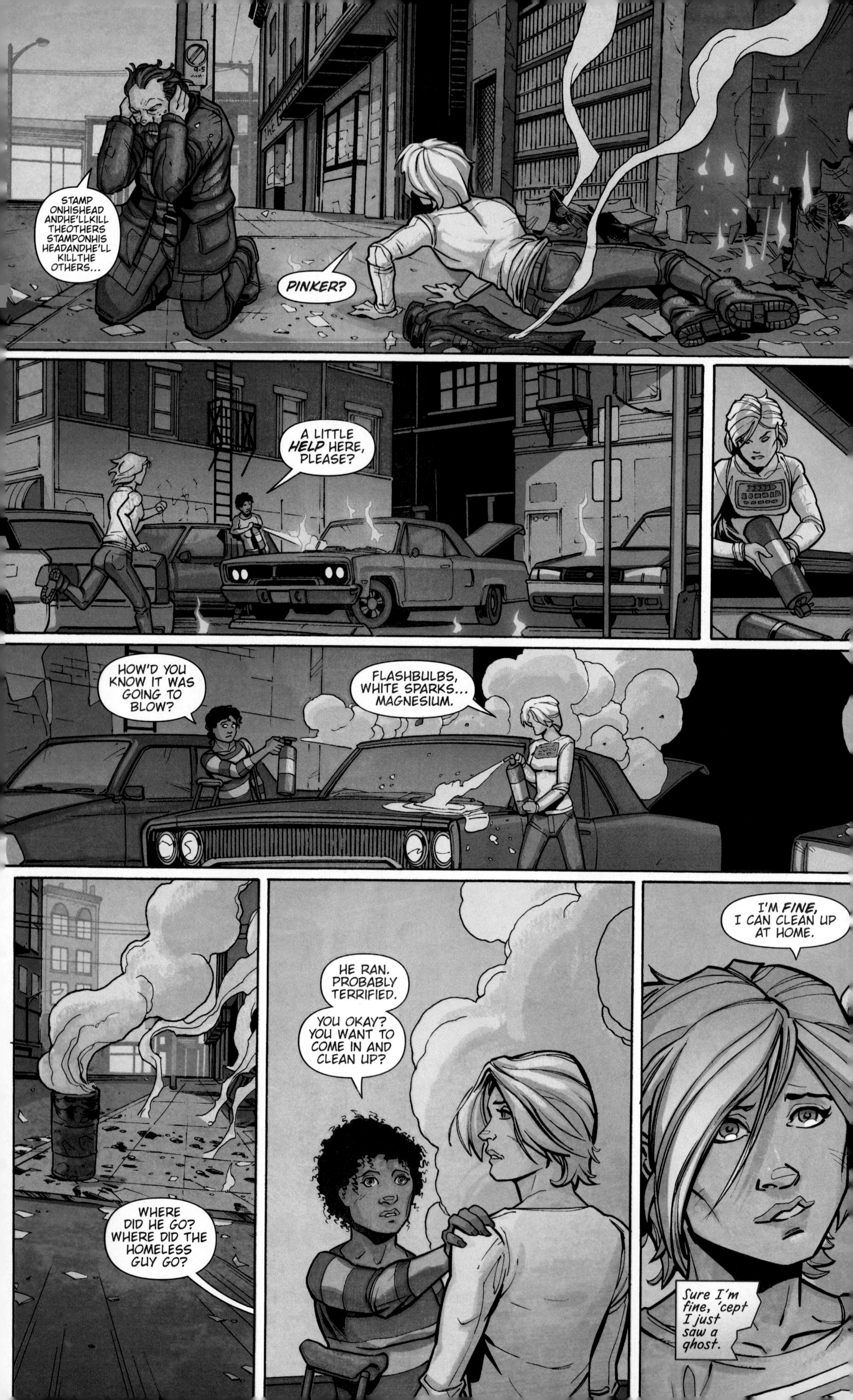
STAMP ONHISHEAD ANDHE'LLKILL THEOTHERS STAMPONHIS HEADANDHE'LL KILLTHE OTHERS...
PINKER?
A LITTLE HELP HERE, PLEASE?
HOW'D YOU KNOW IT WAS GOING TO BLOW?
FLASHBULBS, WHITE SPARKS... MAGNESIUM.
WHERE DID HE GO? WHERE DID THE HOMELESS GUY GO?
HE RAN. PROBABLY TERRIFIED.
YOU OKAY? YOU WANT TO COME IN AND CLEAN UP?
I'M FINE, I CAN CLEAN UP AT HOME.
Sure I'm fine, 'cept I just saw a ghost.

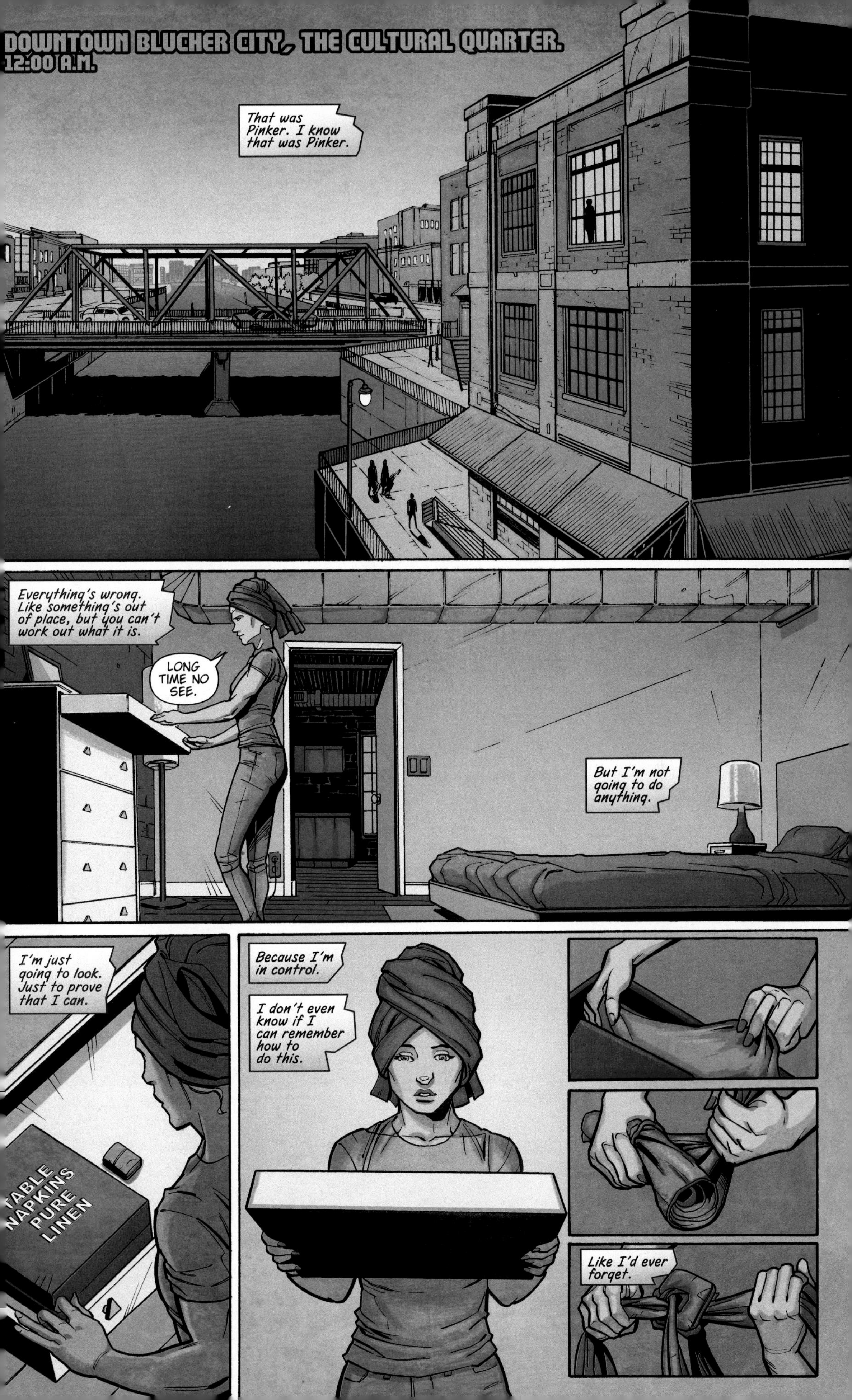
DOWNTOWN BLUCHER CITY, THE CULTURAL QUARTER.
12:00 A.M.
That was Pinker. I know that was Pinker.
Everything's wrong. Like something's out of place, but you can't work out what it is.
LONG TIME NO SEE.
But I'm not going to do anything.
I'm just going to look. Just to prove that I can.
TABLE NAPKINS PURE LINEN
Because I'm in control.
I don't even know if I can remember how to do this.
Like I'd ever forget.

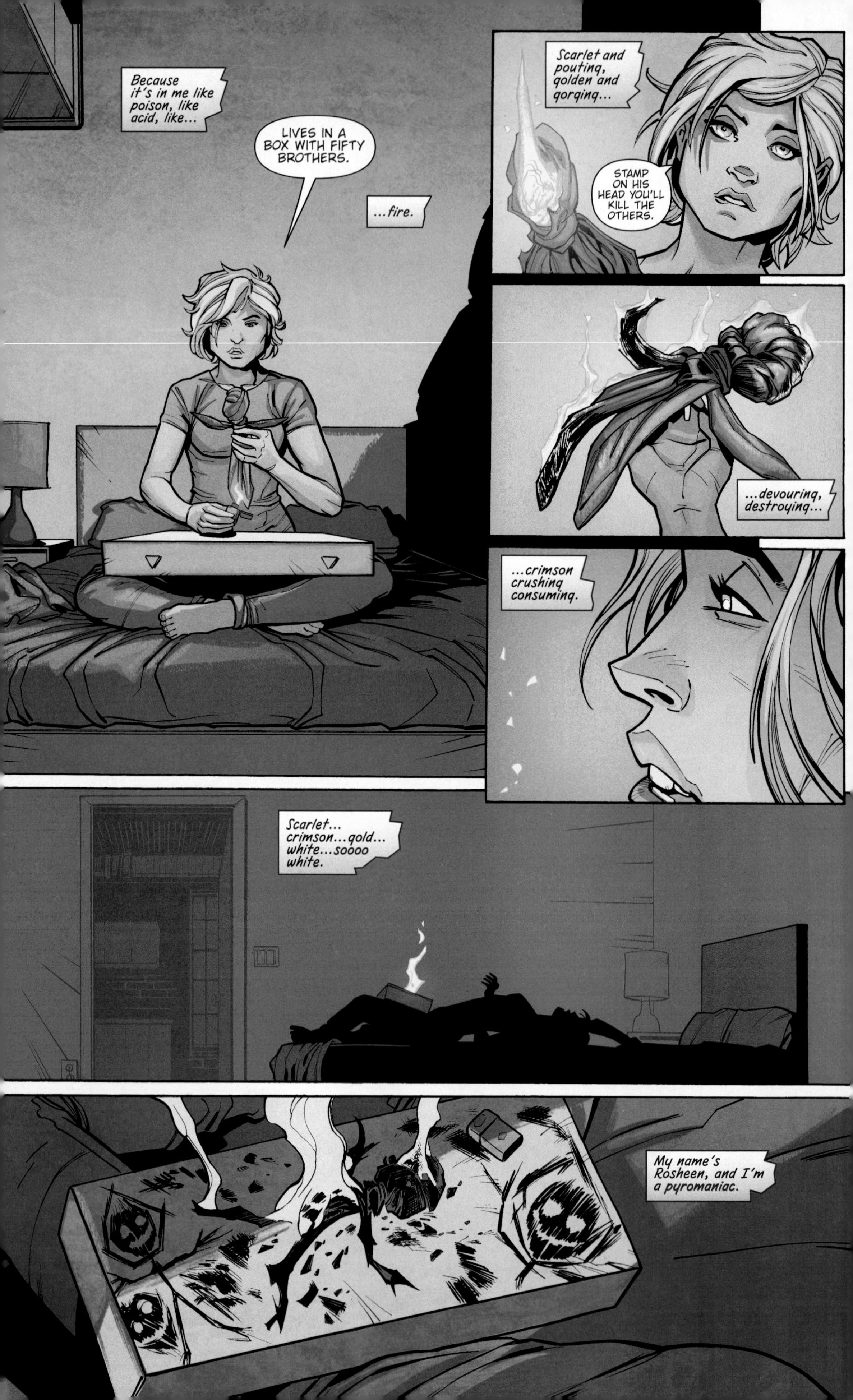
Because it's in me like poison, like acid, like...
LIVES IN A BOX WITH FIFTY BROTHERS.
...fire.
Scarlet and pouting, golden and gorging...
STAMP ON HIS HEAD YOU'LL KILL THE OTHERS.
...devouring, destroying...
...crimson crushing consuming.
Scarlet... crimson...gold... white...soooo white.
My name's Rosheen, and I'm a pyromaniac.

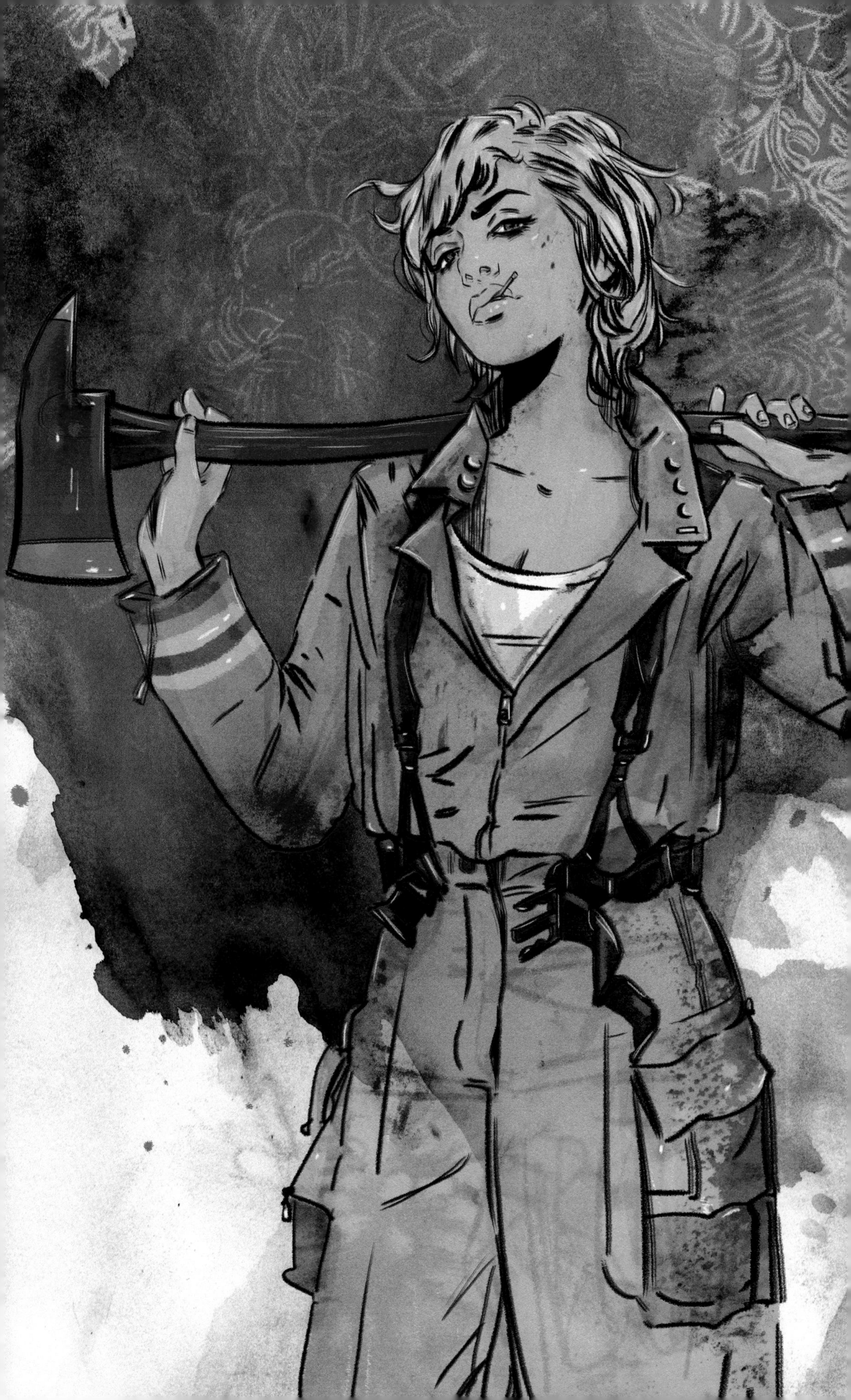

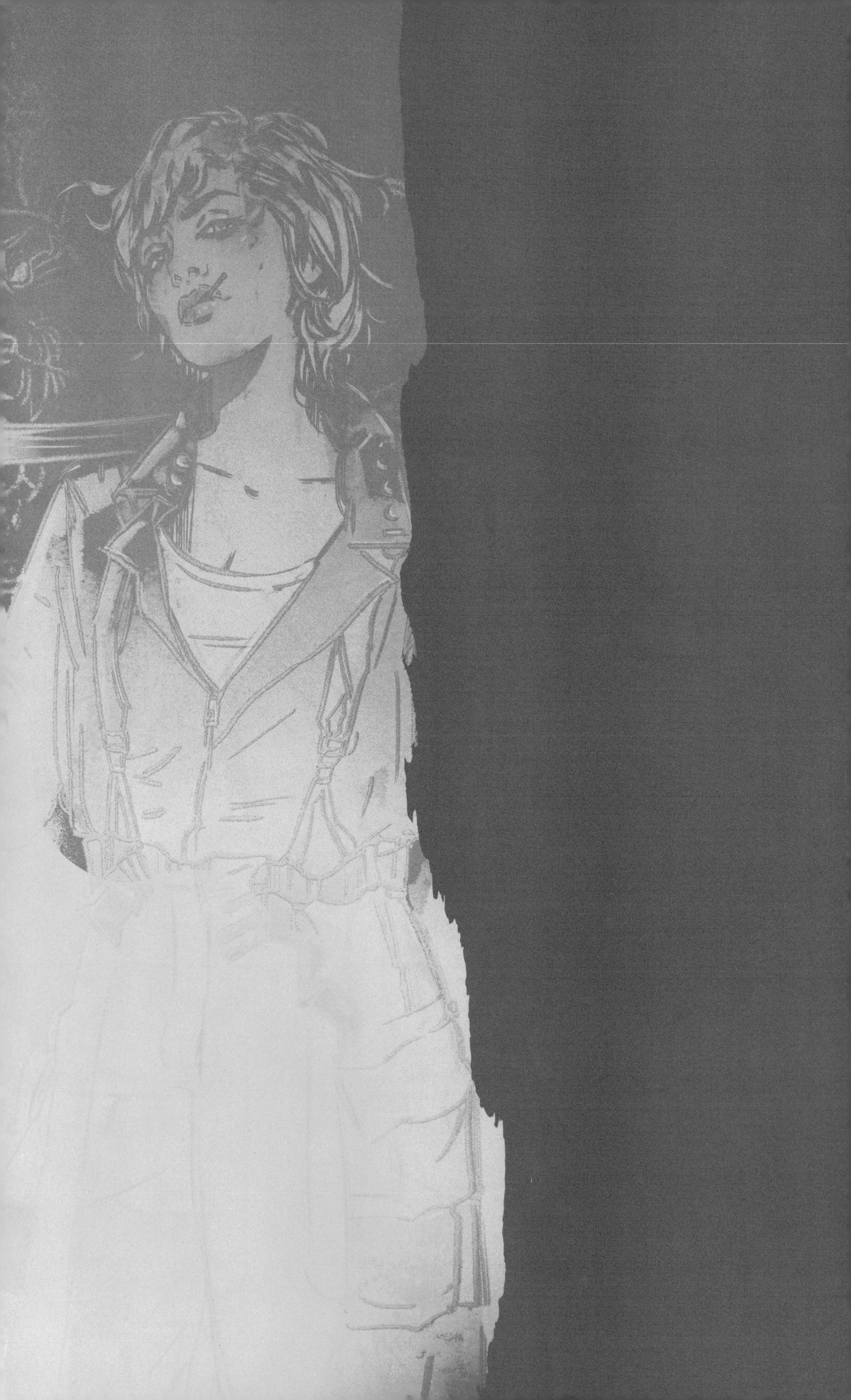

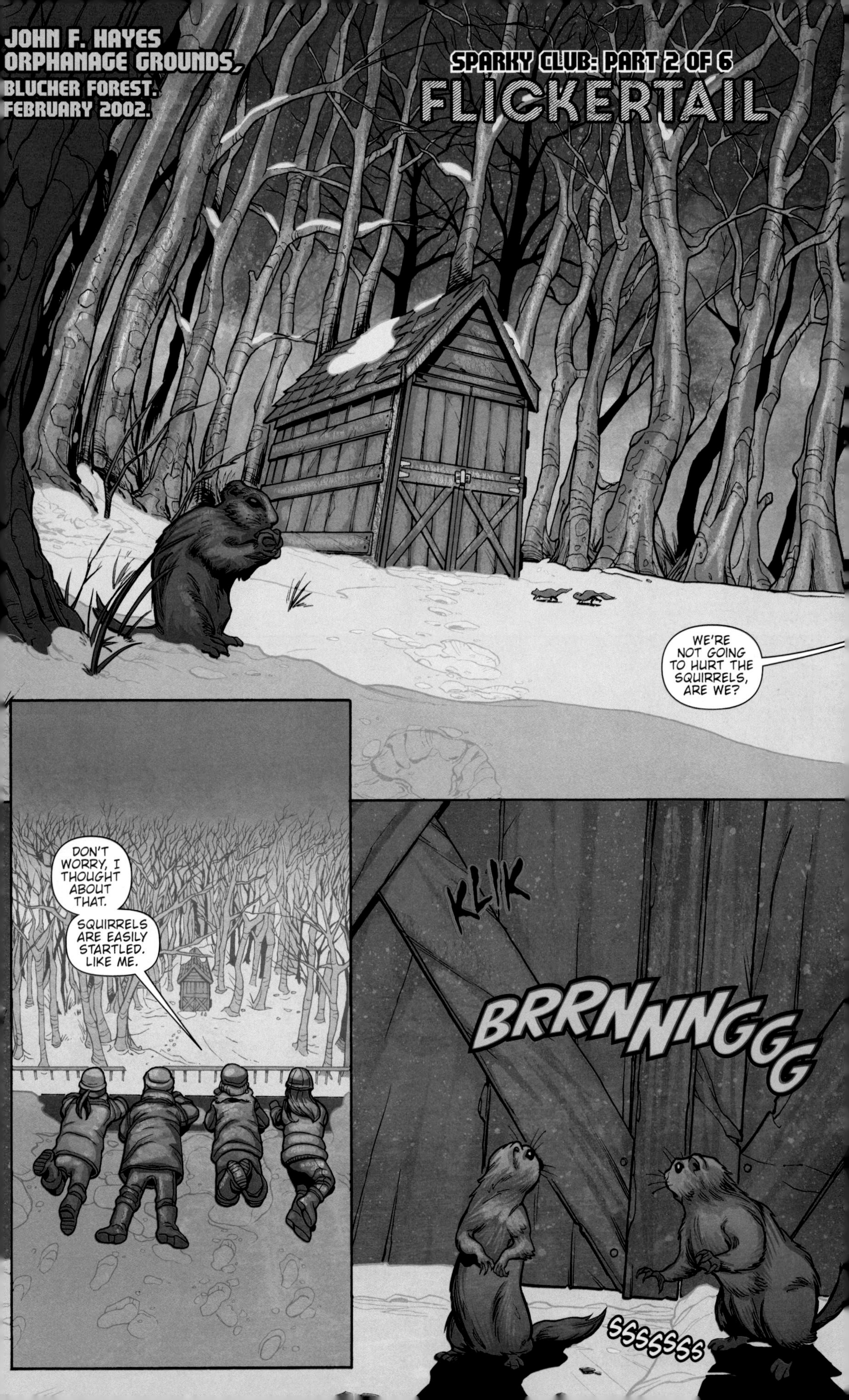
JOHN F. HAYES ORPHANAGE GROUNDS, BLUCHER FOREST. FEBRUARY 2002.
SPARKY CLUB: PART 2 OF 6
FLICKERTAIL
WE'RE NOT GOING TO HURT THE SQUIRRELS, ARE WE?
DON'T WORRY, I THOUGHT ABOUT THAT.
SQUIRRELS ARE EASILY STARTLED. LIKE ME.
KLIK
BRRNNNGGG
SSSSSSS

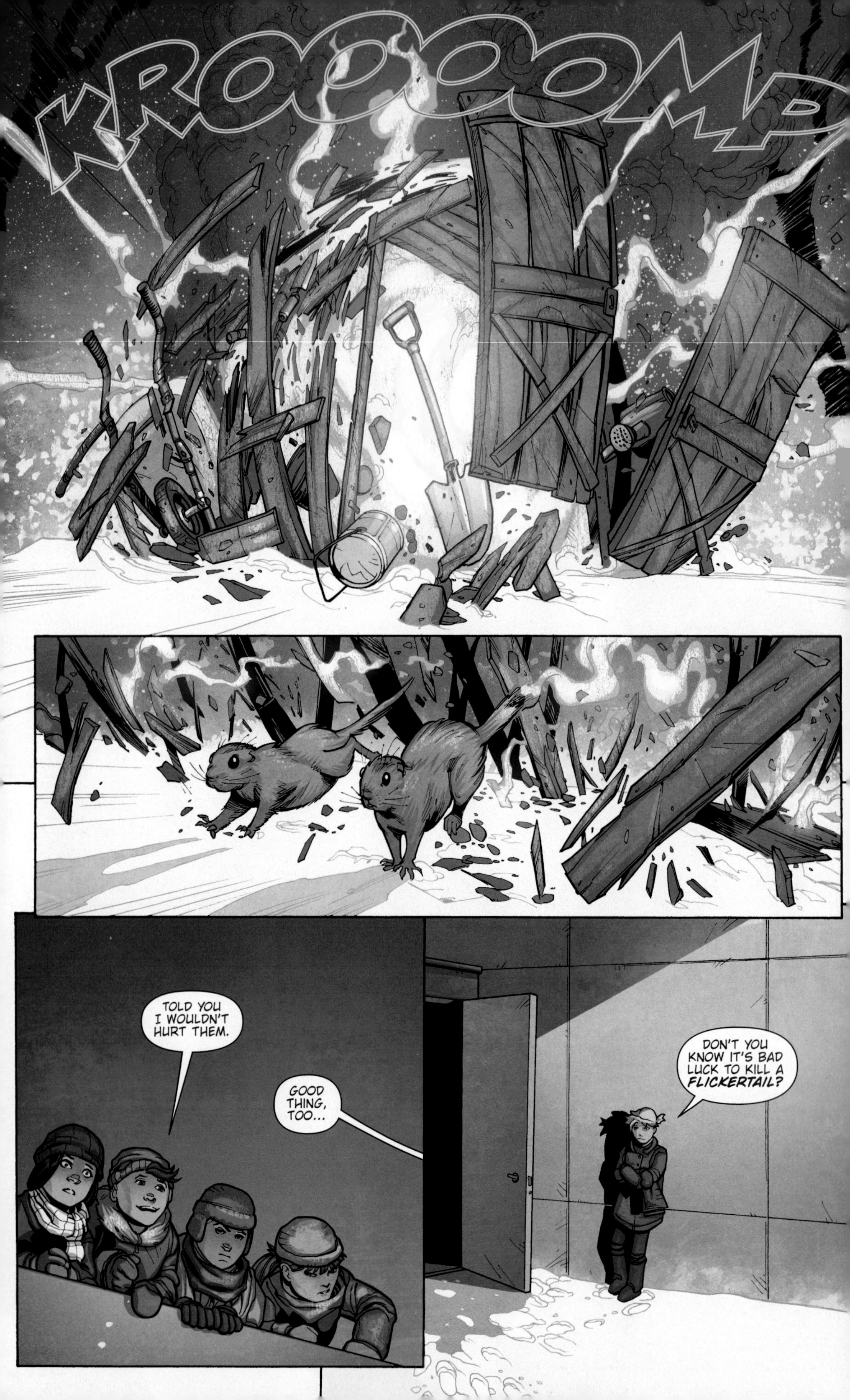
KROOOOMP
TOLD YOU I WOULDN'T HURT THEM.
GOOD THING, TOO...
DON'T YOU KNOW IT'S BAD LUCK TO KILL A *FLICKERTAIL?*

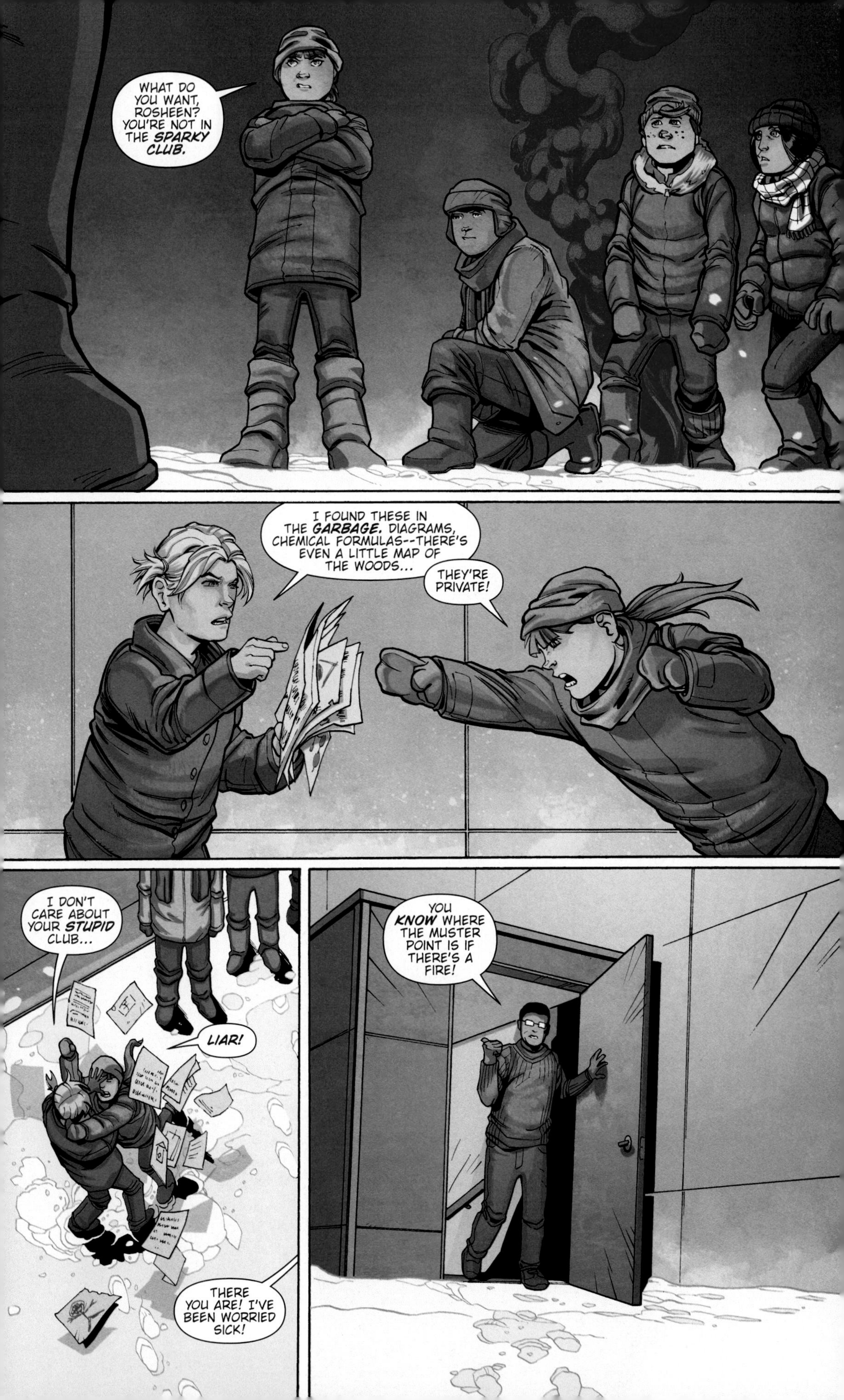
WHAT DO YOU WANT, ROSHEEN? YOU'RE NOT IN THE SPARKY CLUB.
I FOUND THESE IN THE GARBAGE. DIAGRAMS, CHEMICAL FORMULAS--THERE'S EVEN A LITTLE MAP OF THE WOODS...
THEY'RE PRIVATE!
I DON'T CARE ABOUT YOUR STUPID CLUB...
LIAR!
THERE YOU ARE! I'VE BEEN WORRIED SICK!
YOU KNOW WHERE THE MUSTER POINT IS IF THERE'S A FIRE!

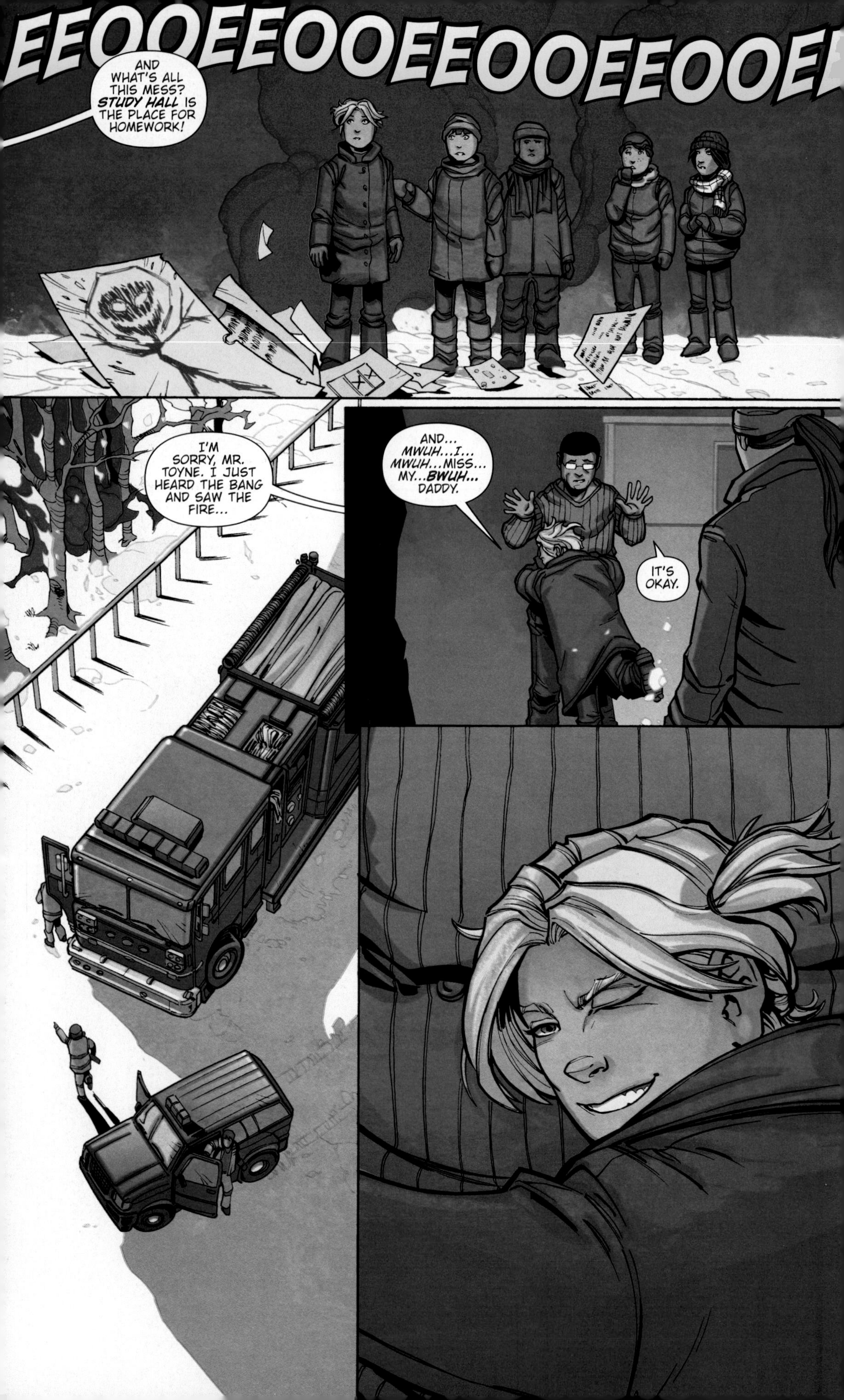
EEOOEEOOEEOOEEOOE
AND WHAT'S ALL THIS MESS? STUDY HALL IS THE PLACE FOR HOMEWORK!
I'M SORRY, MR. TOYNE. I JUST HEARD THE BANG AND SAW THE FIRE...
AND... MWUH...I... MWUH...MISS... MY...BWUH... DADDY.
IT'S OKAY.

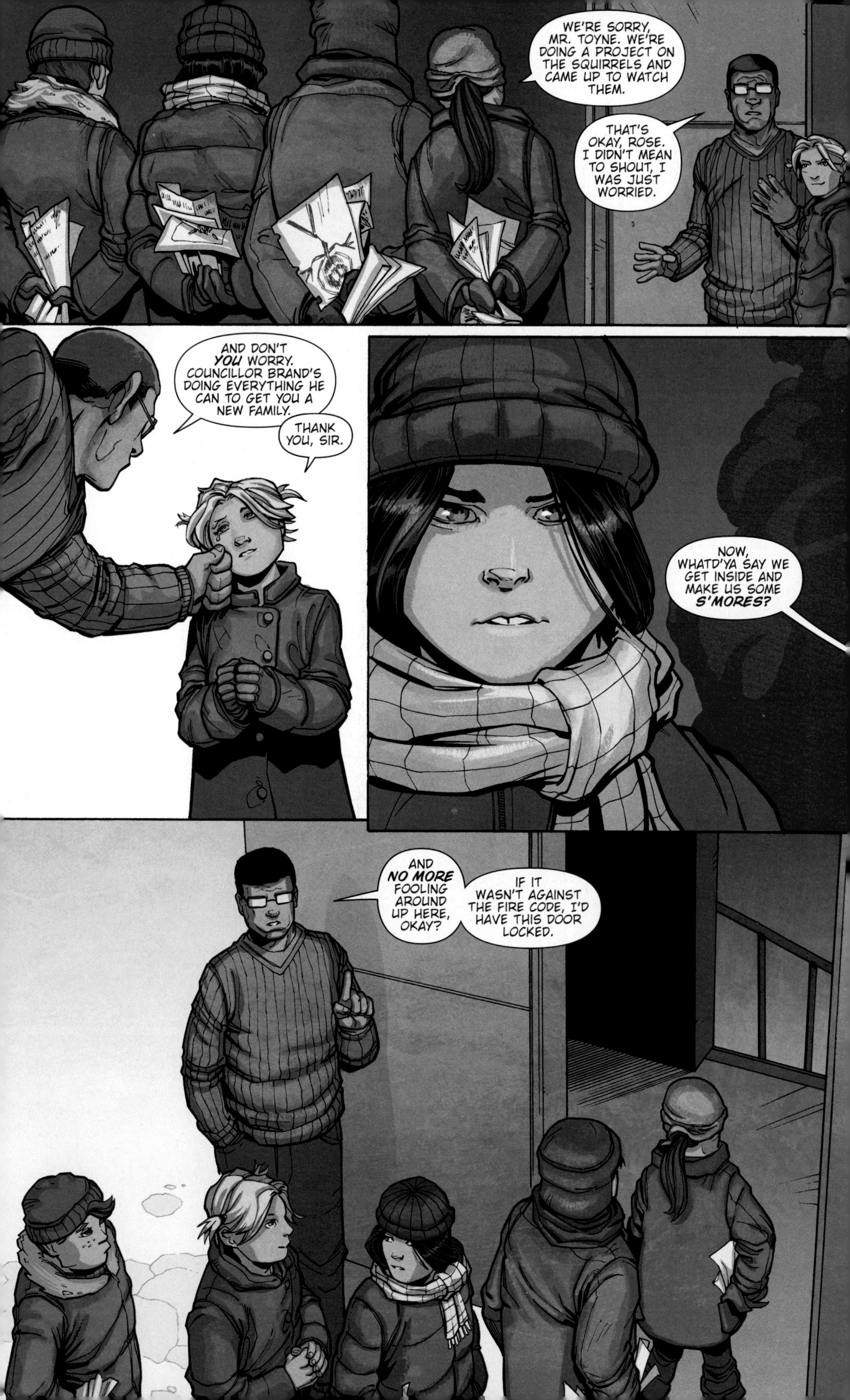
WE'RE SORRY, MR. TOYNE. WE'RE DOING A PROJECT ON THE SQUIRRELS AND CAME UP TO WATCH THEM.
THAT'S OKAY, ROSE. I DIDN'T MEAN TO SHOUT, I WAS JUST WORRIED.
AND DON'T YOU WORRY. COUNCILLOR BRAND'S DOING EVERYTHING HE CAN TO GET YOU A NEW FAMILY.
THANK YOU, SIR.
NOW, WHATD'YA SAY WE GET INSIDE AND MAKE US SOME S'MORES?
AND NO MORE FOOLING AROUND UP HERE, OKAY?
IF IT WASN'T AGAINST THE FIRE CODE, I'D HAVE THIS DOOR LOCKED.

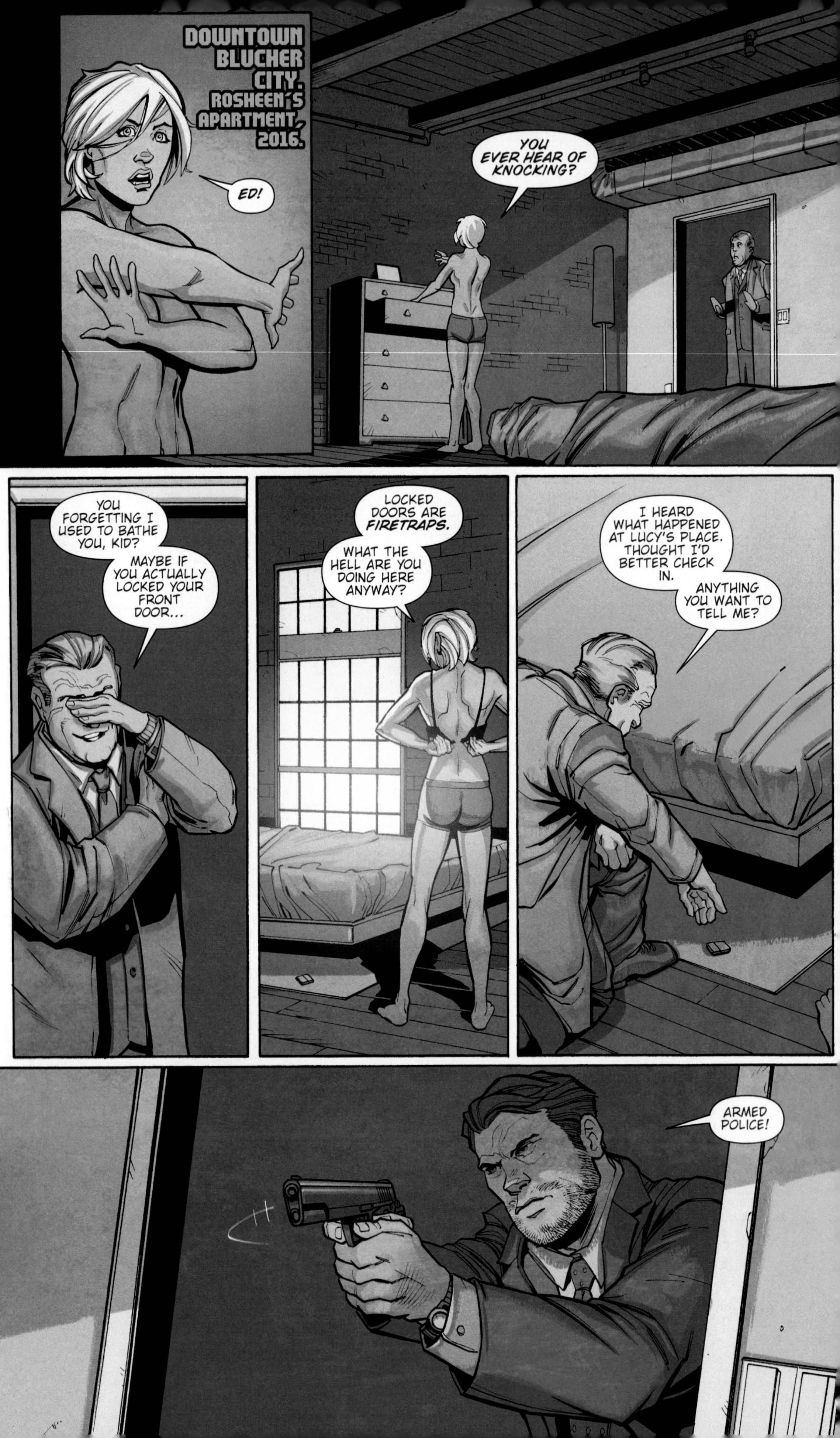
DOWNTOWN BLUCHER CITY. ROSHEEN'S APARTMENT, 2016.
ED!
YOU EVER HEAR OF KNOCKING?
YOU FORGETTING I USED TO BATHE YOU, KID?
MAYBE IF YOU ACTUALLY LOCKED YOUR FRONT DOOR...
LOCKED DOORS ARE FIRETRAPS.
WHAT THE HELL ARE YOU DOING HERE ANYWAY?
I HEARD WHAT HAPPENED AT LUCY'S PLACE. THOUGHT I'D BETTER CHECK IN.
ANYTHING YOU WANT TO TELL ME?
ARMED POLICE!

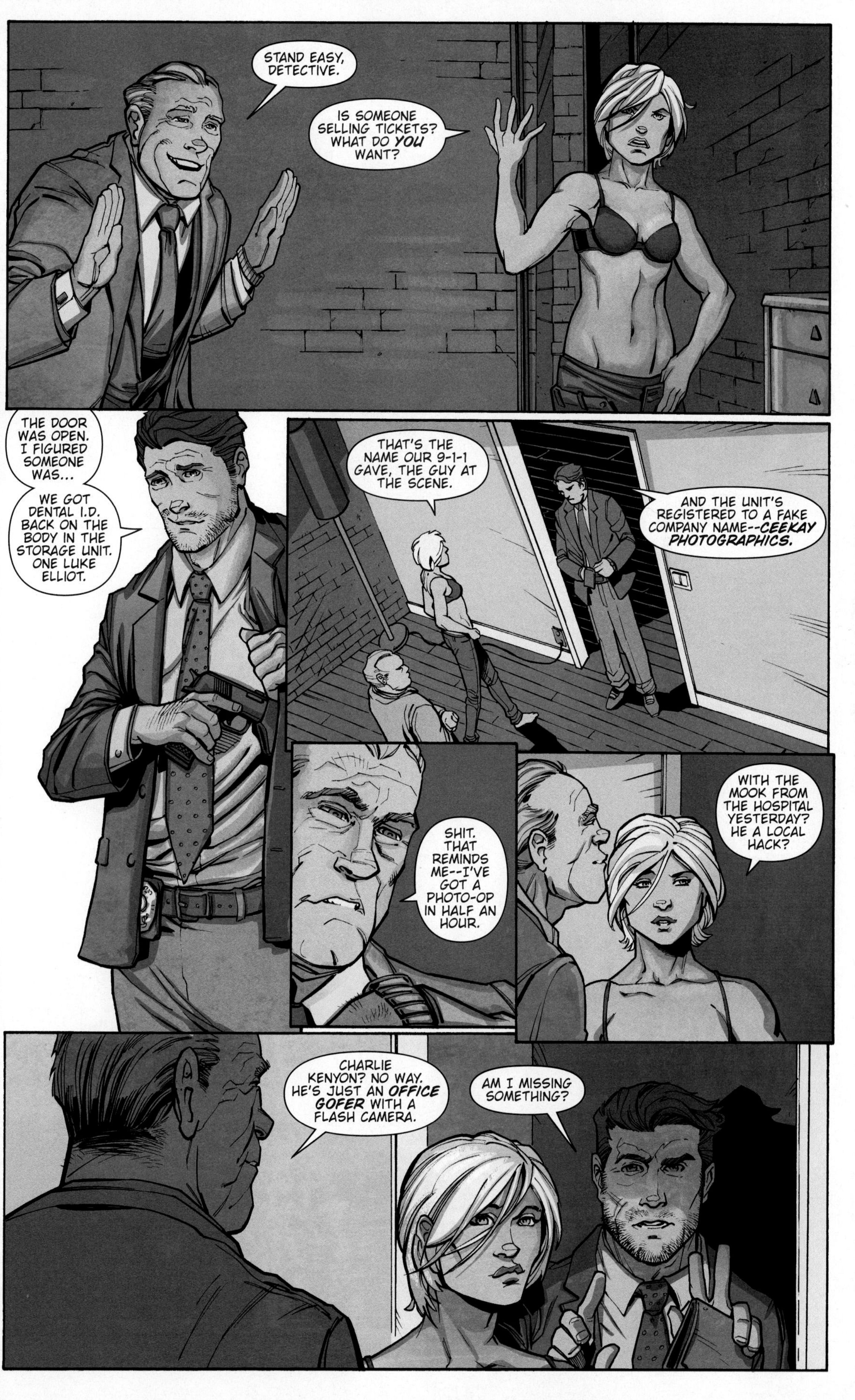
STAND EASY, DETECTIVE.
IS SOMEONE SELLING TICKETS? WHAT DO YOU WANT?
THE DOOR WAS OPEN. I FIGURED SOMEONE WAS...
WE GOT DENTAL I.D. BACK ON THE BODY IN THE STORAGE UNIT. ONE LUKE ELLIOT.
THAT'S THE NAME OUR 9-1-1 GAVE, THE GUY AT THE SCENE.
AND THE UNIT'S REGISTERED TO A FAKE COMPANY NAME--CEEKAY PHOTOGRAPHICS.
SHIT. THAT REMINDS ME--I'VE GOT A PHOTO-OP IN HALF AN HOUR.
WITH THE MOOK FROM THE HOSPITAL YESTERDAY? HE A LOCAL HACK?
CHARLIE KENYON? NO WAY. HE'S JUST AN OFFICE GOFER WITH A FLASH CAMERA.
AM I MISSING SOMETHING?

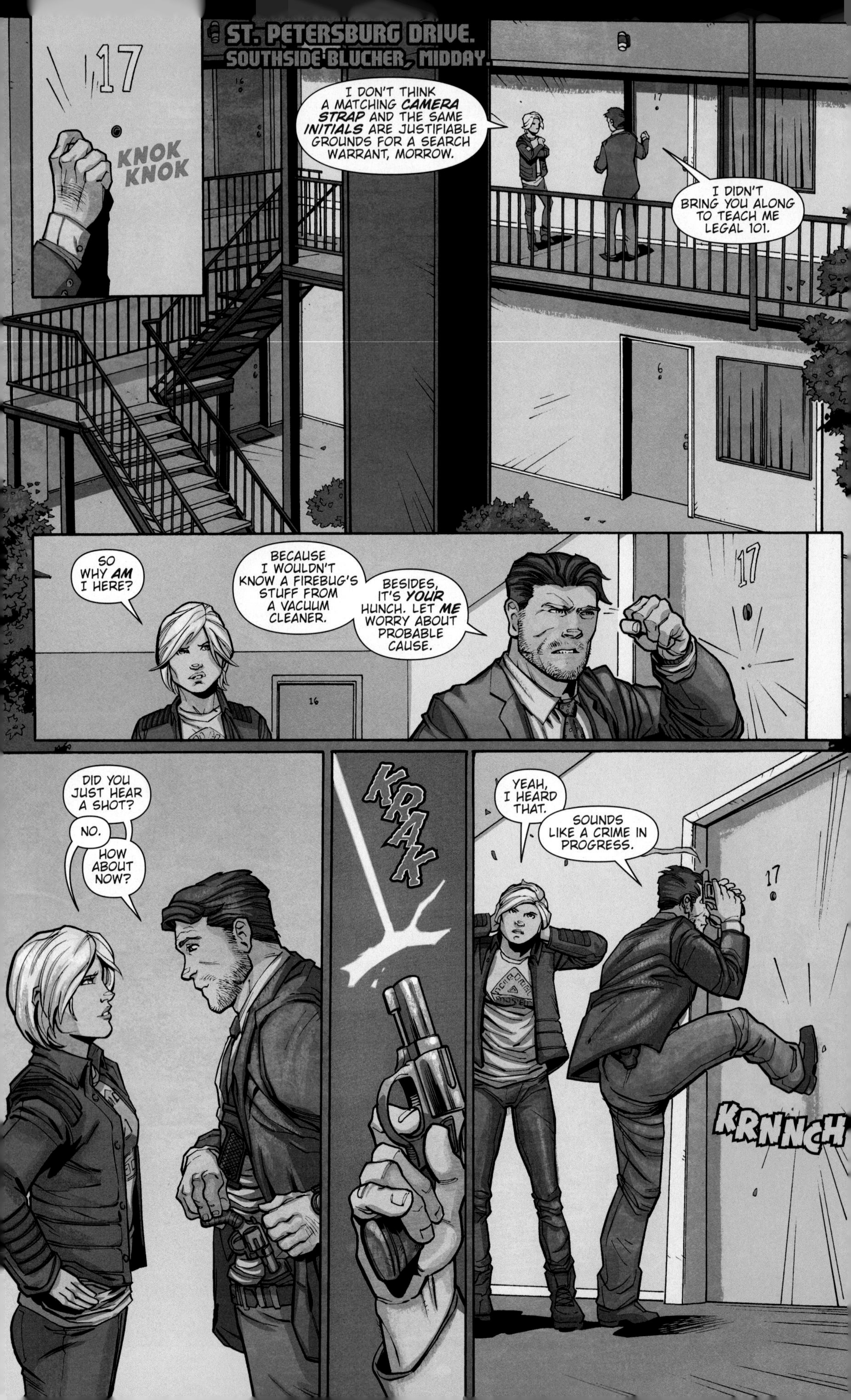

ST. PETERSBURG DRIVE.
SOUTHSIDE BLUCHER, MIDDAY.
17
KNOK KNOK
I DON'T THINK A MATCHING CAMERA STRAP AND THE SAME INITIALS ARE JUSTIFIABLE GROUNDS FOR A SEARCH WARRANT, MORROW.
I DIDN'T BRING YOU ALONG TO TEACH ME LEGAL 101.
SO WHY AM I HERE?
BECAUSE I WOULDN'T KNOW A FIREBUG'S STUFF FROM A VACUUM CLEANER.
BESIDES, IT'S YOUR HUNCH. LET ME WORRY ABOUT PROBABLE CAUSE.
DID YOU JUST HEAR A SHOT?
NO.
HOW ABOUT NOW?
KRAK
YEAH, I HEARD THAT.
SOUNDS LIKE A CRIME IN PROGRESS.
KRNNCH

Dust still rising over the TV, condensation in the cup, Hot Pocket still steaming, three embers glowing on the roach...

HE'S STILL HERE.

THAT'S WHAT I WAS ABOUT TO SAY. HOW DID *YOU* KNOW?

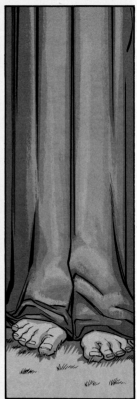

OPEN SESAME.

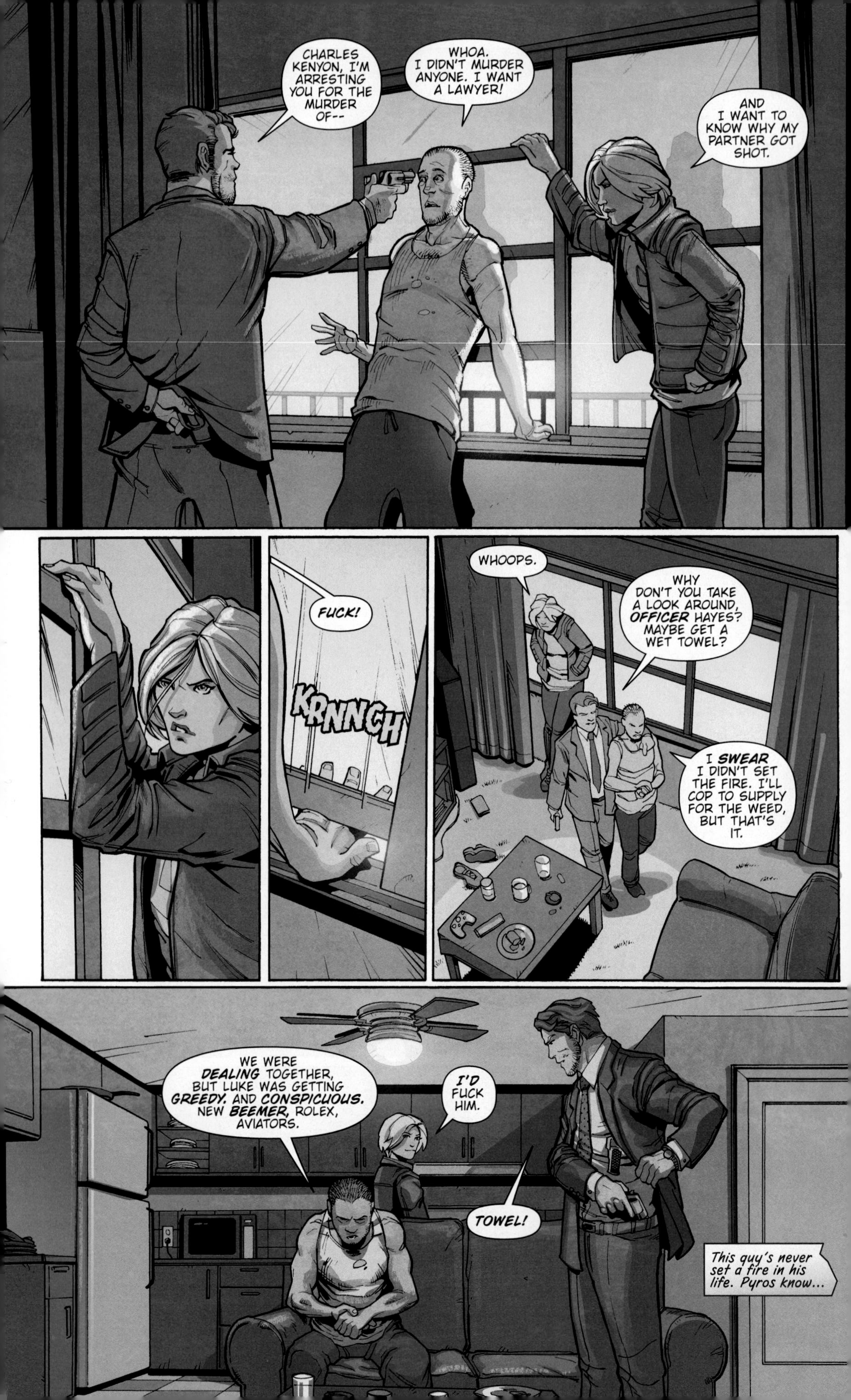
CHARLES KENYON, I'M ARRESTING YOU FOR THE MURDER OF--
WHOA. I DIDN'T MURDER ANYONE. I WANT A LAWYER!
AND I WANT TO KNOW WHY MY PARTNER GOT SHOT.
FUCK!
KRNNCH
WHOOPS.
WHY DON'T YOU TAKE A LOOK AROUND, OFFICER HAYES? MAYBE GET A WET TOWEL?
I SWEAR I DIDN'T SET THE FIRE. I'LL COP TO SUPPLY FOR THE WEED, BUT THAT'S IT.
WE WERE DEALING TOGETHER, BUT LUKE WAS GETTING GREEDY. AND CONSPICUOUS. NEW BEEMER, ROLEX, AVIATORS.
I'D FUCK HIM.
TOWEL!
This guy's never set a fire in his life. Pyros know...

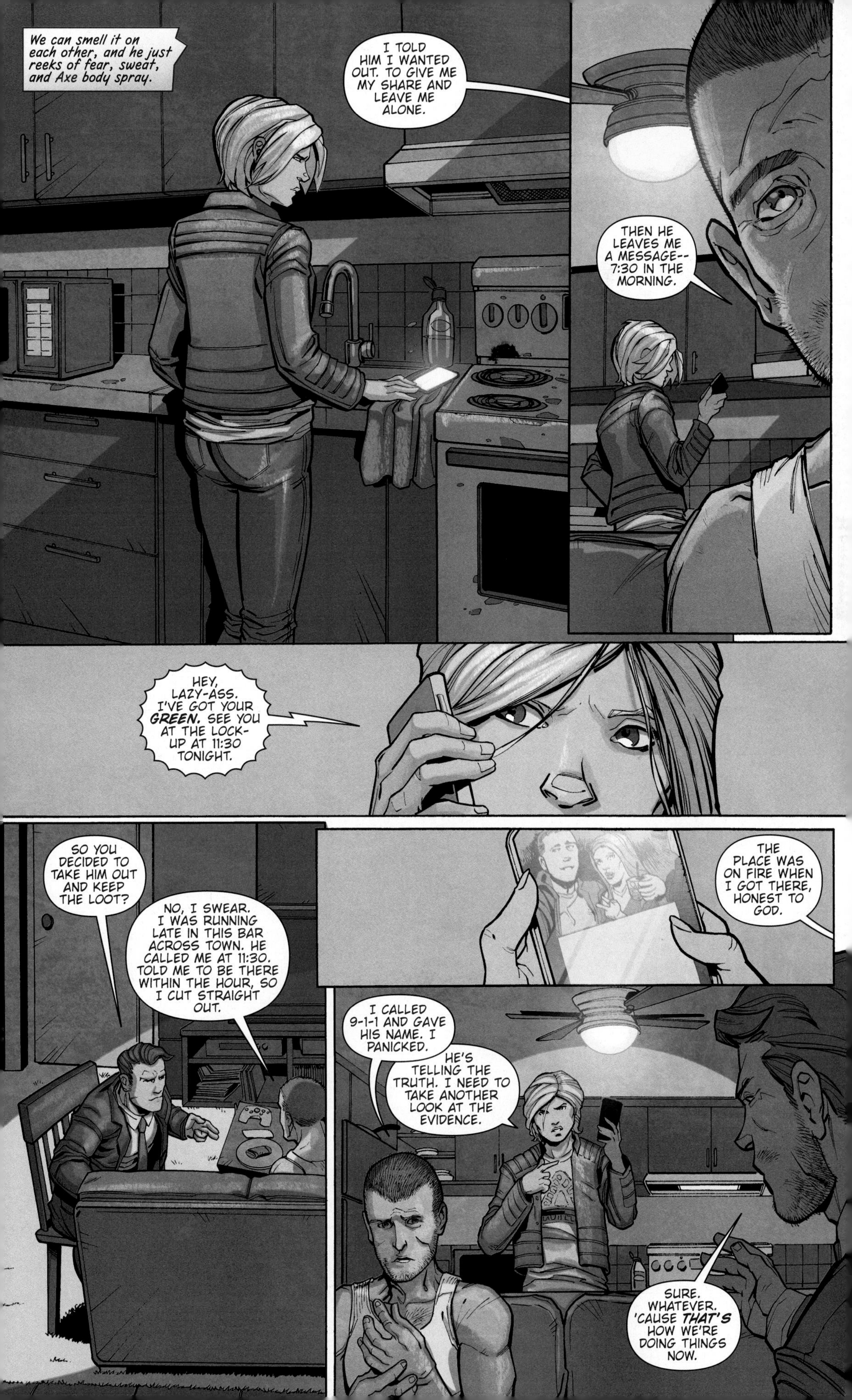
We can smell it on each other, and he just reeks of fear, sweat, and Axe body spray.
I TOLD HIM I WANTED OUT. TO GIVE ME MY SHARE AND LEAVE ME ALONE.
THEN HE LEAVES ME A MESSAGE-- 7:30 IN THE MORNING.
HEY, LAZY-ASS. I'VE GOT YOUR GREEN. SEE YOU AT THE LOCK-UP AT 11:30 TONIGHT.
SO YOU DECIDED TO TAKE HIM OUT AND KEEP THE LOOT?
NO, I SWEAR. I WAS RUNNING LATE IN THIS BAR ACROSS TOWN. HE CALLED ME AT 11:30. TOLD ME TO BE THERE WITHIN THE HOUR, SO I CUT STRAIGHT OUT.
THE PLACE WAS ON FIRE WHEN I GOT THERE, HONEST TO GOD.
I CALLED 9-1-1 AND GAVE HIS NAME. I PANICKED.
HE'S TELLING THE TRUTH. I NEED TO TAKE ANOTHER LOOK AT THE EVIDENCE.
SURE. WHATEVER. 'CAUSE THAT'S HOW WE'RE DOING THINGS NOW.

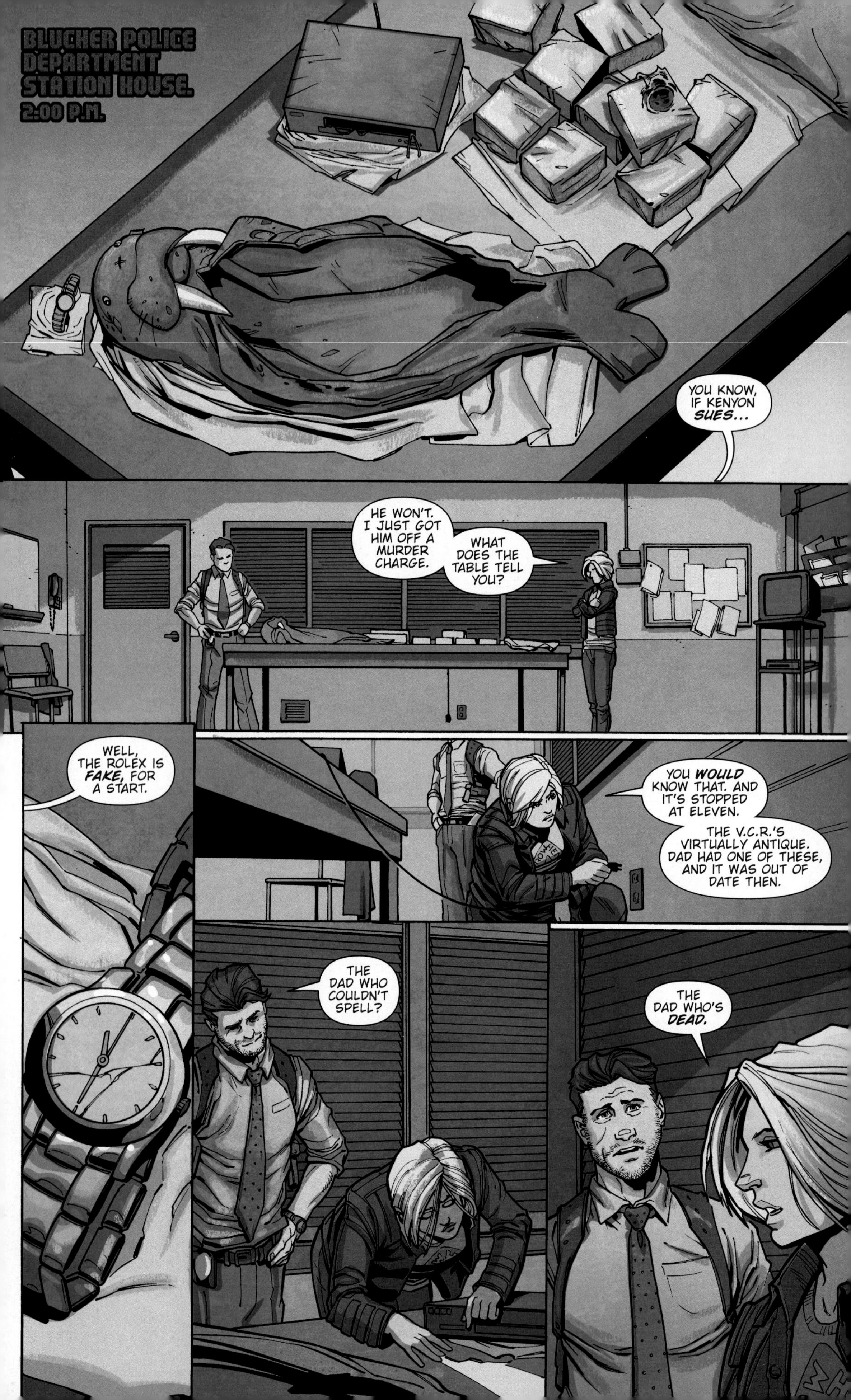

BLUCHER POLICE DEPARTMENT STATION HOUSE. 2:00 P.M.
YOU KNOW, IF KENYON SUES...
HE WON'T. I JUST GOT HIM OFF A MURDER CHARGE.
WHAT DOES THE TABLE TELL YOU?
WELL, THE ROLEX IS FAKE, FOR A START.
YOU WOULD KNOW THAT. AND IT'S STOPPED AT ELEVEN.
THE V.C.R.'S VIRTUALLY ANTIQUE. DAD HAD ONE OF THESE, AND IT WAS OUT OF DATE THEN.
THE DAD WHO COULDN'T SPELL?
THE DAD WHO'S DEAD.

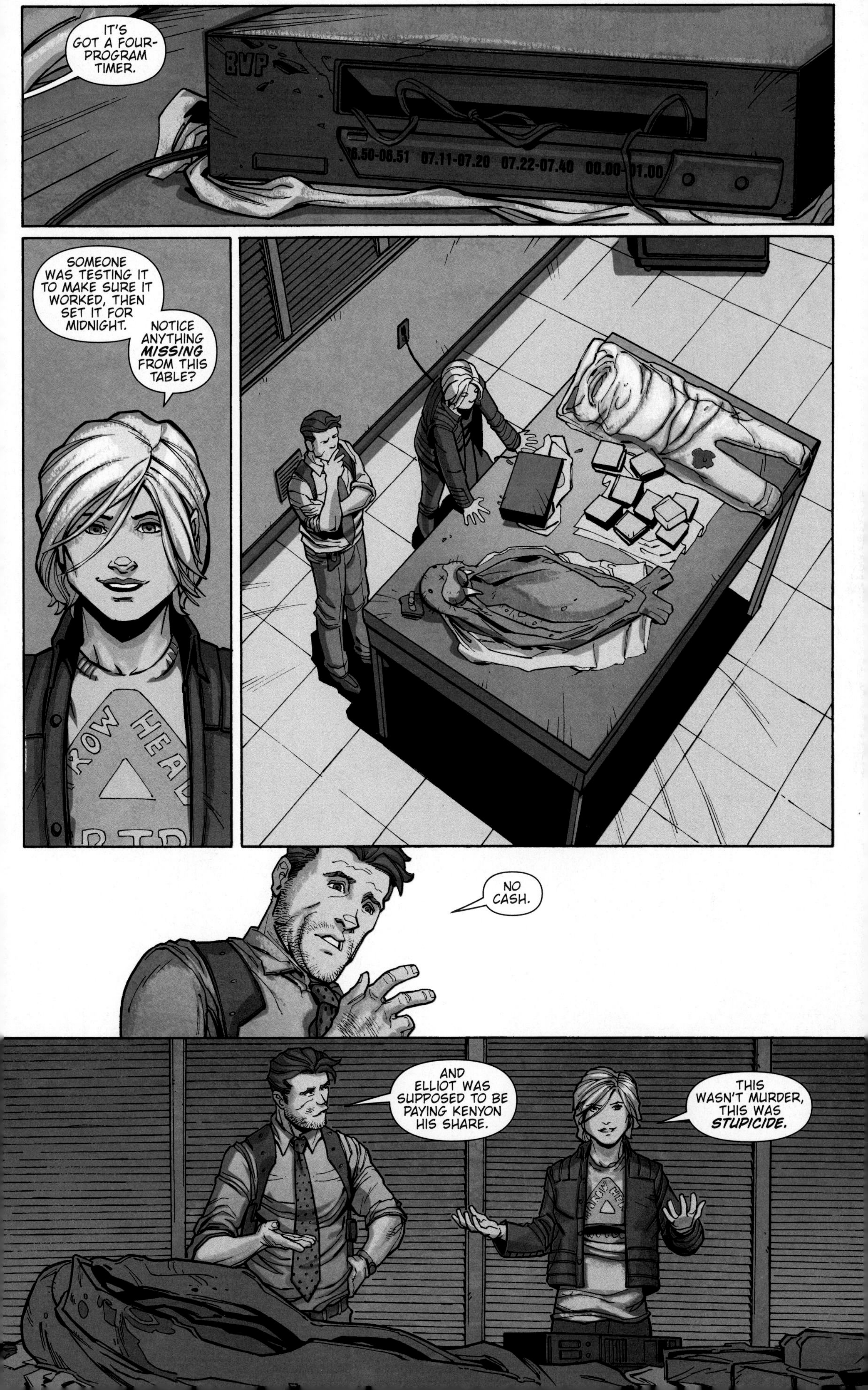
IT'S GOT A FOUR-PROGRAM TIMER.
BVP
06.50-06.51 07.11-07.20 07.22-07.40 00.00-01.00
SOMEONE WAS TESTING IT TO MAKE SURE IT WORKED, THEN SET IT FOR MIDNIGHT.
NOTICE ANYTHING *MISSING* FROM THIS TABLE?
NO CASH.
AND ELLIOT WAS SUPPOSED TO BE PAYING KENYON HIS SHARE.
THIS WASN'T MURDER, THIS WAS *STUPICIDE.*

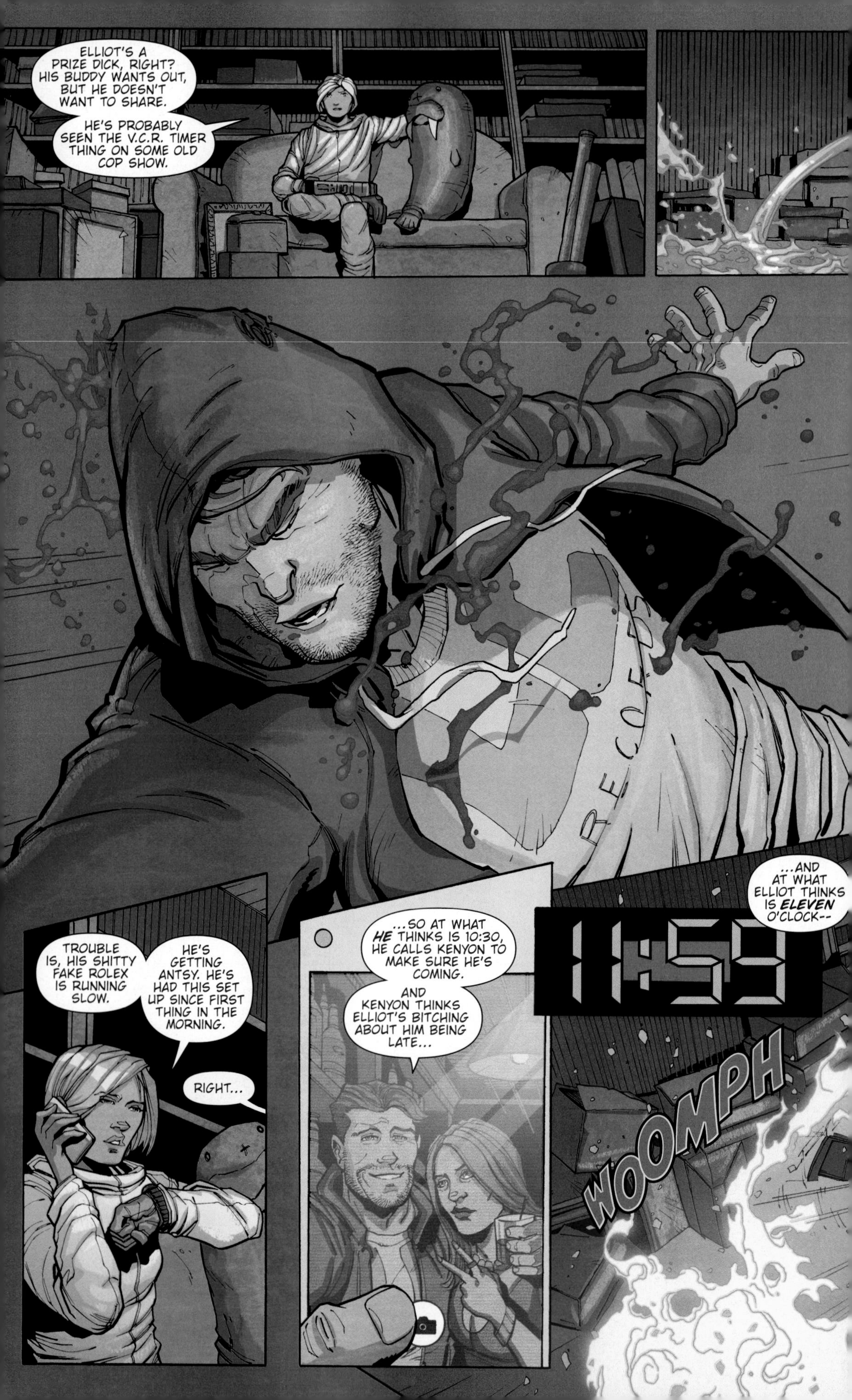

ELLIOT'S A PRIZE DICK, RIGHT? HIS BUDDY WANTS OUT, BUT HE DOESN'T WANT TO SHARE.
HE'S PROBABLY SEEN THE V.C.R. TIMER THING ON SOME OLD COP SHOW.
TROUBLE IS, HIS SHITTY FAKE ROLEX IS RUNNING SLOW.
HE'S GETTING ANTSY. HE'S HAD THIS SET UP SINCE FIRST THING IN THE MORNING.
RIGHT...
...SO AT WHAT HE THINKS IS 10:30, HE CALLS KENYON TO MAKE SURE HE'S COMING.
AND KENYON THINKS ELLIOT'S BITCHING ABOUT HIM BEING LATE...
...AND AT WHAT ELLIOT THINKS IS ELEVEN O'CLOCK--
11:59
WOOMPH

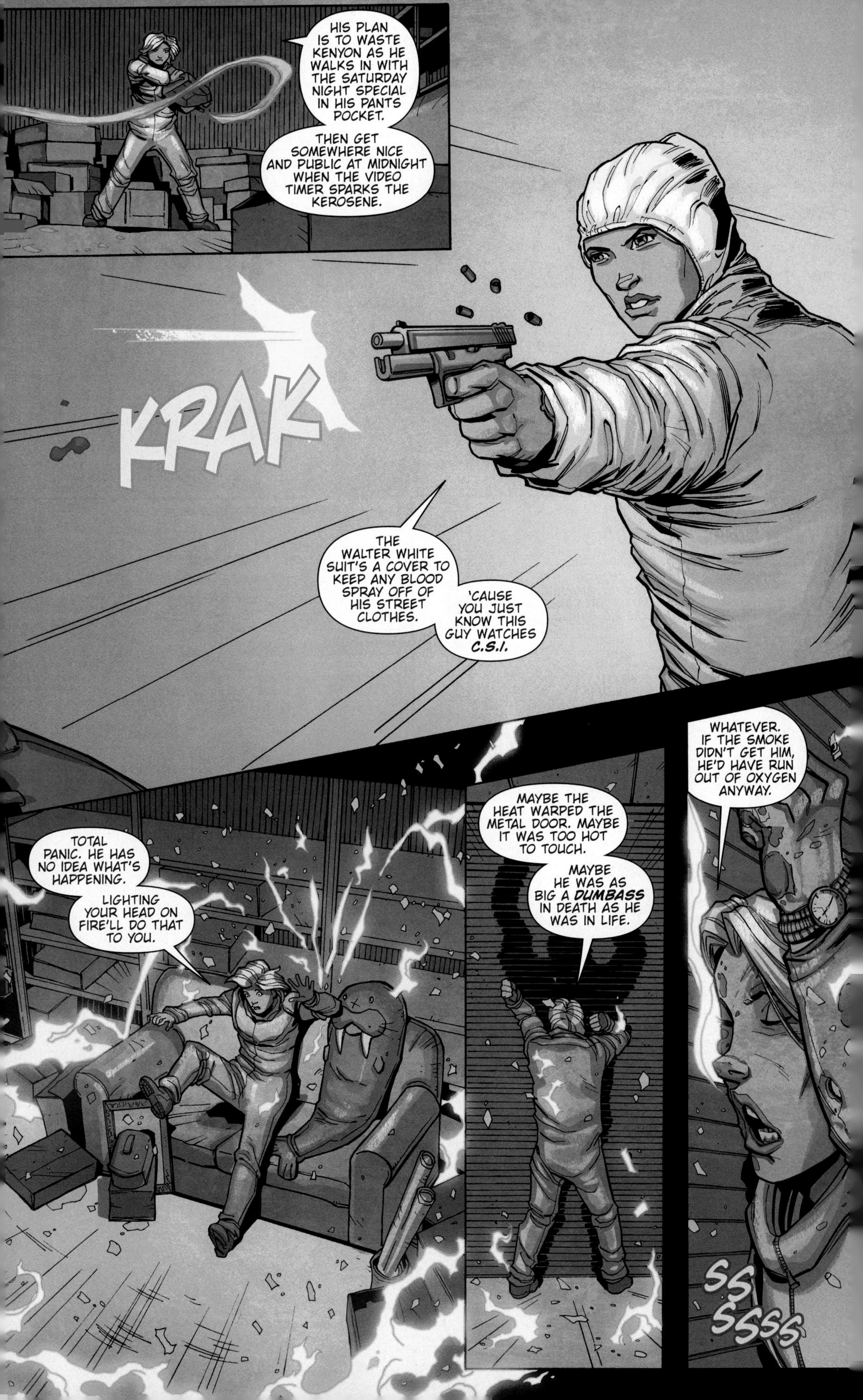
HIS PLAN IS TO WASTE KENYON AS HE WALKS IN WITH THE SATURDAY NIGHT SPECIAL IN HIS PANTS POCKET.
THEN GET SOMEWHERE NICE AND PUBLIC AT MIDNIGHT WHEN THE VIDEO TIMER SPARKS THE KEROSENE.
KRAK
THE WALTER WHITE SUIT'S A COVER TO KEEP ANY BLOOD SPRAY OFF OF HIS STREET CLOTHES.
'CAUSE YOU JUST KNOW THIS GUY WATCHES *C.S.I.*
TOTAL PANIC. HE HAS NO IDEA WHAT'S HAPPENING.
LIGHTING YOUR HEAD ON FIRE'LL DO THAT TO YOU.
MAYBE THE HEAT WARPED THE METAL DOOR. MAYBE IT WAS TOO HOT TO TOUCH.
MAYBE HE WAS AS BIG A ***DUMBASS*** IN DEATH AS HE WAS IN LIFE.
WHATEVER. IF THE SMOKE DIDN'T GET HIM, HE'D HAVE RUN OUT OF OXYGEN ANYWAY.
SSSSSS

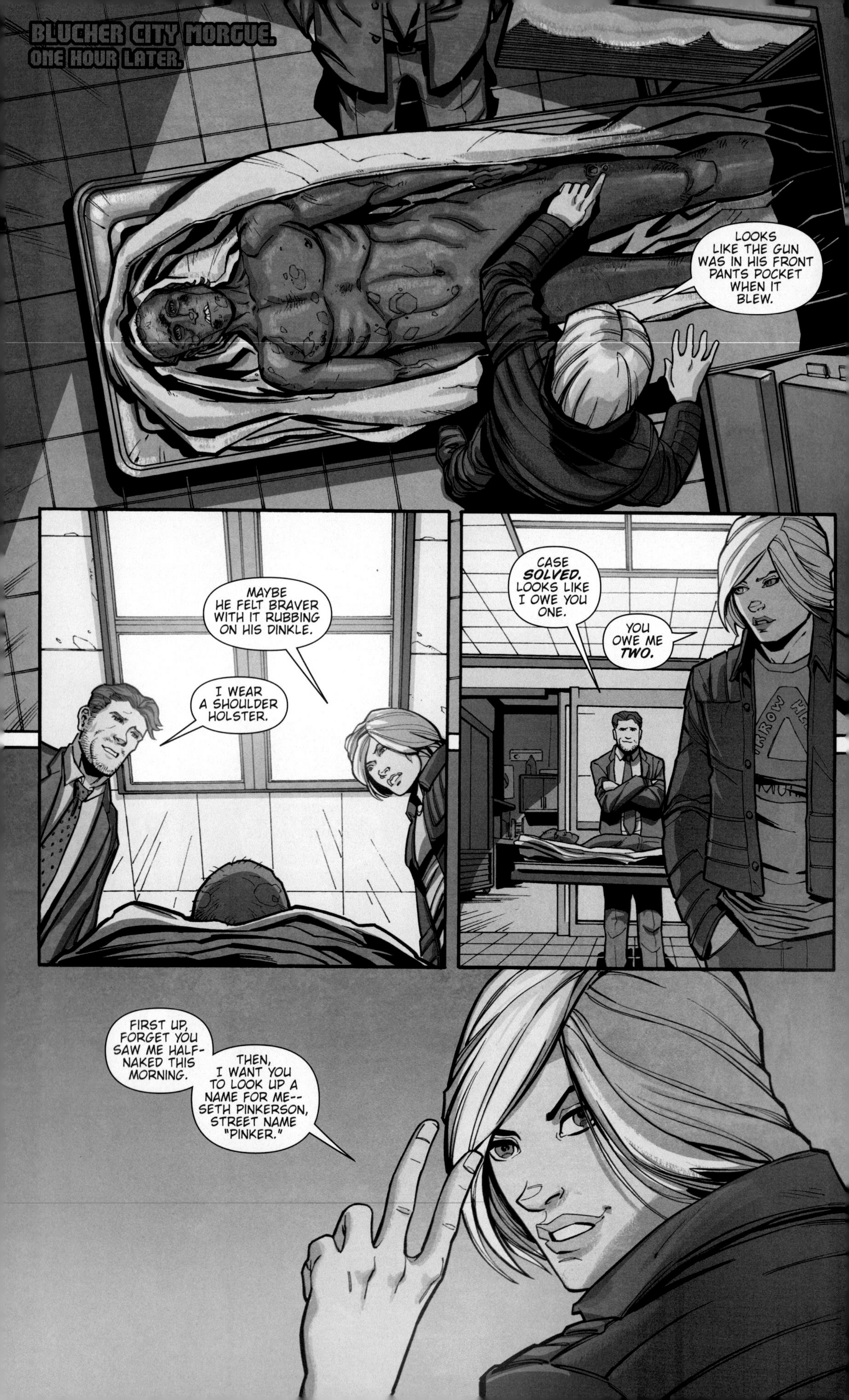

BLUCHER CITY MORGUE. ONE HOUR LATER.
LOOKS LIKE THE GUN WAS IN HIS FRONT PANTS POCKET WHEN IT BLEW.
MAYBE HE FELT BRAVER WITH IT RUBBING ON HIS DINKLE.
I WEAR A SHOULDER HOLSTER.
CASE SOLVED. LOOKS LIKE I OWE YOU ONE.
YOU OWE ME TWO.
FIRST UP, FORGET YOU SAW ME HALF-NAKED THIS MORNING.
THEN, I WANT YOU TO LOOK UP A NAME FOR ME-- SETH PINKERSON, STREET NAME "PINKER."

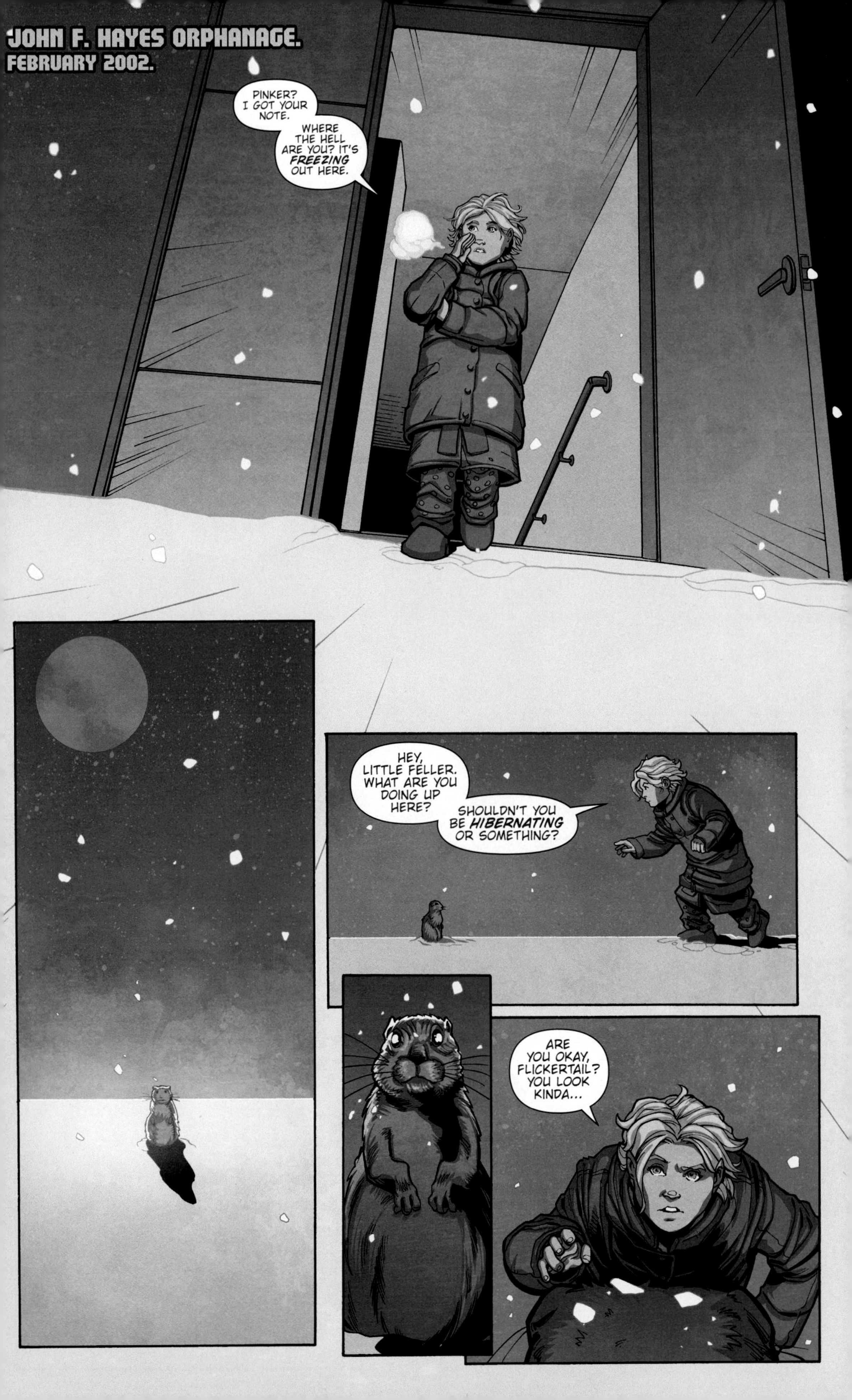
JOHN F. HAYES ORPHANAGE.
FEBRUARY 2002.
PINKER? I GOT YOUR NOTE.
WHERE THE HELL ARE YOU? IT'S *FREEZING* OUT HERE.
HEY, LITTLE FELLER. WHAT ARE YOU DOING UP HERE?
SHOULDN'T YOU BE *HIBERNATING* OR SOMETHING?
ARE YOU OKAY, FLICKERTAIL? YOU LOOK KINDA...

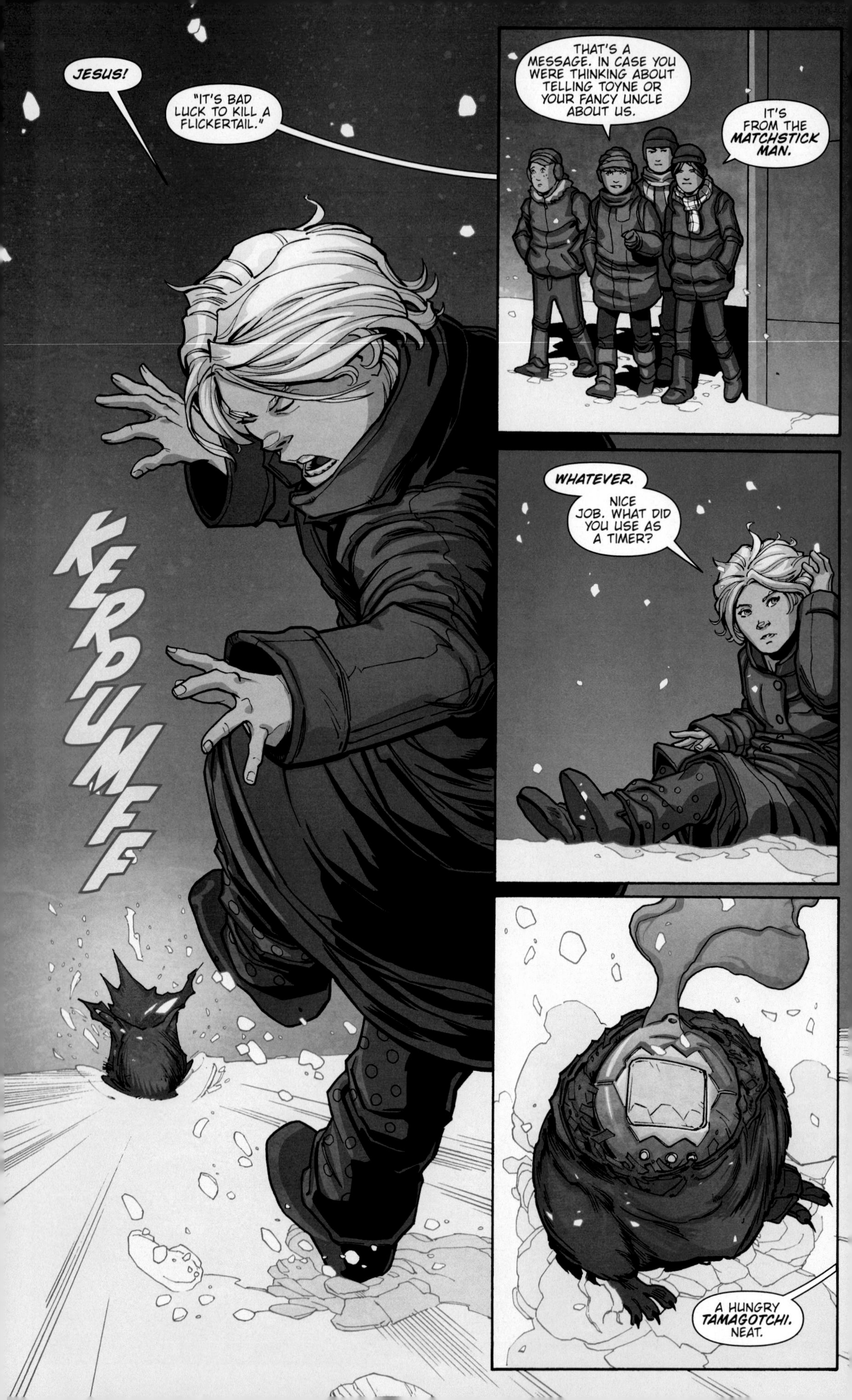
JESUS!
"IT'S BAD LUCK TO KILL A FLICKERTAIL."
KERPUMFF
THAT'S A MESSAGE. IN CASE YOU WERE THINKING ABOUT TELLING TOYNE OR YOUR FANCY UNCLE ABOUT US.
IT'S FROM THE MATCHSTICK MAN.
WHATEVER.
NICE JOB. WHAT DID YOU USE AS A TIMER?
A HUNGRY TAMAGOTCHI. NEAT.

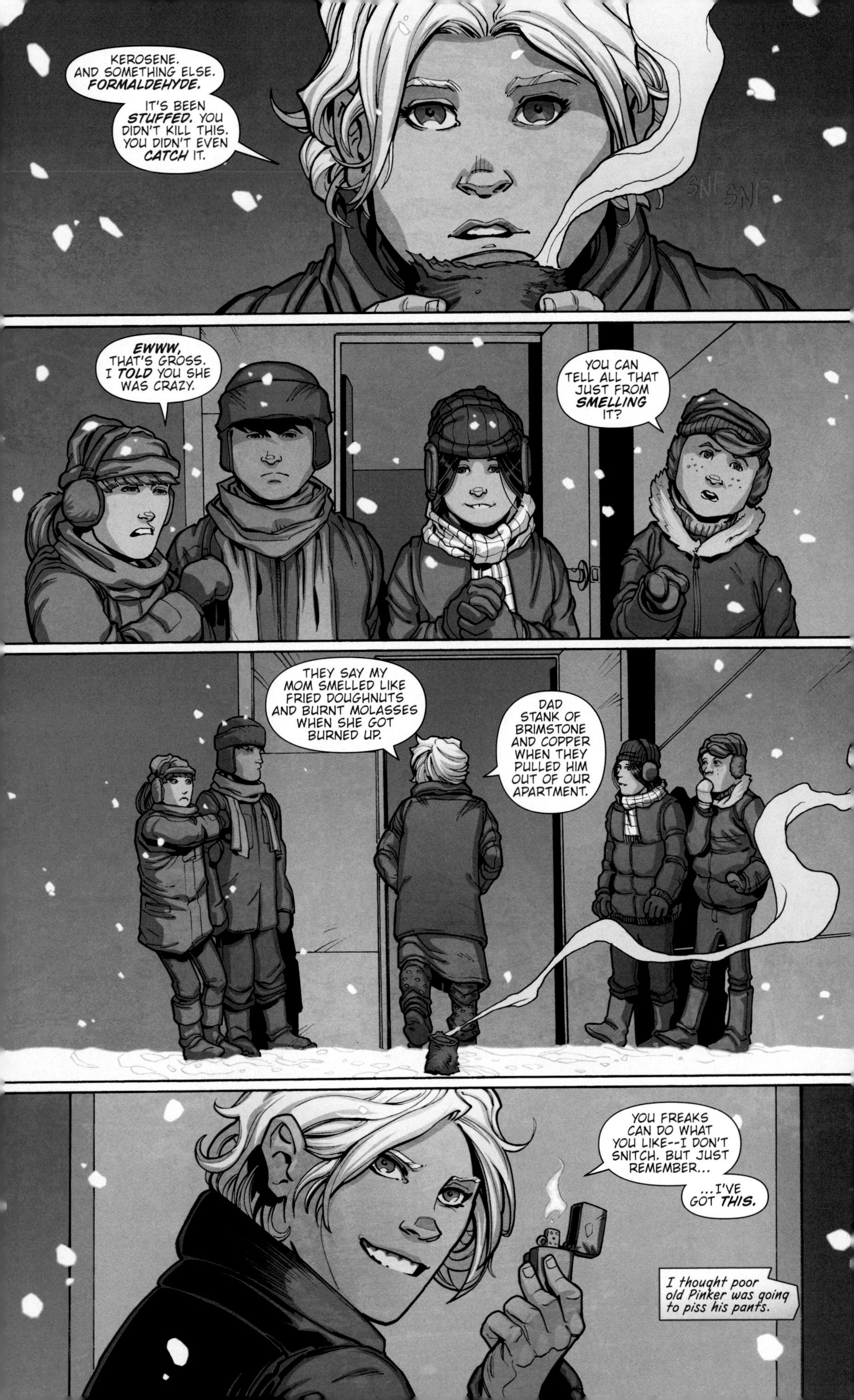
KEROSENE. AND SOMETHING ELSE. FORMALDEHYDE.
IT'S BEEN STUFFED. YOU DIDN'T KILL THIS. YOU DIDN'T EVEN CATCH IT.
SNF SNF
EWWW, THAT'S GROSS. I TOLD YOU SHE WAS CRAZY.
YOU CAN TELL ALL THAT JUST FROM SMELLING IT?
THEY SAY MY MOM SMELLED LIKE FRIED DOUGHNUTS AND BURNT MOLASSES WHEN SHE GOT BURNED UP.
DAD STANK OF BRIMSTONE AND COPPER WHEN THEY PULLED HIM OUT OF OUR APARTMENT.
YOU FREAKS CAN DO WHAT YOU LIKE--I DON'T SNITCH. BUT JUST REMEMBER...
...I'VE GOT THIS.
I thought poor old Pinker was going to piss his pants.

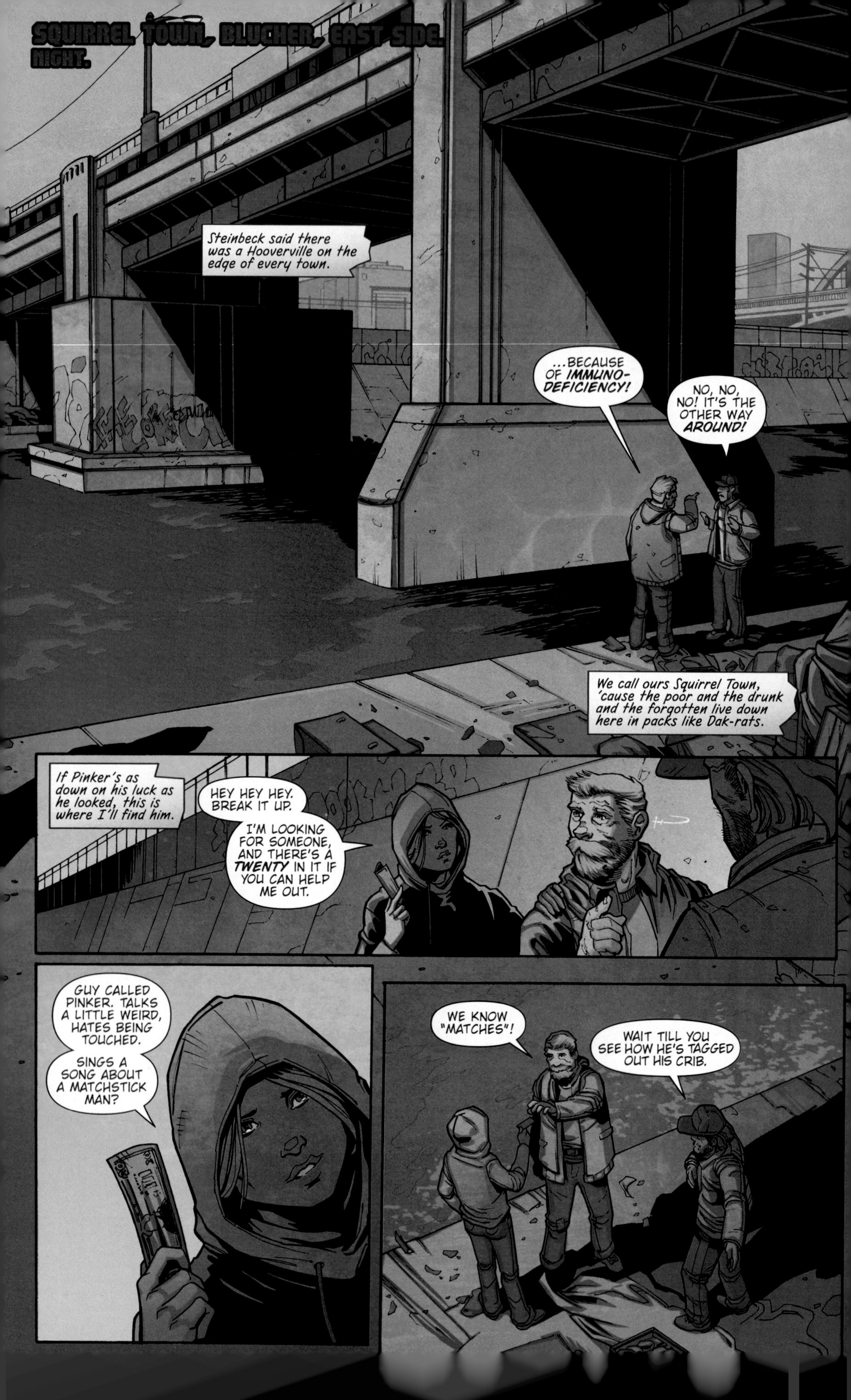
SQUIRREL TOWN, BLUCHER, EAST SIDE. NIGHT.
Steinbeck said there was a Hooverville on the edge of every town.
...BECAUSE OF IMMUNO-DEFICIENCY!
NO, NO, NO! IT'S THE OTHER WAY AROUND!
We call ours Squirrel Town, 'cause the poor and the drunk and the forgotten live down here in packs like Dak-rats.
If Pinker's as down on his luck as he looked, this is where I'll find him.
HEY HEY HEY. BREAK IT UP.
I'M LOOKING FOR SOMEONE, AND THERE'S A TWENTY IN IT IF YOU CAN HELP ME OUT.
GUY CALLED PINKER. TALKS A LITTLE WEIRD, HATES BEING TOUCHED.
SINGS A SONG ABOUT A MATCHSTICK MAN?
WE KNOW "MATCHES"!
WAIT TILL YOU SEE HOW HE'S TAGGED OUT HIS CRIB.

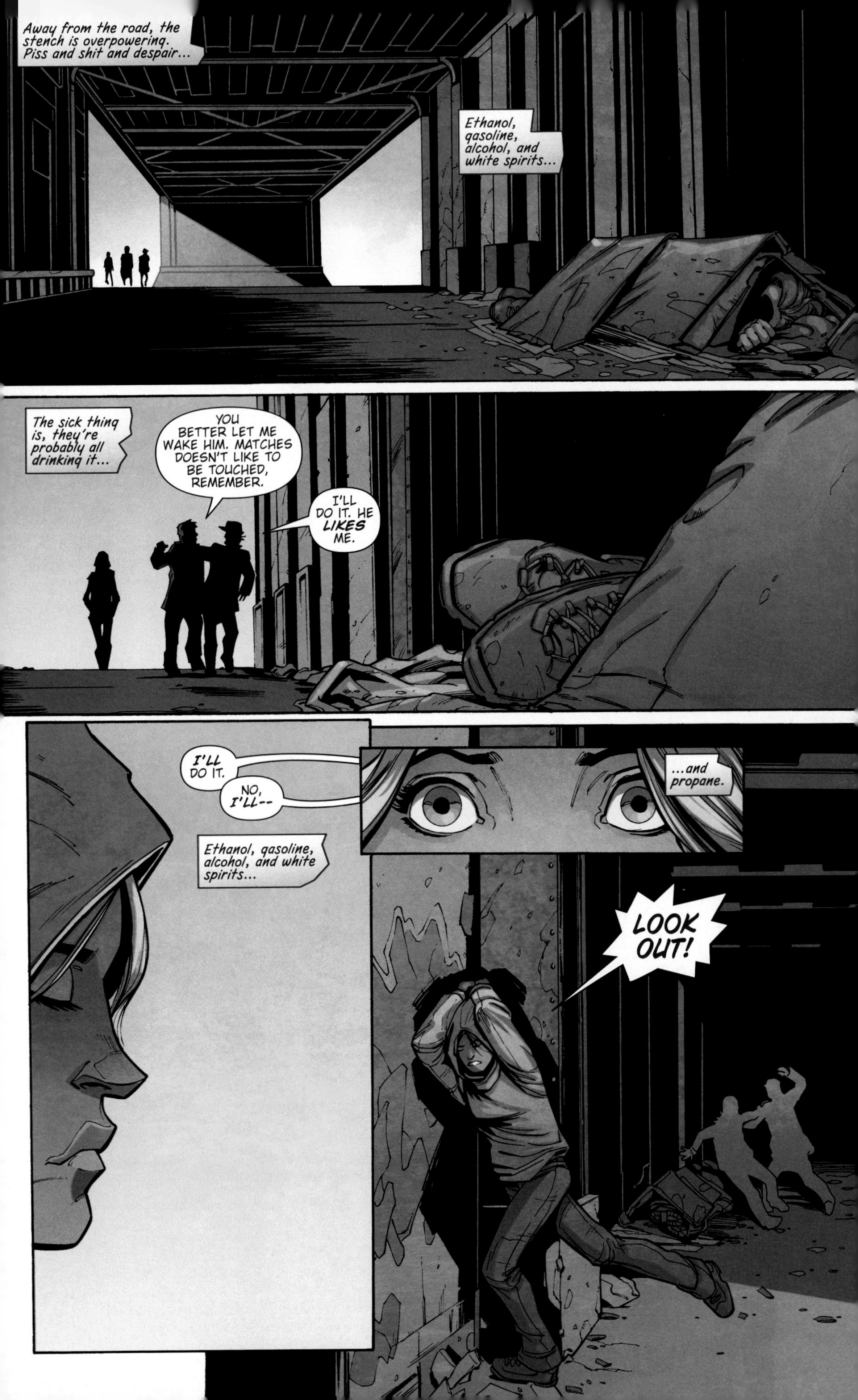
Away from the road, the stench is overpowering. Piss and shit and despair...
Ethanol, gasoline, alcohol, and white spirits...
The sick thing is, they're probably all drinking it...
YOU BETTER LET ME WAKE HIM. MATCHES DOESN'T LIKE TO BE TOUCHED, REMEMBER.
I'LL DO IT. HE LIKES ME.
I'LL DO IT.
NO, I'LL--
...and propane.
Ethanol, gasoline, alcohol, and white spirits...
LOOK OUT!

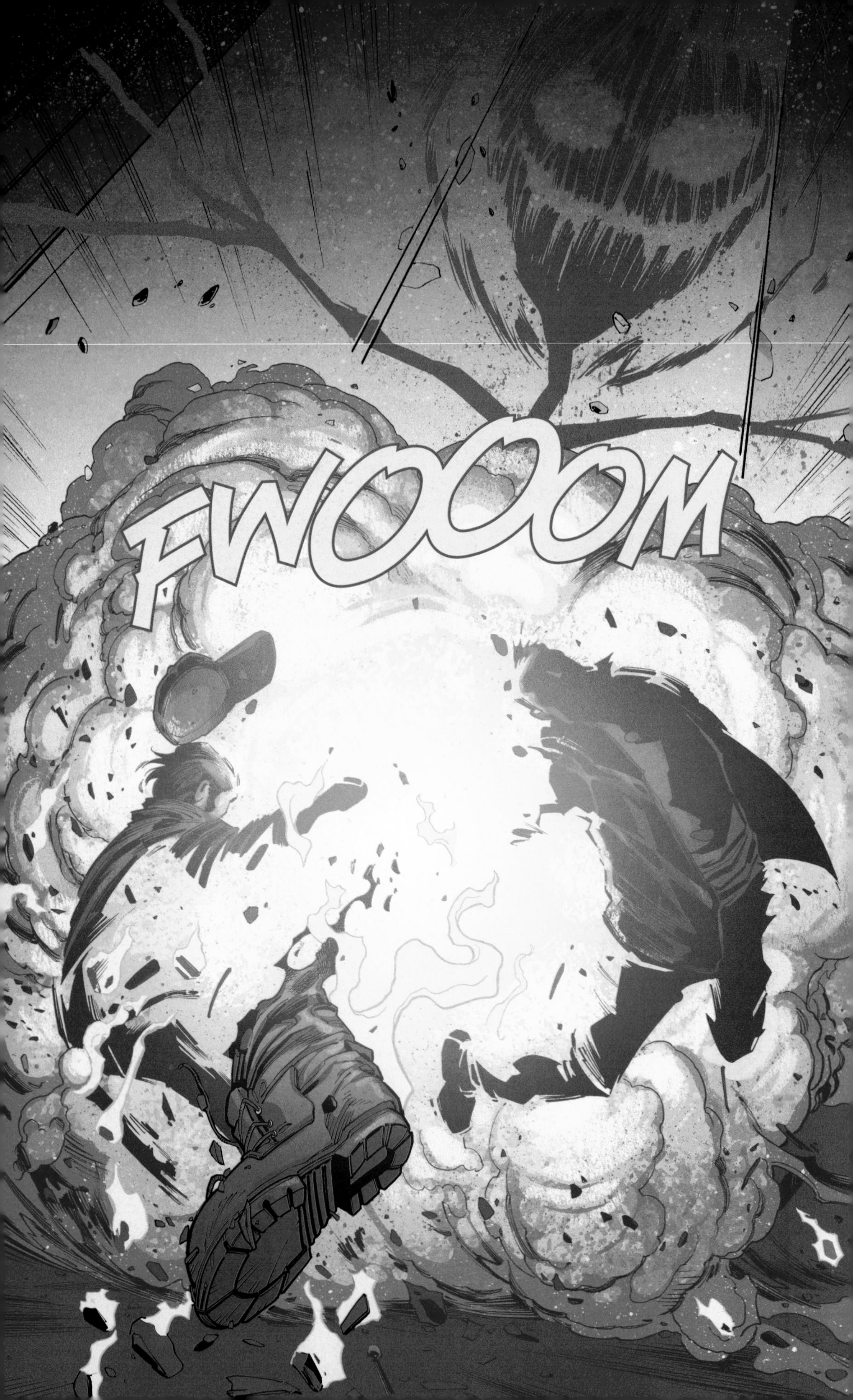
FWOOOM

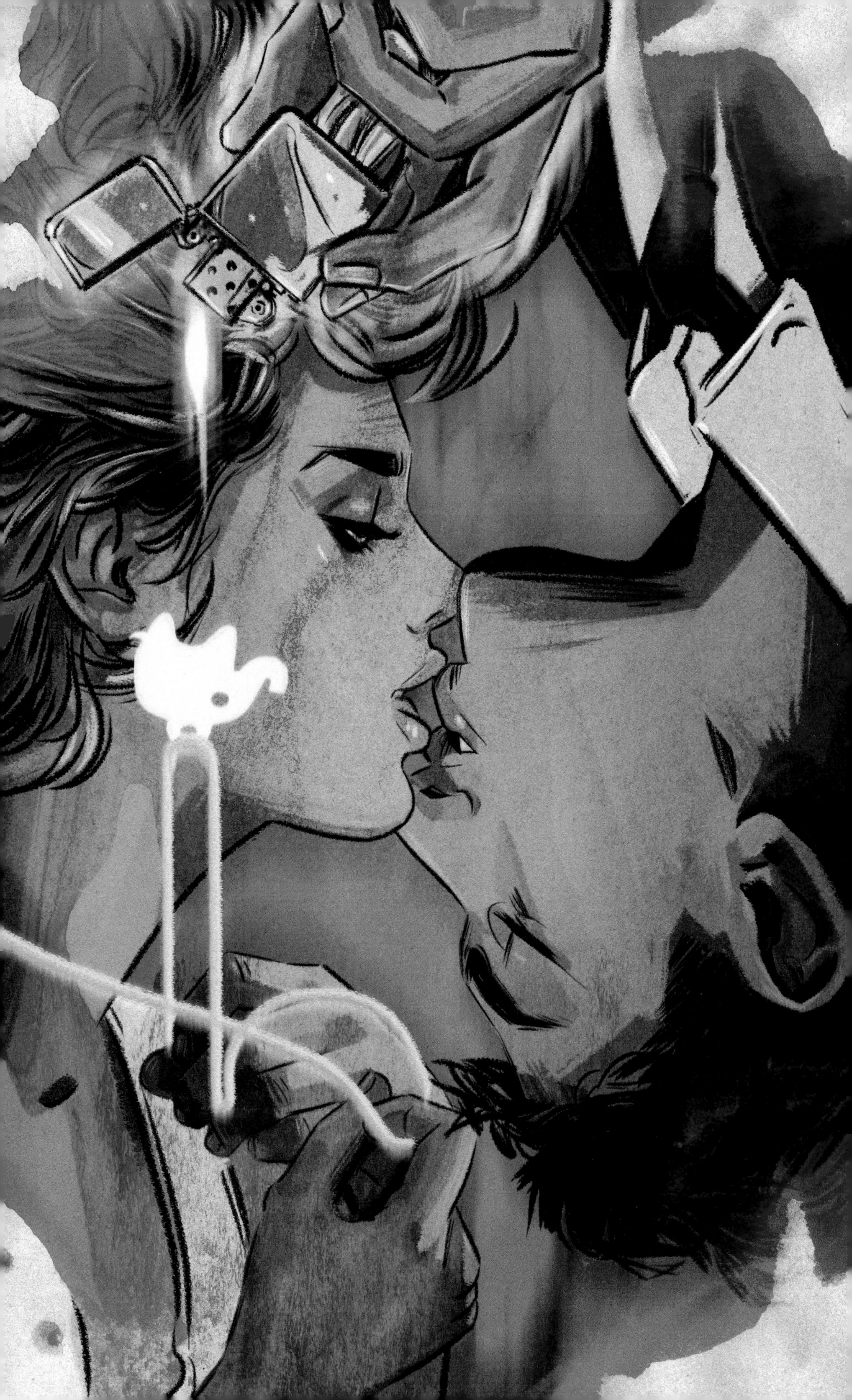

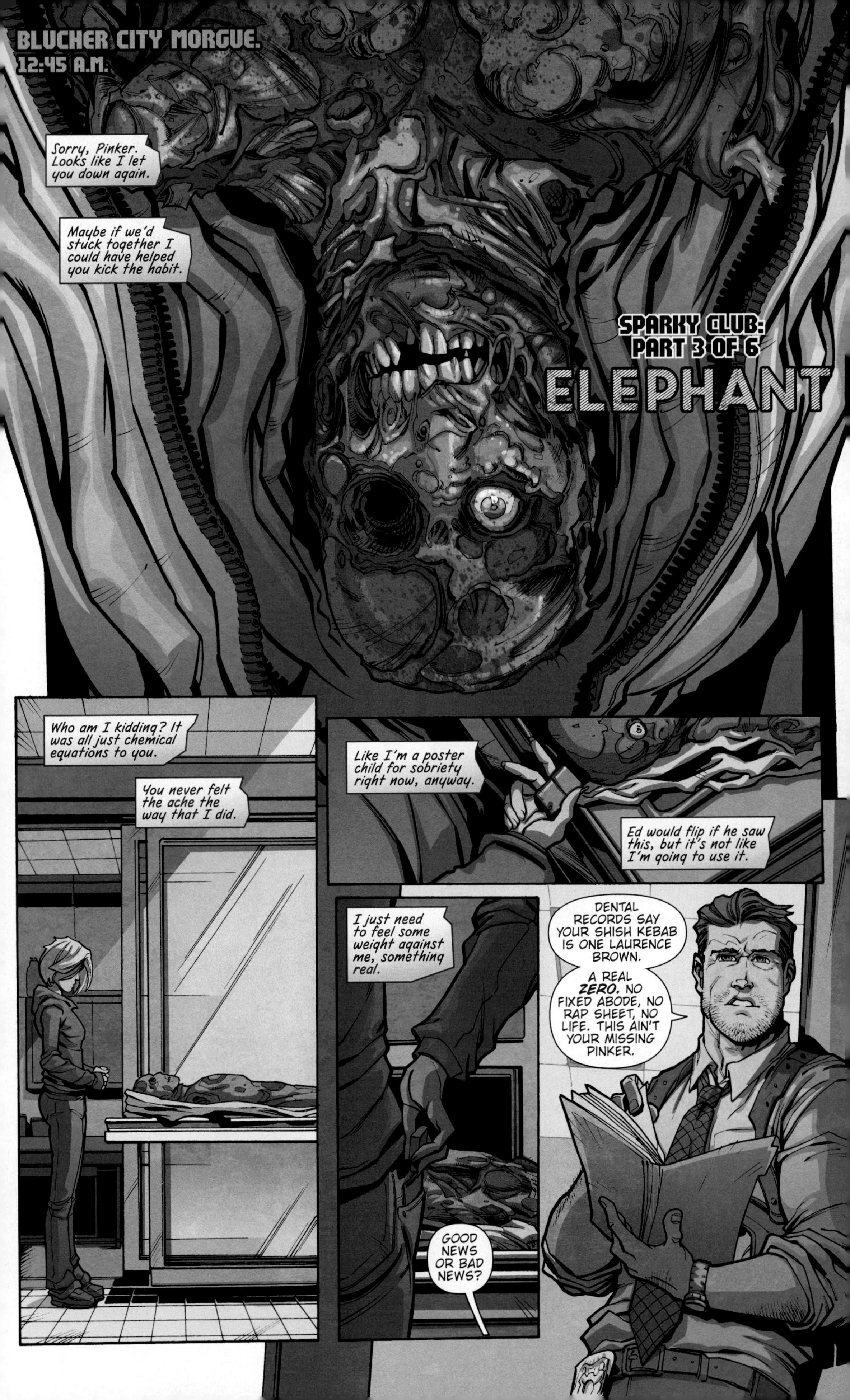
BLUCHER CITY MORGUE.
12:45 A.M.
Sorry, Pinker. Looks like I let you down again.
Maybe if we'd stuck together I could have helped you kick the habit.
SPARKY CLUB: PART 3 OF 6
ELEPHANT
Who am I kidding? It was all just chemical equations to you.
You never felt the ache the way that I did.
Like I'm a poster child for sobriety right now, anyway.
Ed would flip if he saw this, but it's not like I'm going to use it.
I just need to feel some weight against me, something real.
GOOD NEWS OR BAD NEWS?
DENTAL RECORDS SAY YOUR SHISH KEBAB IS ONE LAURENCE BROWN.
A REAL ZERO. NO FIXED ABODE, NO RAP SHEET, NO LIFE. THIS AIN'T YOUR MISSING PINKER.

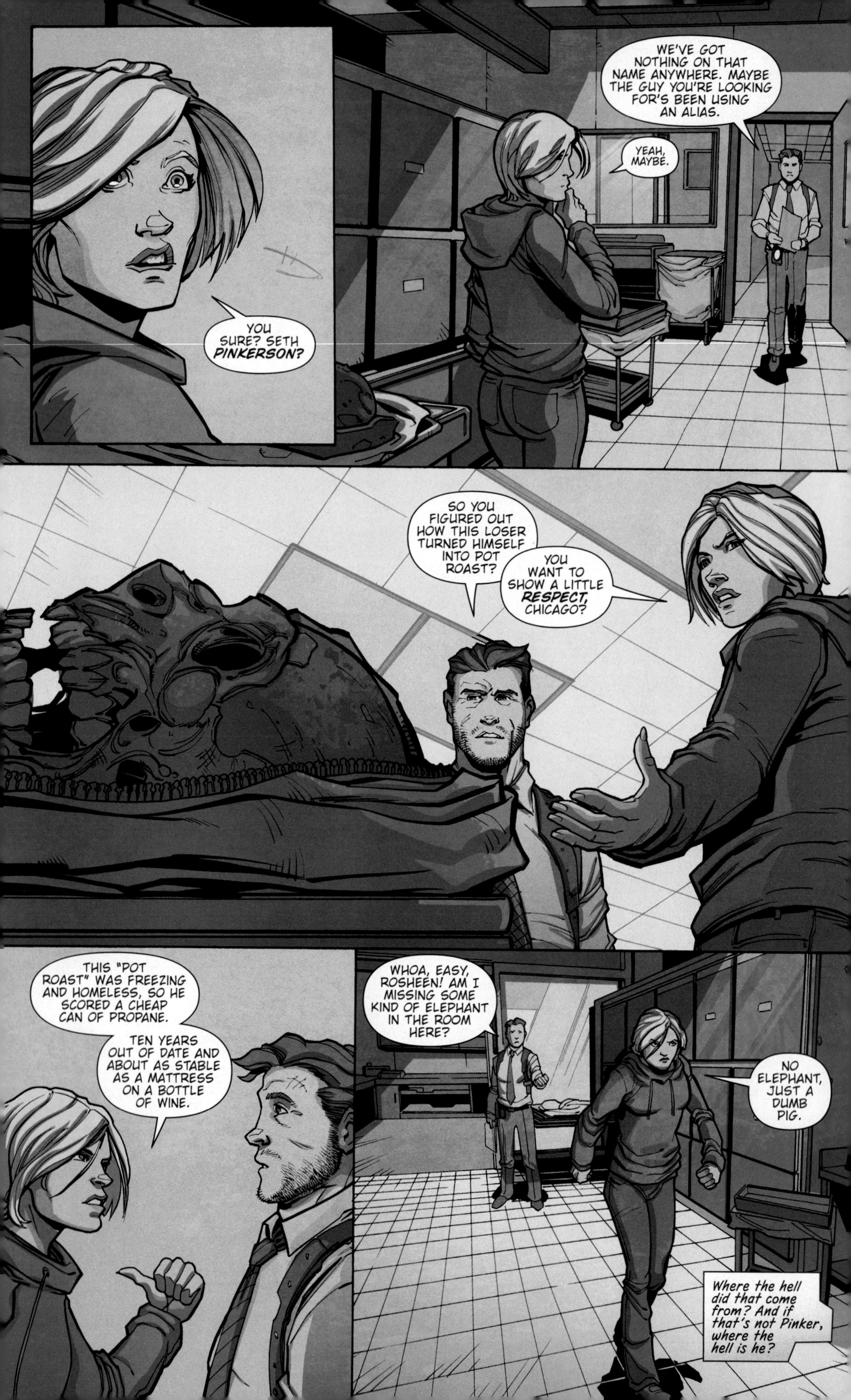
YOU SURE? SETH PINKERSON?
WE'VE GOT NOTHING ON THAT NAME ANYWHERE. MAYBE THE GUY YOU'RE LOOKING FOR'S BEEN USING AN ALIAS.
YEAH, MAYBE.
SO YOU FIGURED OUT HOW THIS LOSER TURNED HIMSELF INTO POT ROAST?
YOU WANT TO SHOW A LITTLE RESPECT, CHICAGO?
THIS "POT ROAST" WAS FREEZING AND HOMELESS, SO HE SCORED A CHEAP CAN OF PROPANE.
TEN YEARS OUT OF DATE AND ABOUT AS STABLE AS A MATTRESS ON A BOTTLE OF WINE.
WHOA, EASY, ROSHEEN! AM I MISSING SOME KIND OF ELEPHANT IN THE ROOM HERE?
NO ELEPHANT, JUST A DUMB PIG.
Where the hell did that come from? And if that's not Pinker, where the hell is he?

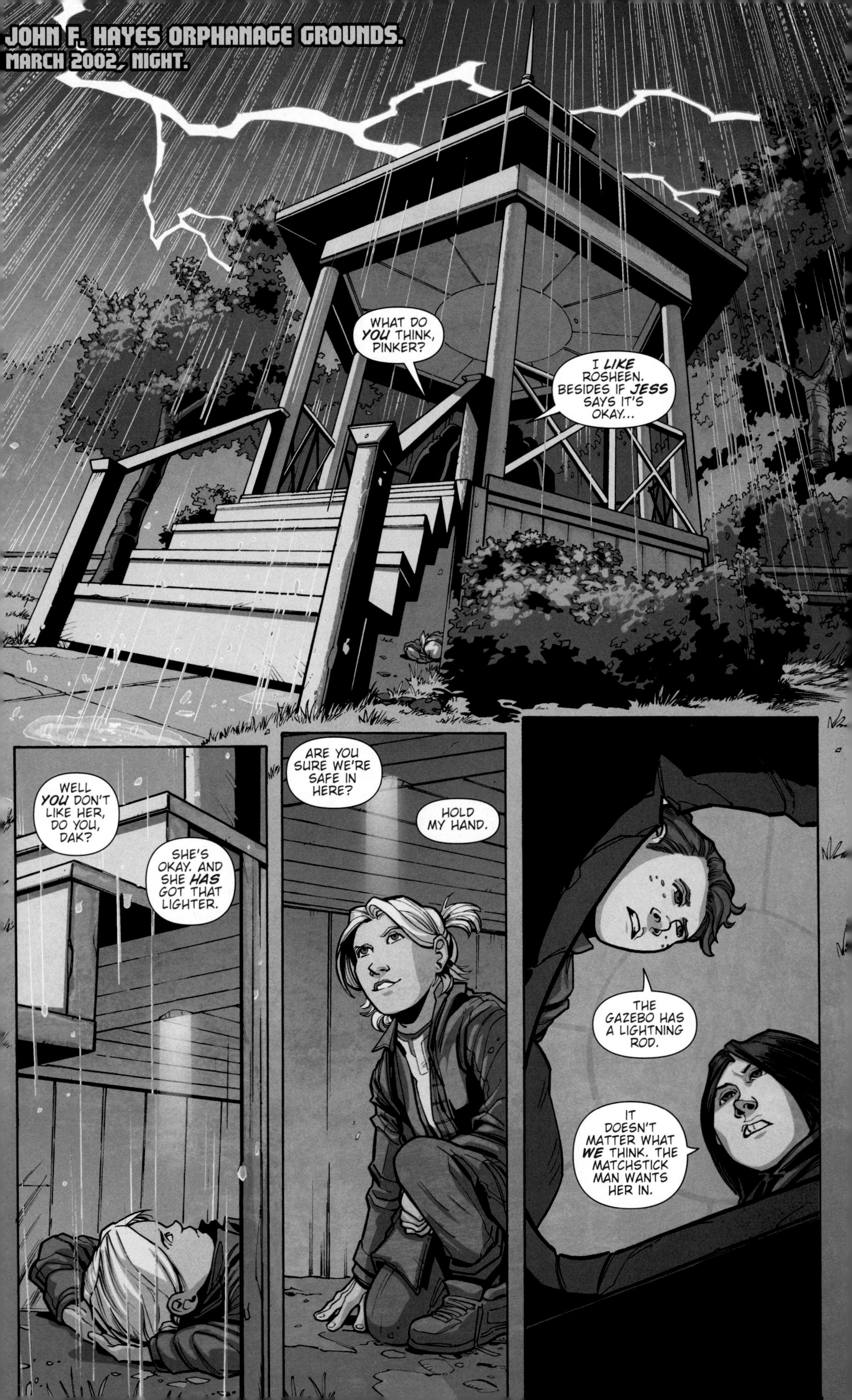

JOHN F. HAYES ORPHANAGE GROUNDS.
MARCH 2002, NIGHT.
WHAT DO YOU THINK, PINKER?
I LIKE ROSHEEN. BESIDES IF JESS SAYS IT'S OKAY...
WELL YOU DON'T LIKE HER, DO YOU, DAK?
SHE'S OKAY. AND SHE HAS GOT THAT LIGHTER.
ARE YOU SURE WE'RE SAFE IN HERE?
HOLD MY HAND.
THE GAZEBO HAS A LIGHTNING ROD.
IT DOESN'T MATTER WHAT WE THINK. THE MATCHSTICK MAN WANTS HER IN.

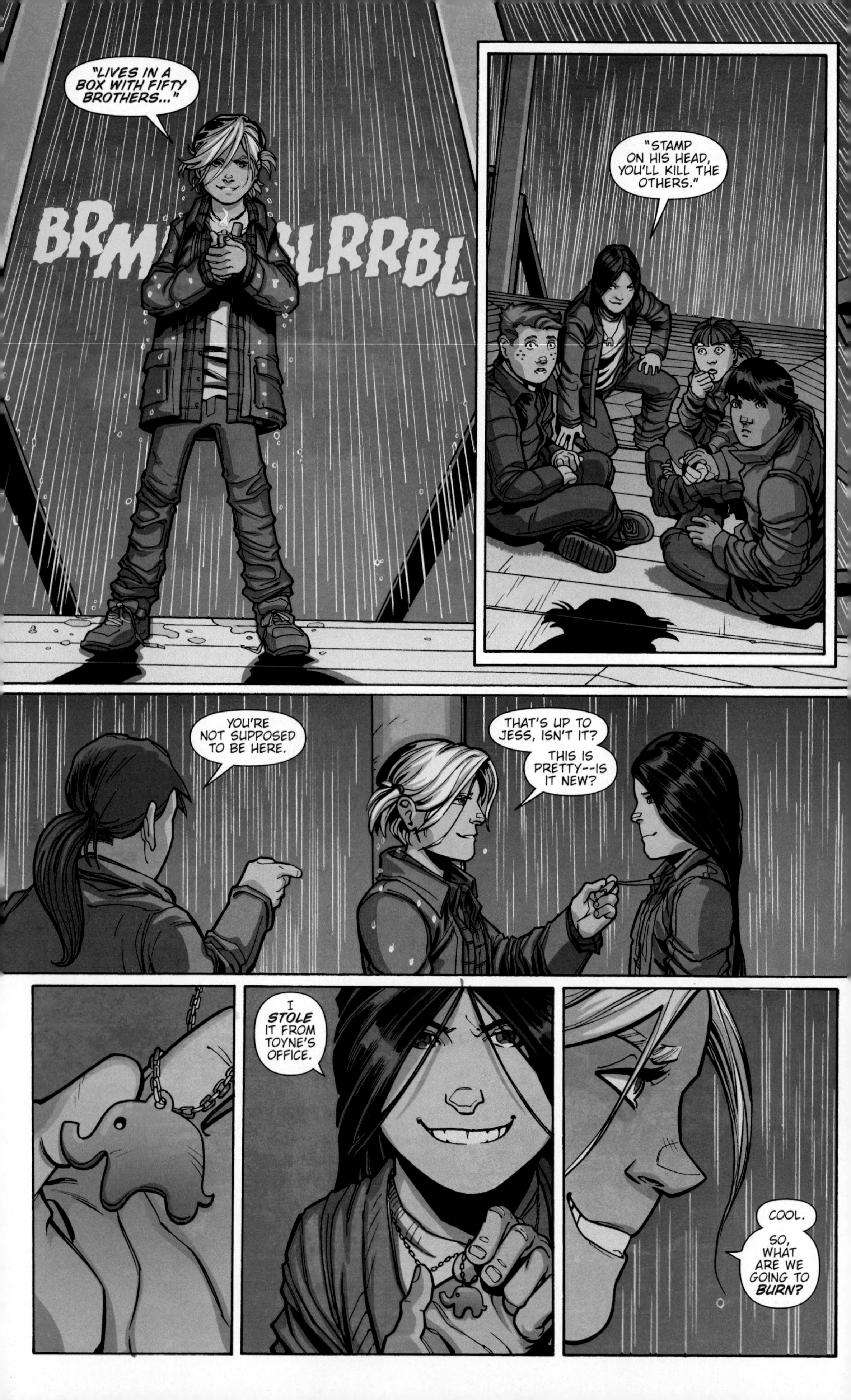
"LIVES IN A BOX WITH FIFTY BROTHERS..."
BRMBLLRRRBL
"STAMP ON HIS HEAD, YOU'LL KILL THE OTHERS."
YOU'RE NOT SUPPOSED TO BE HERE.
THAT'S UP TO JESS, ISN'T IT?
THIS IS PRETTY--IS IT NEW?
I STOLE IT FROM TOYNE'S OFFICE.
COOL.
SO, WHAT ARE WE GOING TO BURN?

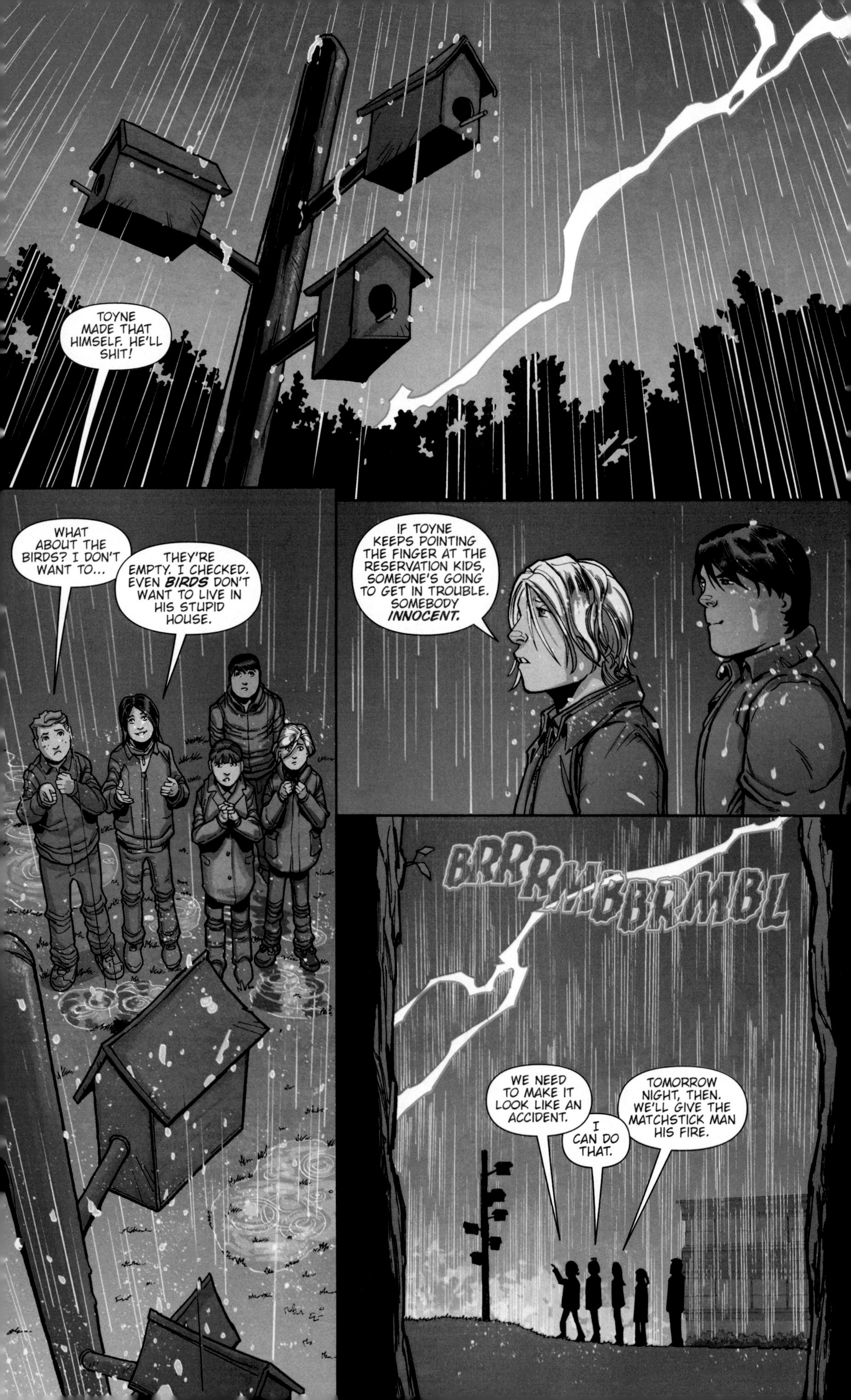
TOYNE MADE THAT HIMSELF. HE'LL SHIT!
WHAT ABOUT THE BIRDS? I DON'T WANT TO...
THEY'RE EMPTY. I CHECKED. EVEN **BIRDS** DON'T WANT TO LIVE IN HIS STUPID HOUSE.
IF TOYNE KEEPS POINTING THE FINGER AT THE RESERVATION KIDS, SOMEONE'S GOING TO GET IN TROUBLE. SOMEBODY ***INNOCENT.***
BRRRMBBRMBL
WE NEED TO MAKE IT LOOK LIKE AN ACCIDENT.
I CAN DO THAT.
TOMORROW NIGHT, THEN. WE'LL GIVE THE MATCHSTICK MAN HIS FIRE.

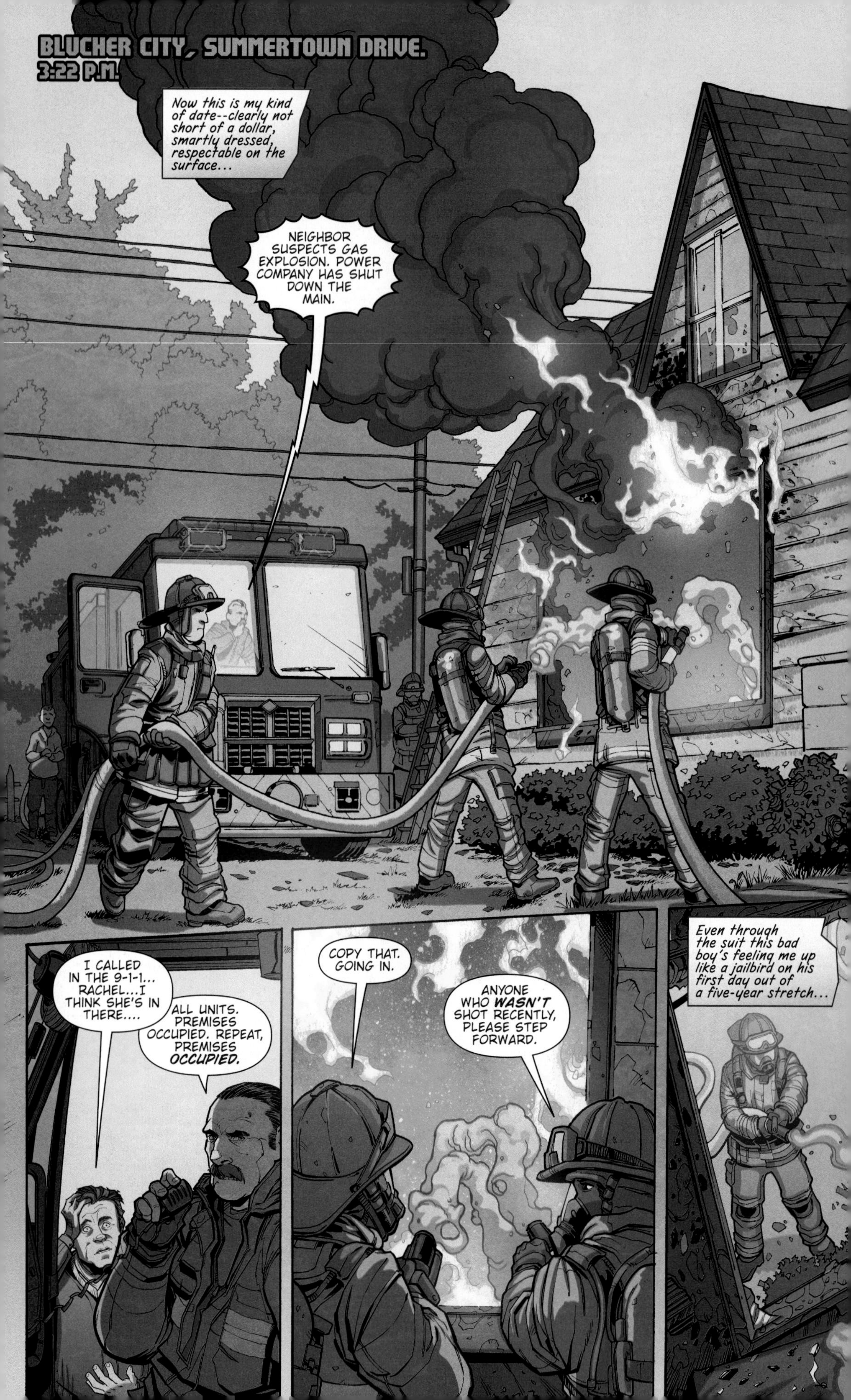
BLUCHER CITY, SUMMERTOWN DRIVE.
3:22 P.M.
Now this is my kind of date--clearly not short of a dollar, smartly dressed, respectable on the surface...
NEIGHBOR SUSPECTS GAS EXPLOSION. POWER COMPANY HAS SHUT DOWN THE MAIN.
I CALLED IN THE 9-1-1... RACHEL...I THINK SHE'S IN THERE....
ALL UNITS. PREMISES OCCUPIED. REPEAT, PREMISES OCCUPIED.
COPY THAT. GOING IN.
ANYONE WHO WASN'T SHOT RECENTLY, PLEASE STEP FORWARD.
Even through the suit this bad boy's feeling me up like a jailbird on his first day out of a five-year stretch...

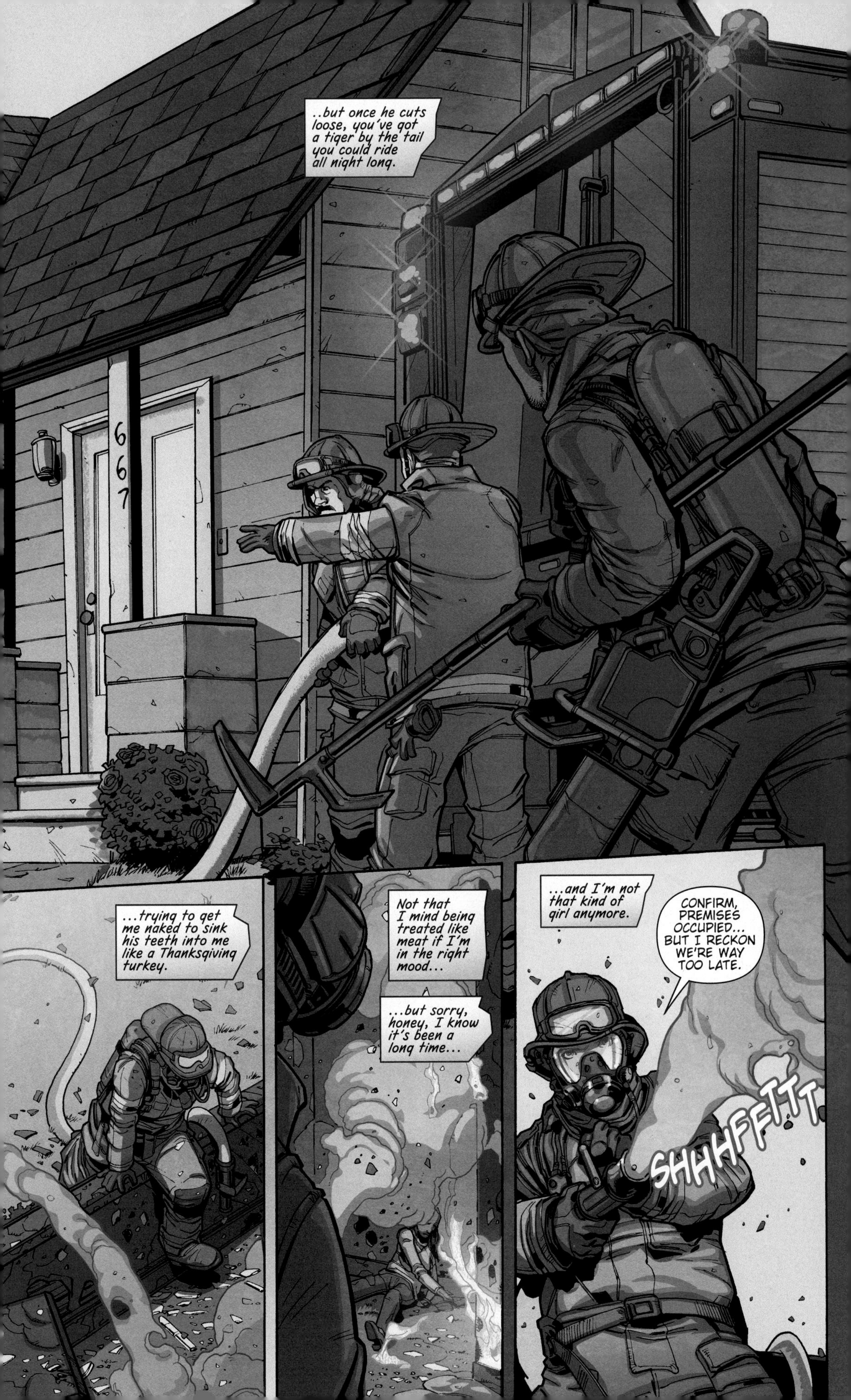
..but once he cuts loose, you've got a tiger by the tail you could ride all night long.
667
...trying to get me naked to sink his teeth into me like a Thanksgiving turkey.
Not that I mind being treated like meat if I'm in the right mood...
...but sorry, honey, I know it's been a long time...
...and I'm not that kind of girl anymore.
CONFIRM, PREMISES OCCUPIED... BUT I RECKON WE'RE WAY TOO LATE.
SHHHFFTTT

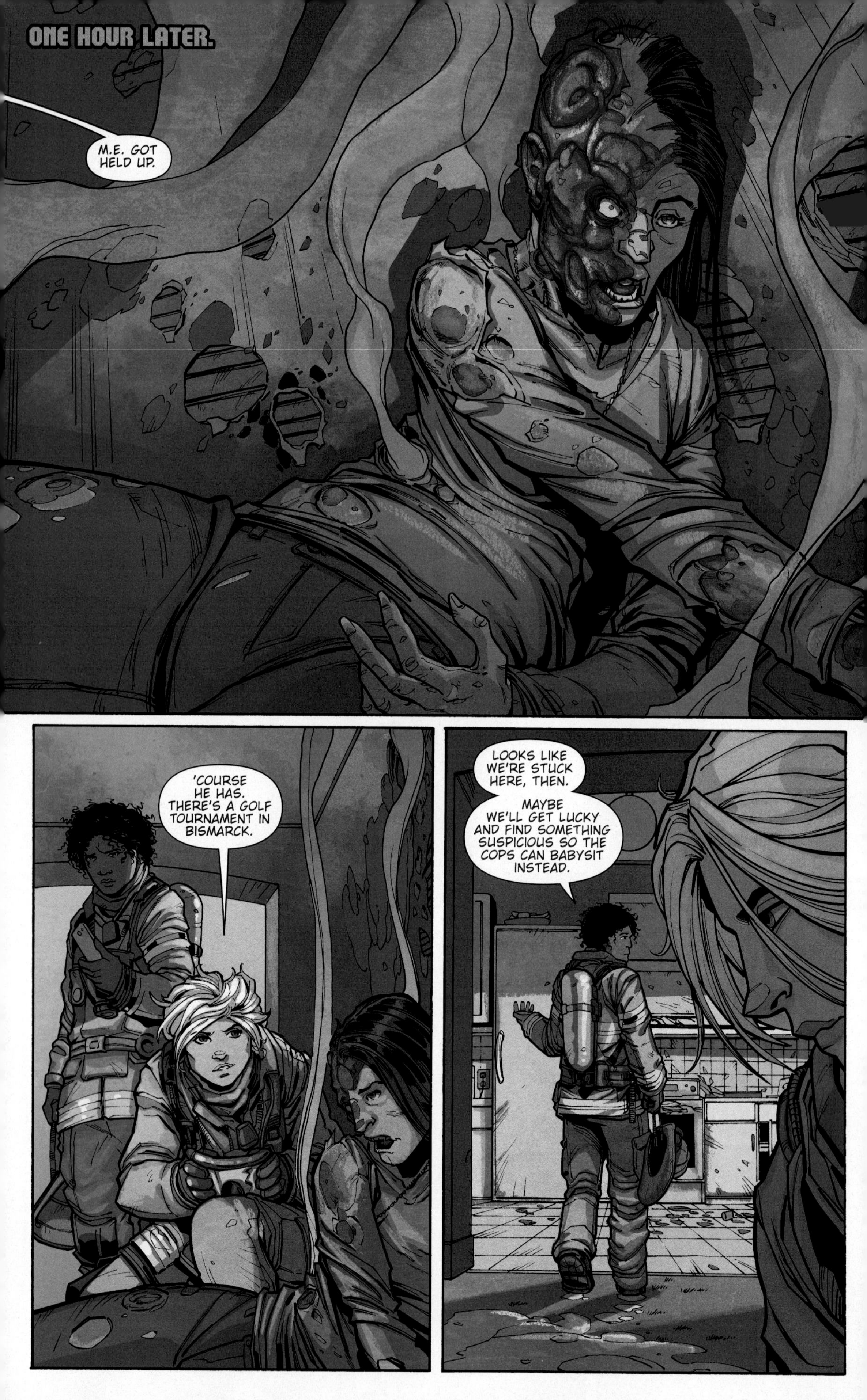
ONE HOUR LATER.
M.E. GOT HELD UP.
'COURSE HE HAS. THERE'S A GOLF TOURNAMENT IN BISMARCK.
LOOKS LIKE WE'RE STUCK HERE, THEN.
MAYBE WE'LL GET LUCKY AND FIND SOMETHING SUSPICIOUS SO THE COPS CAN BABYSIT INSTEAD.

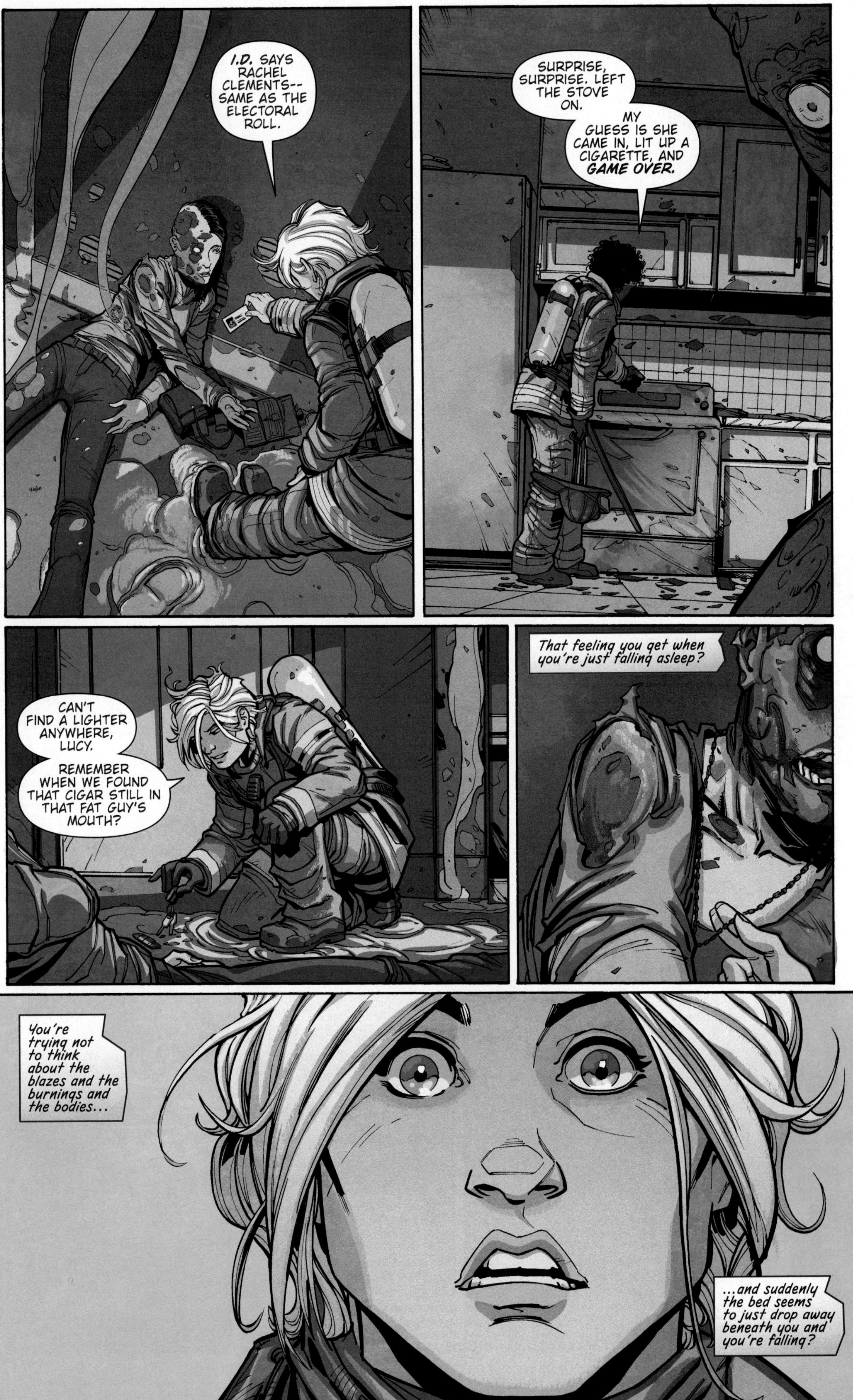
I.D. SAYS RACHEL CLEMENTS-- SAME AS THE ELECTORAL ROLL.
SURPRISE, SURPRISE. LEFT THE STOVE ON.
MY GUESS IS SHE CAME IN, LIT UP A CIGARETTE, AND GAME OVER.
CAN'T FIND A LIGHTER ANYWHERE, LUCY.
REMEMBER WHEN WE FOUND THAT CIGAR STILL IN THAT FAT GUY'S MOUTH?
That feeling you get when you're just falling asleep?
You're trying not to think about the blazes and the burnings and the bodies...
...and suddenly the bed seems to just drop away beneath you and you're falling?

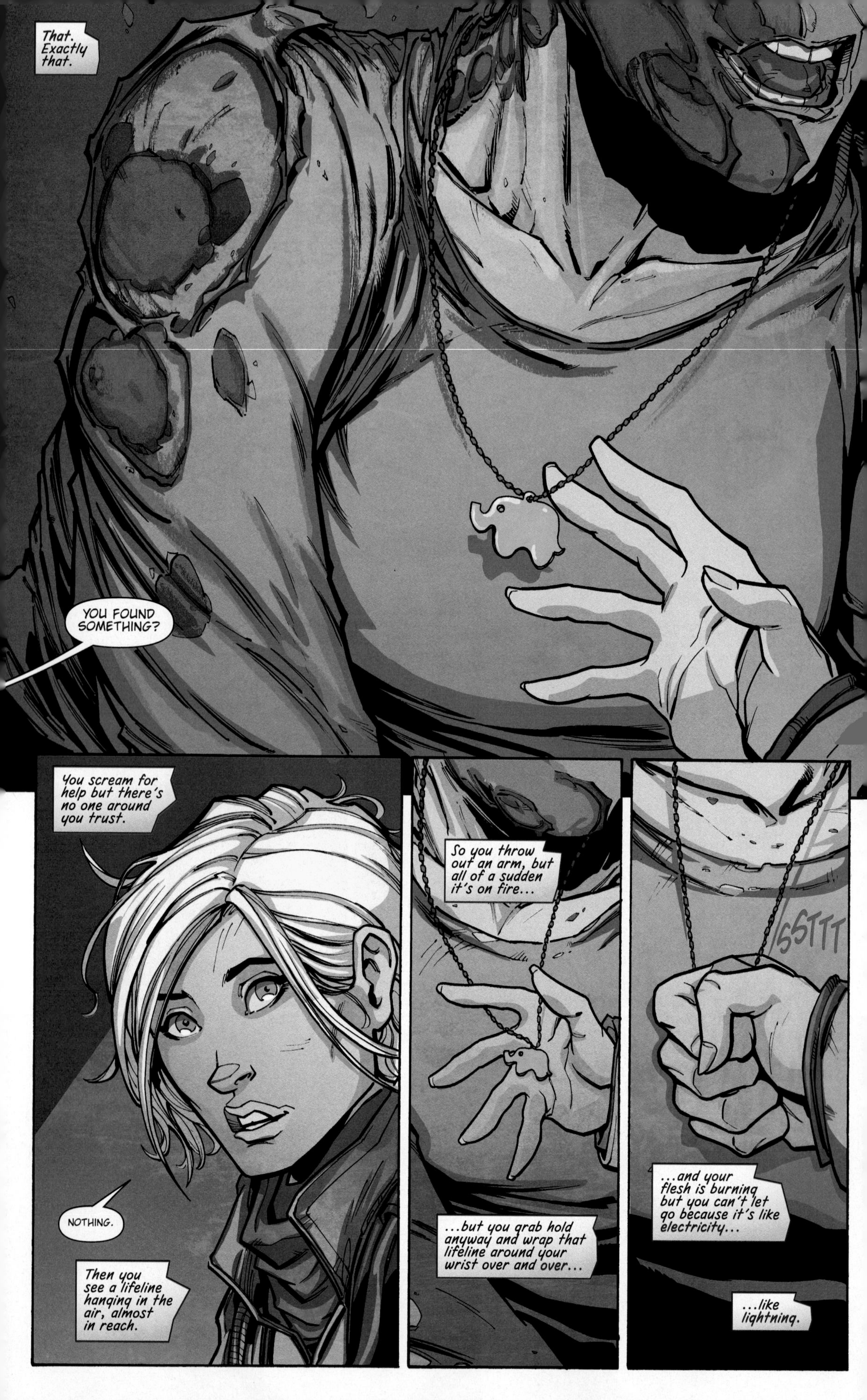

That. Exactly that.
YOU FOUND SOMETHING?
You scream for help but there's no one around you trust.
NOTHING.
Then you see a lifeline hanging in the air, almost in reach.
So you throw out an arm, but all of a sudden it's on fire...
...but you grab hold anyway and wrap that lifeline around your wrist over and over...
SSTTT
...and your flesh is burning but you can't let go because it's like electricity...
...like lightning.

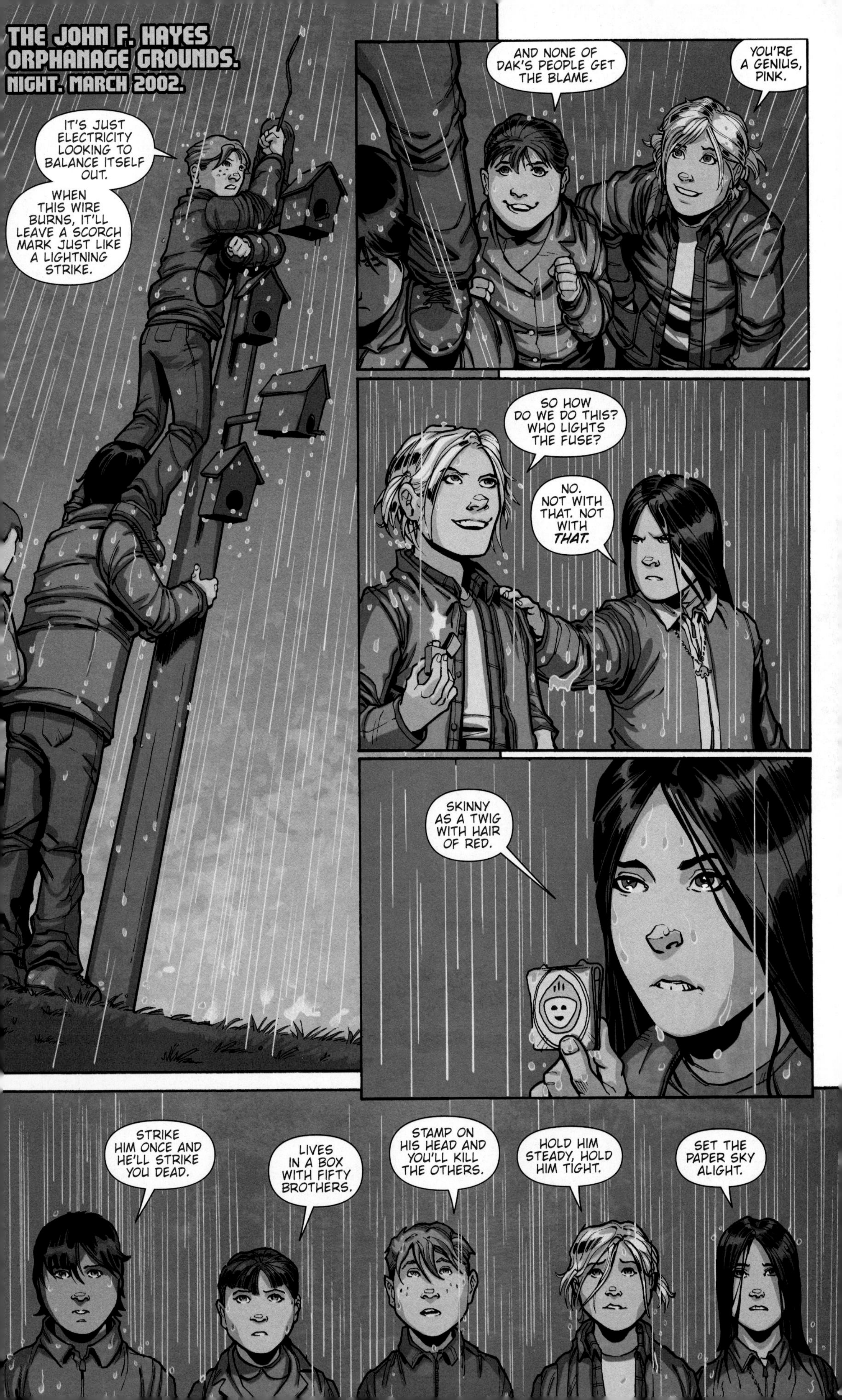
THE JOHN F. HAYES ORPHANAGE GROUNDS. NIGHT. MARCH 2002.
IT'S JUST ELECTRICITY LOOKING TO BALANCE ITSELF OUT.
WHEN THIS WIRE BURNS, IT'LL LEAVE A SCORCH MARK JUST LIKE A LIGHTNING STRIKE.
AND NONE OF DAK'S PEOPLE GET THE BLAME.
YOU'RE A GENIUS, PINK.
SO HOW DO WE DO THIS? WHO LIGHTS THE FUSE?
NO. NOT WITH THAT. NOT WITH *THAT.*
SKINNY AS A TWIG WITH HAIR OF RED.
STRIKE HIM ONCE AND HE'LL STRIKE YOU DEAD.
LIVES IN A BOX WITH FIFTY BROTHERS.
STAMP ON HIS HEAD AND YOU'LL KILL THE OTHERS.
HOLD HIM STEADY, HOLD HIM TIGHT.
SET THE PAPER SKY ALIGHT.

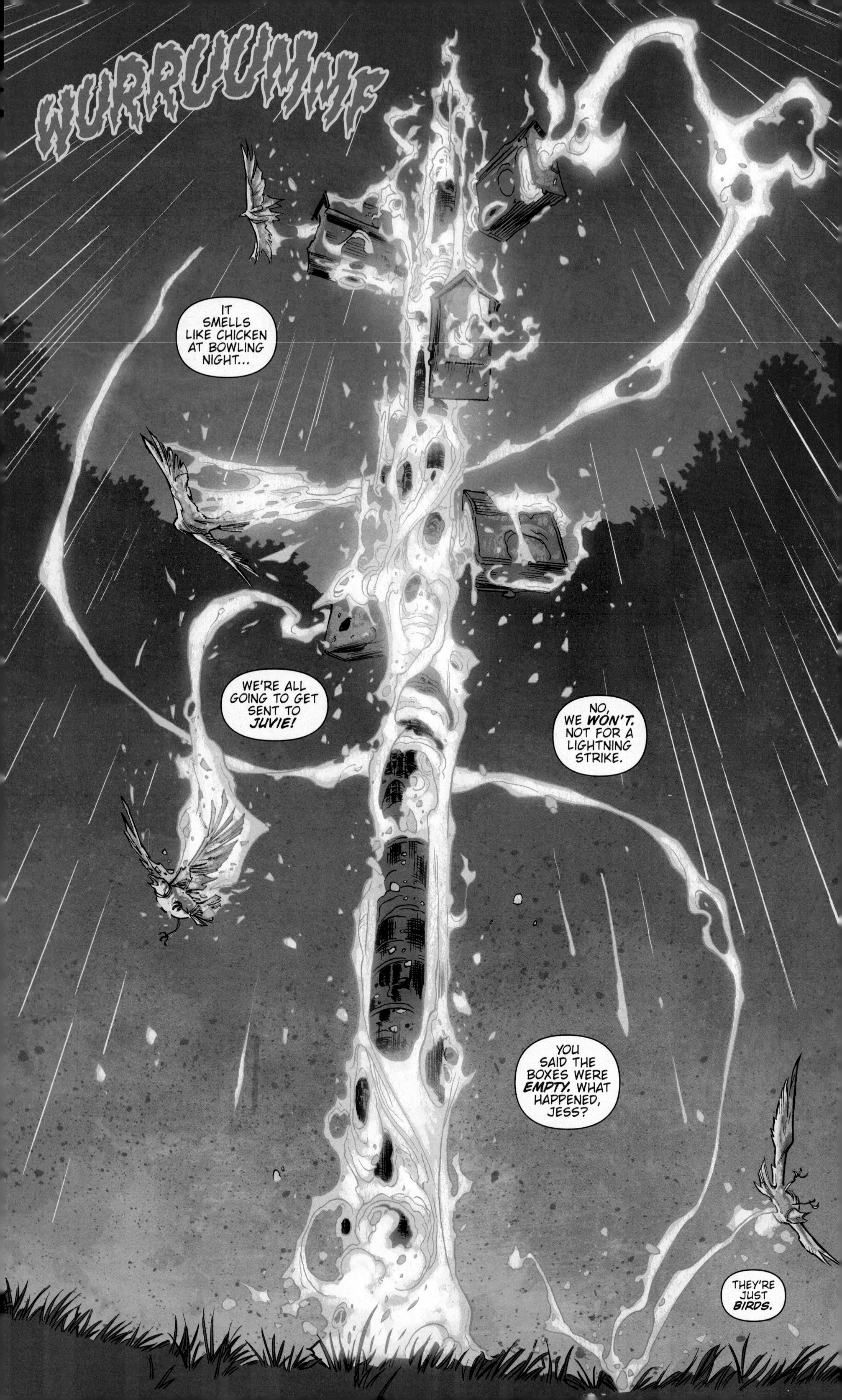
WURRUUMMF
IT SMELLS LIKE CHICKEN AT BOWLING NIGHT...
WE'RE ALL GOING TO GET SENT TO JUVIE!
NO, WE WON'T. NOT FOR A LIGHTNING STRIKE.
YOU SAID THE BOXES WERE EMPTY. WHAT HAPPENED, JESS?
THEY'RE JUST BIRDS.

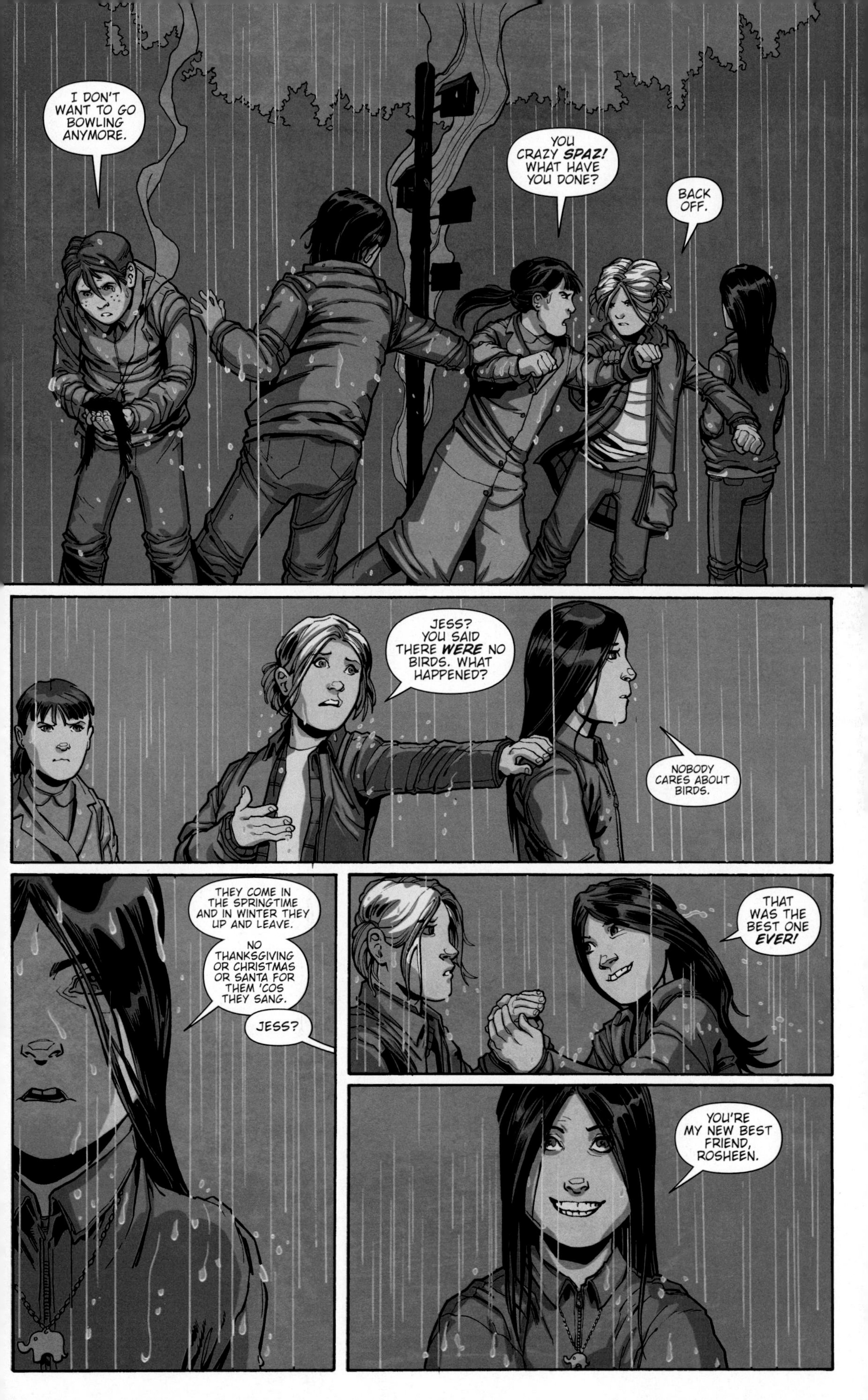
I DON'T WANT TO GO BOWLING ANYMORE.
YOU CRAZY SPAZ! WHAT HAVE YOU DONE?
BACK OFF.
JESS? YOU SAID THERE WERE NO BIRDS. WHAT HAPPENED?
NOBODY CARES ABOUT BIRDS.
THEY COME IN THE SPRINGTIME AND IN WINTER THEY UP AND LEAVE.
NO THANKSGIVING OR CHRISTMAS OR SANTA FOR THEM 'COS THEY SANG.
JESS?
THAT WAS THE BEST ONE EVER!
YOU'RE MY NEW BEST FRIEND, ROSHEEN.

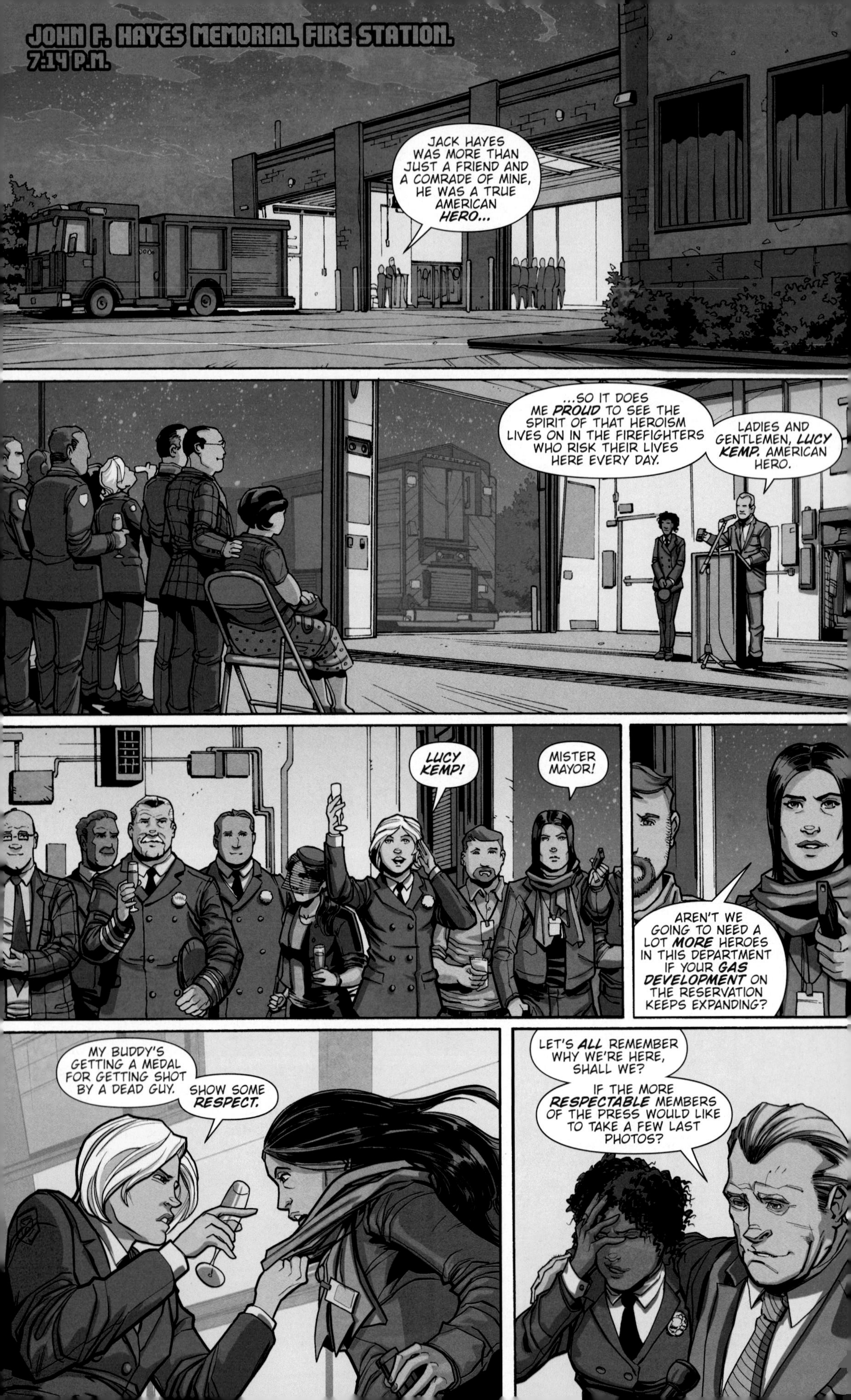
JOHN F. HAYES MEMORIAL FIRE STATION.
7:14 P.M.
JACK HAYES WAS MORE THAN JUST A FRIEND AND A COMRADE OF MINE, HE WAS A TRUE AMERICAN HERO...
...SO IT DOES ME PROUD TO SEE THE SPIRIT OF THAT HEROISM LIVES ON IN THE FIREFIGHTERS WHO RISK THEIR LIVES HERE EVERY DAY.
LADIES AND GENTLEMEN, LUCY KEMP. AMERICAN HERO.
LUCY KEMP!
MISTER MAYOR!
AREN'T WE GOING TO NEED A LOT MORE HEROES IN THIS DEPARTMENT IF YOUR GAS DEVELOPMENT ON THE RESERVATION KEEPS EXPANDING?
MY BUDDY'S GETTING A MEDAL FOR GETTING SHOT BY A DEAD GUY.
SHOW SOME RESPECT.
LET'S ALL REMEMBER WHY WE'RE HERE, SHALL WE?
IF THE MORE RESPECTABLE MEMBERS OF THE PRESS WOULD LIKE TO TAKE A FEW LAST PHOTOS?

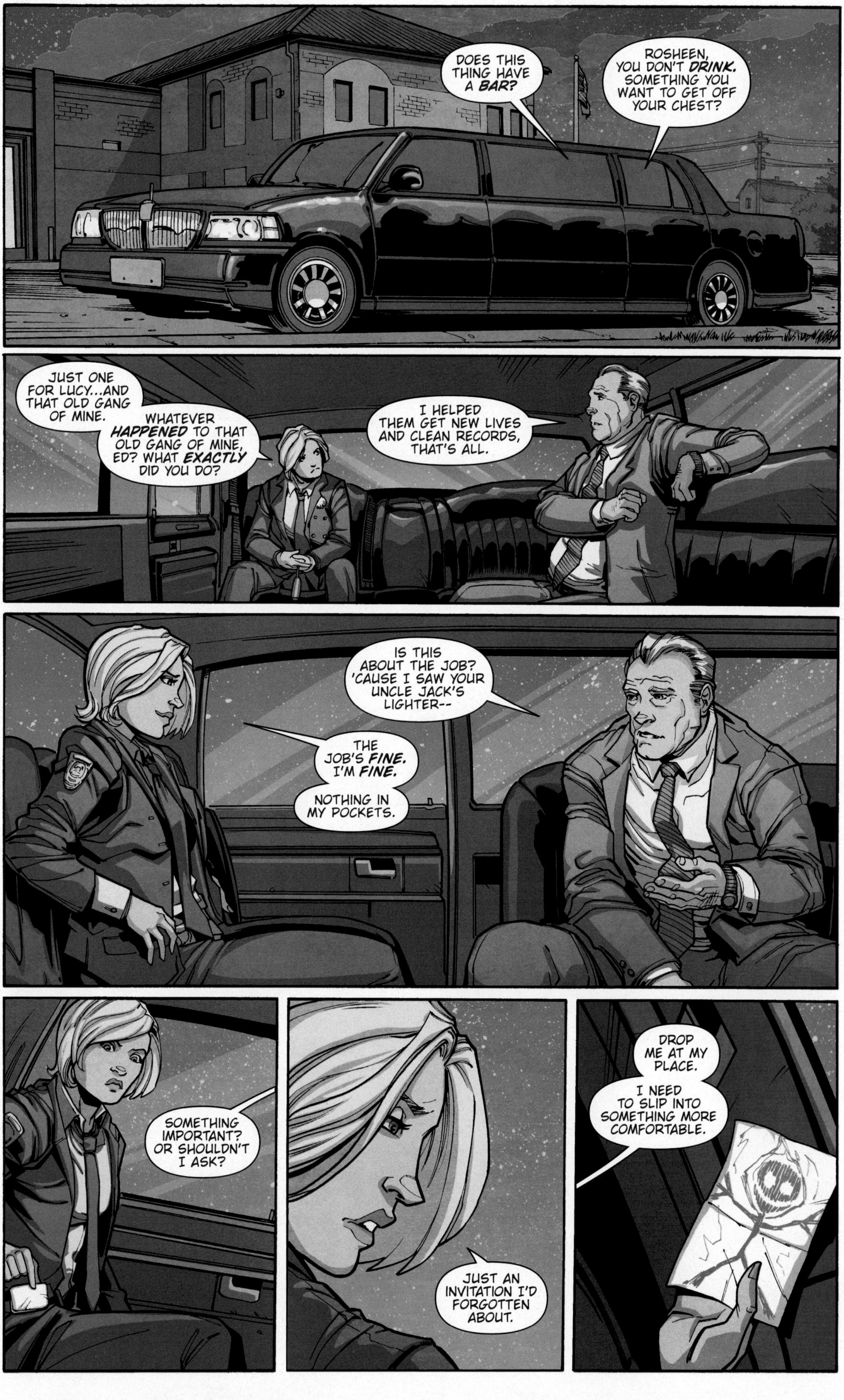
DOES THIS THING HAVE A *BAR?*
ROSHEEN, YOU DON'T *DRINK.* SOMETHING YOU WANT TO GET OFF YOUR CHEST?
JUST ONE FOR LUCY...AND THAT OLD GANG OF MINE.
WHATEVER *HAPPENED* TO THAT OLD GANG OF MINE, ED? WHAT *EXACTLY* DID YOU DO?
I HELPED THEM GET NEW LIVES AND CLEAN RECORDS, THAT'S ALL.
IS THIS ABOUT THE JOB? 'CAUSE I SAW YOUR UNCLE JACK'S LIGHTER--
THE JOB'S *FINE.* I'M *FINE.*
NOTHING IN MY POCKETS.
SOMETHING IMPORTANT? OR SHOULDN'T I ASK?
JUST AN INVITATION I'D FORGOTTEN ABOUT.
DROP ME AT MY PLACE.
I NEED TO SLIP INTO SOMETHING MORE COMFORTABLE.

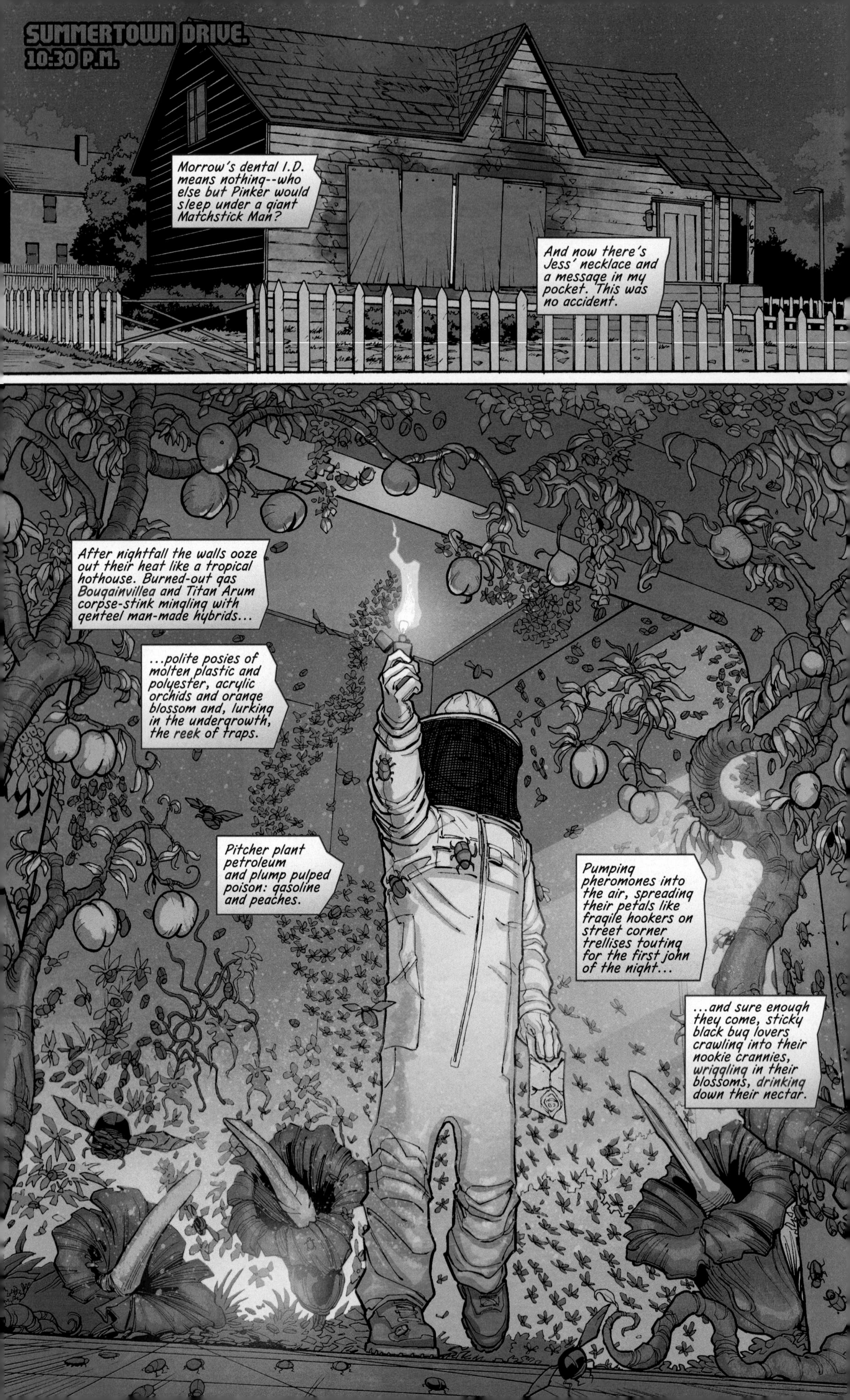
SUMMERTOWN DRIVE.
10:30 P.M.
Morrow's dental I.D. means nothing--who else but Pinker would sleep under a giant Matchstick Man?
And now there's Jess' necklace and a message in my pocket. This was no accident.
After nightfall the walls ooze out their heat like a tropical hothouse. Burned-out gas Bougainvillea and Titan Arum corpse-stink mingling with genteel man-made hybrids...
...polite posies of molten plastic and polyester, acrylic orchids and orange blossom and, lurking in the undergrowth, the reek of traps.
Pitcher plant petroleum and plump pulped poison: gasoline and peaches.
Pumping pheromones into the air, spreading their petals like fragile hookers on street corner trellises touting for the first john of the night...
...and sure enough they come, sticky black bug lovers crawling into their nookie crannies, wriggling in their blossoms, drinking down their nectar.

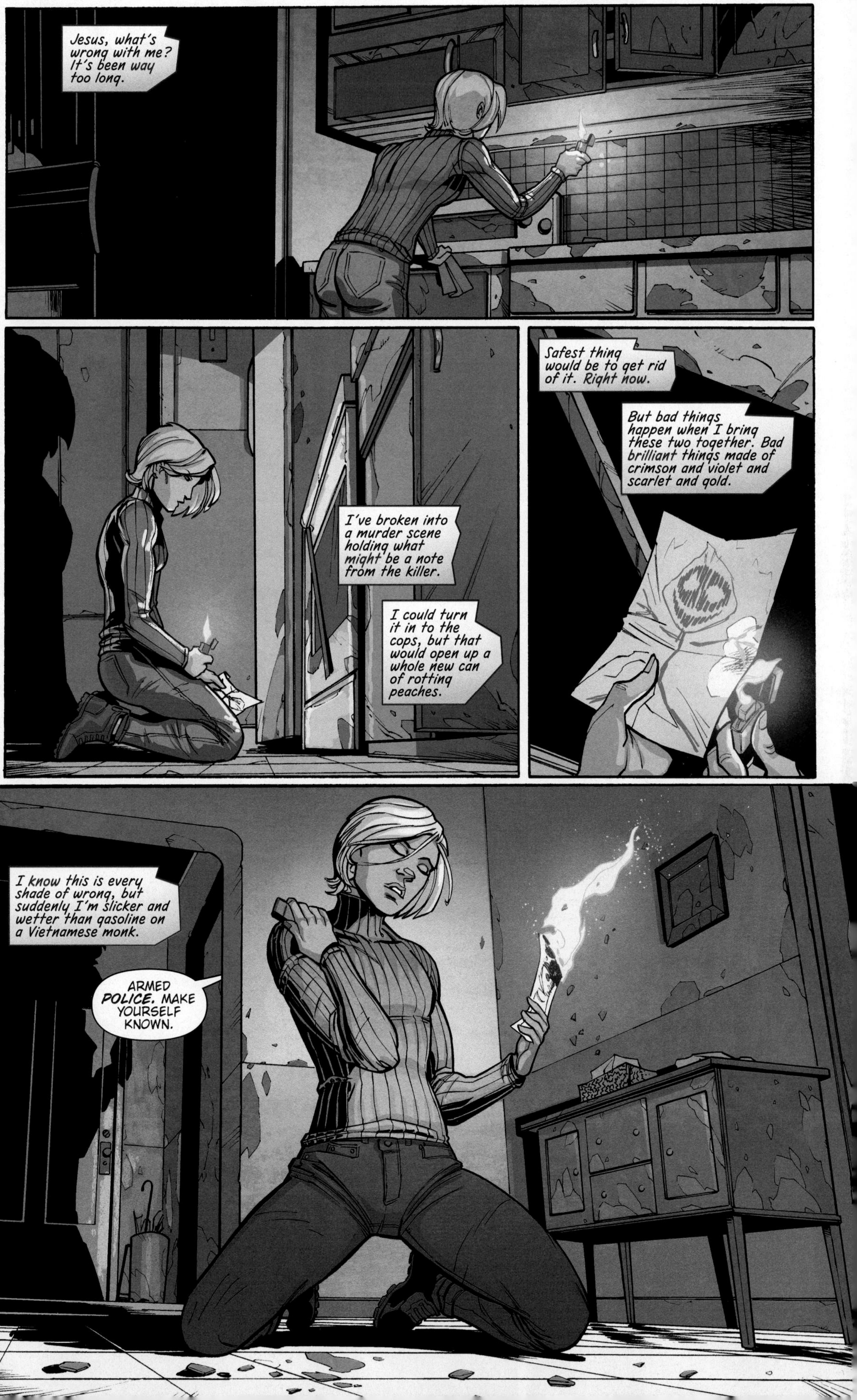
Jesus, what's wrong with me? It's been way too long.
I've broken into a murder scene holding what might be a note from the killer.
I could turn it in to the cops, but that would open up a whole new can of rotting peaches.
Safest thing would be to get rid of it. Right now.
But bad things happen when I bring these two together. Bad brilliant things made of crimson and violet and scarlet and gold.
I know this is every shade of wrong, but suddenly I'm slicker and wetter than gasoline on a Vietnamese monk.
ARMED POLICE. MAKE YOURSELF KNOWN.

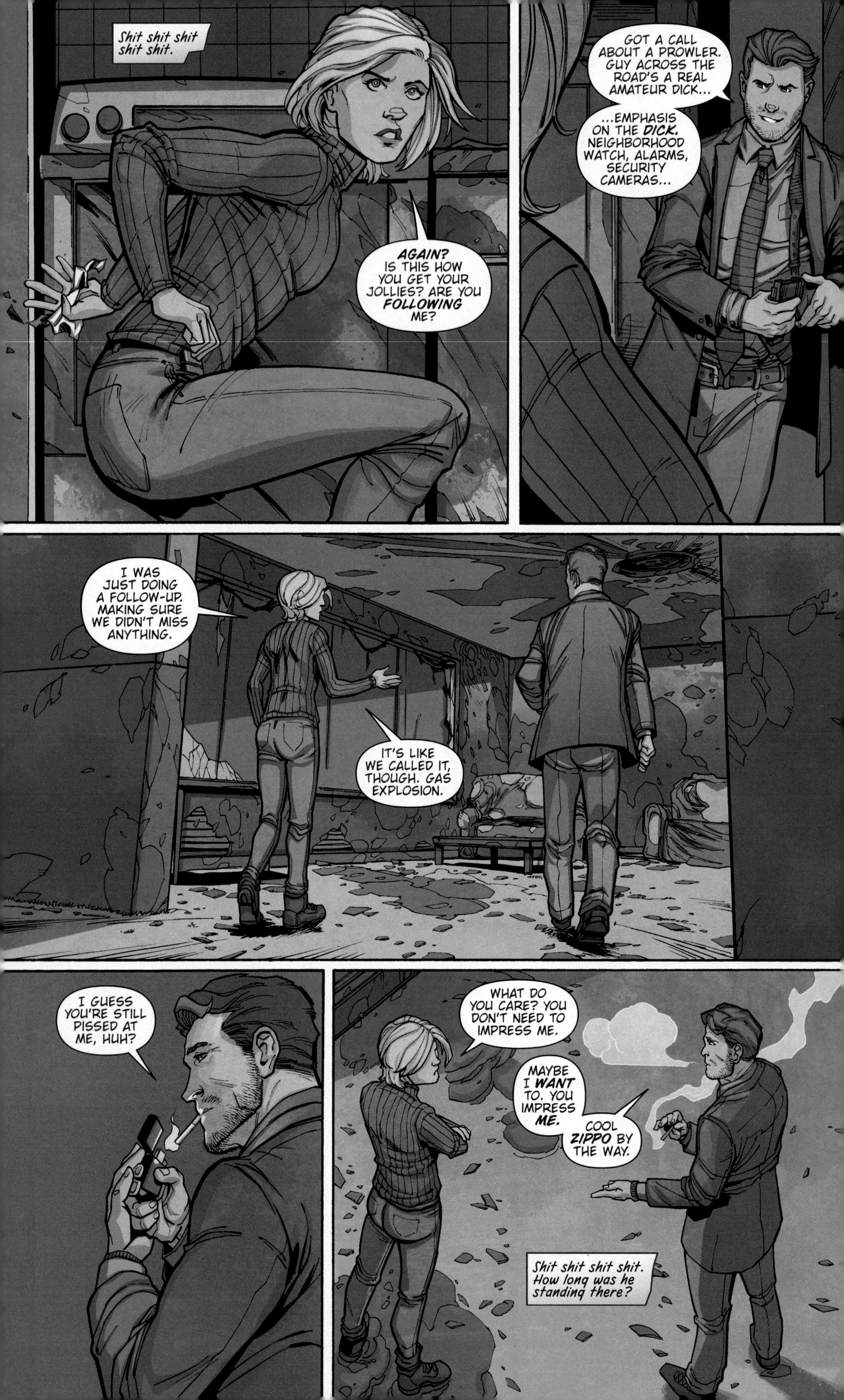
Shit shit shit shit shit.
GOT A CALL ABOUT A PROWLER. GUY ACROSS THE ROAD'S A REAL AMATEUR DICK...
...EMPHASIS ON THE DICK. NEIGHBORHOOD WATCH, ALARMS, SECURITY CAMERAS...
AGAIN? IS THIS HOW YOU GET YOUR JOLLIES? ARE YOU FOLLOWING ME?
I WAS JUST DOING A FOLLOW-UP. MAKING SURE WE DIDN'T MISS ANYTHING.
IT'S LIKE WE CALLED IT, THOUGH. GAS EXPLOSION.
I GUESS YOU'RE STILL PISSED AT ME, HUH?
WHAT DO YOU CARE? YOU DON'T NEED TO IMPRESS ME.
MAYBE I WANT TO. YOU IMPRESS ME.
COOL ZIPPO BY THE WAY.
Shit shit shit shit. How long was he standing there?

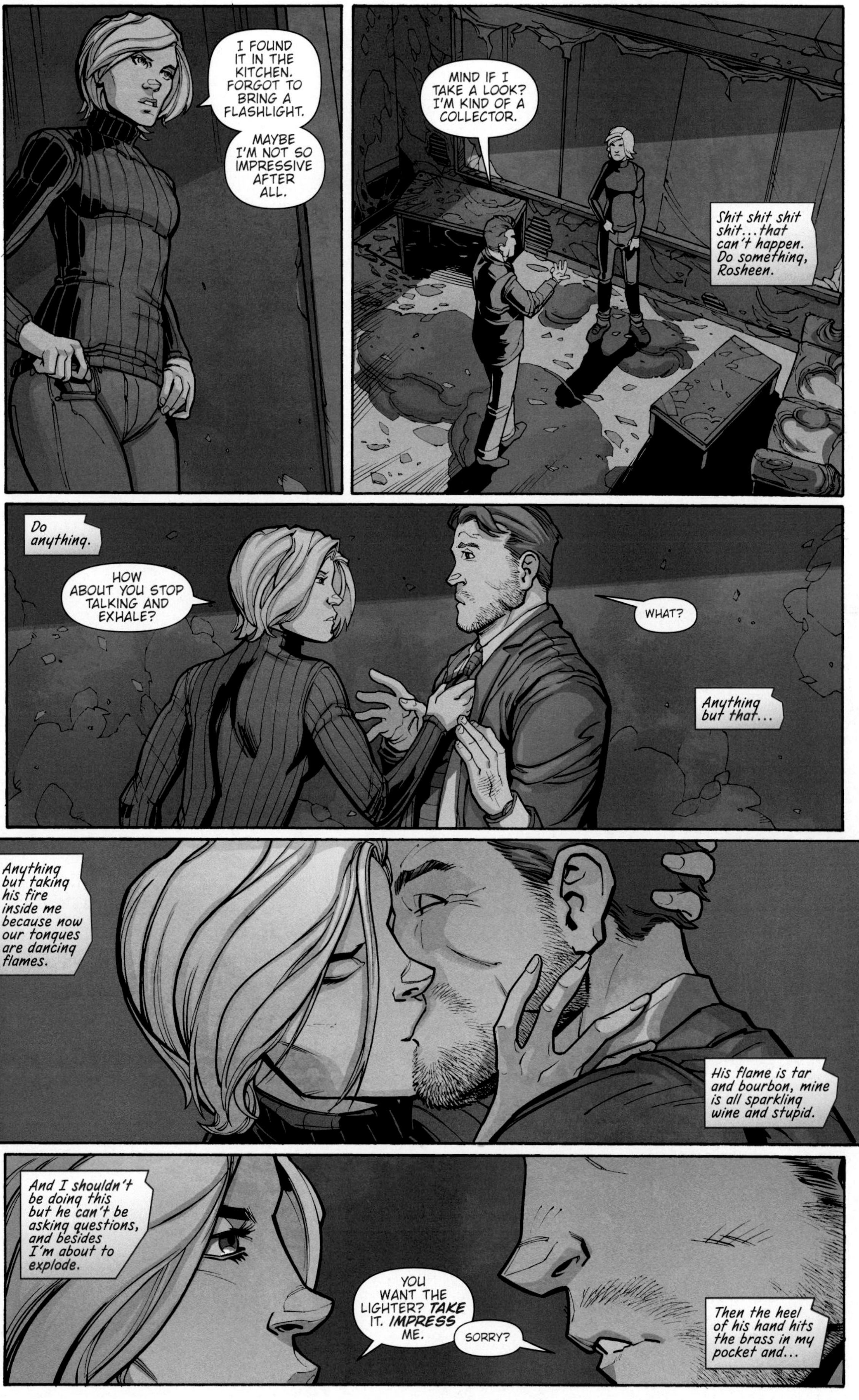
I FOUND IT IN THE KITCHEN. FORGOT TO BRING A FLASHLIGHT.
MAYBE I'M NOT SO IMPRESSIVE AFTER ALL.
MIND IF I TAKE A LOOK? I'M KIND OF A COLLECTOR.
Shit shit shit shit...that can't happen. Do something, Rosheen.
Do anything.
HOW ABOUT YOU STOP TALKING AND EXHALE?
WHAT?
Anything but that...
Anything but taking his fire inside me because now our tongues are dancing flames.
His flame is tar and bourbon, mine is all sparkling wine and stupid.
And I shouldn't be doing this but he can't be asking questions, and besides I'm about to explode.
YOU WANT THE LIGHTER? TAKE IT. IMPRESS ME.
SORRY?
Then the heel of his hand hits the brass in my pocket and...

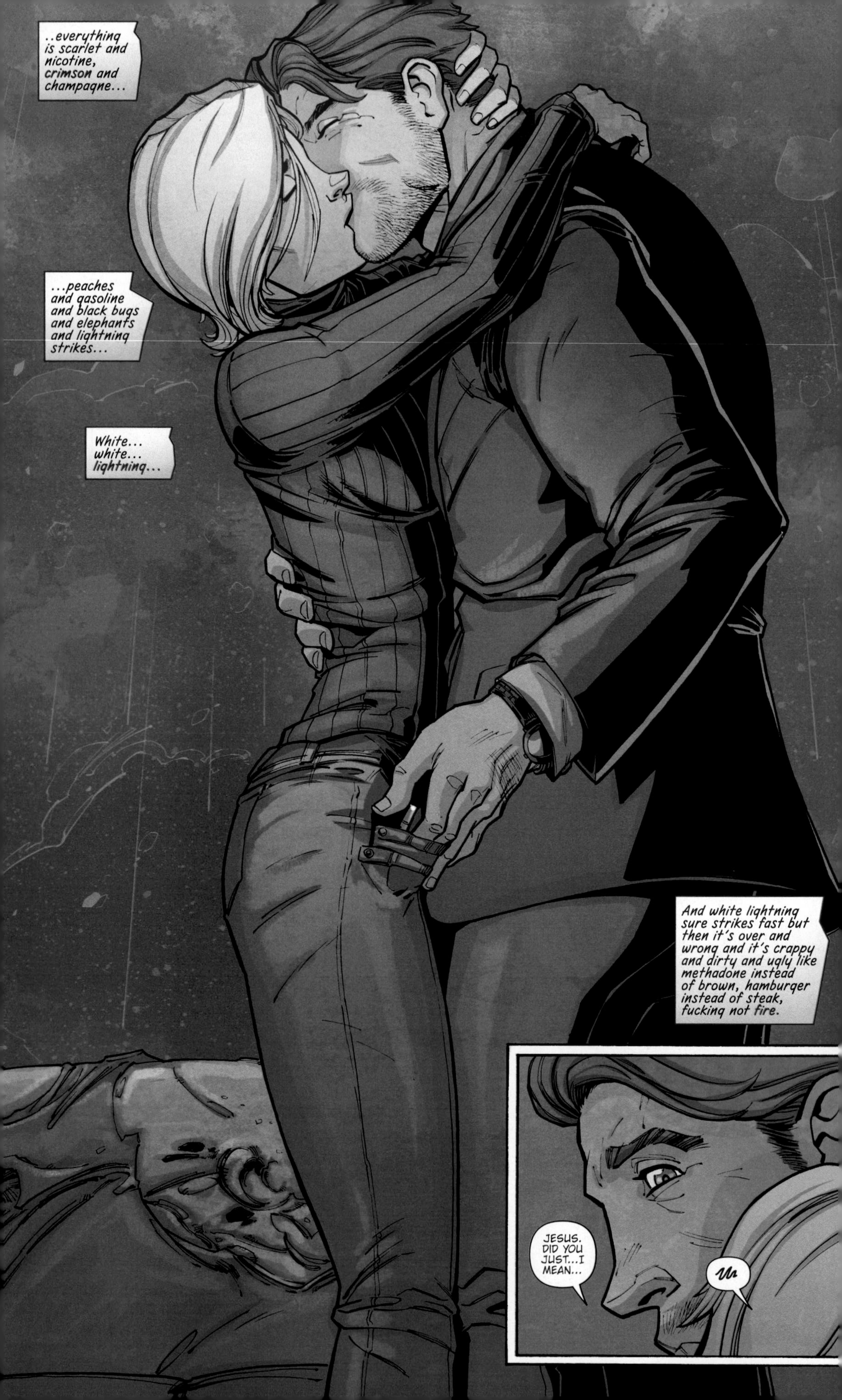
...everything is scarlet and nicotine, crimson and champagne...
...peaches and gasoline and black bugs and elephants and lightning strikes...
White... white... lightning...
And white lightning sure strikes fast but then it's over and wrong and it's crappy and dirty and ugly like methadone instead of brown, hamburger instead of steak, fucking not fire.
JESUS. DID YOU JUST...I MEAN...

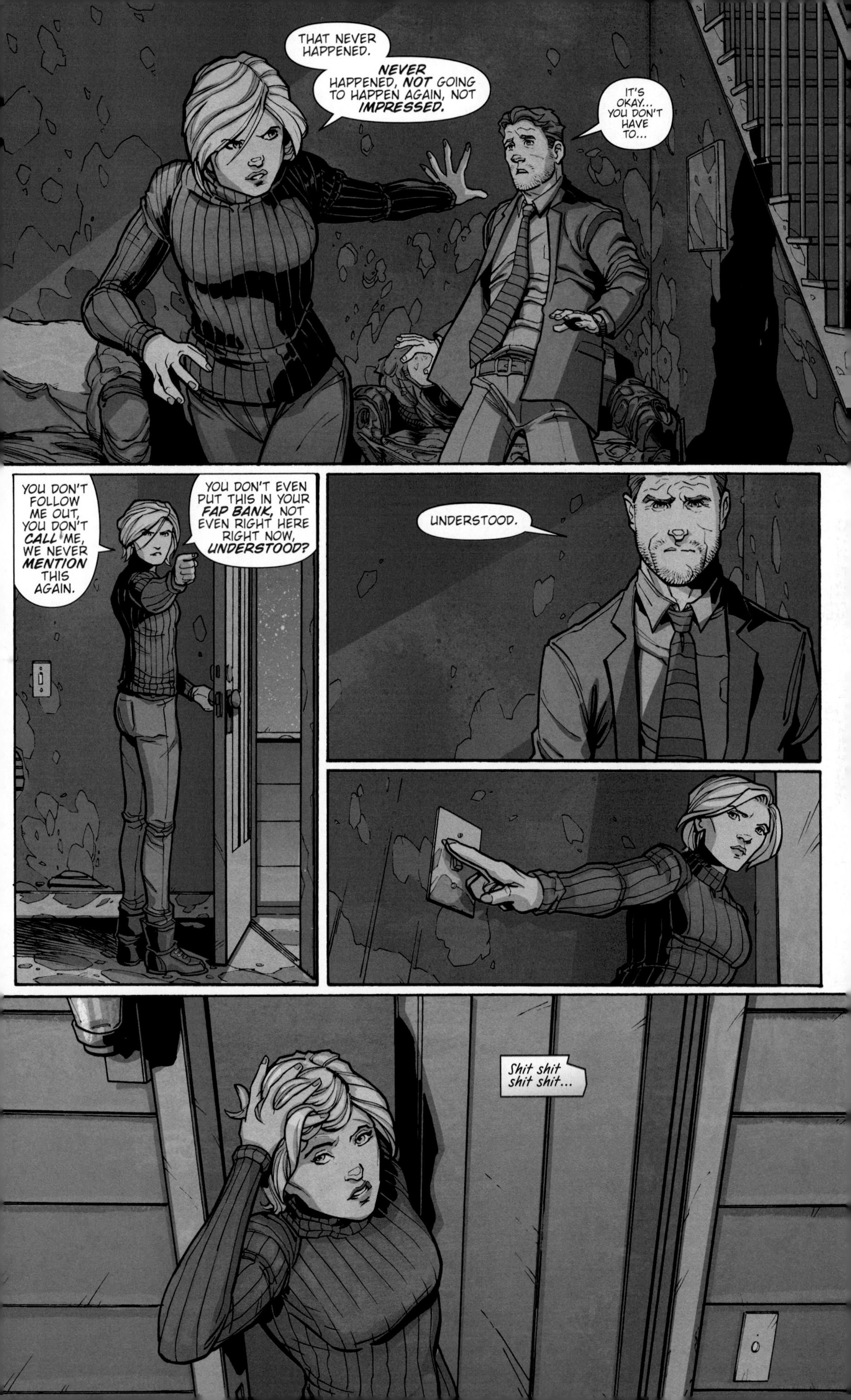
THAT NEVER HAPPENED.
NEVER HAPPENED, NOT GOING TO HAPPEN AGAIN, NOT IMPRESSED.
IT'S OKAY... YOU DON'T HAVE TO...
YOU DON'T FOLLOW ME OUT, YOU DON'T CALL ME, WE NEVER MENTION THIS AGAIN.
YOU DON'T EVEN PUT THIS IN YOUR FAP BANK, NOT EVEN RIGHT HERE RIGHT NOW, UNDERSTOOD?
UNDERSTOOD.
Shit shit shit shit...

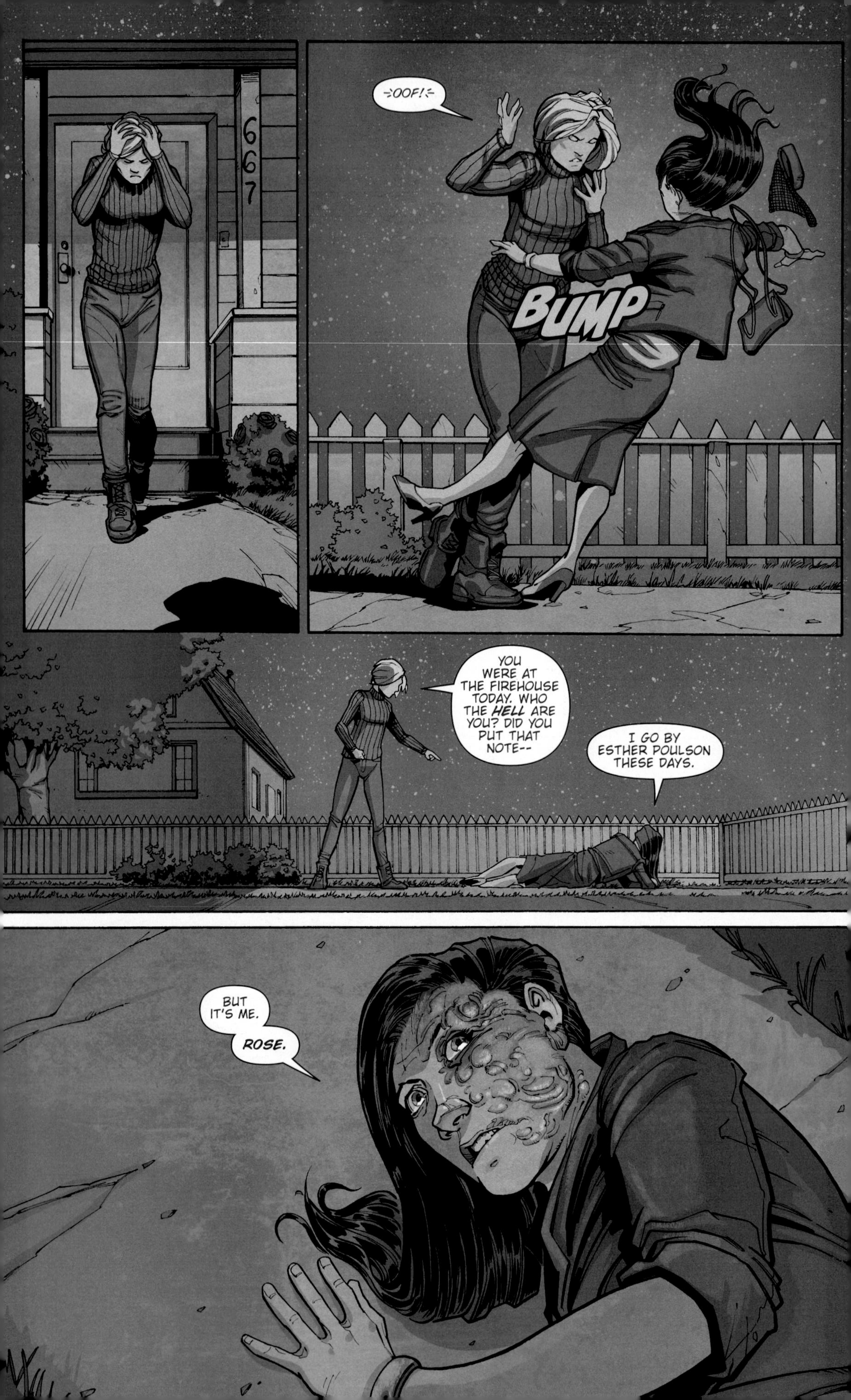
667
-OOF!-
BUMP
YOU WERE AT THE FIREHOUSE TODAY. WHO THE HELL ARE YOU? DID YOU PUT THAT NOTE--
I GO BY ESTHER POULSON THESE DAYS.
BUT IT'S ME.
ROSE.

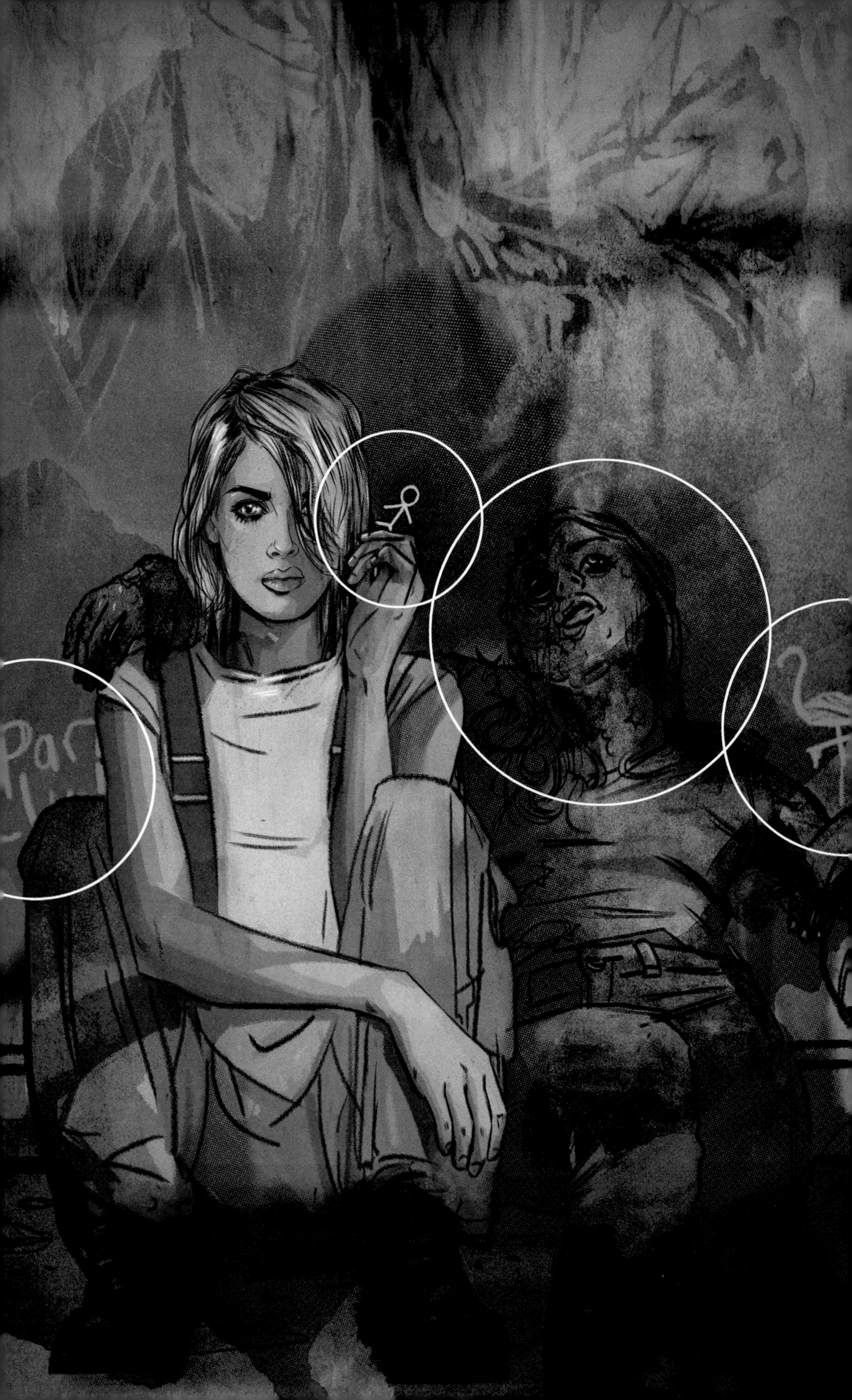

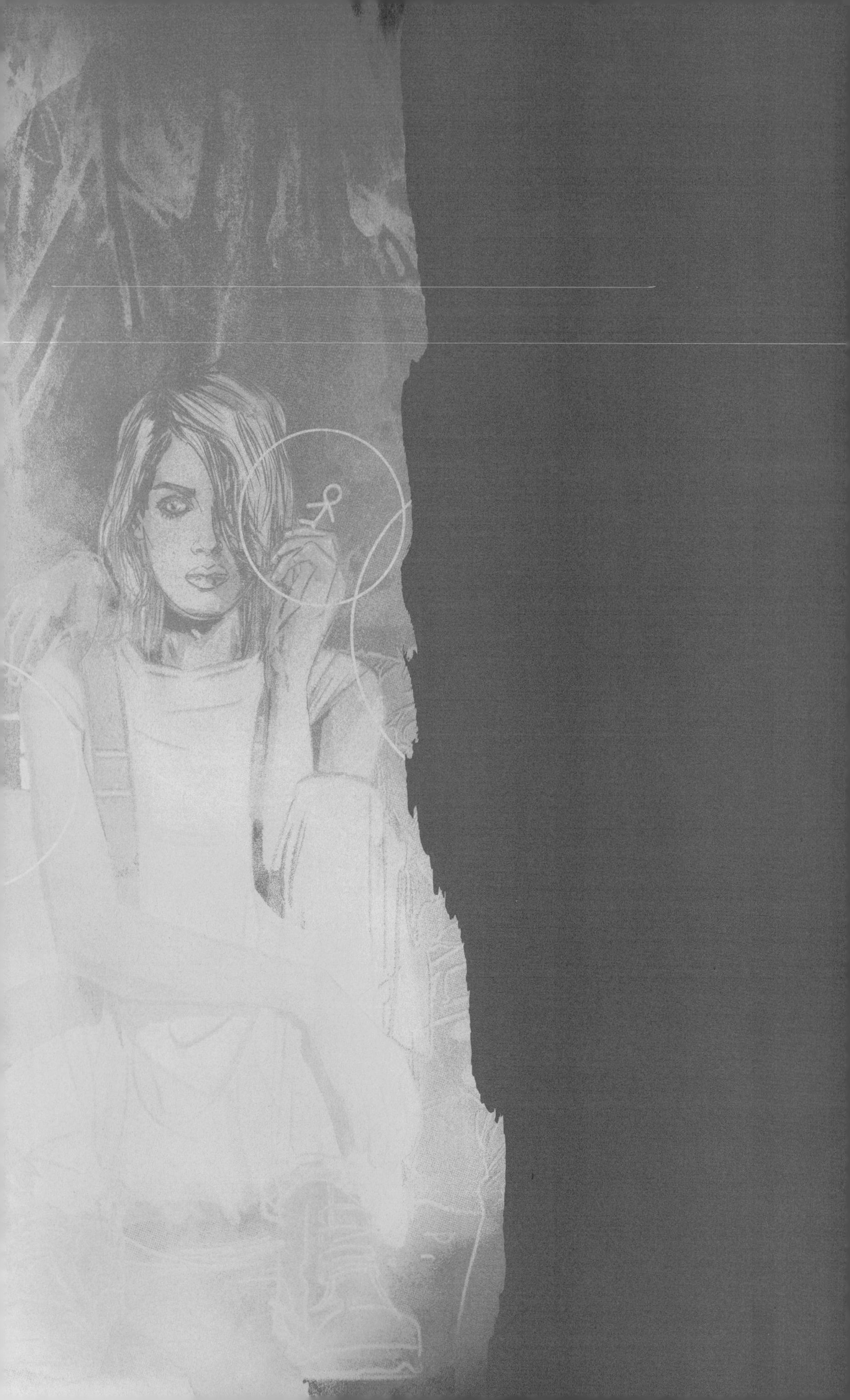

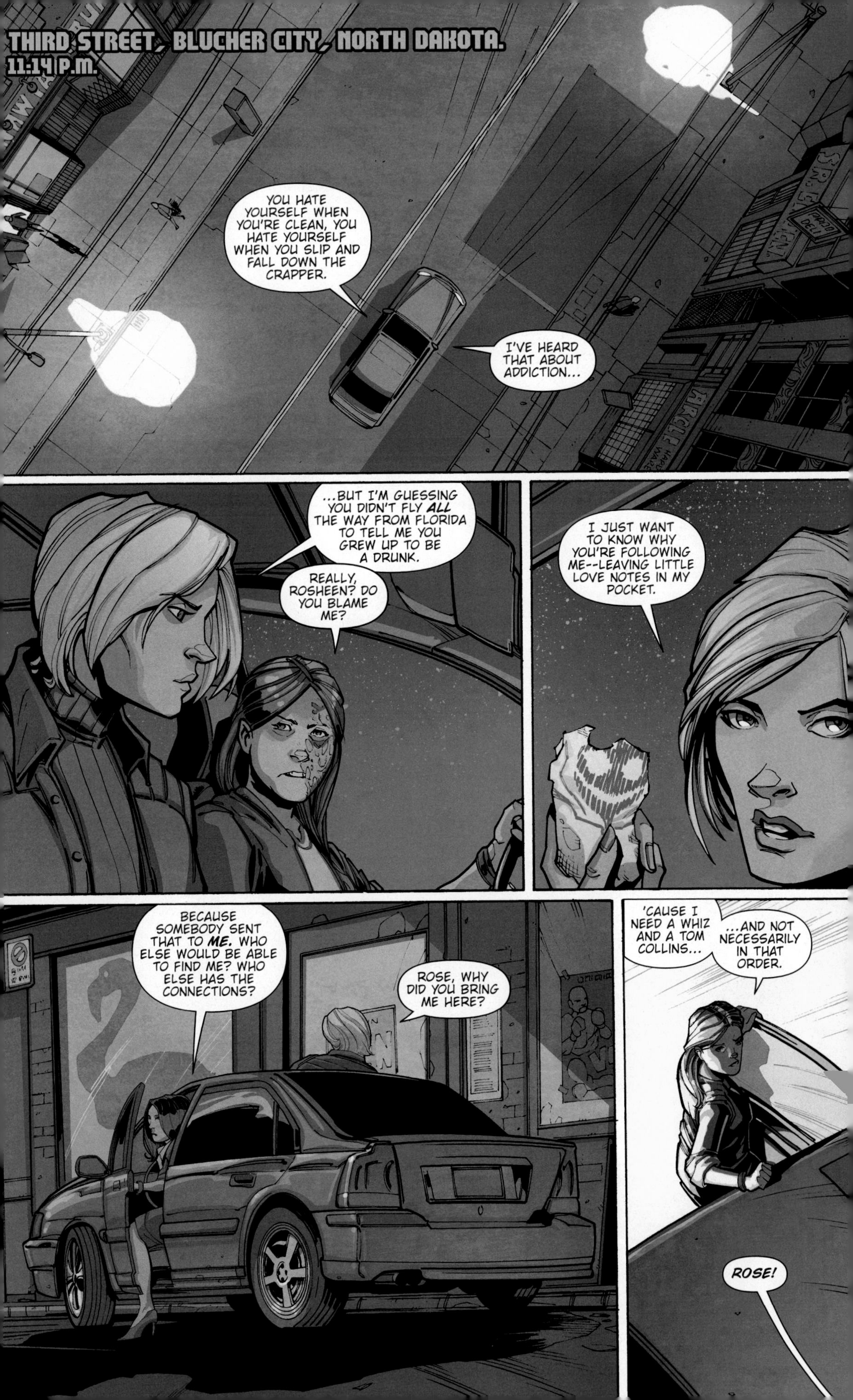
THIRD STREET, BLUCHER CITY, NORTH DAKOTA.
11:14 P.M.
YOU HATE YOURSELF WHEN YOU'RE CLEAN, YOU HATE YOURSELF WHEN YOU SLIP AND FALL DOWN THE CRAPPER.
I'VE HEARD THAT ABOUT ADDICTION...
...BUT I'M GUESSING YOU DIDN'T FLY ALL THE WAY FROM FLORIDA TO TELL ME YOU GREW UP TO BE A DRUNK.
REALLY, ROSHEEN? DO YOU BLAME ME?
I JUST WANT TO KNOW WHY YOU'RE FOLLOWING ME--LEAVING LITTLE LOVE NOTES IN MY POCKET.
BECAUSE SOMEBODY SENT THAT TO ME. WHO ELSE WOULD BE ABLE TO FIND ME? WHO ELSE HAS THE CONNECTIONS?
ROSE, WHY DID YOU BRING ME HERE?
'CAUSE I NEED A WHIZ AND A TOM COLLINS...
...AND NOT NECESSARILY IN THAT ORDER.
ROSE!

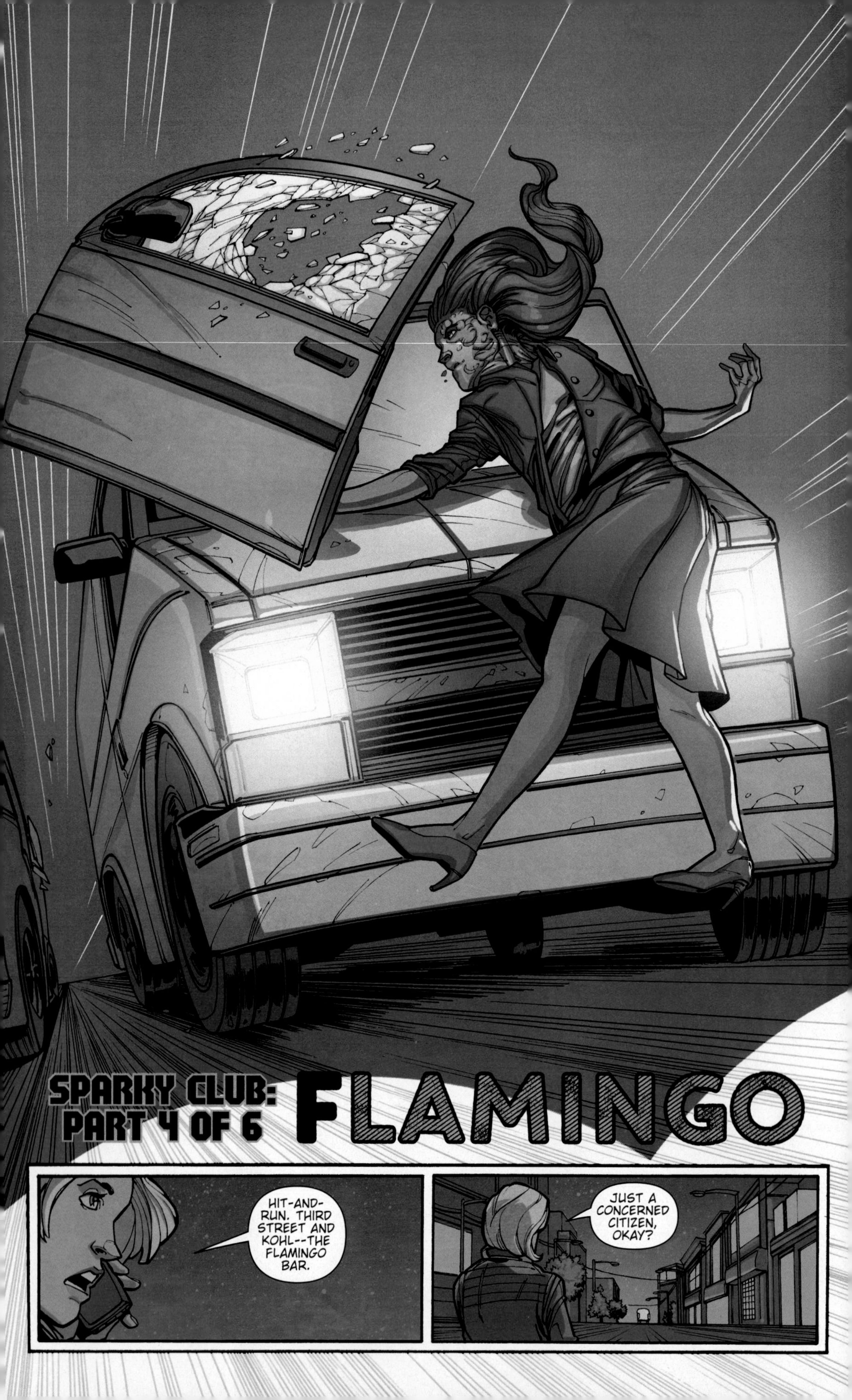
SPARKY CLUB: PART 4 OF 6
FLAMINGO
HIT-AND-RUN. THIRD STREET AND KOHL--THE FLAMINGO BAR.
JUST A CONCERNED CITIZEN, OKAY?

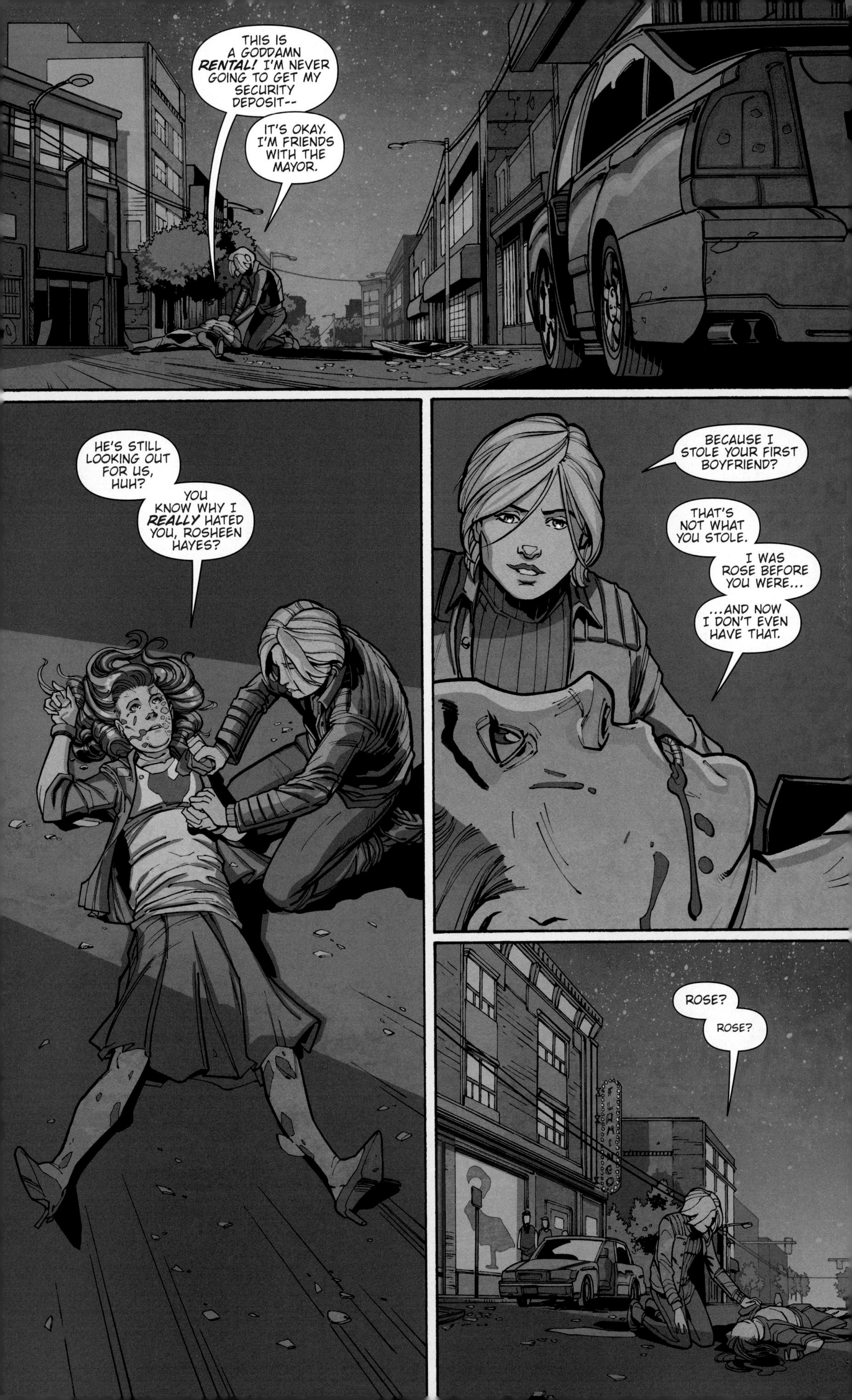
THIS IS A GODDAMN RENTAL! I'M NEVER GOING TO GET MY SECURITY DEPOSIT--
IT'S OKAY. I'M FRIENDS WITH THE MAYOR.
HE'S STILL LOOKING OUT FOR US, HUH?
YOU KNOW WHY I REALLY HATED YOU, ROSHEEN HAYES?
BECAUSE I STOLE YOUR FIRST BOYFRIEND?
THAT'S NOT WHAT YOU STOLE.
I WAS ROSE BEFORE YOU WERE...
...AND NOW I DON'T EVEN HAVE THAT.
ROSE?
ROSE?

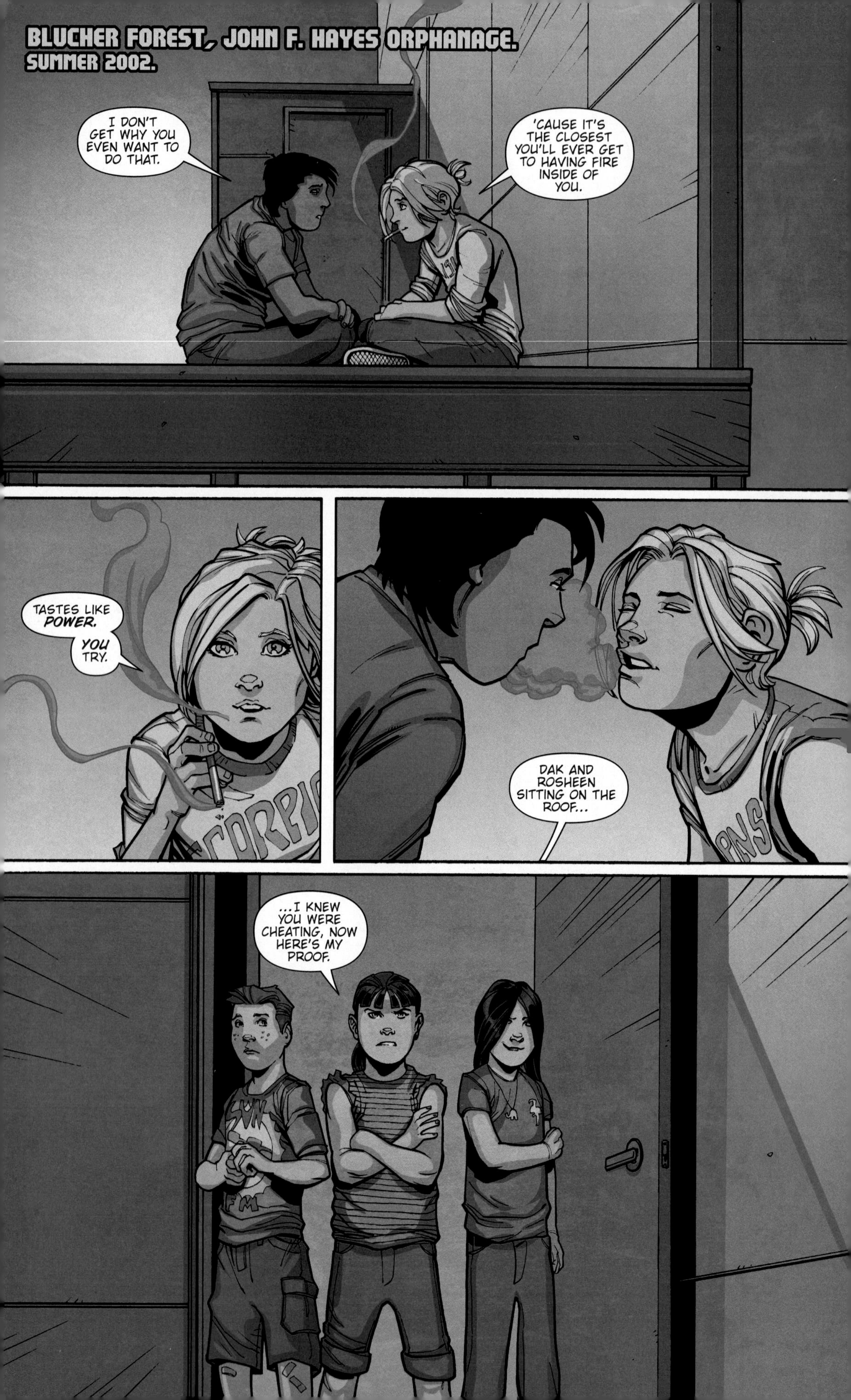
BLUCHER FOREST, JOHN F. HAYES ORPHANAGE.
SUMMER 2002.
I DON'T GET WHY YOU EVEN WANT TO DO THAT.
'CAUSE IT'S THE CLOSEST YOU'LL EVER GET TO HAVING FIRE INSIDE OF YOU.
TASTES LIKE *POWER.*
YOU TRY.
DAK AND ROSHEEN SITTING ON THE ROOF...
...I KNEW YOU WERE CHEATING, NOW HERE'S MY PROOF.

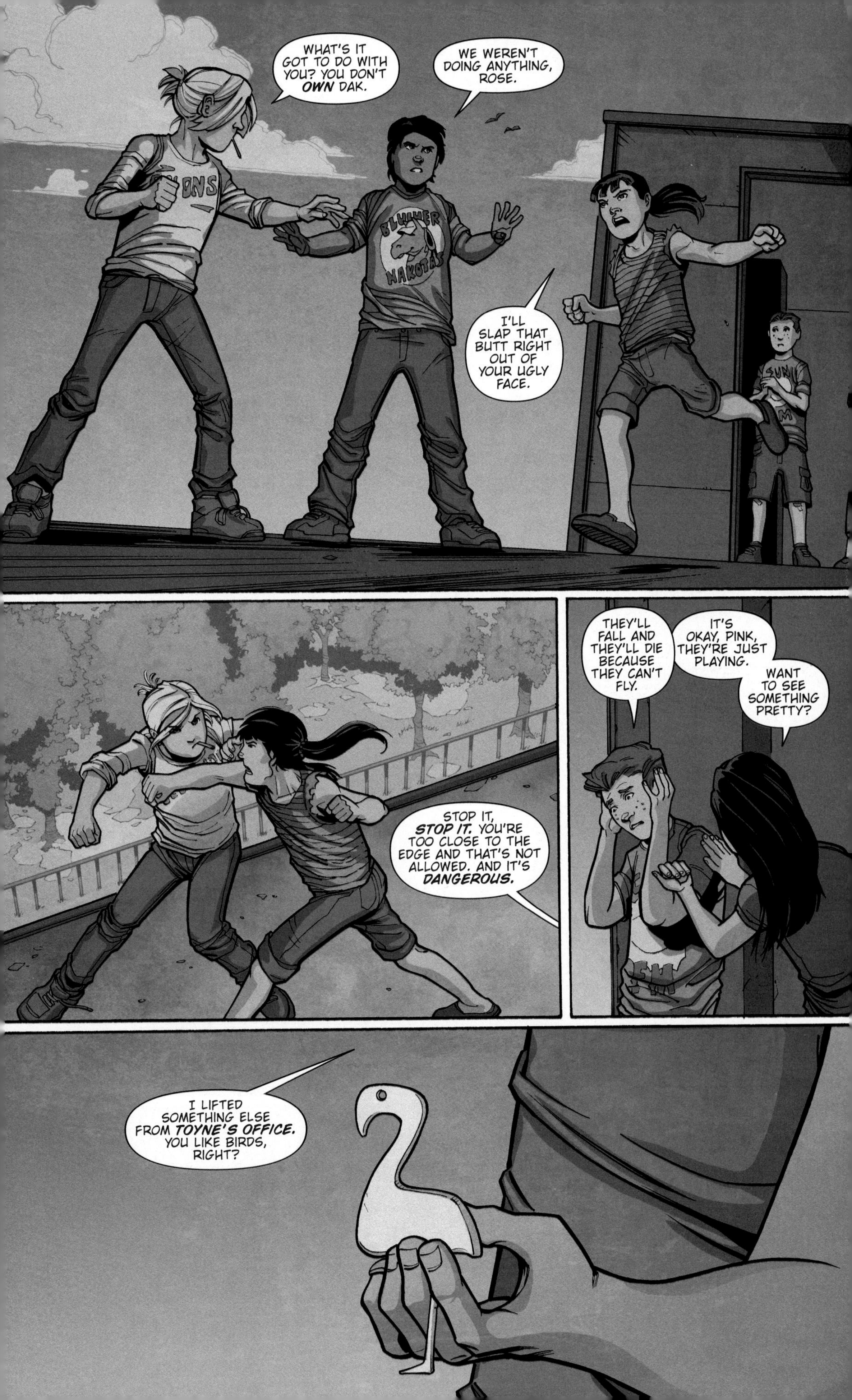
WHAT'S IT GOT TO DO WITH YOU? YOU DON'T **OWN** DAK.
WE WEREN'T DOING ANYTHING, ROSE.
I'LL SLAP THAT BUTT RIGHT OUT OF YOUR UGLY FACE.
STOP IT, **STOP IT.** YOU'RE TOO CLOSE TO THE EDGE AND THAT'S NOT ALLOWED. AND IT'S **DANGEROUS.**
THEY'LL FALL AND THEY'LL DIE BECAUSE THEY CAN'T FLY.
IT'S OKAY, PINK, THEY'RE JUST PLAYING.
WANT TO SEE SOMETHING PRETTY?
I LIFTED SOMETHING ELSE FROM **TOYNE'S OFFICE.** YOU LIKE BIRDS, RIGHT?

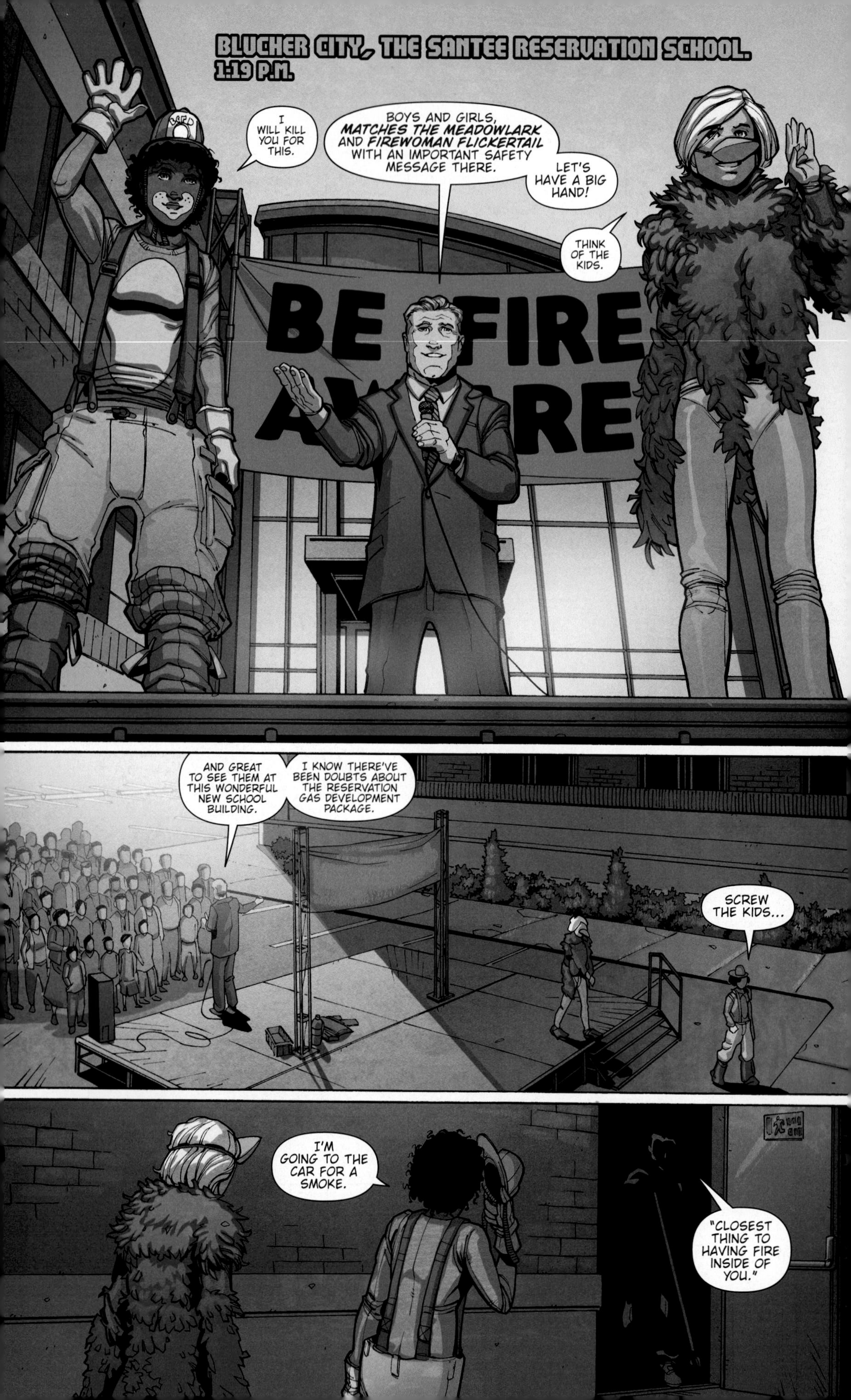
BLUCHER CITY, THE SANTEE RESERVATION SCHOOL. 1:19 P.M.
I WILL KILL YOU FOR THIS.
BOYS AND GIRLS, MATCHES THE MEADOWLARK AND FIREWOMAN FLICKERTAIL WITH AN IMPORTANT SAFETY MESSAGE THERE.
LET'S HAVE A BIG HAND!
THINK OF THE KIDS.
BE FIRE AWARE
AND GREAT TO SEE THEM AT THIS WONDERFUL NEW SCHOOL BUILDING.
I KNOW THERE'VE BEEN DOUBTS ABOUT THE RESERVATION GAS DEVELOPMENT PACKAGE.
SCREW THE KIDS...
I'M GOING TO THE CAR FOR A SMOKE.
"CLOSEST THING TO HAVING FIRE INSIDE OF YOU."

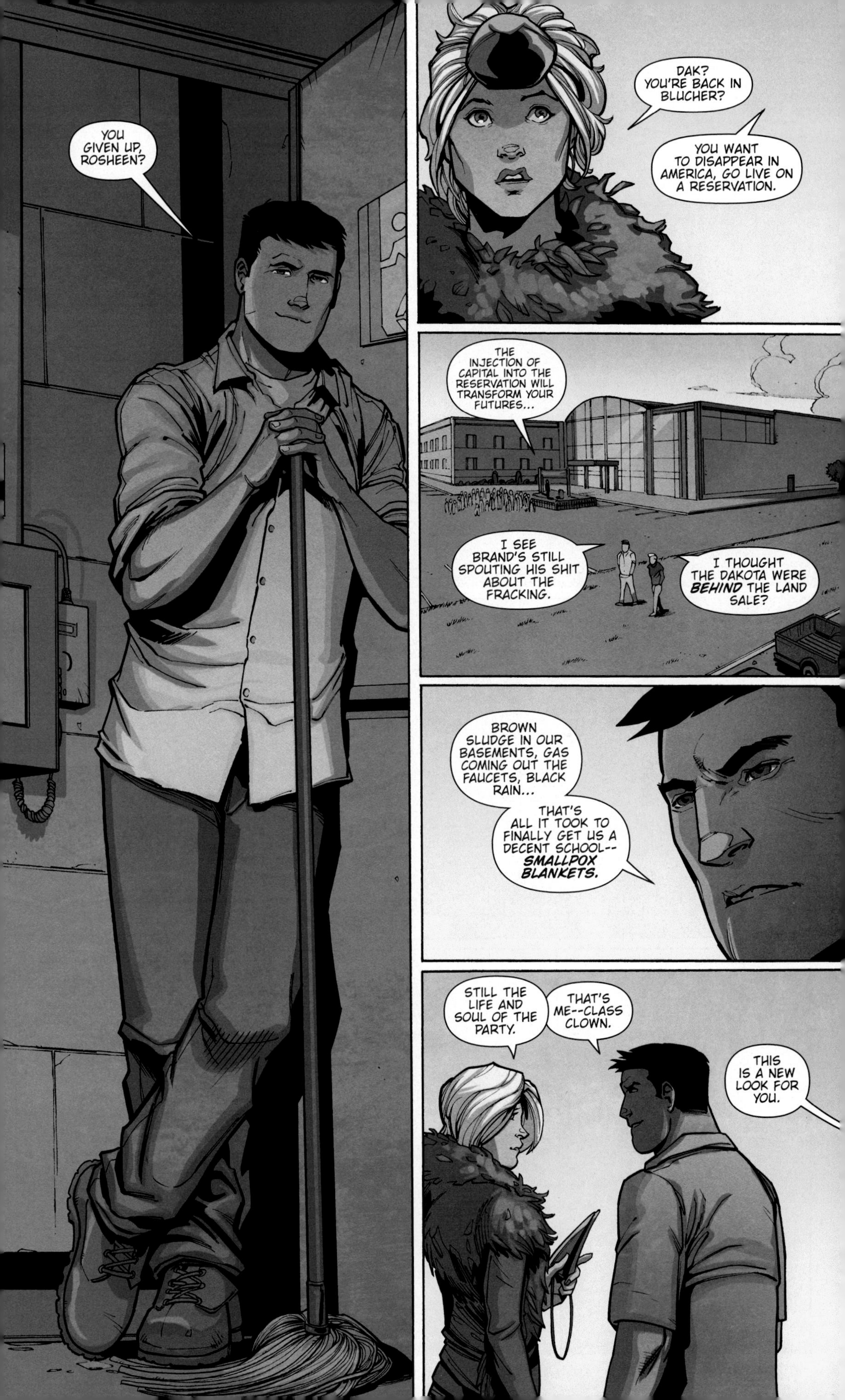
YOU GIVEN UP, ROSHEEN?
DAK? YOU'RE BACK IN BLUCHER?
YOU WANT TO DISAPPEAR IN AMERICA, GO LIVE ON A RESERVATION.
THE INJECTION OF CAPITAL INTO THE RESERVATION WILL TRANSFORM YOUR FUTURES...
I SEE BRAND'S STILL SPOUTING HIS SHIT ABOUT THE FRACKING.
I THOUGHT THE DAKOTA WERE *BEHIND* THE LAND SALE?
BROWN SLUDGE IN OUR BASEMENTS, GAS COMING OUT THE FAUCETS, BLACK RAIN...
THAT'S ALL IT TOOK TO FINALLY GET US A DECENT SCHOOL-- *SMALLPOX BLANKETS.*
STILL THE LIFE AND SOUL OF THE PARTY.
THAT'S ME--CLASS CLOWN.
THIS IS A NEW LOOK FOR YOU.

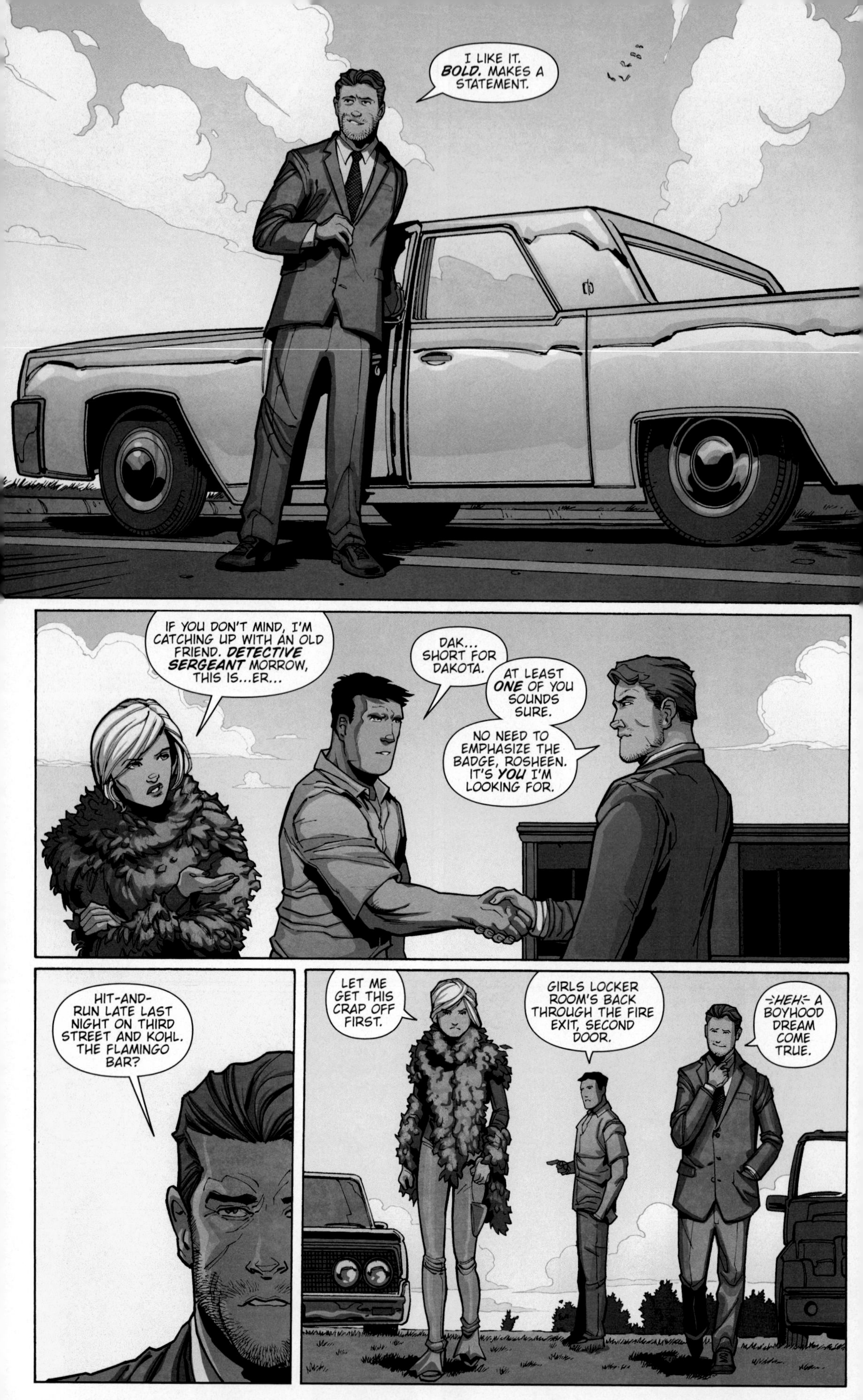
I LIKE IT. BOLD. MAKES A STATEMENT.
IF YOU DON'T MIND, I'M CATCHING UP WITH AN OLD FRIEND. DETECTIVE SERGEANT MORROW, THIS IS...ER...
DAK... SHORT FOR DAKOTA.
AT LEAST ONE OF YOU SOUNDS SURE.
NO NEED TO EMPHASIZE THE BADGE, ROSHEEN. IT'S YOU I'M LOOKING FOR.
HIT-AND-RUN LATE LAST NIGHT ON THIRD STREET AND KOHL. THE FLAMINGO BAR?
LET ME GET THIS CRAP OFF FIRST.
GIRLS LOCKER ROOM'S BACK THROUGH THE FIRE EXIT, SECOND DOOR.
HEH A BOYHOOD DREAM COME TRUE.

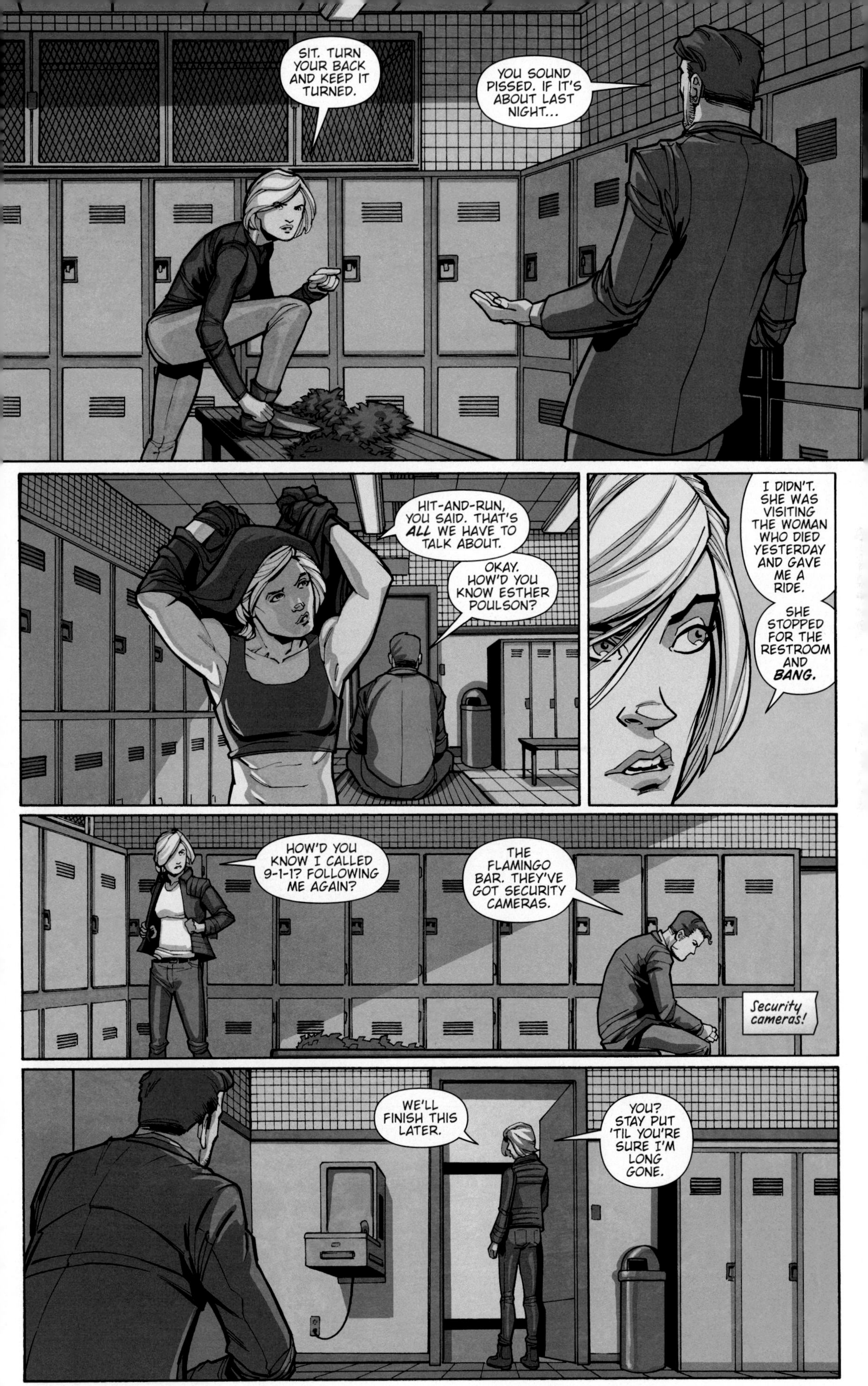
SIT. TURN YOUR BACK AND KEEP IT TURNED.
YOU SOUND PISSED. IF IT'S ABOUT LAST NIGHT...
HIT-AND-RUN, YOU SAID. THAT'S **ALL** WE HAVE TO TALK ABOUT.
OKAY. HOW'D YOU KNOW ESTHER POULSON?
I DIDN'T. SHE WAS VISITING THE WOMAN WHO DIED YESTERDAY AND GAVE ME A RIDE.
SHE STOPPED FOR THE RESTROOM AND **BANG.**
HOW'D YOU KNOW I CALLED 9-1-1? FOLLOWING ME AGAIN?
THE FLAMINGO BAR. THEY'VE GOT SECURITY CAMERAS.
Security cameras!
WE'LL FINISH THIS LATER.
YOU? STAY PUT 'TIL YOU'RE SURE I'M LONG GONE.

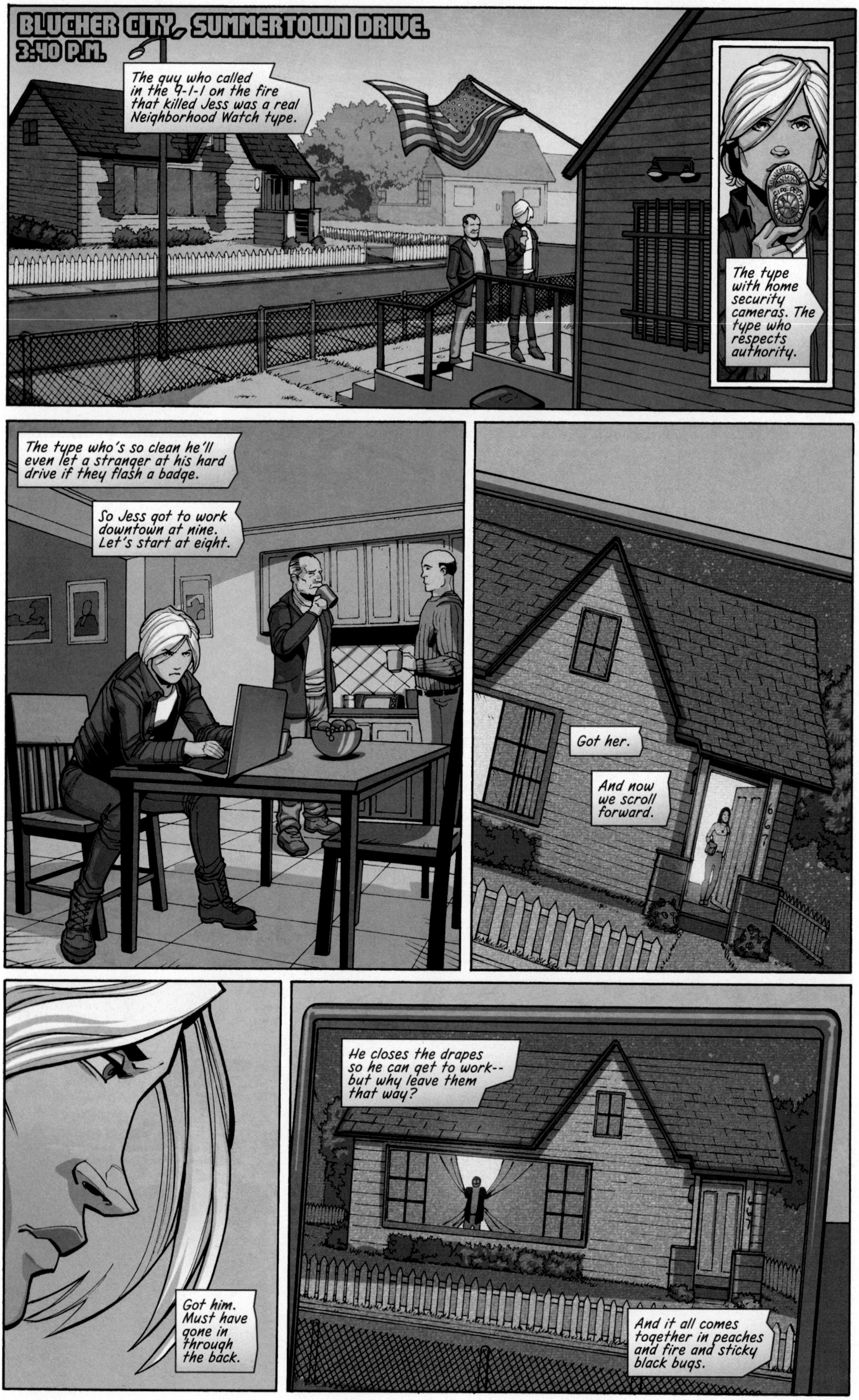
BLUCHER CITY, SUMMERTOWN DRIVE.
3:40 P.M.
The guy who called in the 9-1-1 on the fire that killed Jess was a real Neighborhood Watch type.
The type with home security cameras. The type who respects authority.
The type who's so clean he'll even let a stranger at his hard drive if they flash a badge.
So Jess got to work downtown at nine. Let's start at eight.
Got her.
And now we scroll forward.
Got him. Must have gone in through the back.
He closes the drapes so he can get to work-- but why leave them that way?
And it all comes together in peaches and fire and sticky black bugs.

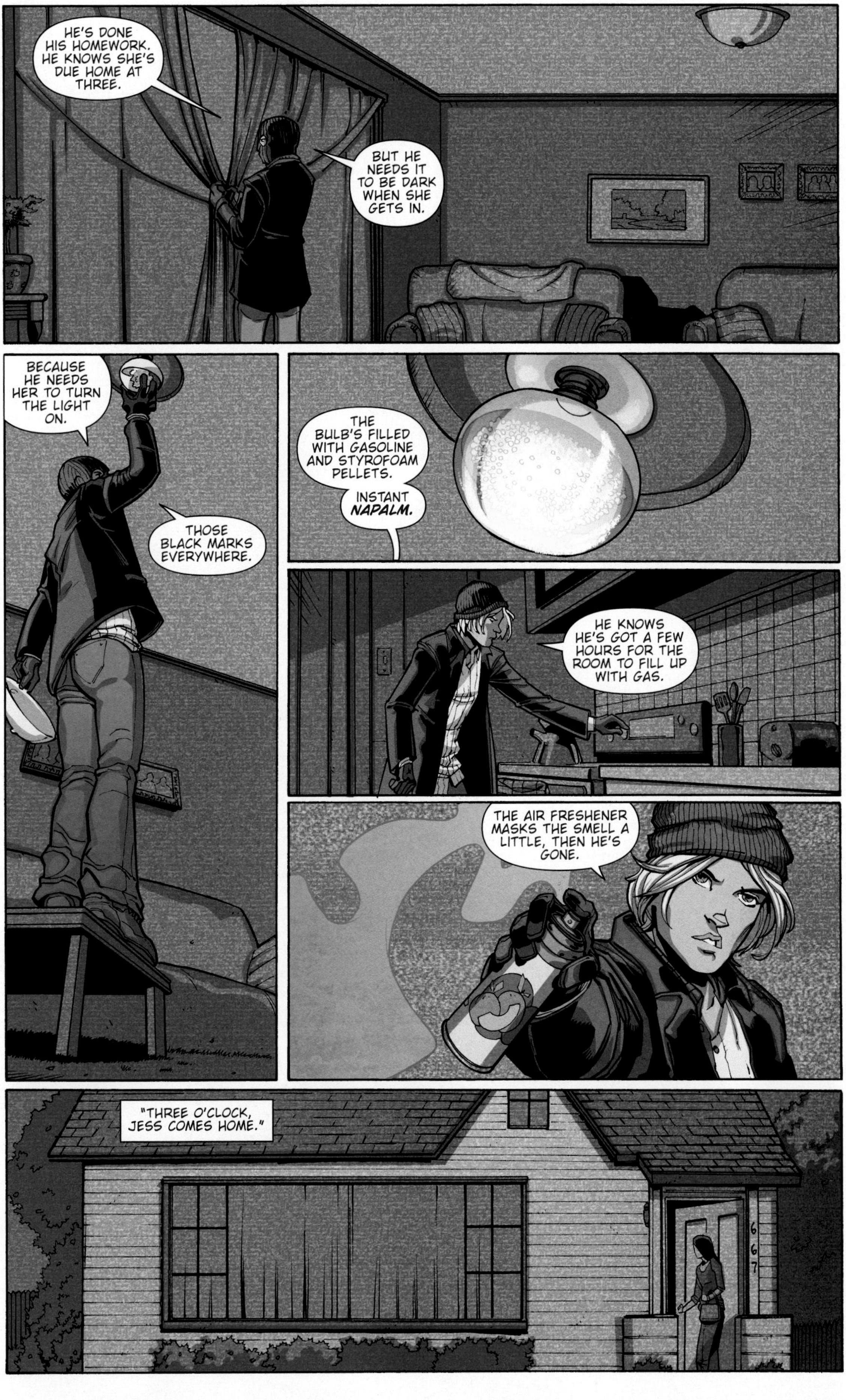
HE'S DONE HIS HOMEWORK. HE KNOWS SHE'S DUE HOME AT THREE.
BUT HE NEEDS IT TO BE DARK WHEN SHE GETS IN.
BECAUSE HE NEEDS HER TO TURN THE LIGHT ON.
THOSE BLACK MARKS EVERYWHERE.
THE BULB'S FILLED WITH GASOLINE AND STYROFOAM PELLETS.
INSTANT NAPALM.
HE KNOWS HE'S GOT A FEW HOURS FOR THE ROOM TO FILL UP WITH GAS.
THE AIR FRESHENER MASKS THE SMELL A LITTLE, THEN HE'S GONE.
"THREE O'CLOCK, JESS COMES HOME."
667

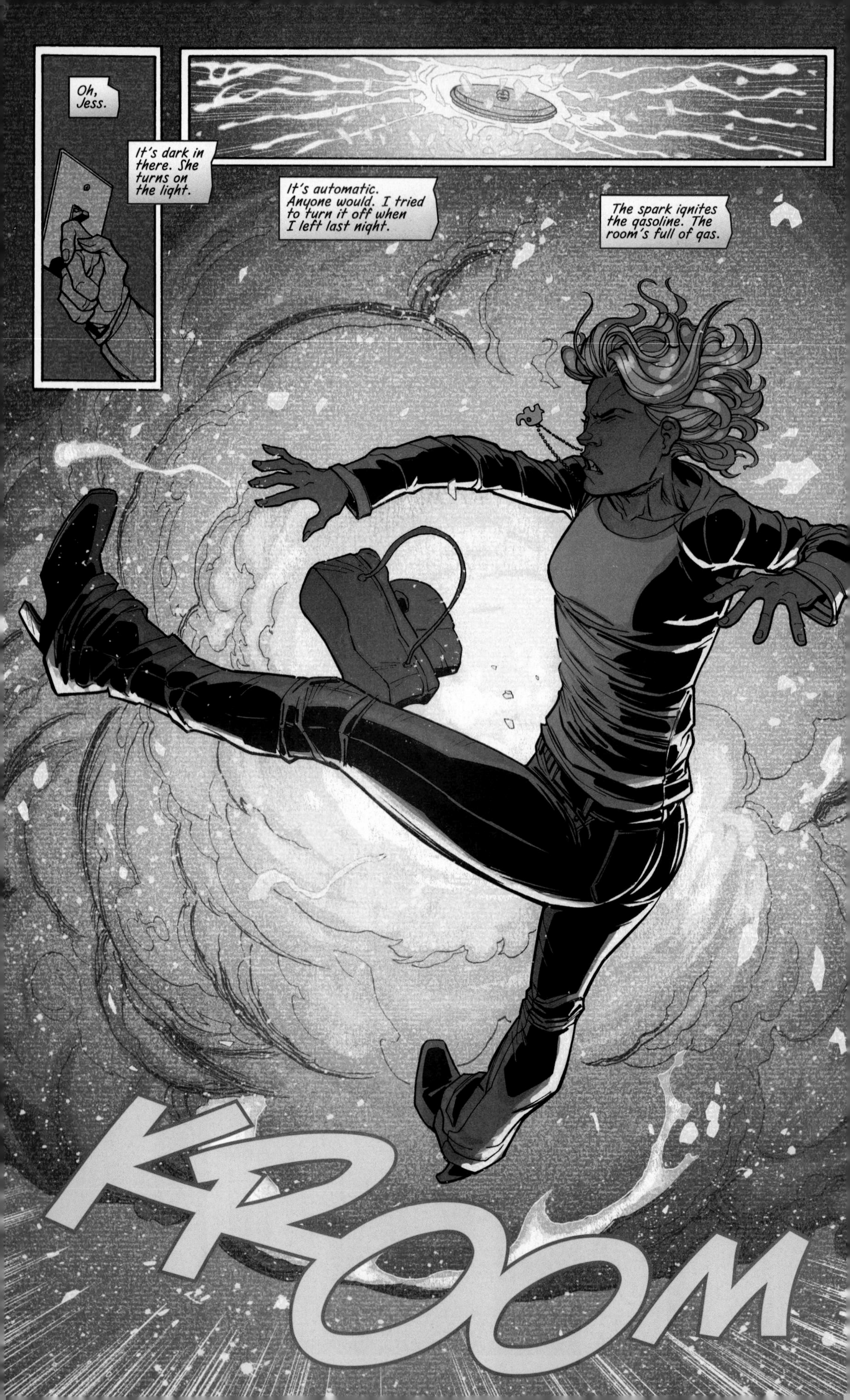
Oh, Jess.
It's dark in there. She turns on the light.
It's automatic. Anyone would. I tried to turn it off when I left last night.
The spark ignites the gasoline. The room's full of gas.
KROOM

BLUCHER FOREST, JOHN F. HAYES ORPHANAGE GROUNDS. SUMMER 2002.

I GUESS WE'LL NEVER KNOW THE LORD'S PLAN IN TAKING THESE LITTLE BIRDS.

JUST LIKE WE'LL NEVER KNOW WHY HE TOOK YOUR FAMILIES.

TOYNE'S BROOCH!

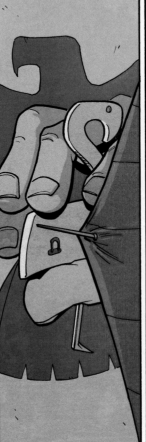

IT'S GOOD TO SEE YOU KIDS LOOKING OUT FOR EACH OTHER.

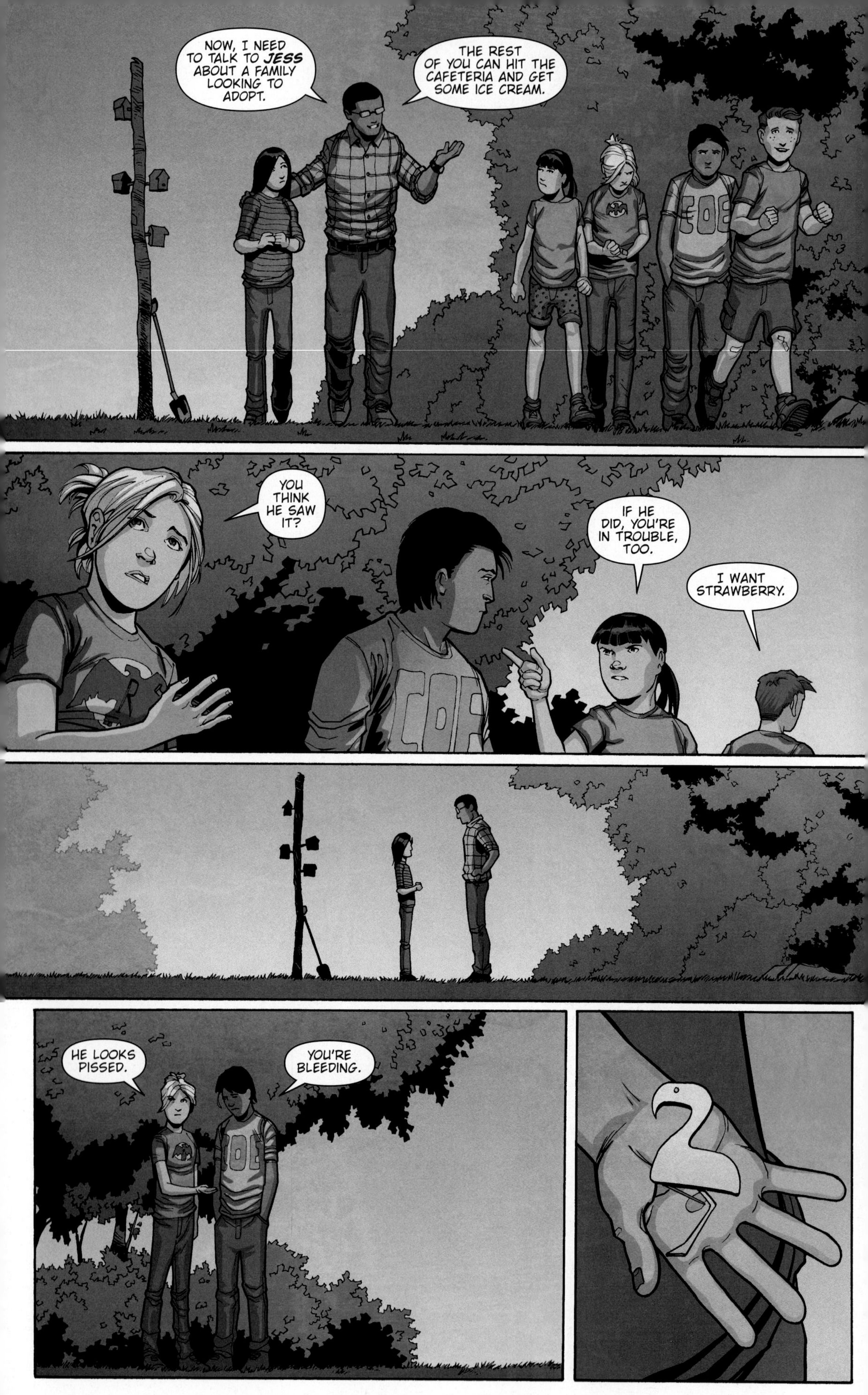
NOW, I NEED TO TALK TO JESS ABOUT A FAMILY LOOKING TO ADOPT.
THE REST OF YOU CAN HIT THE CAFETERIA AND GET SOME ICE CREAM.
YOU THINK HE SAW IT?
IF HE DID, YOU'RE IN TROUBLE, TOO.
I WANT STRAWBERRY.
HE LOOKS PISSED.
YOU'RE BLEEDING.

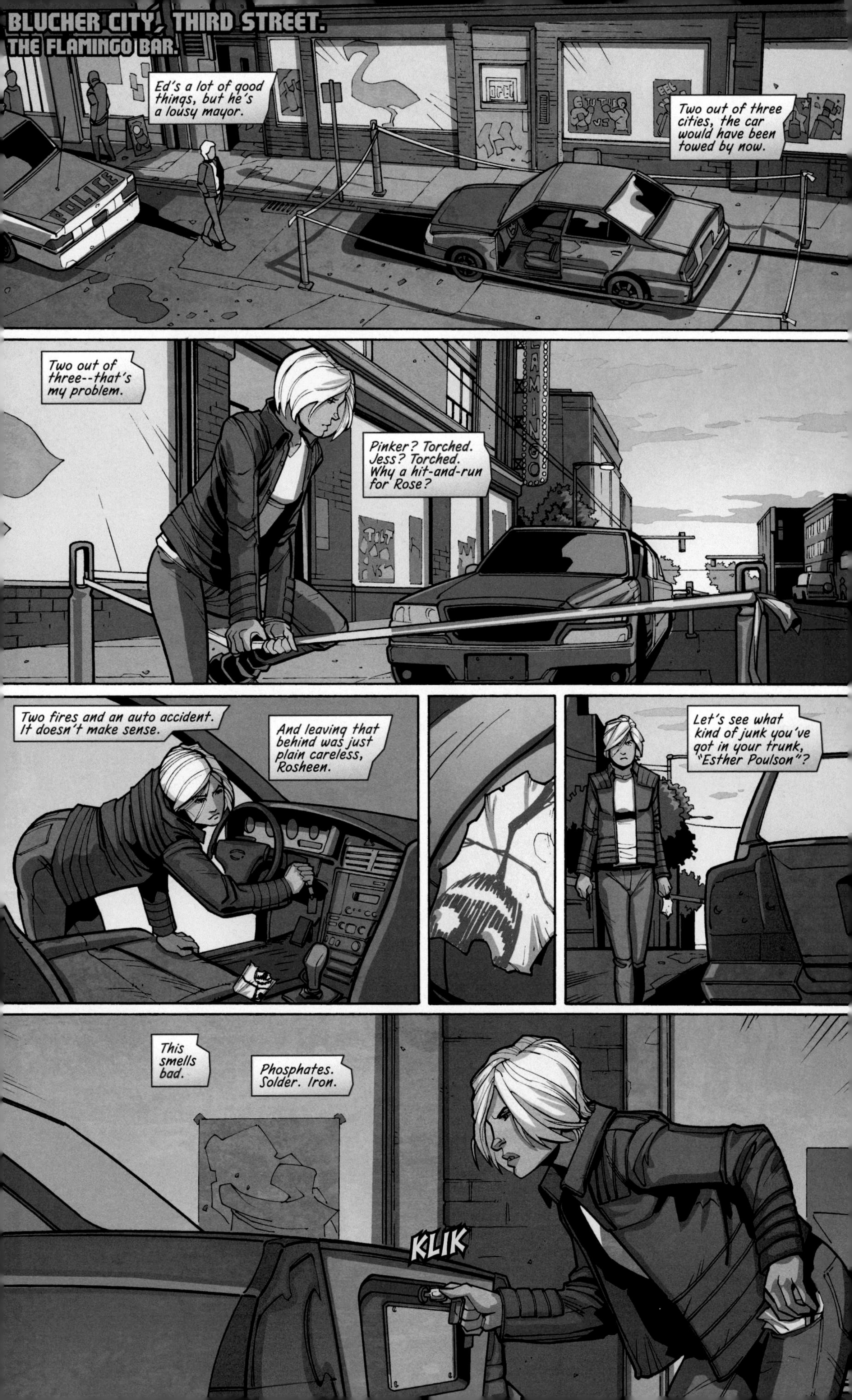
BLUCHER CITY, THIRD STREET.
THE FLAMINGO BAR.
Ed's a lot of good things, but he's a lousy mayor.
Two out of three cities, the car would have been towed by now.
Two out of three--that's my problem.
Pinker? Torched. Jess? Torched. Why a hit-and-run for Rose?
Two fires and an auto accident. It doesn't make sense.
And leaving that behind was just plain careless, Rosheen.
Let's see what kind of junk you've got in your trunk, "Esther Poulson"?
This smells bad.
Phosphates. Solder. Iron.
KLIK

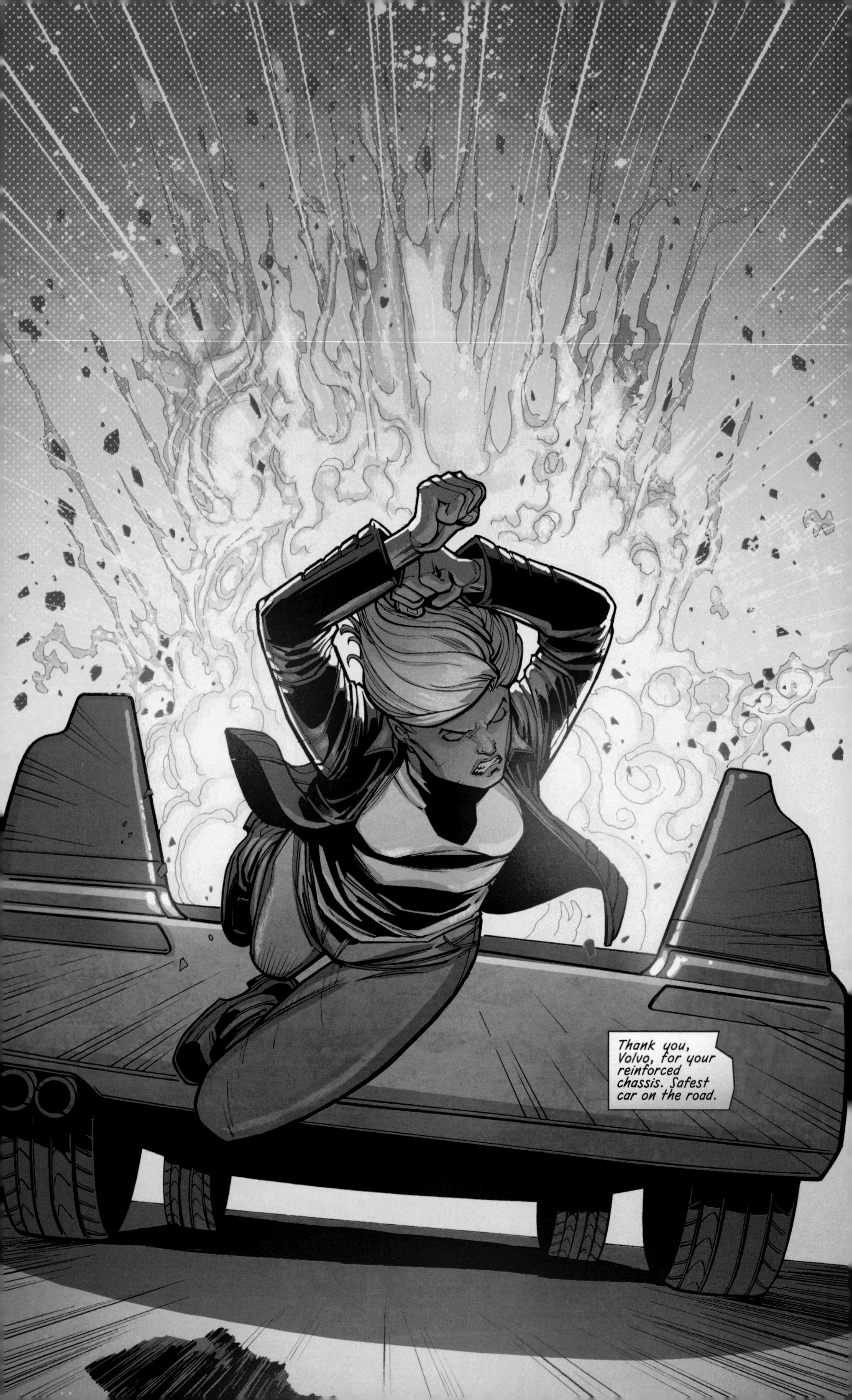
Thank you, Volvo, for your reinforced chassis. Safest car on the road.

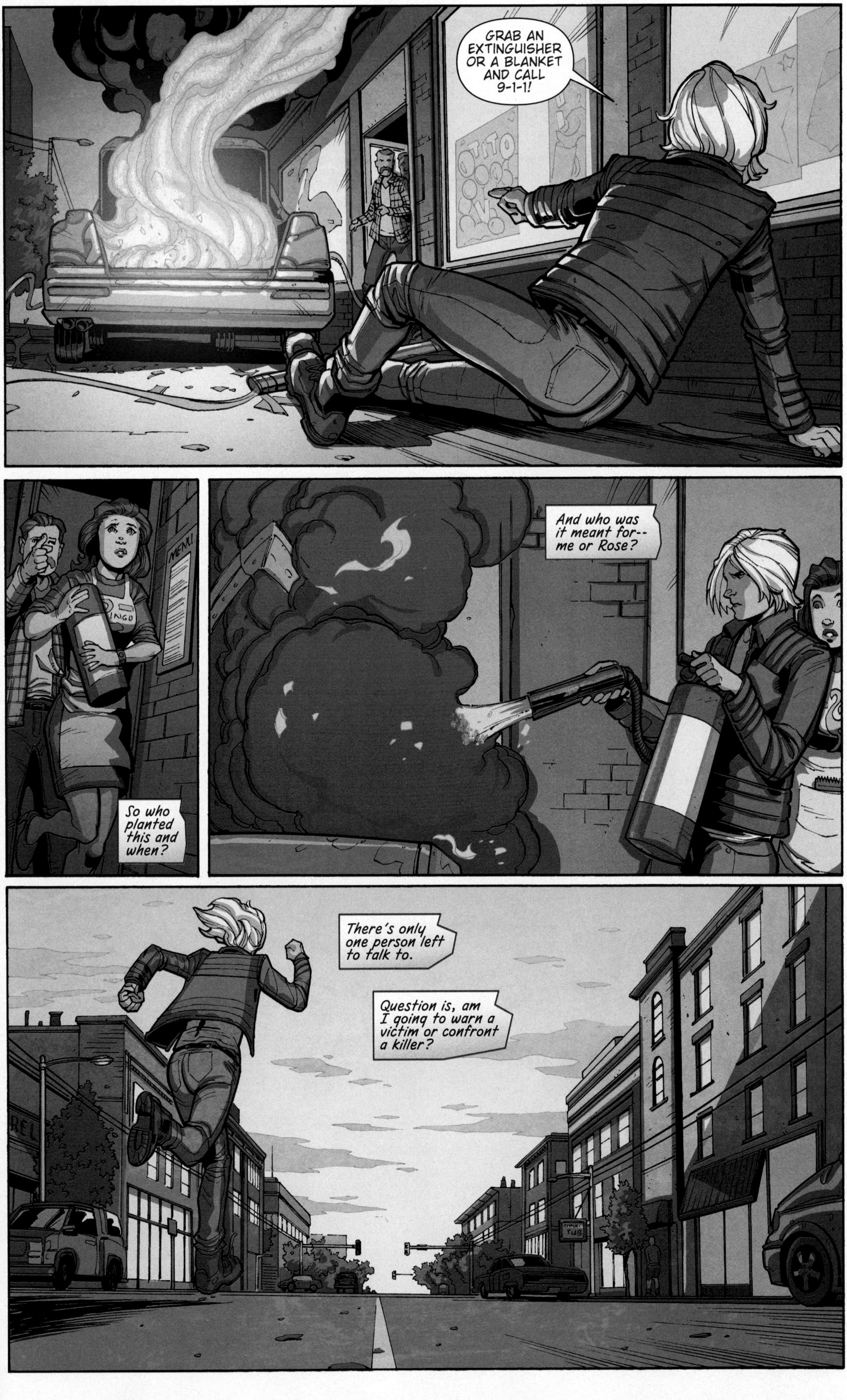
GRAB AN EXTINGUISHER OR A BLANKET AND CALL 9-1-1!
So who planted this and when?
And who was it meant for-- me or Rose?
There's only one person left to talk to.
Question is, am I going to warn a victim or confront a killer?

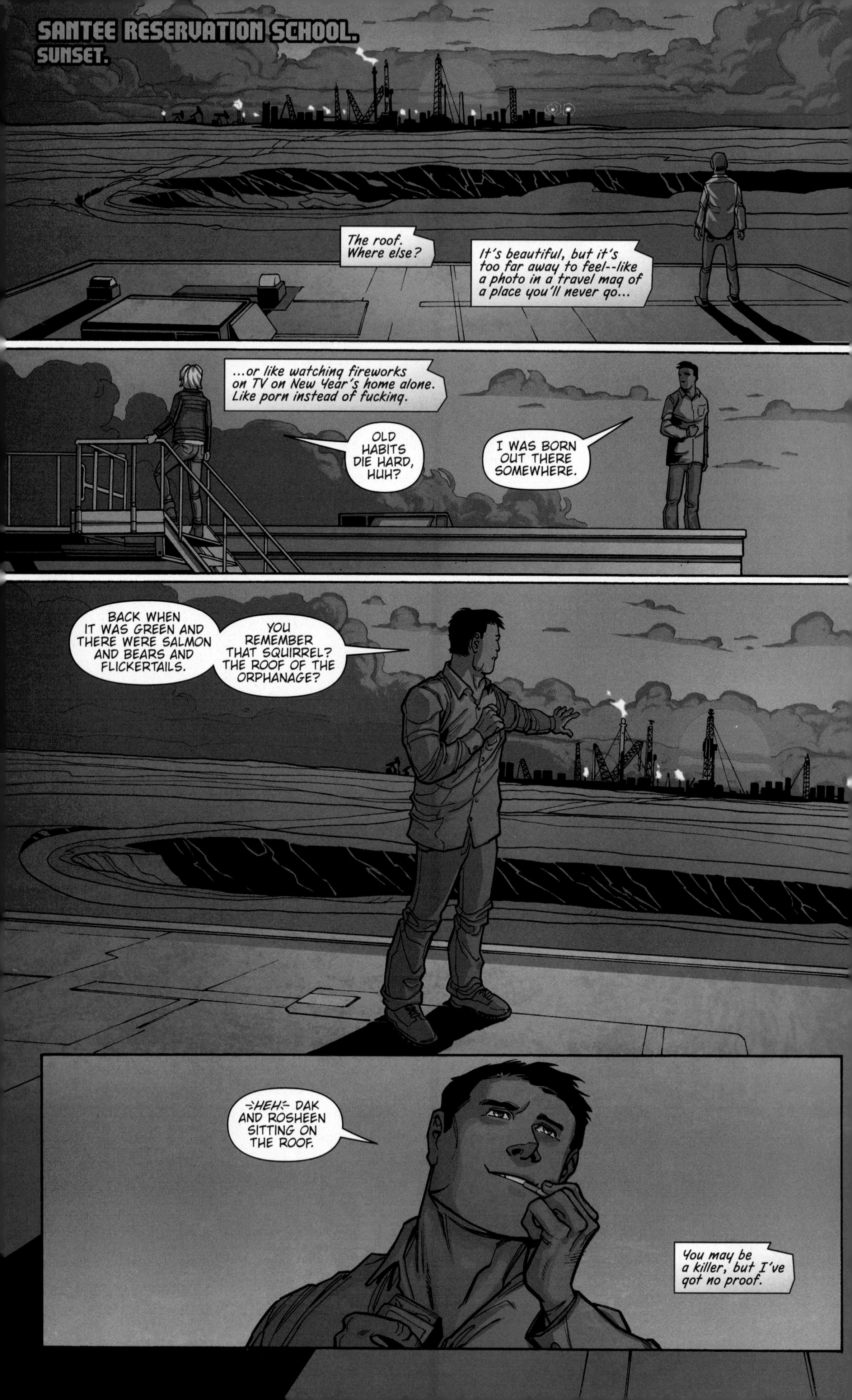
SANTEE RESERVATION SCHOOL.
SUNSET.
The roof. Where else?
It's beautiful, but it's too far away to feel--like a photo in a travel mag of a place you'll never go...
...or like watching fireworks on TV on New Year's home alone. Like porn instead of fucking.
OLD HABITS DIE HARD, HUH?
I WAS BORN OUT THERE SOMEWHERE.
BACK WHEN IT WAS GREEN AND THERE WERE SALMON AND BEARS AND FLICKERTAILS.
YOU REMEMBER THAT SQUIRREL? THE ROOF OF THE ORPHANAGE?
HEH DAK AND ROSHEEN SITTING ON THE ROOF.
You may be a killer, but I've got no proof.

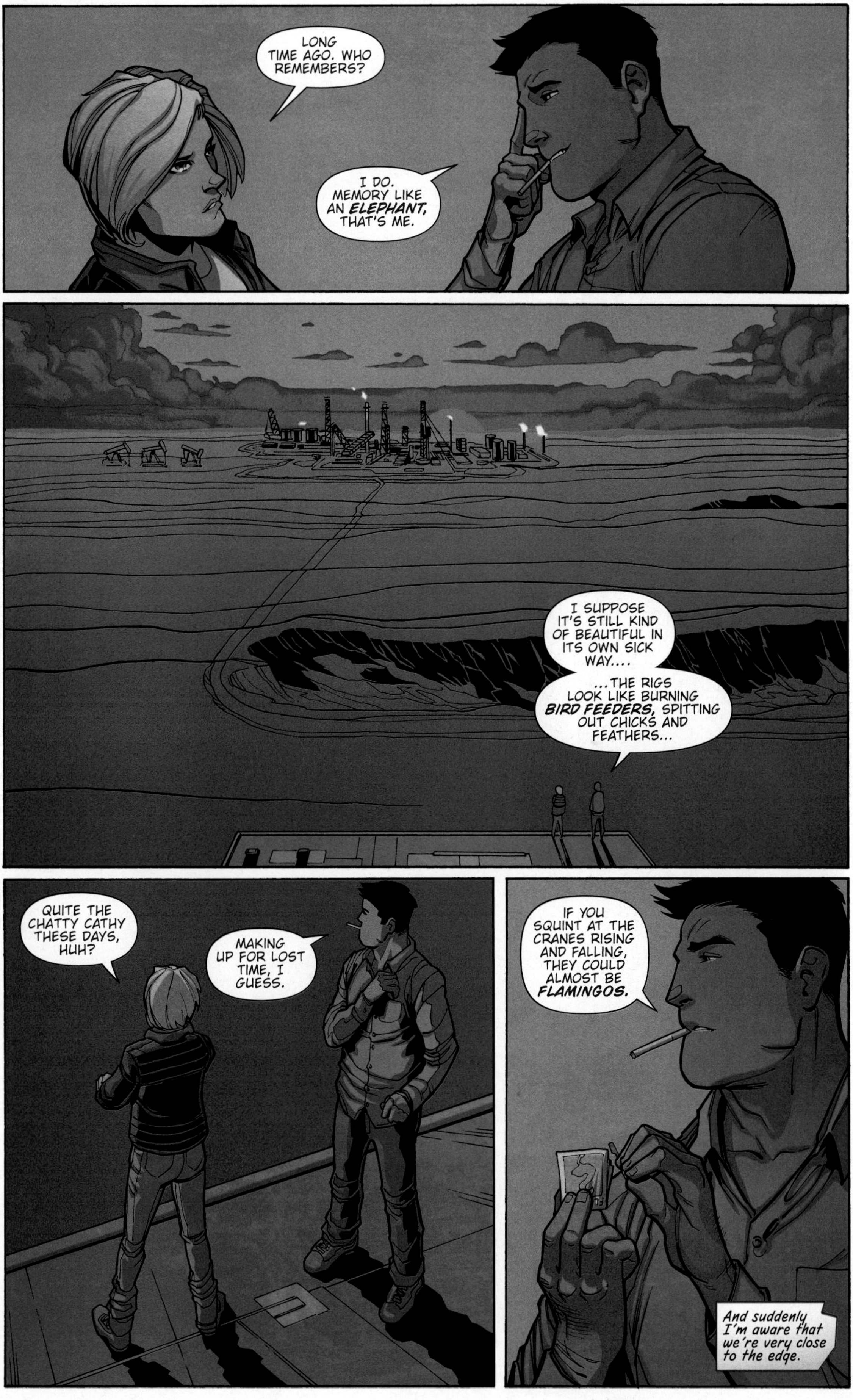
LONG TIME AGO. WHO REMEMBERS?
I DO. MEMORY LIKE AN *ELEPHANT,* THAT'S ME.
I SUPPOSE IT'S STILL KIND OF BEAUTIFUL IN ITS OWN SICK WAY....
...THE RIGS LOOK LIKE BURNING *BIRD FEEDERS,* SPITTING OUT CHICKS AND FEATHERS...
QUITE THE CHATTY CATHY THESE DAYS, HUH?
MAKING UP FOR LOST TIME, I GUESS.
IF YOU SQUINT AT THE CRANES RISING AND FALLING, THEY COULD ALMOST BE *FLAMINGOS.*
And suddenly I'm aware that we're very close to the edge.

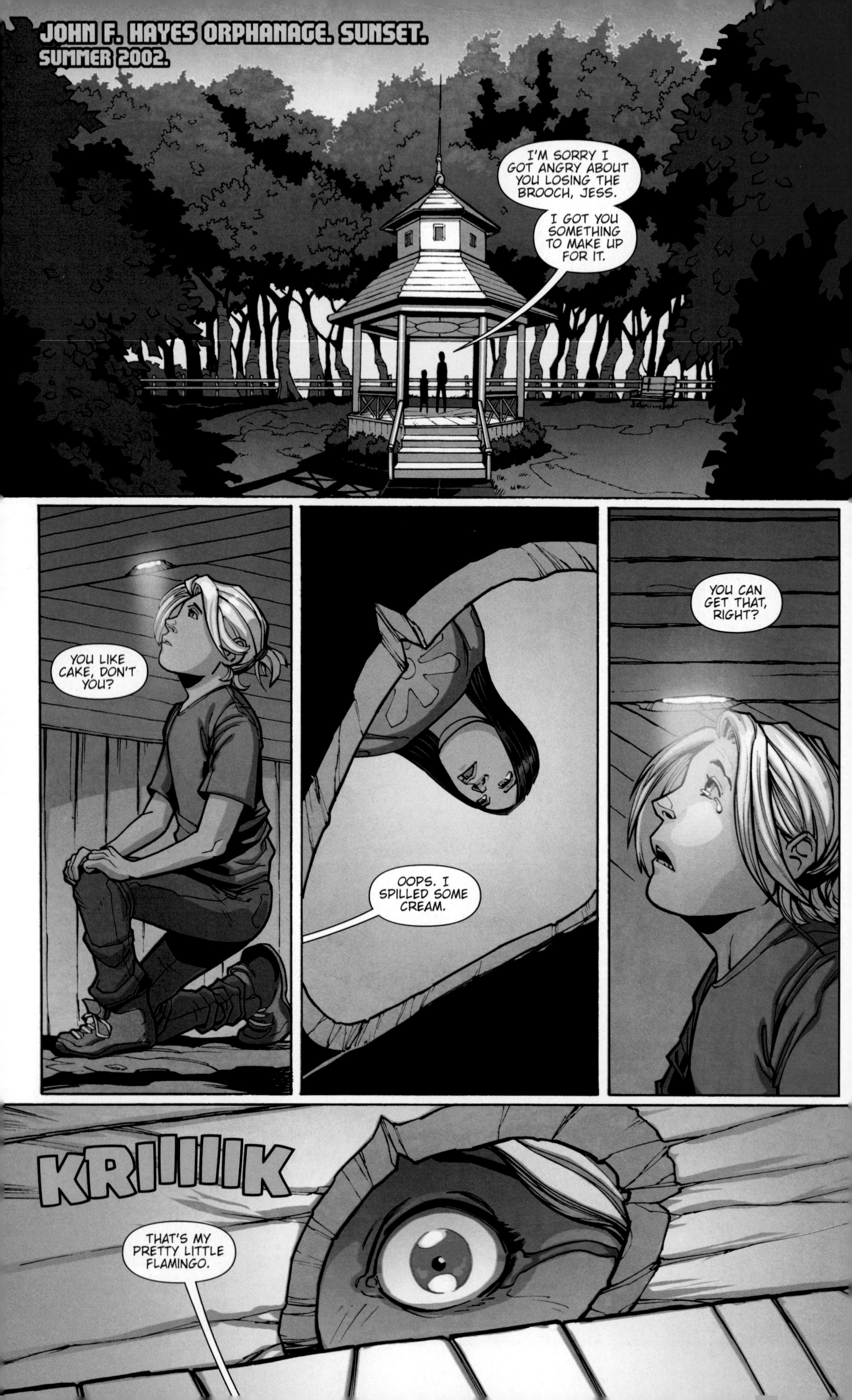
JOHN F. HAYES ORPHANAGE. SUNSET. SUMMER 2002.
I'M SORRY I GOT ANGRY ABOUT YOU LOSING THE BROOCH, JESS.
I GOT YOU SOMETHING TO MAKE UP FOR IT.
YOU LIKE CAKE, DON'T YOU?
OOPS. I SPILLED SOME CREAM.
YOU CAN GET THAT, RIGHT?
KRIIIIIK
THAT'S MY PRETTY LITTLE FLAMINGO.

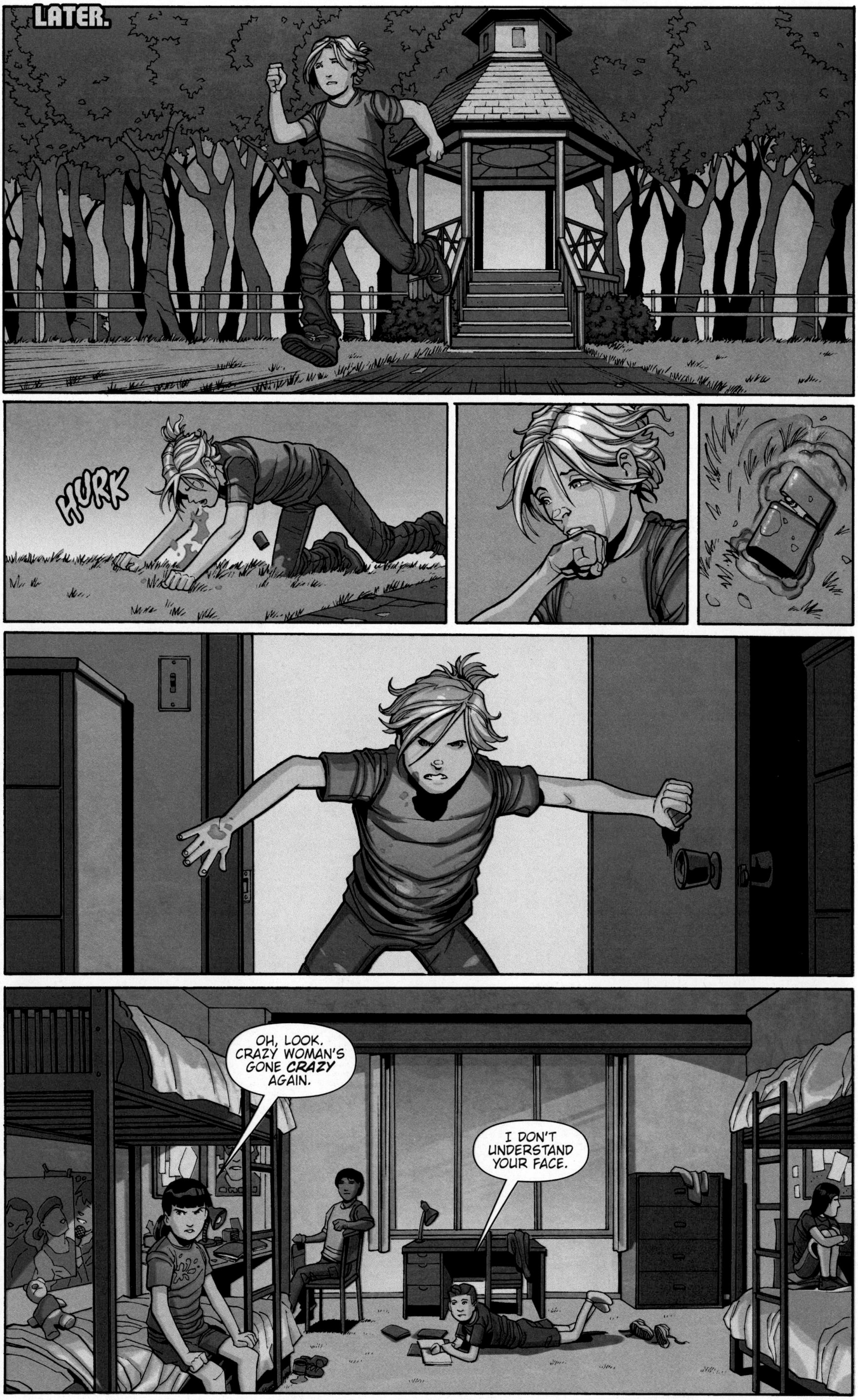
LATER.
HURK
OH, LOOK. CRAZY WOMAN'S GONE CRAZY AGAIN.
I DON'T UNDERSTAND YOUR FACE.

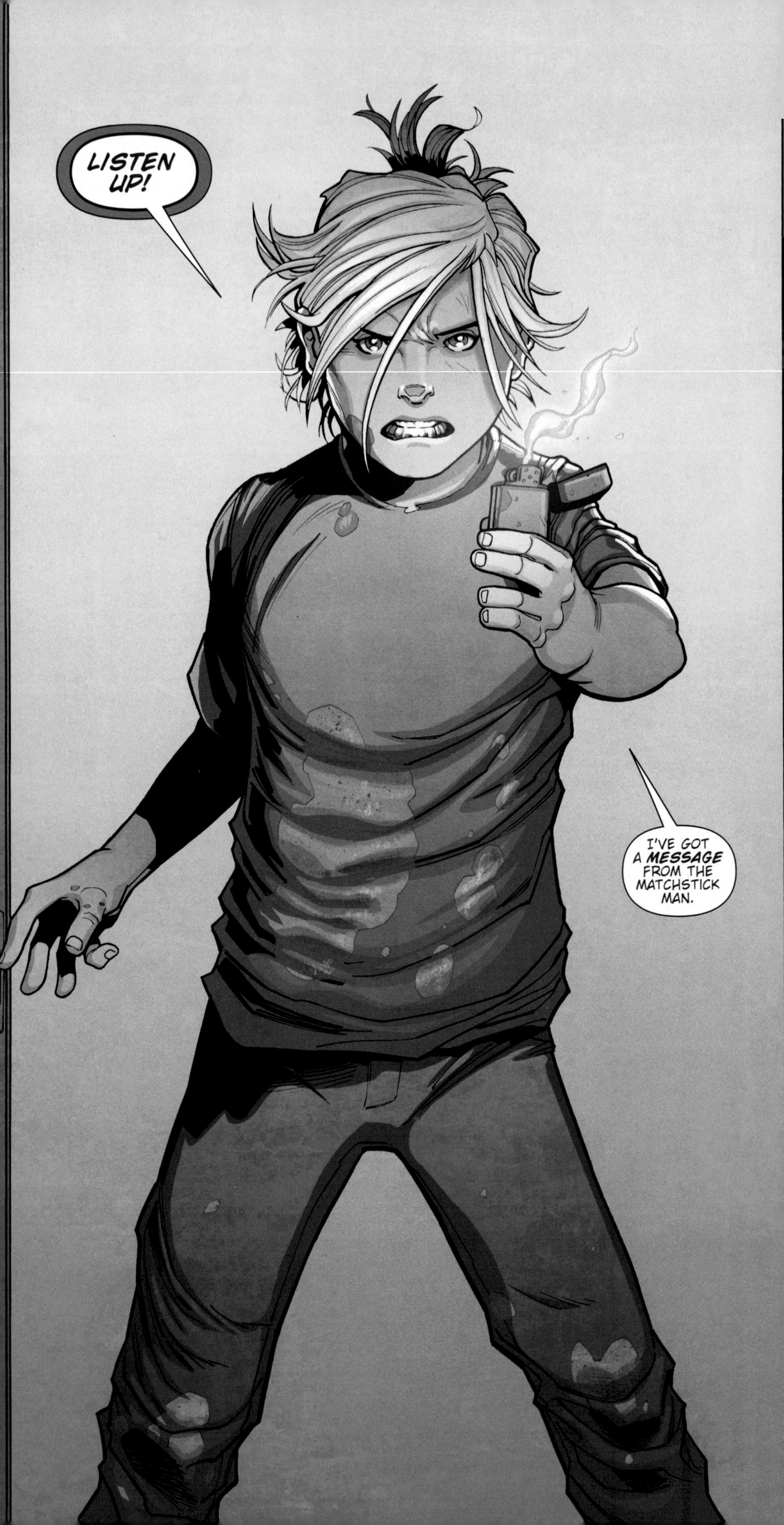
LISTEN UP!
I'VE GOT A MESSAGE FROM THE MATCHSTICK MAN.

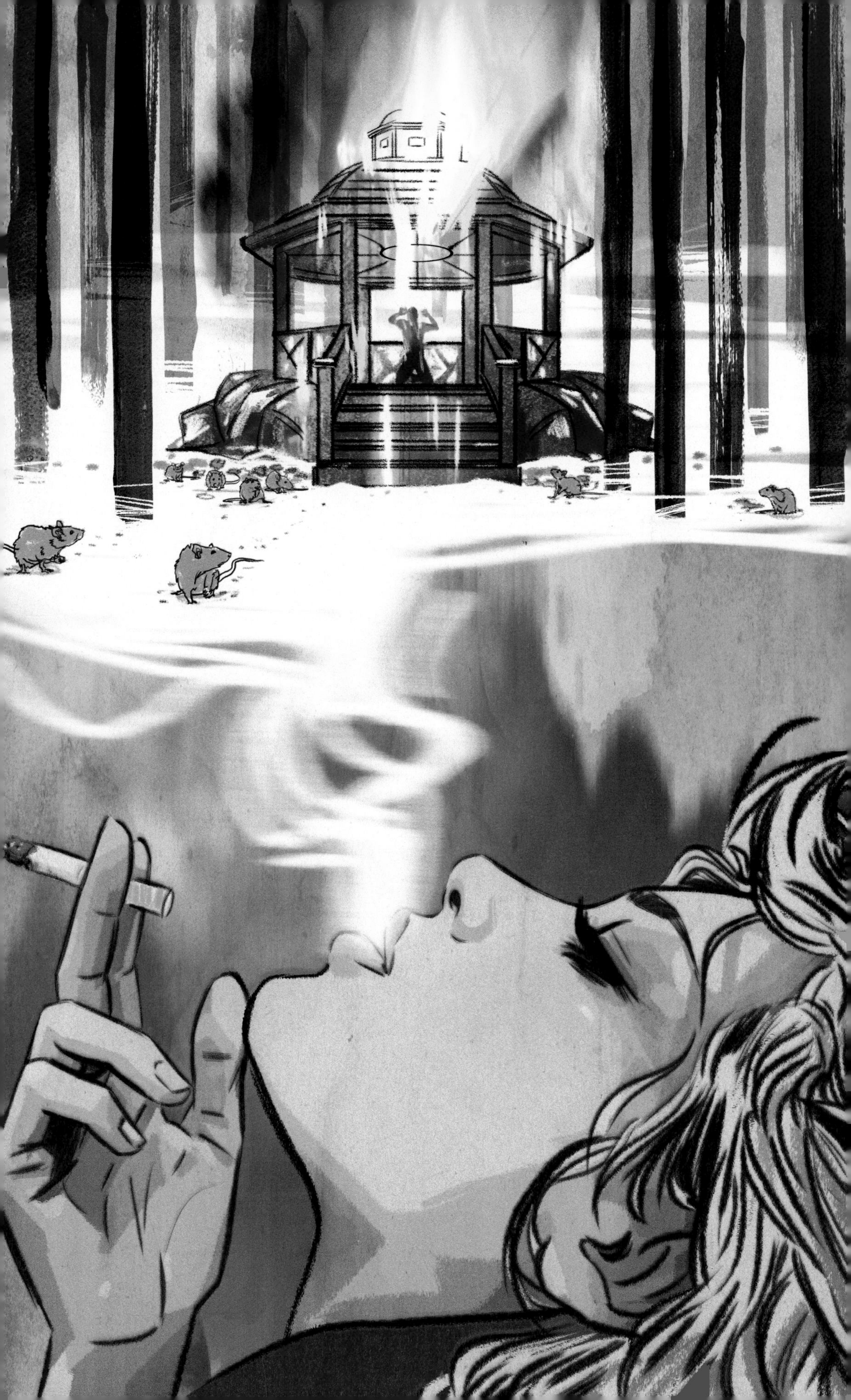

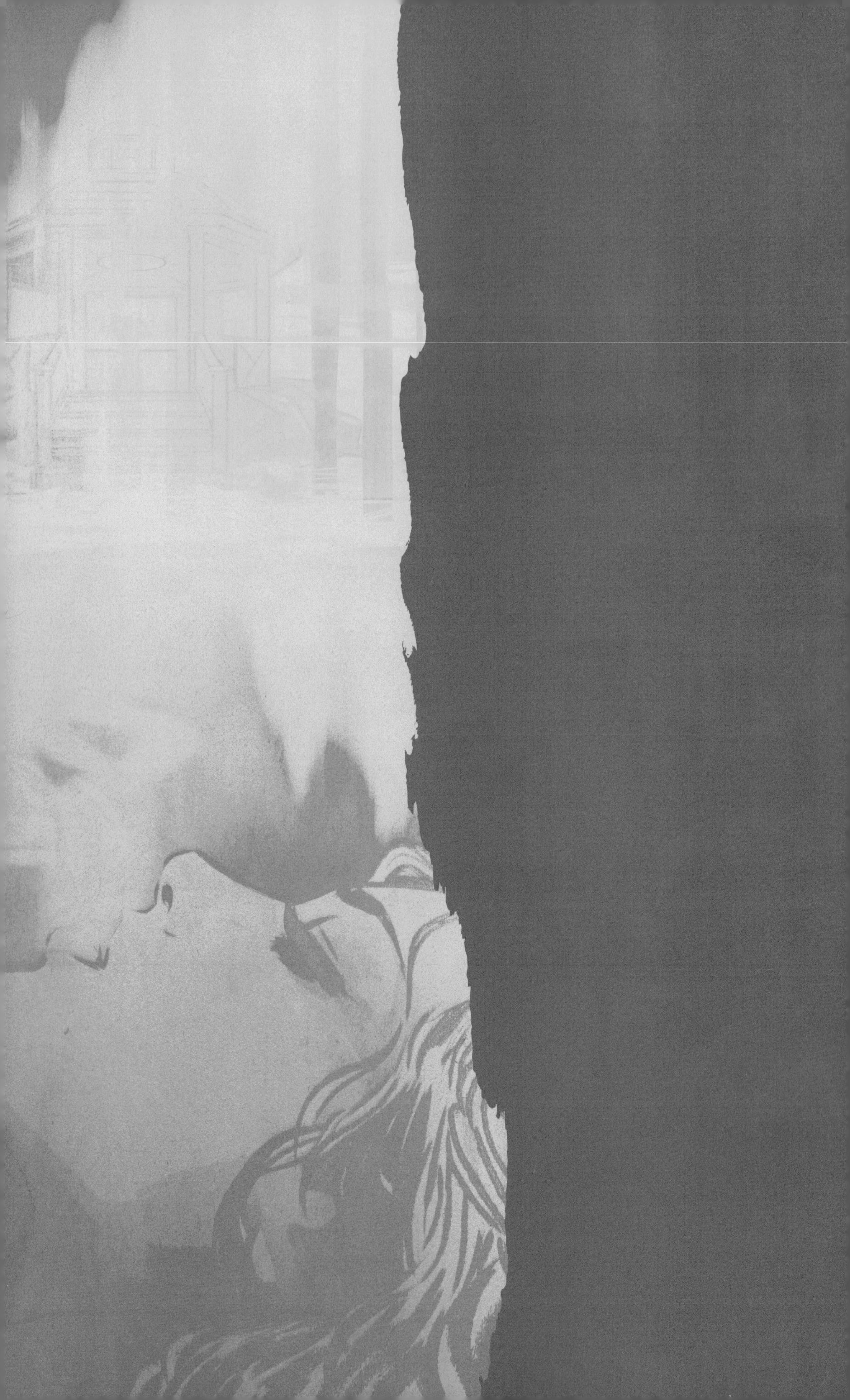

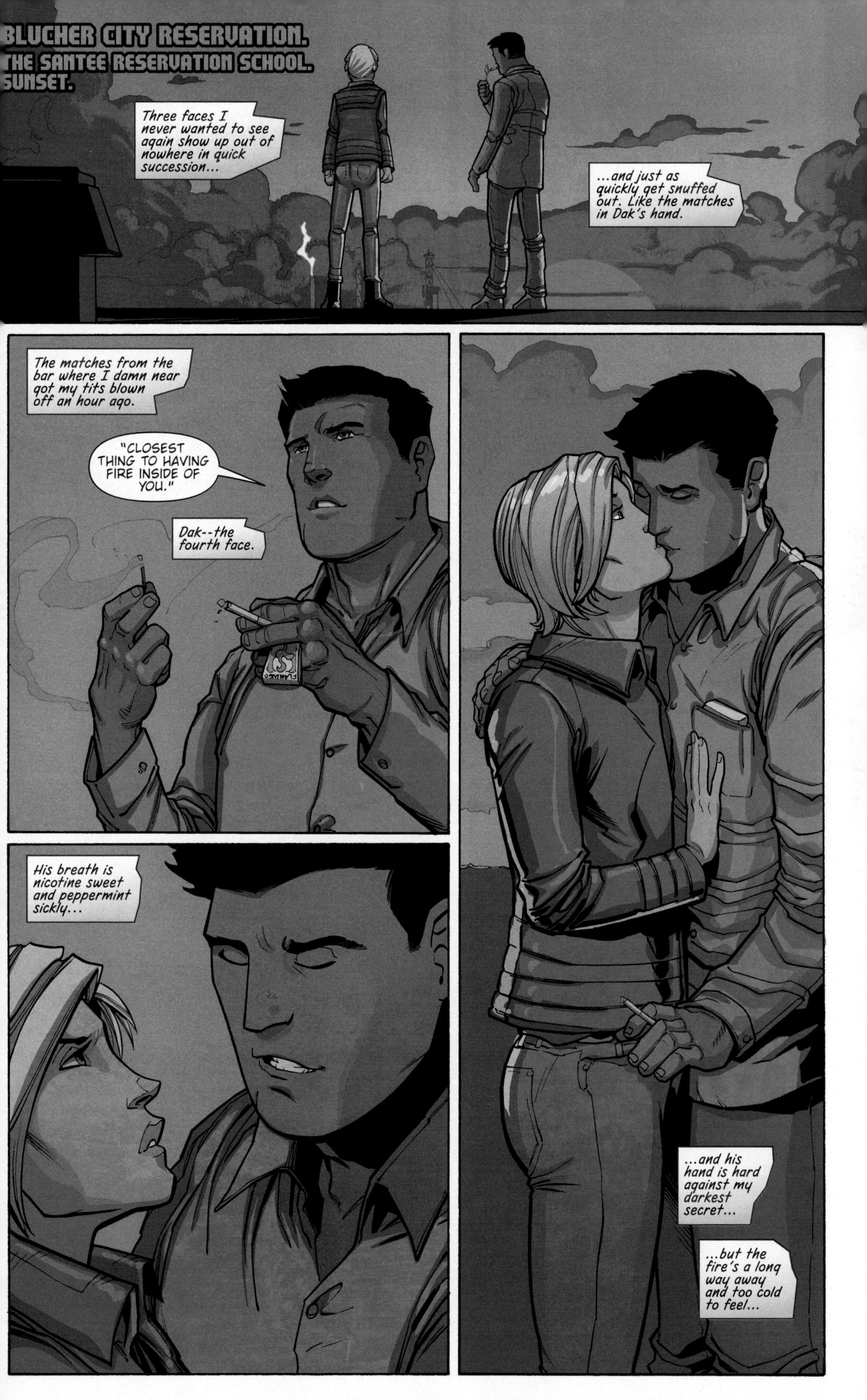
BLUCHER CITY RESERVATION.
THE SANTEE RESERVATION SCHOOL.
SUNSET.
Three faces I never wanted to see again show up out of nowhere in quick succession...
...and just as quickly get snuffed out. Like the matches in Dak's hand.
The matches from the bar where I damn near got my tits blown off an hour ago.
"CLOSEST THING TO HAVING FIRE INSIDE OF YOU."
Dak--the fourth face.
His breath is nicotine sweet and peppermint sickly...
...and his hand is hard against my darkest secret...
...but the fire's a long way away and too cold to feel...

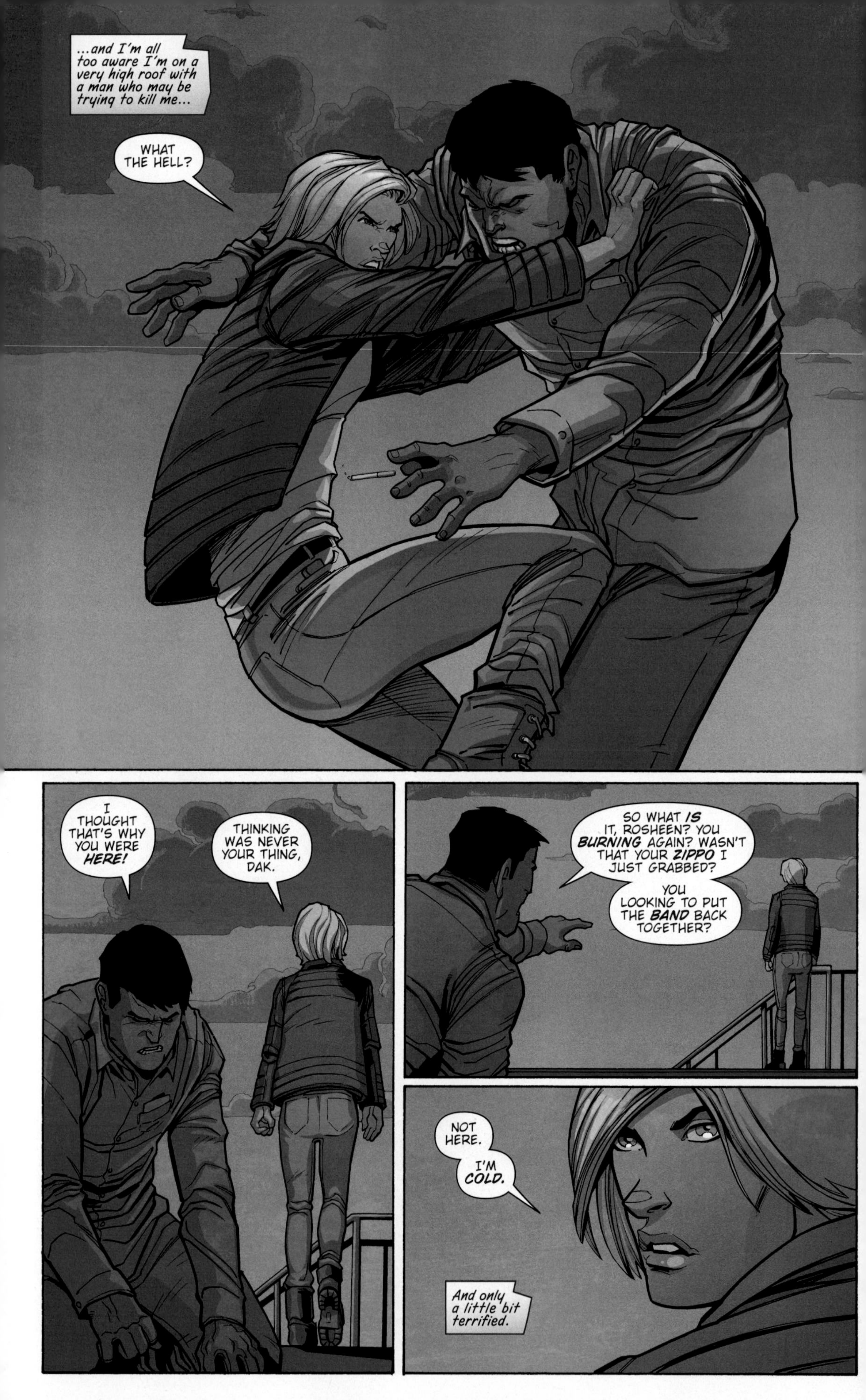
...and I'm all too aware I'm on a very high roof with a man who may be trying to kill me...
WHAT THE HELL?
I THOUGHT THAT'S WHY YOU WERE HERE!
THINKING WAS NEVER YOUR THING, DAK.
SO WHAT IS IT, ROSHEEN? YOU BURNING AGAIN? WASN'T THAT YOUR ZIPPO I JUST GRABBED?
YOU LOOKING TO PUT THE BAND BACK TOGETHER?
NOT HERE.
I'M COLD.
And only a little bit terrified.

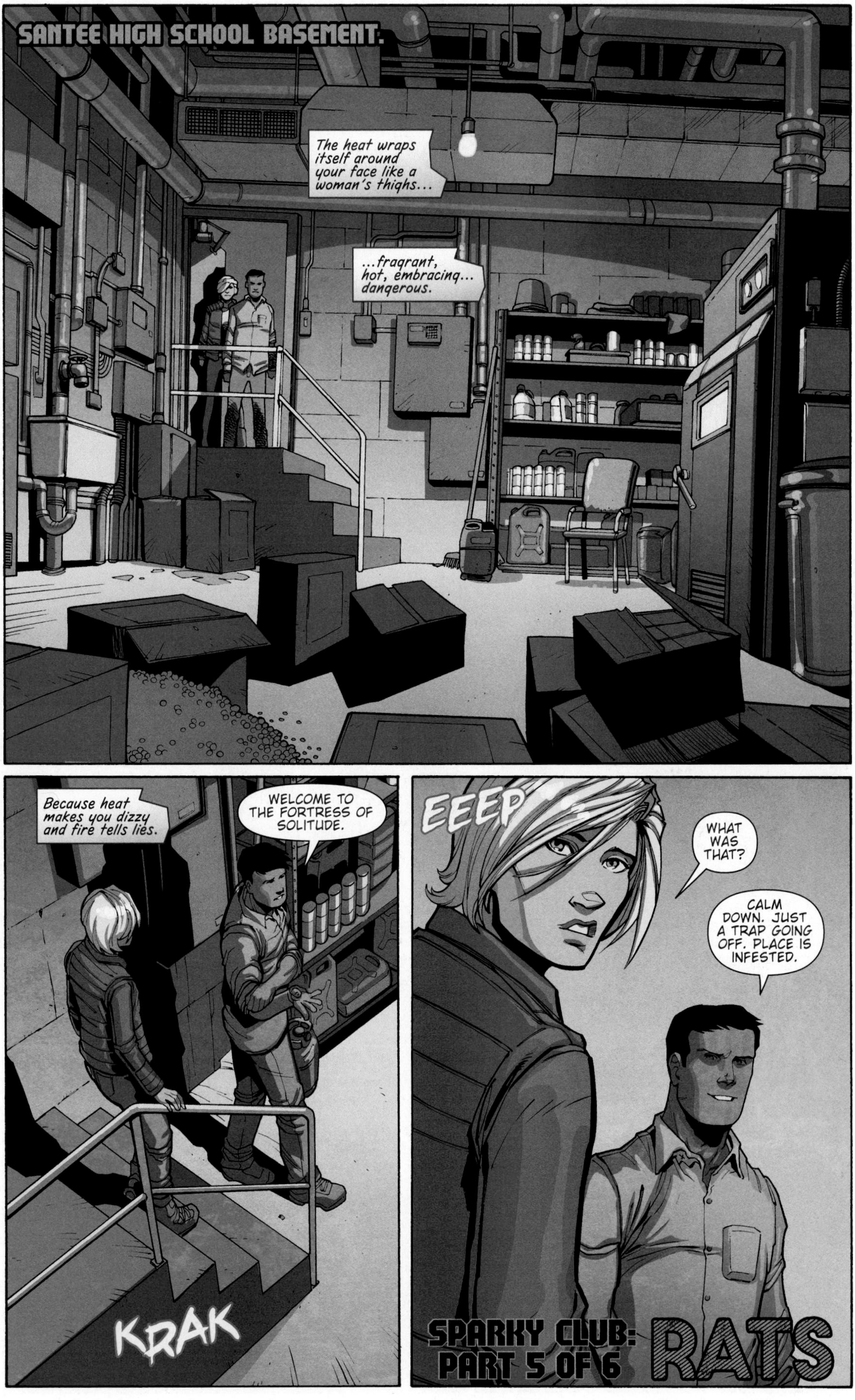
SANTEE HIGH SCHOOL BASEMENT.
The heat wraps itself around your face like a woman's thighs...
...fragrant, hot, embracing... dangerous.
Because heat makes you dizzy and fire tells lies.
WELCOME TO THE FORTRESS OF SOLITUDE.
KRAK
EEEP
WHAT WAS THAT?
CALM DOWN. JUST A TRAP GOING OFF. PLACE IS INFESTED.
SPARKY CLUB: PART 5 OF 6
RATS

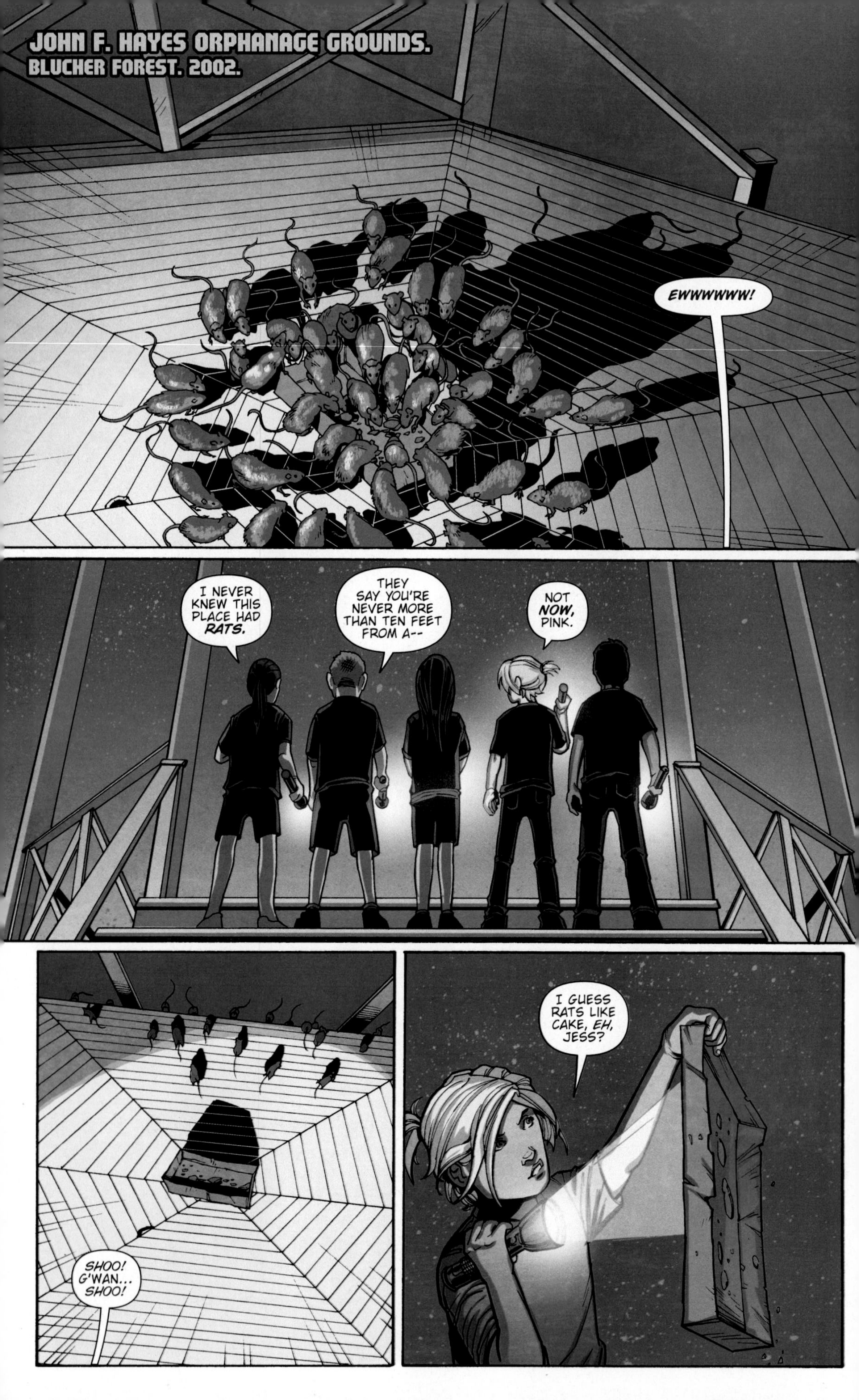
JOHN F. HAYES ORPHANAGE GROUNDS.
BLUCHER FOREST. 2002.
EWWWWWW!
I NEVER KNEW THIS PLACE HAD RATS.
THEY SAY YOU'RE NEVER MORE THAN TEN FEET FROM A--
NOT NOW, PINK.
SHOO! G'WAN... SHOO!
I GUESS RATS LIKE CAKE, EH, JESS?

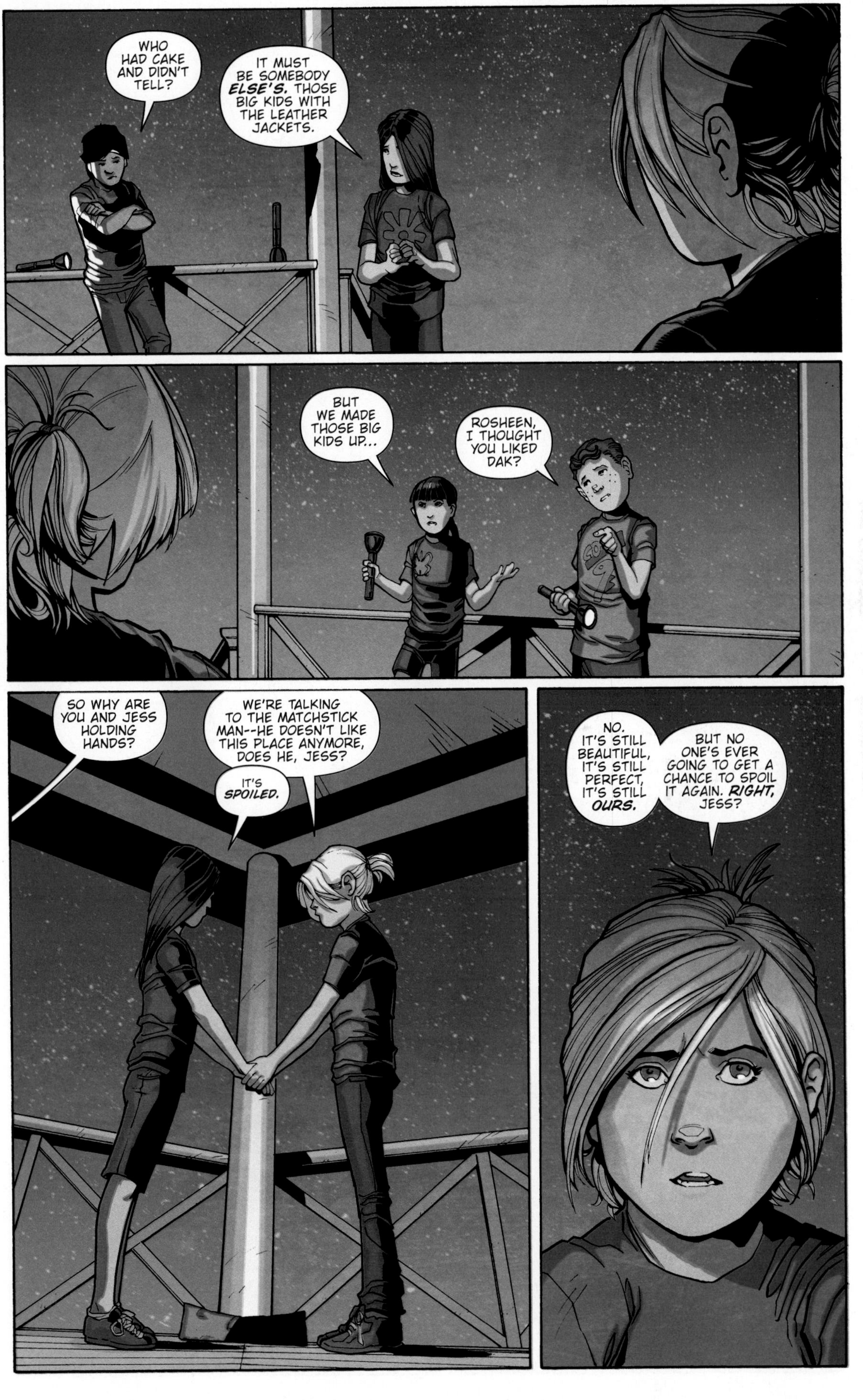
WHO HAD CAKE AND DIDN'T TELL?
IT MUST BE SOMEBODY ***ELSE'S.*** THOSE BIG KIDS WITH THE LEATHER JACKETS.
BUT WE MADE THOSE BIG KIDS UP...
ROSHEEN, I THOUGHT YOU LIKED DAK?
SO WHY ARE YOU AND JESS HOLDING HANDS?
WE'RE TALKING TO THE MATCHSTICK MAN--HE DOESN'T LIKE THIS PLACE ANYMORE, DOES HE, JESS?
IT'S ***SPOILED.***
NO. IT'S STILL BEAUTIFUL, IT'S STILL PERFECT, IT'S STILL ***OURS.***
BUT NO ONE'S EVER GOING TO GET A CHANCE TO SPOIL IT AGAIN. ***RIGHT,*** JESS?

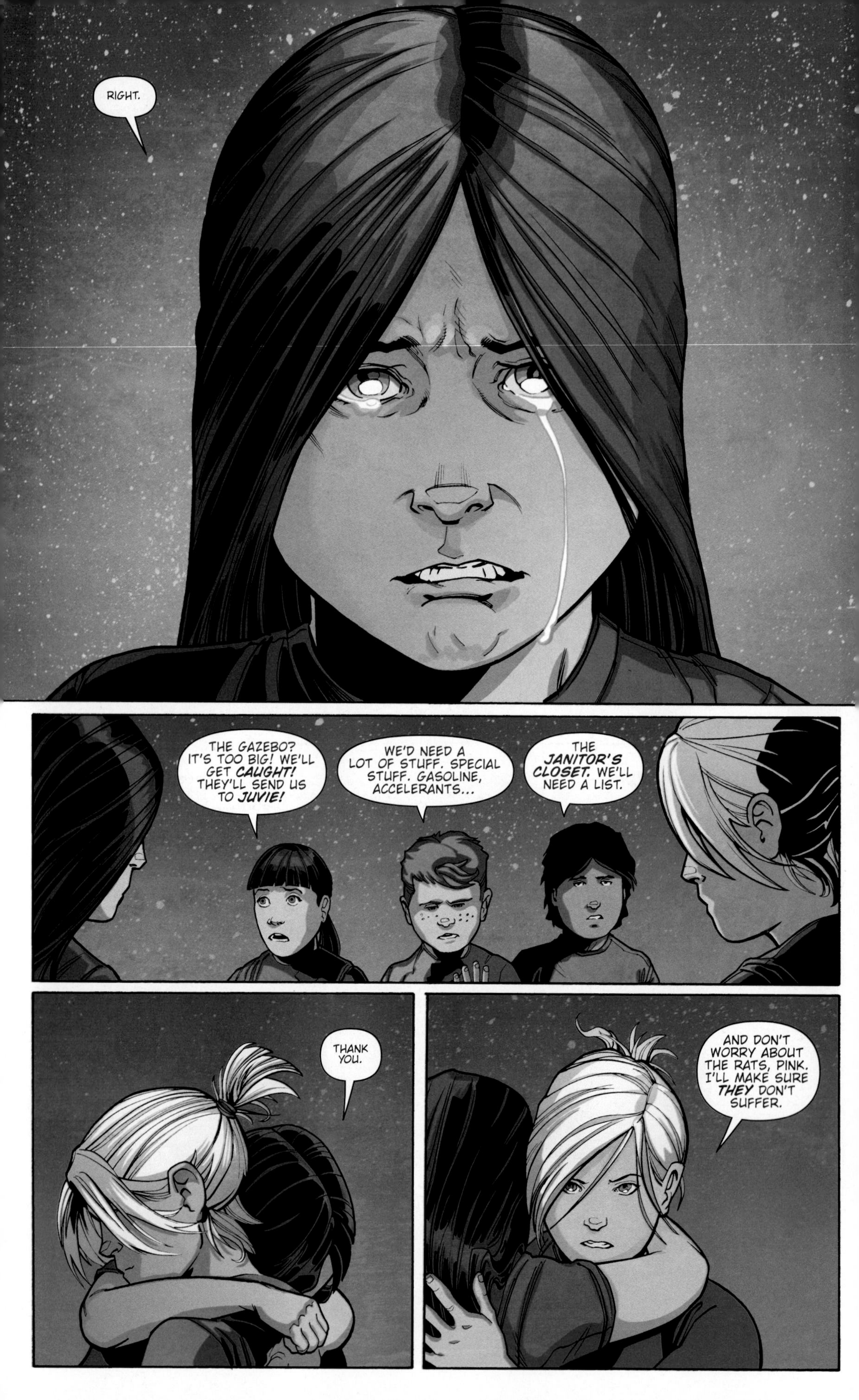
RIGHT.
THE GAZEBO? IT'S TOO BIG! WE'LL GET CAUGHT! THEY'LL SEND US TO JUVIE!
WE'D NEED A LOT OF STUFF. SPECIAL STUFF. GASOLINE, ACCELERANTS...
THE JANITOR'S CLOSET. WE'LL NEED A LIST.
THANK YOU.
AND DON'T WORRY ABOUT THE RATS, PINK. I'LL MAKE SURE THEY DON'T SUFFER.

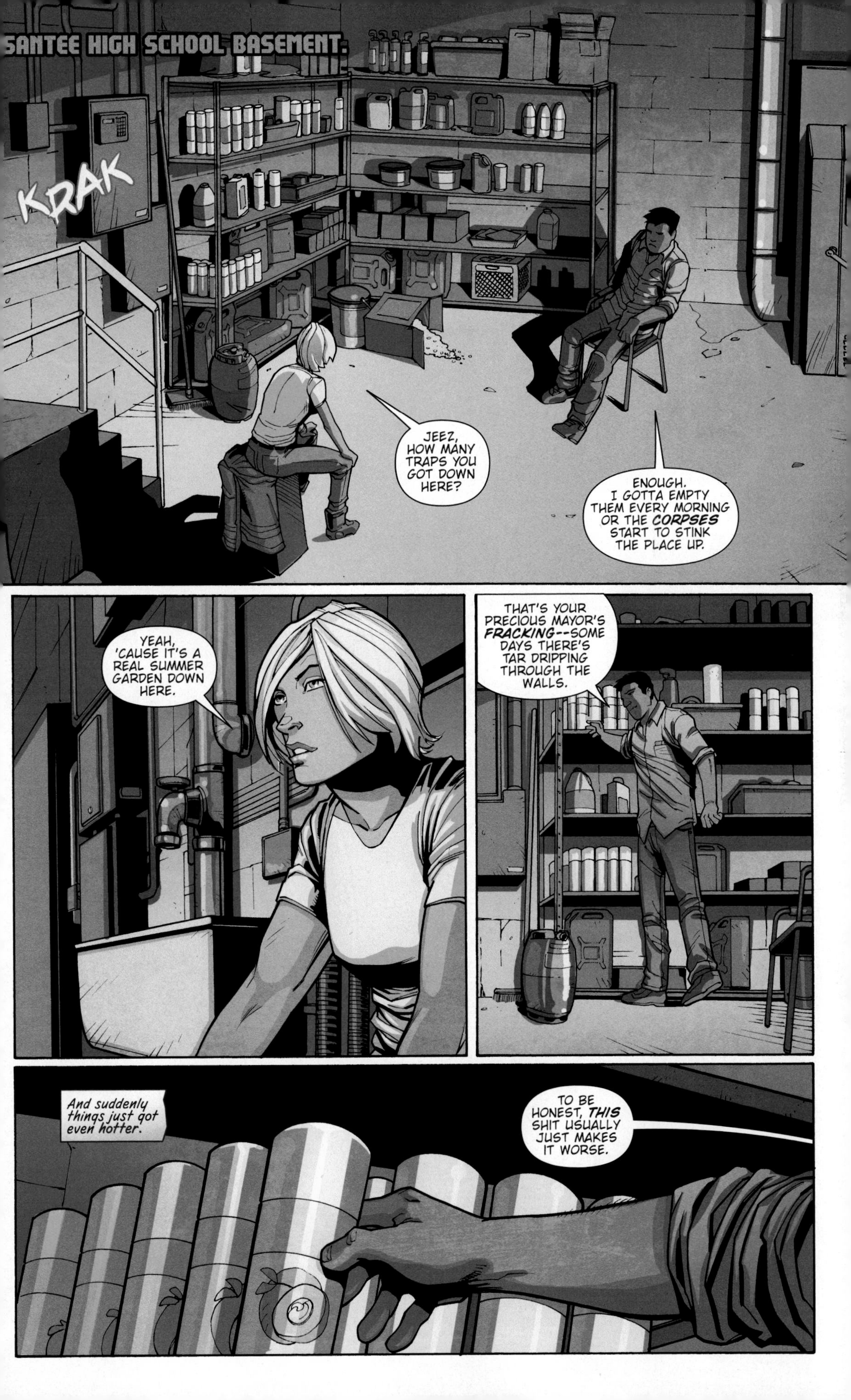
SANTEE HIGH SCHOOL BASEMENT.
KRAK
JEEZ, HOW MANY TRAPS YOU GOT DOWN HERE?
ENOUGH. I GOTTA EMPTY THEM EVERY MORNING OR THE CORPSES START TO STINK THE PLACE UP.
YEAH, 'CAUSE IT'S A REAL SUMMER GARDEN DOWN HERE.
THAT'S YOUR PRECIOUS MAYOR'S FRACKING--SOME DAYS THERE'S TAR DRIPPING THROUGH THE WALLS.
And suddenly things just got even hotter.
TO BE HONEST, THIS SHIT USUALLY JUST MAKES IT WORSE.

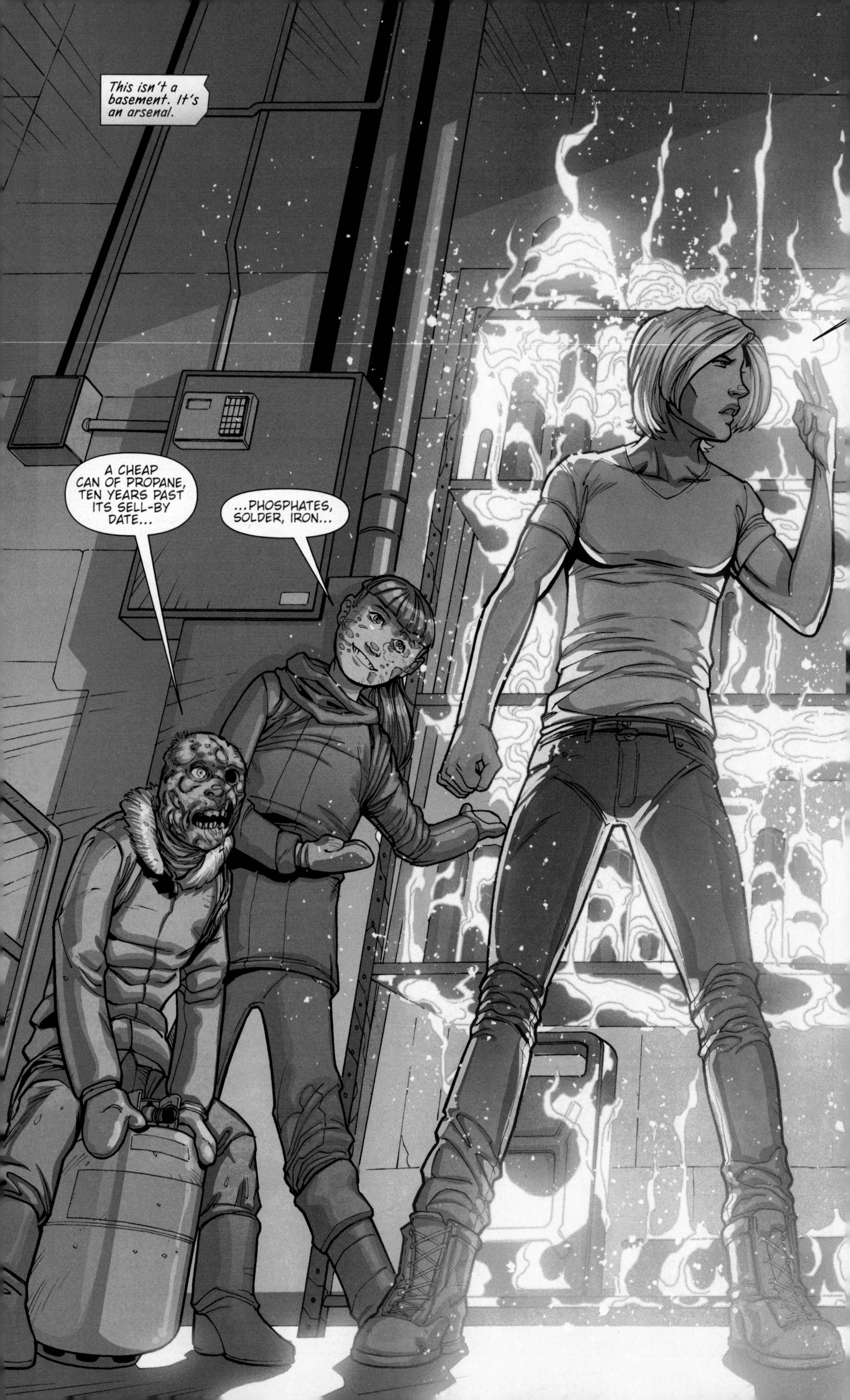
This isn't a basement. It's an arsenal.
A CHEAP CAN OF PROPANE, TEN YEARS PAST ITS SELL-BY DATE...
...PHOSPHATES, SOLDER, IRON...

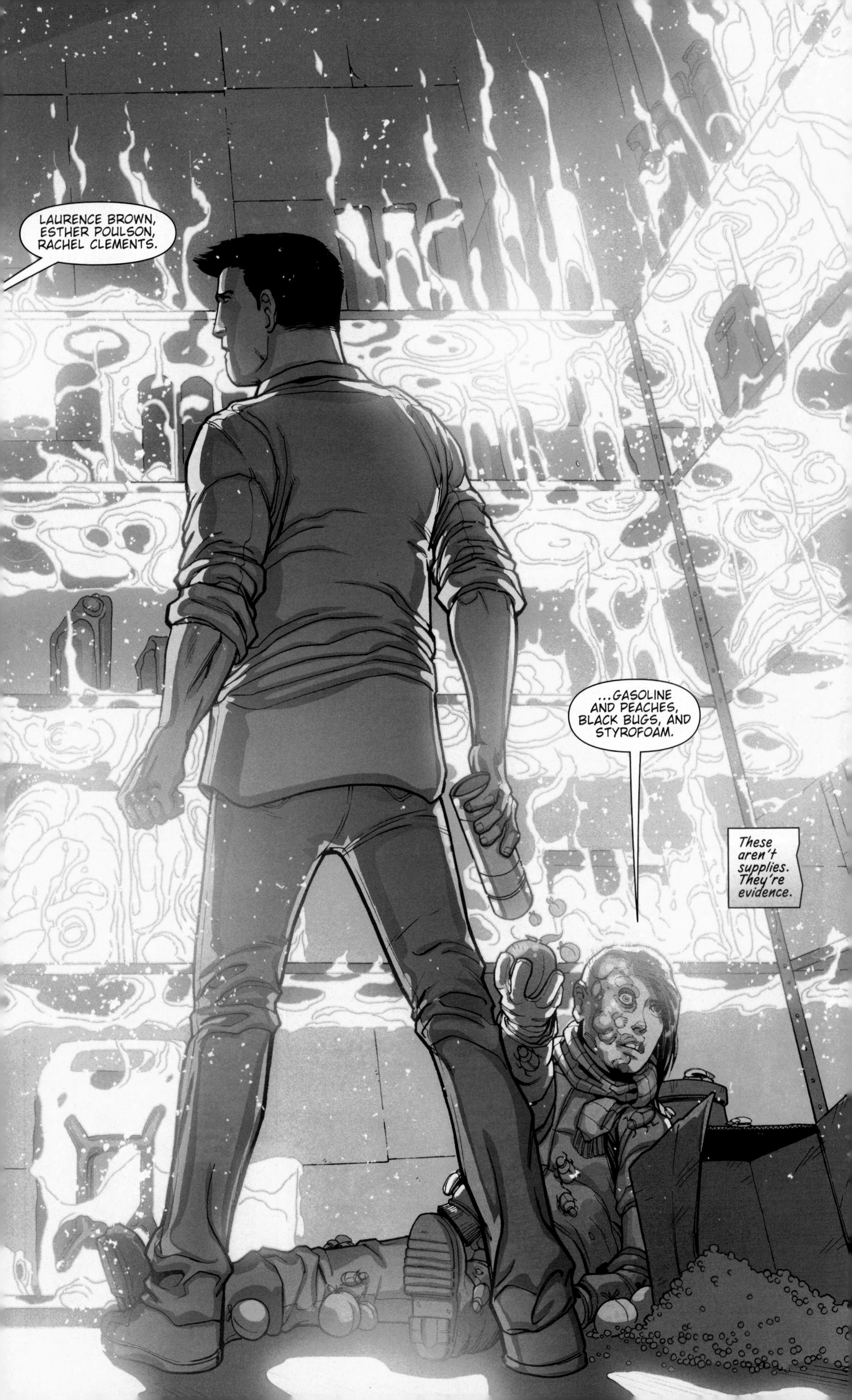
LAURENCE BROWN,
ESTHER POULSON,
RACHEL CLEMENTS.
...GASOLINE AND PEACHES, BLACK BUGS, AND STYROFOAM.
These aren't supplies. They're evidence.

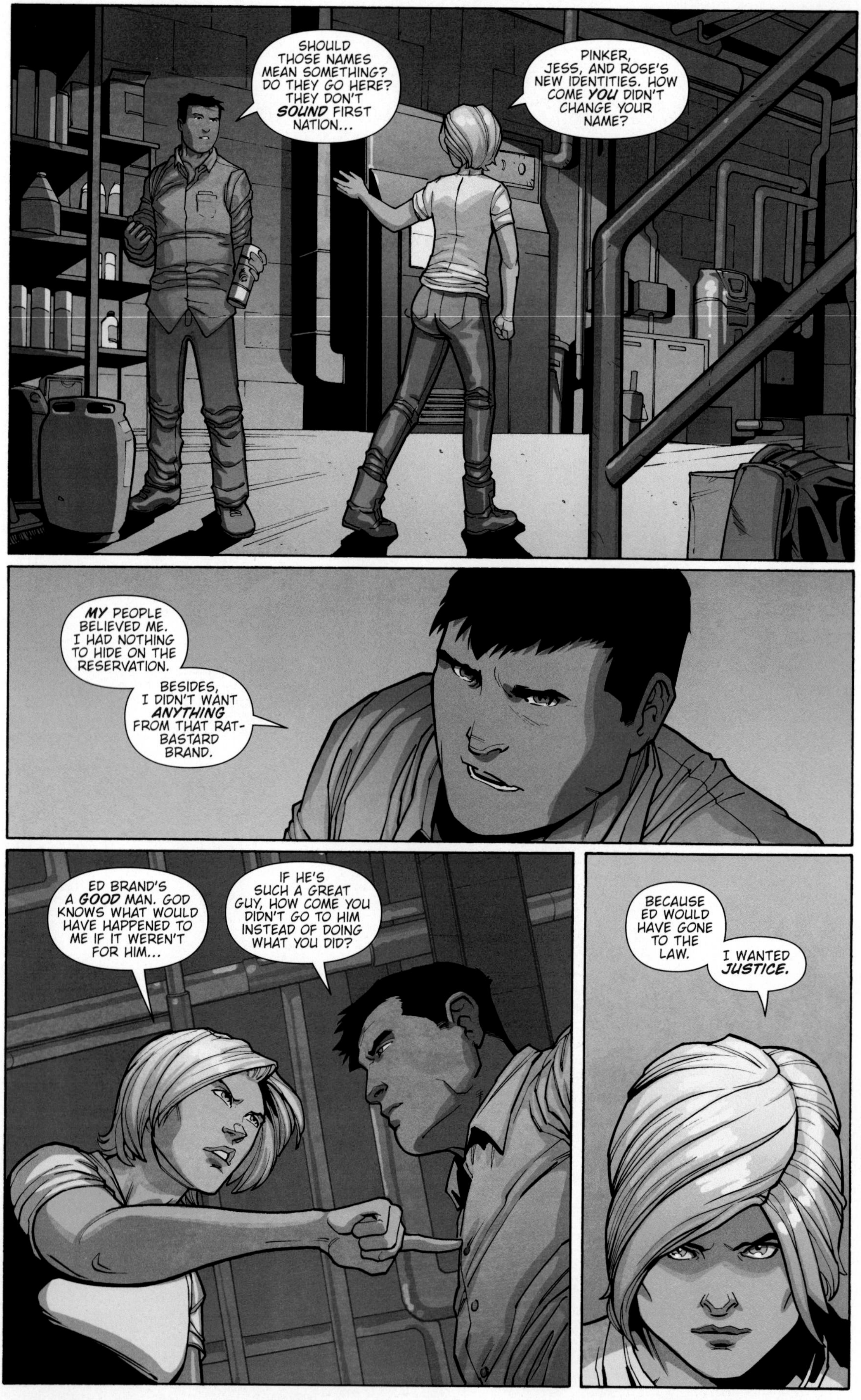
SHOULD THOSE NAMES MEAN SOMETHING? DO THEY GO HERE? THEY DON'T SOUND FIRST NATION...
PINKER, JESS, AND ROSE'S NEW IDENTITIES. HOW COME YOU DIDN'T CHANGE YOUR NAME?
MY PEOPLE BELIEVED ME. I HAD NOTHING TO HIDE ON THE RESERVATION.
BESIDES, I DIDN'T WANT ANYTHING FROM THAT RAT-BASTARD BRAND.
ED BRAND'S A GOOD MAN. GOD KNOWS WHAT WOULD HAVE HAPPENED TO ME IF IT WEREN'T FOR HIM...
IF HE'S SUCH A GREAT GUY, HOW COME YOU DIDN'T GO TO HIM INSTEAD OF DOING WHAT YOU DID?
BECAUSE ED WOULD HAVE GONE TO THE LAW.
I WANTED JUSTICE.

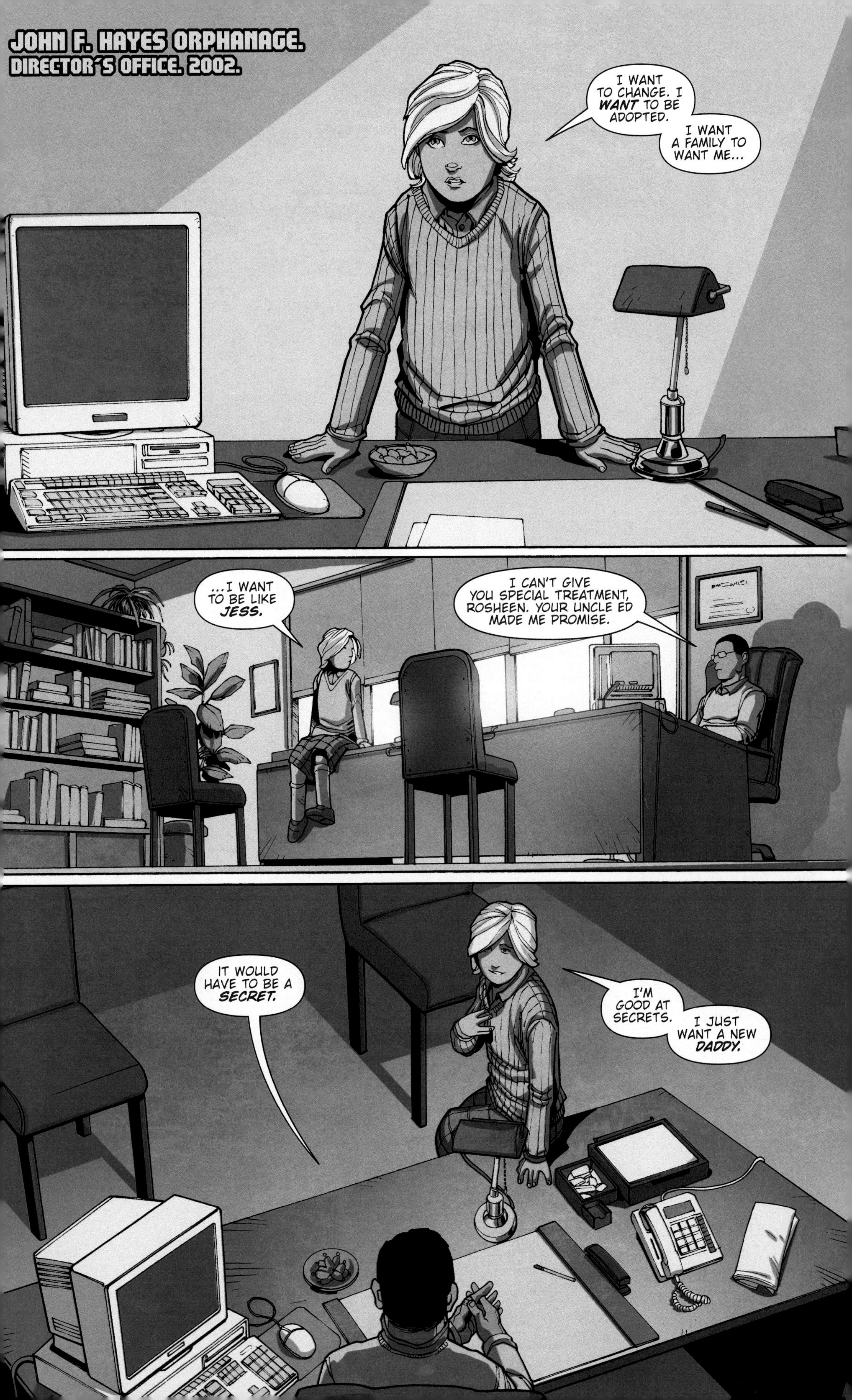
JOHN F. HAYES ORPHANAGE. DIRECTOR'S OFFICE. 2002.
I WANT TO CHANGE. I WANT TO BE ADOPTED.
I WANT A FAMILY TO WANT ME...
...I WANT TO BE LIKE JESS.
I CAN'T GIVE YOU SPECIAL TREATMENT, ROSHEEN. YOUR UNCLE ED MADE ME PROMISE.
IT WOULD HAVE TO BE A SECRET.
I'M GOOD AT SECRETS.
I JUST WANT A NEW DADDY.

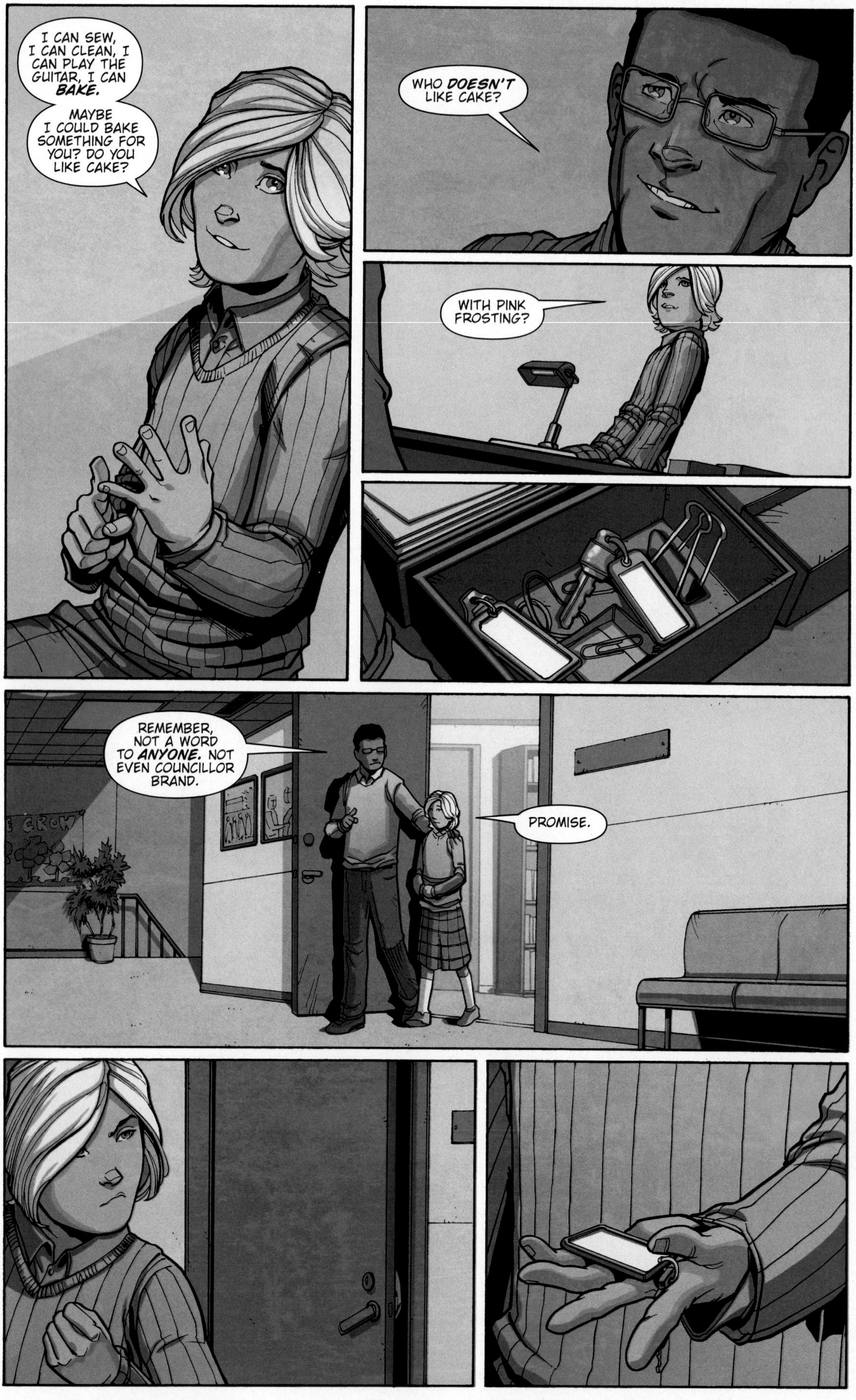

I CAN SEW, I CAN CLEAN, I CAN PLAY THE GUITAR, I CAN *BAKE.*
MAYBE I COULD BAKE SOMETHING FOR YOU? DO YOU LIKE CAKE?
WHO *DOESN'T* LIKE CAKE?
WITH PINK FROSTING?
REMEMBER, NOT A WORD TO *ANYONE.* NOT EVEN COUNCILLOR BRAND.
PROMISE.

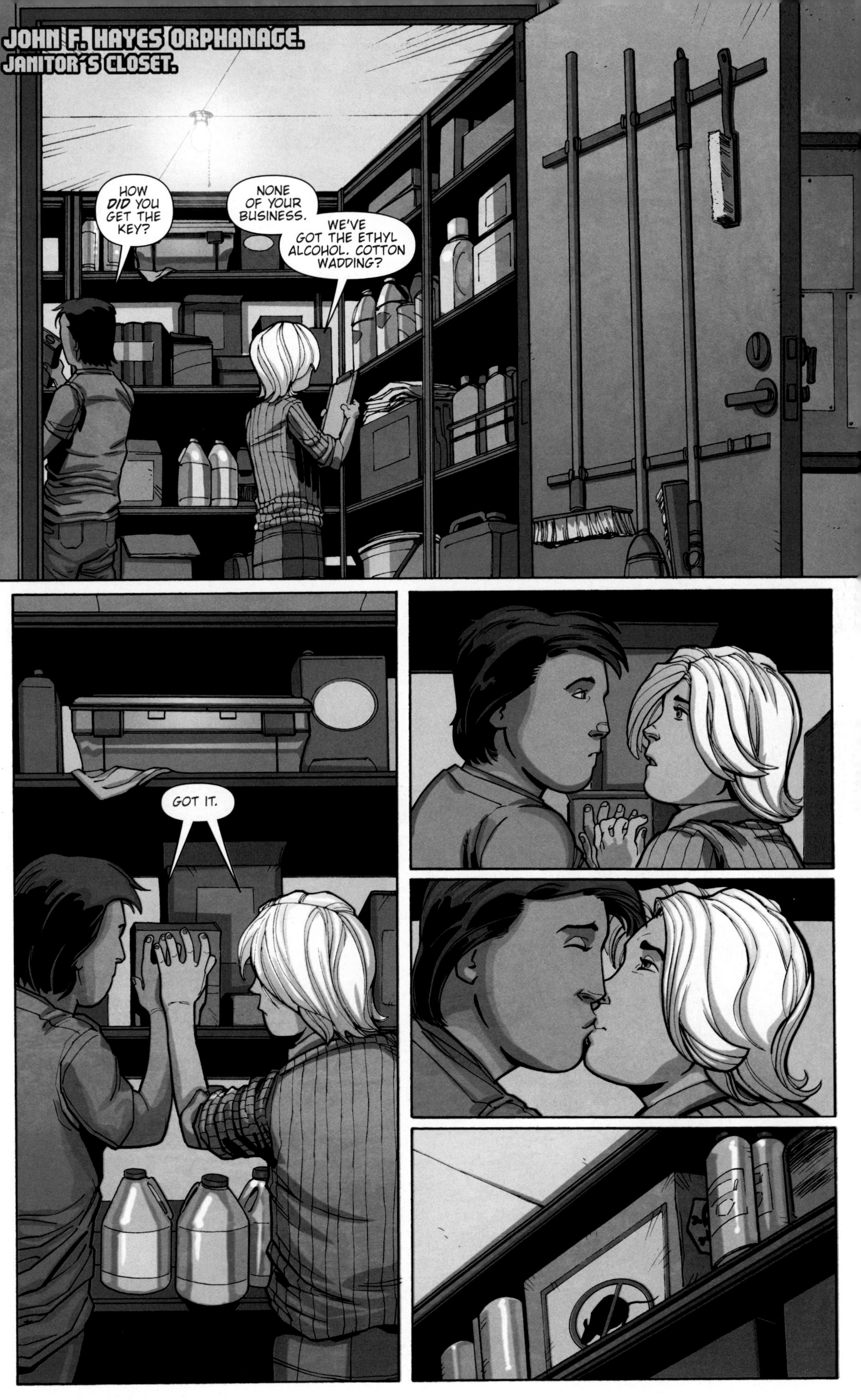
JOHN F. HAYES ORPHANAGE.
JANITOR'S CLOSET.
HOW *DID* YOU GET THE KEY?
NONE OF YOUR BUSINESS.
WE'VE GOT THE ETHYL ALCOHOL. COTTON WADDING?
GOT IT.

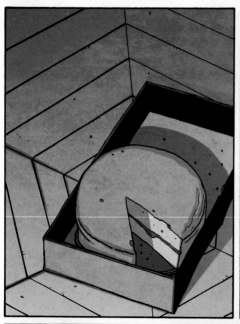

YOU DIDN'T SAY THERE'D BE CAKE.

I LIKE CAKE. ESPECIALLY WITH FROSTING THAT'S LIKE MY NAME.

NOT THIS ONE, PINK. THIS ONE'S BAD. THE RATS HAVE BEEN AT IT.

WE SHOULD GET TO WORK. WHAT DO WE NEED TO DO?

WE NEED TO SOAK THE CIRCUMFERENCE WITH THINNERS, GENERATE ENOUGH HEAT FOR THE MAIN SUPPORTS TO CATCH.

THE GASOLINE SHOULD GO UNDER THE **CRAWL SPACE** TO CREATE A CENTRAL HEAT TOWER.

I'LL DO THE CRAWL SPACE.

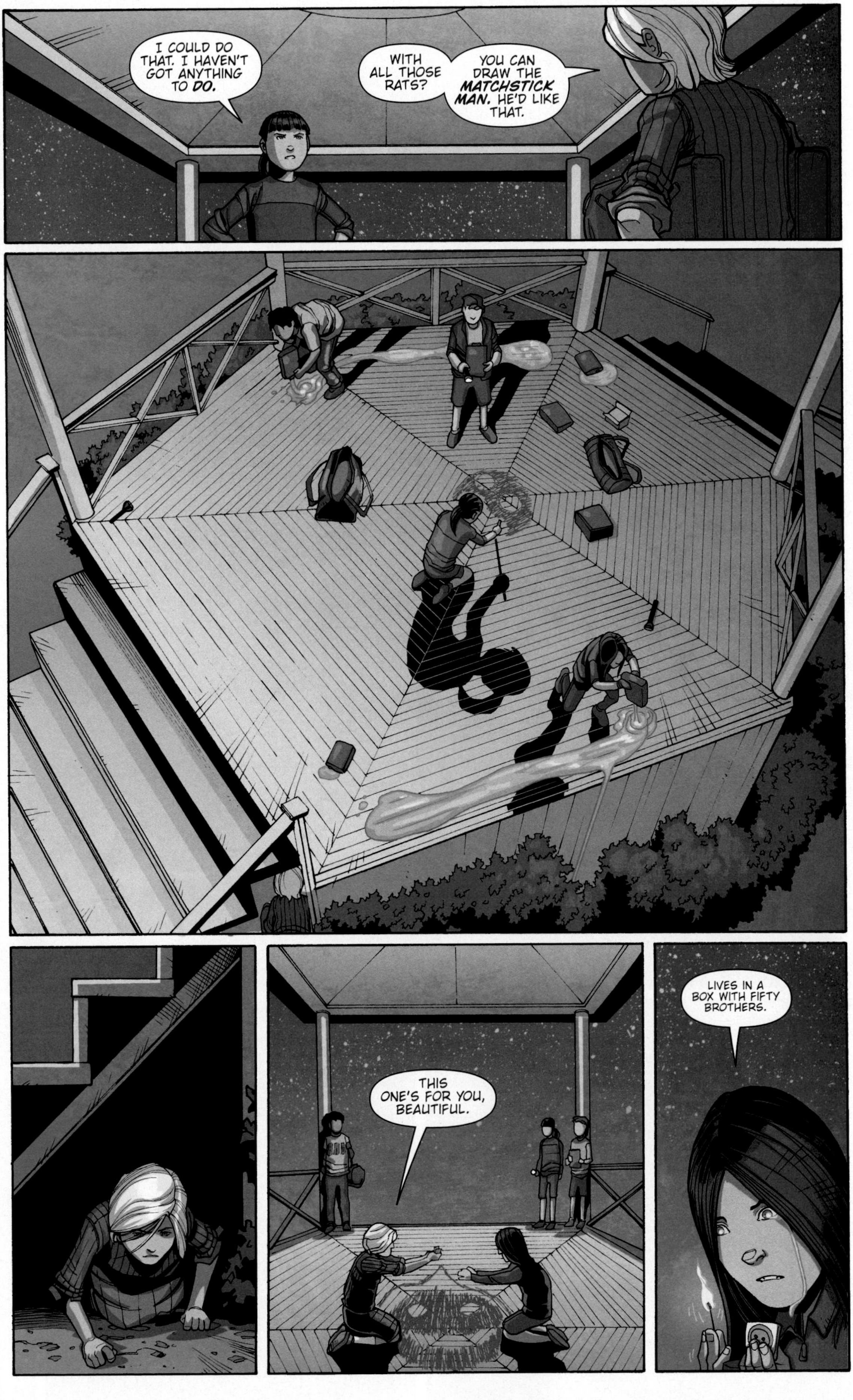
I COULD DO THAT. I HAVEN'T GOT ANYTHING TO DO.
WITH ALL THOSE RATS?
YOU CAN DRAW THE MATCHSTICK MAN. HE'D LIKE THAT.
THIS ONE'S FOR YOU, BEAUTIFUL.
LIVES IN A BOX WITH FIFTY BROTHERS.

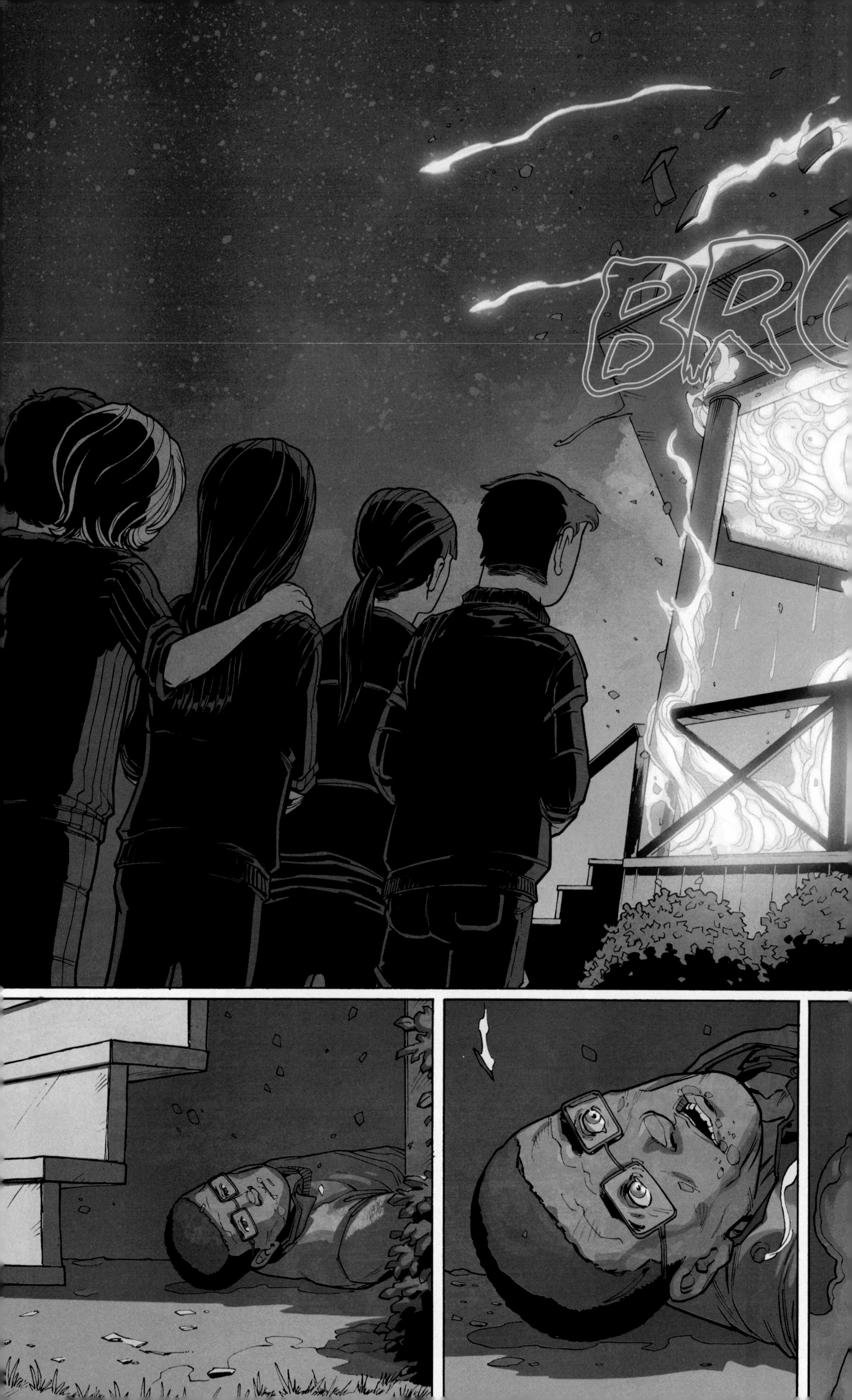
BRO

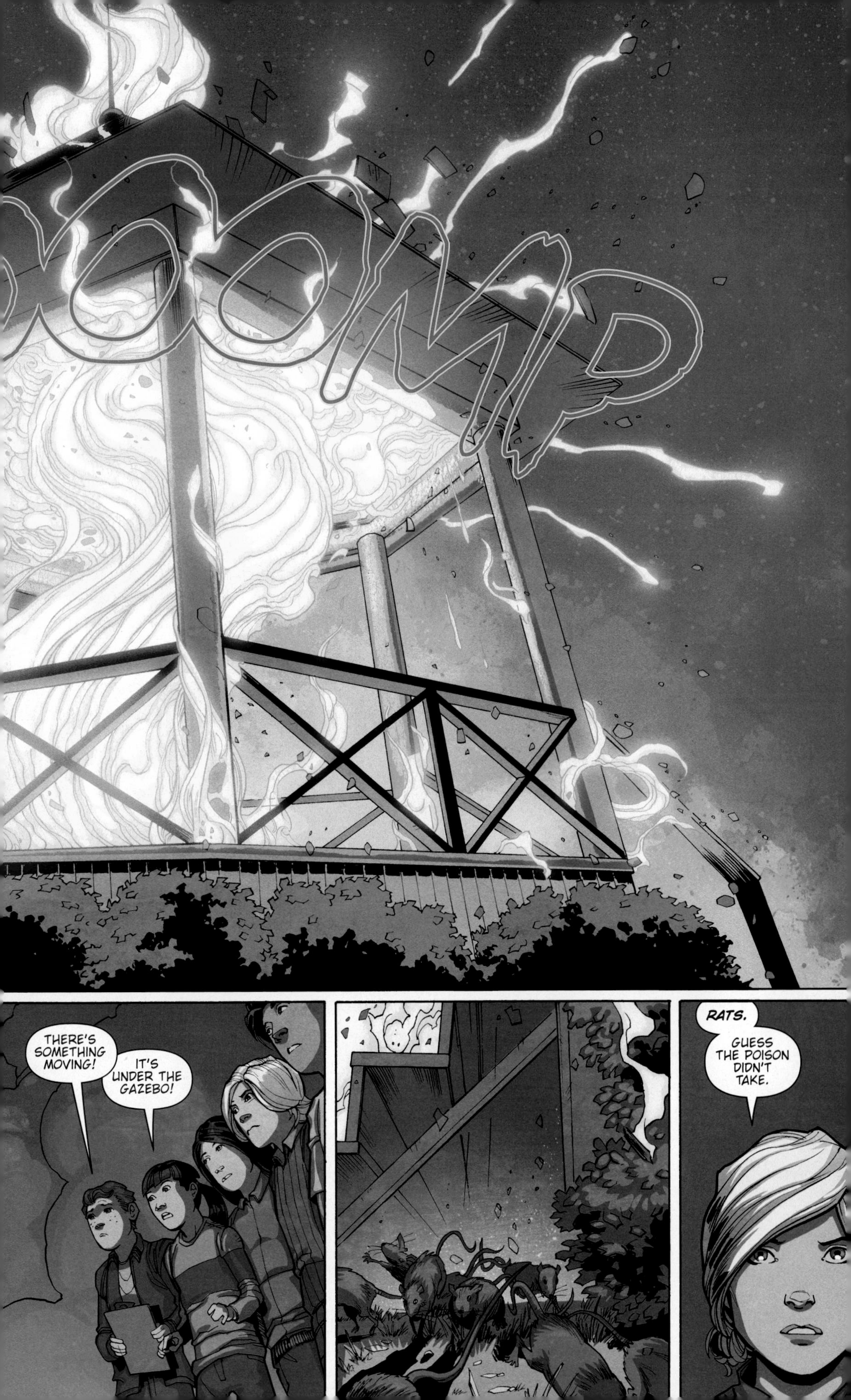
OOMP
THERE'S SOMETHING MOVING!
IT'S UNDER THE GAZEBO!
RATS.
GUESS THE POISON DIDN'T TAKE.

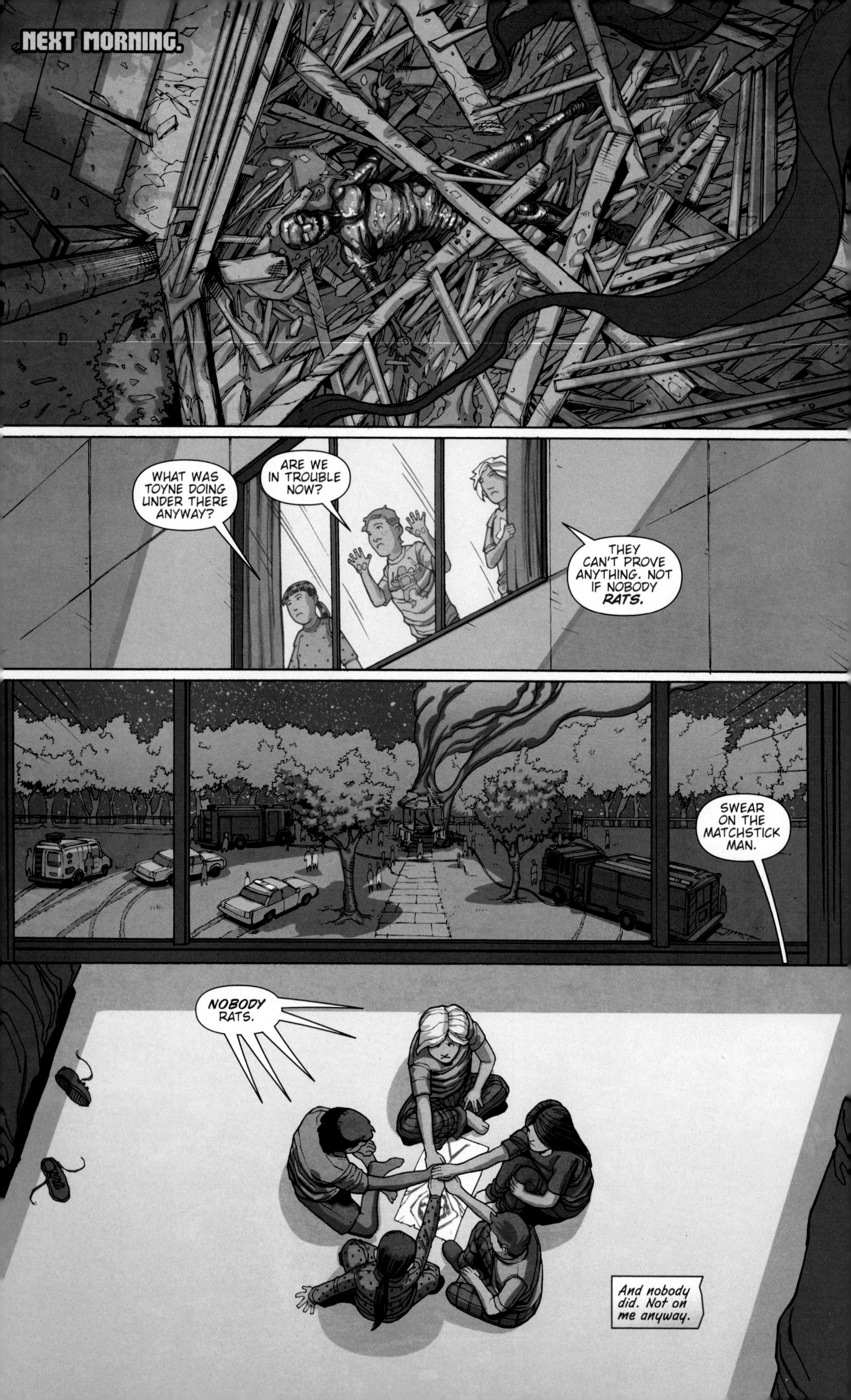
NEXT MORNING.
WHAT WAS TOYNE DOING UNDER THERE ANYWAY?
ARE WE IN TROUBLE NOW?
THEY CAN'T PROVE ANYTHING. NOT IF NOBODY RATS.
SWEAR ON THE MATCHSTICK MAN.
NOBODY RATS.
And nobody did. Not on me anyway.

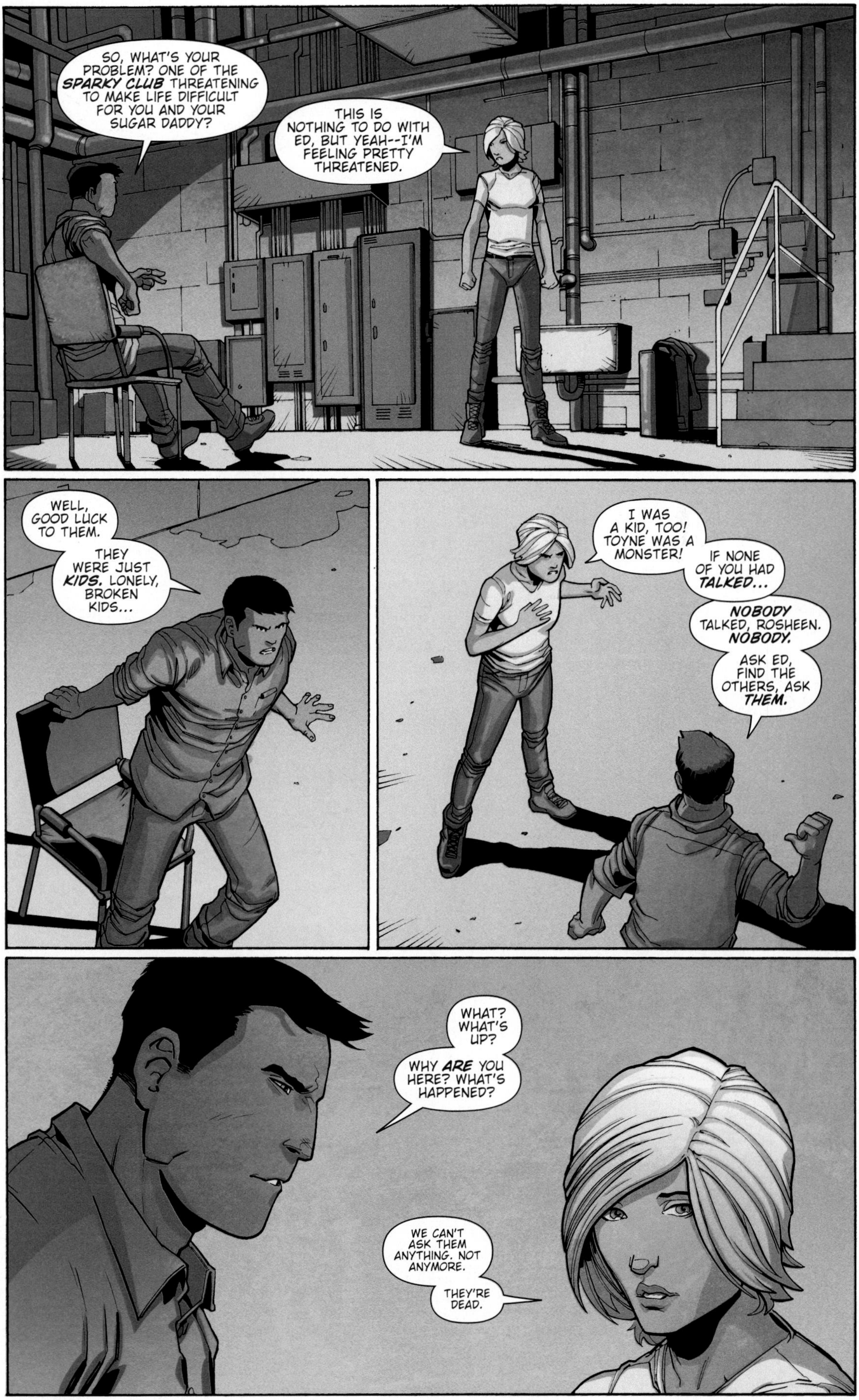
SO, WHAT'S YOUR PROBLEM? ONE OF THE SPARKY CLUB THREATENING TO MAKE LIFE DIFFICULT FOR YOU AND YOUR SUGAR DADDY?
THIS IS NOTHING TO DO WITH ED, BUT YEAH--I'M FEELING PRETTY THREATENED.
WELL, GOOD LUCK TO THEM.
THEY WERE JUST KIDS. LONELY, BROKEN KIDS...
I WAS A KID, TOO! TOYNE WAS A MONSTER!
IF NONE OF YOU HAD TALKED...
NOBODY TALKED, ROSHEEN. NOBODY.
ASK ED, FIND THE OTHERS, ASK THEM.
WHAT? WHAT'S UP?
WHY ARE YOU HERE? WHAT'S HAPPENED?
WE CAN'T ASK THEM ANYTHING. NOT ANYMORE.
THEY'RE DEAD.

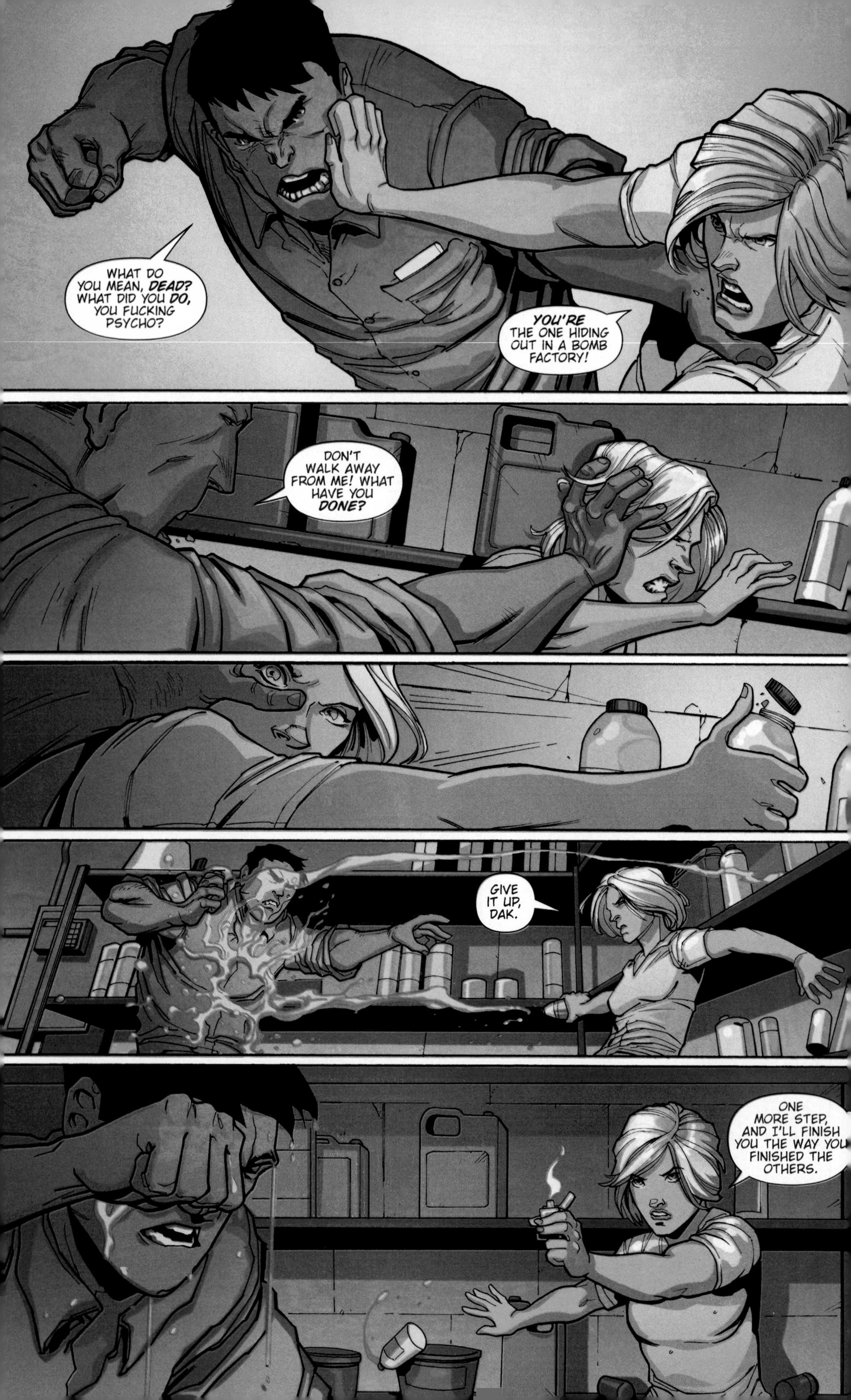

WHAT DO YOU MEAN, **DEAD?** WHAT DID YOU **DO,** YOU FUCKING PSYCHO?
YOU'RE THE ONE HIDING OUT IN A BOMB FACTORY!
DON'T WALK AWAY FROM ME! WHAT HAVE YOU **DONE?**
GIVE IT UP, DAK.
ONE MORE STEP, AND I'LL FINISH YOU THE WAY YOU FINISHED THE OTHERS.

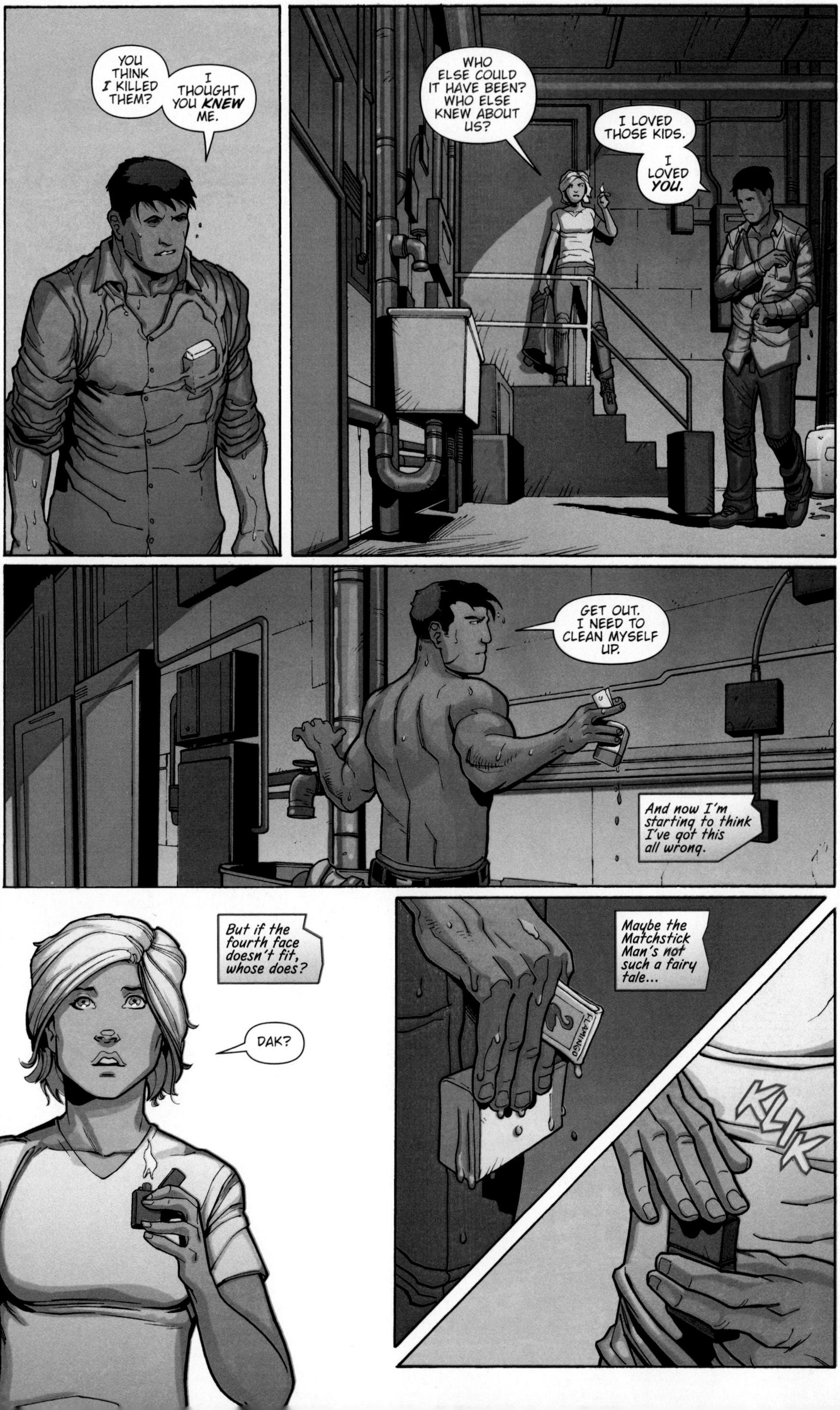

YOU THINK I KILLED THEM?
I THOUGHT YOU KNEW ME.
WHO ELSE COULD IT HAVE BEEN? WHO ELSE KNEW ABOUT US?
I LOVED THOSE KIDS.
I LOVED YOU.
GET OUT. I NEED TO CLEAN MYSELF UP.
And now I'm starting to think I've got this all wrong.
But if the fourth face doesn't fit, whose does?
DAK?
Maybe the Matchstick Man's not such a fairy tale...
FLAMINGO
KLIK

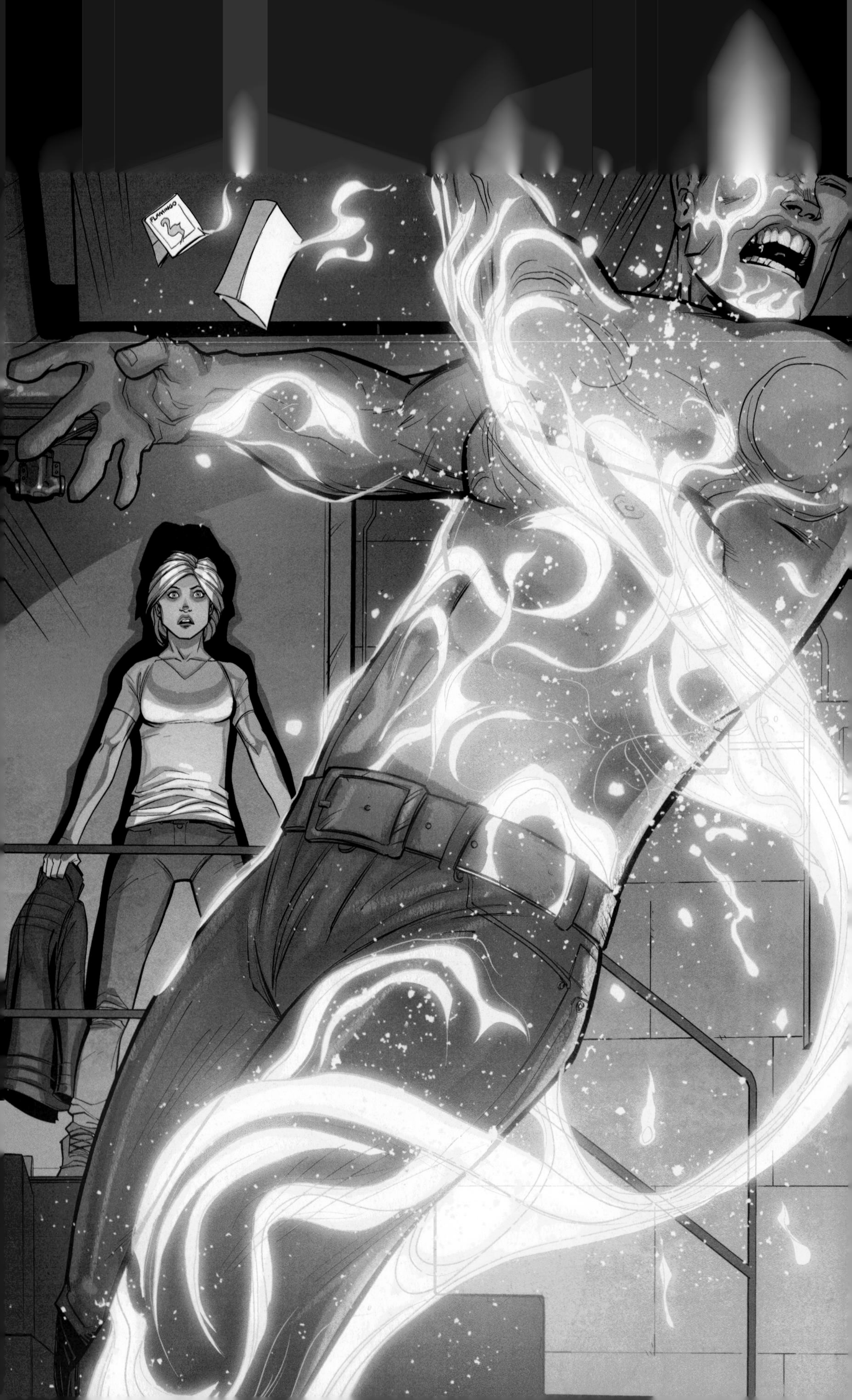
FLAMINGO

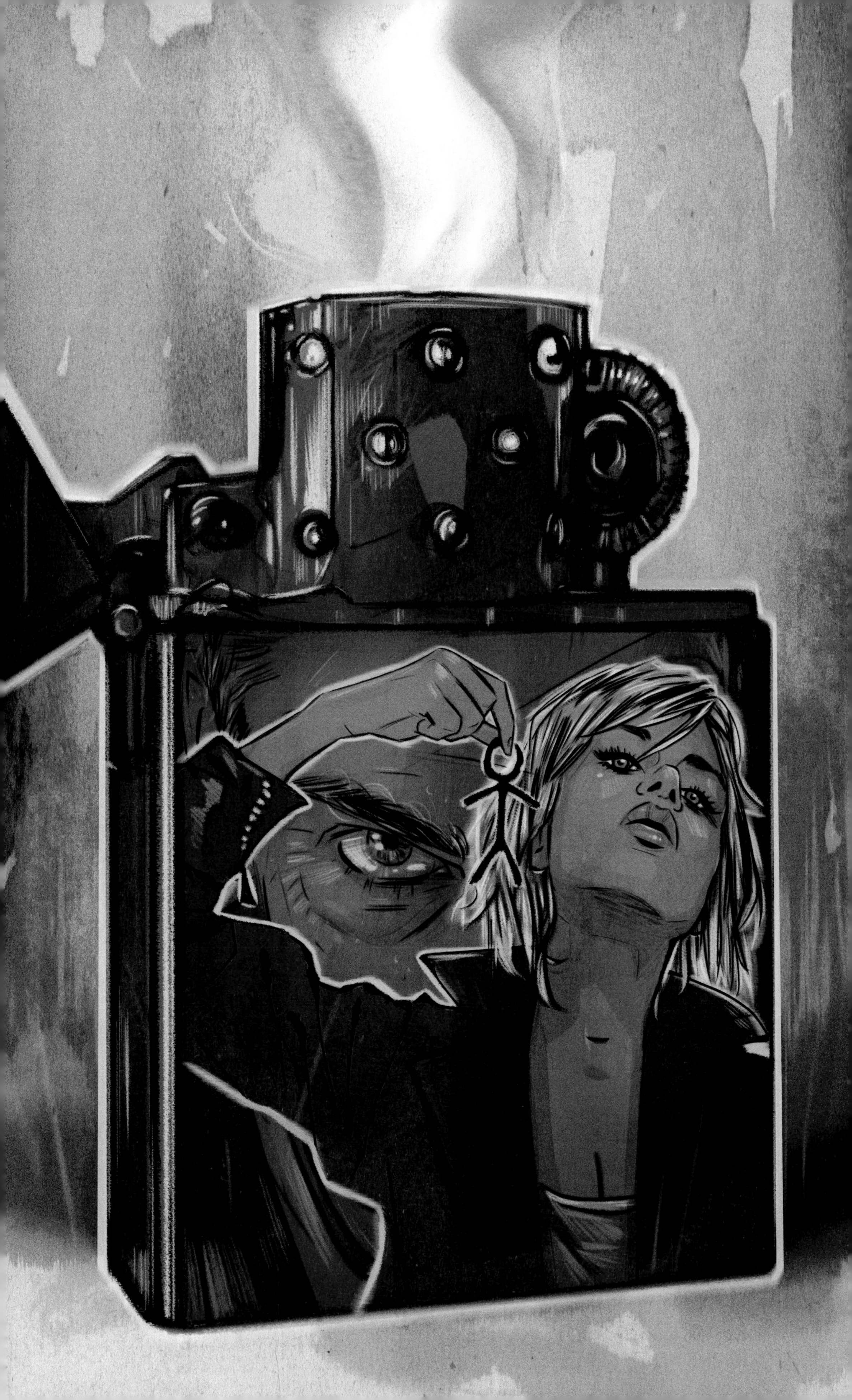

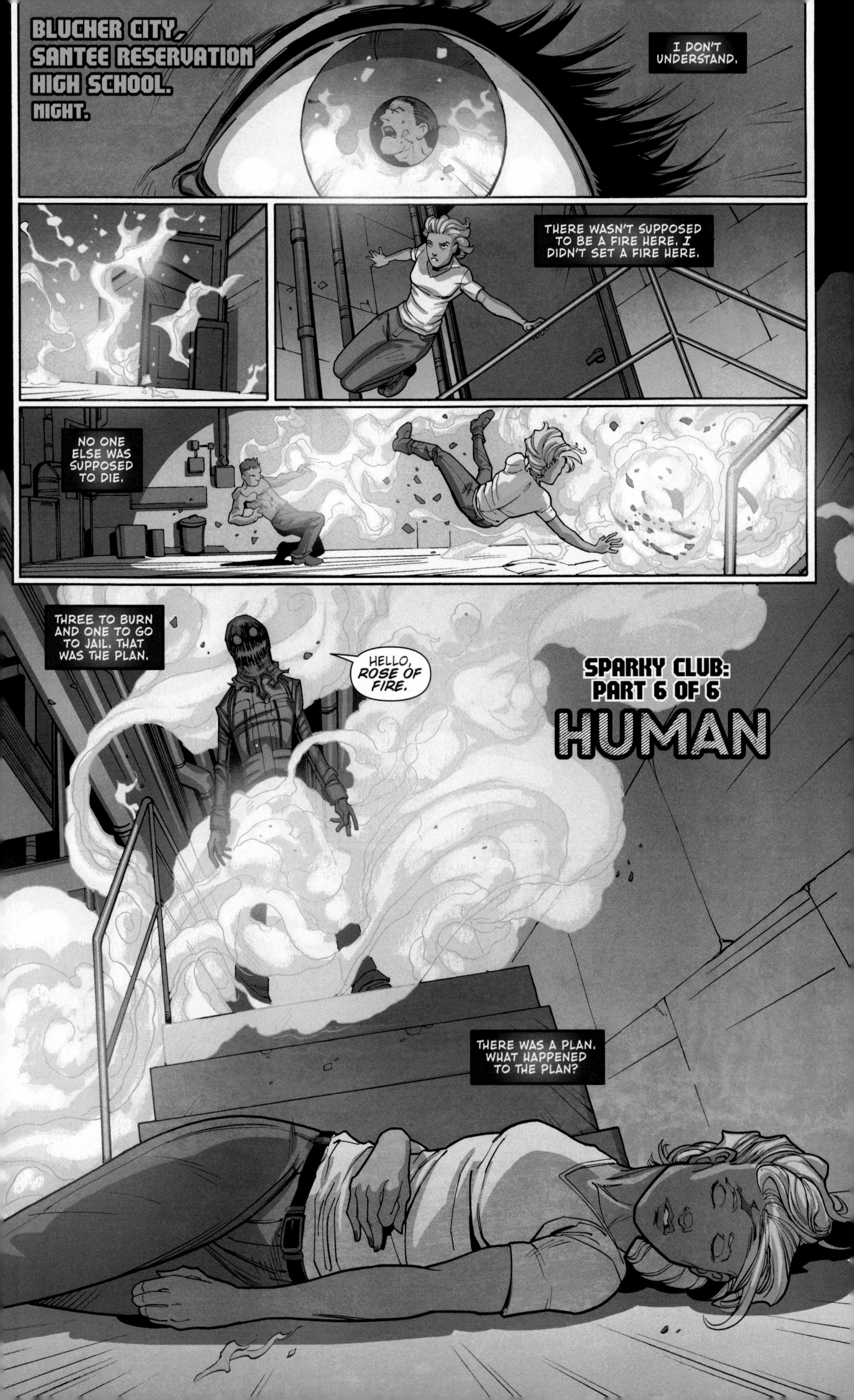
BLUCHER CITY, SANTEE RESERVATION HIGH SCHOOL. NIGHT.
I DON'T UNDERSTAND.
THERE WASN'T SUPPOSED TO BE A FIRE HERE. I DIDN'T SET A FIRE HERE.
NO ONE ELSE WAS SUPPOSED TO DIE.
THREE TO BURN AND ONE TO GO TO JAIL. THAT WAS THE PLAN.
HELLO, ROSE OF FIRE.
SPARKY CLUB: PART 6 OF 6
HUMAN
THERE WAS A PLAN. WHAT HAPPENED TO THE PLAN?

HOW'S *DAK* GOING TO TAKE THE BLAME NOW? AND HOW DID HE *BURN* IN THE FIRST PLACE?

MATCHSTICK MAN WOULD WANT ME TO SAVE ROSHEEN. HE *ALWAYS* WANTS TO SAVE ROSHEEN.

HAVE TO TOUCH HER BUT I DON'T LIKE TO TOUCH. DON'T LIKE TO BE TOUCHED.

I'M GOING TO HAVE TO GIVE YOU *CPR* NOW.

I WON'T LIKE IT.

BUT I ALWAYS WISHED I COULD TOUCH HER IF I DIDN'T *NOT* LIKE TO TOUCH.

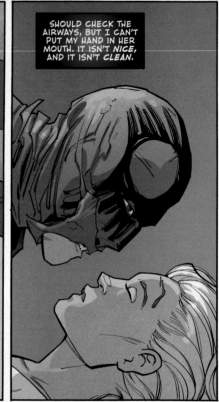

SHOULD CHECK THE AIRWAYS, BUT I CAN'T PUT MY HAND IN HER MOUTH. IT ISN'T *NICE*, AND IT ISN'T *CLEAN*.

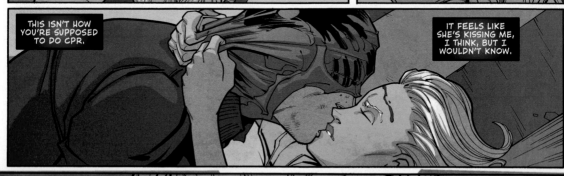

THIS ISN'T HOW YOU'RE SUPPOSED TO DO CPR.

IT FEELS LIKE SHE'S KISSING ME, I THINK, BUT I WOULDN'T KNOW,

I DON'T THINK SHE WAS KISSING ME.

HELLO, *PINKER.*

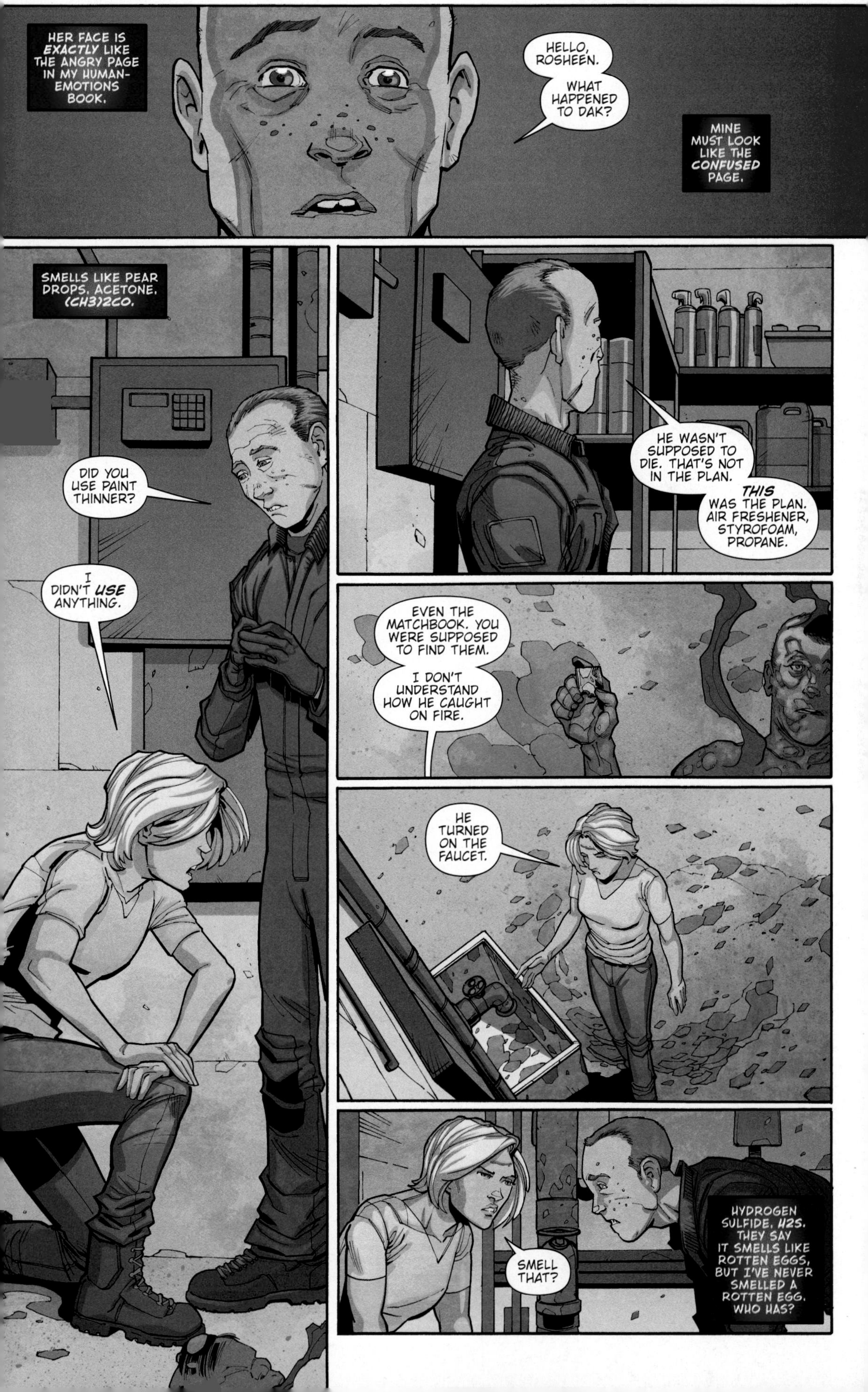

HER FACE IS EXACTLY LIKE THE ANGRY PAGE IN MY HUMAN-EMOTIONS BOOK.
HELLO, ROSHEEN.
WHAT HAPPENED TO DAK?
MINE MUST LOOK LIKE THE CONFUSED PAGE.
SMELLS LIKE PEAR DROPS. ACETONE. (CH3)2CO.
DID YOU USE PAINT THINNER?
I DIDN'T USE ANYTHING.
HE WASN'T SUPPOSED TO DIE. THAT'S NOT IN THE PLAN.
THIS WAS THE PLAN. AIR FRESHENER, STYROFOAM, PROPANE.
EVEN THE MATCHBOOK. YOU WERE SUPPOSED TO FIND THEM.
I DON'T UNDERSTAND HOW HE CAUGHT ON FIRE.
HE TURNED ON THE FAUCET.
SMELL THAT?
HYDROGEN SULFIDE. H2S. THEY SAY IT SMELLS LIKE ROTTEN EGGS, BUT I'VE NEVER SMELLED A ROTTEN EGG. WHO HAS?

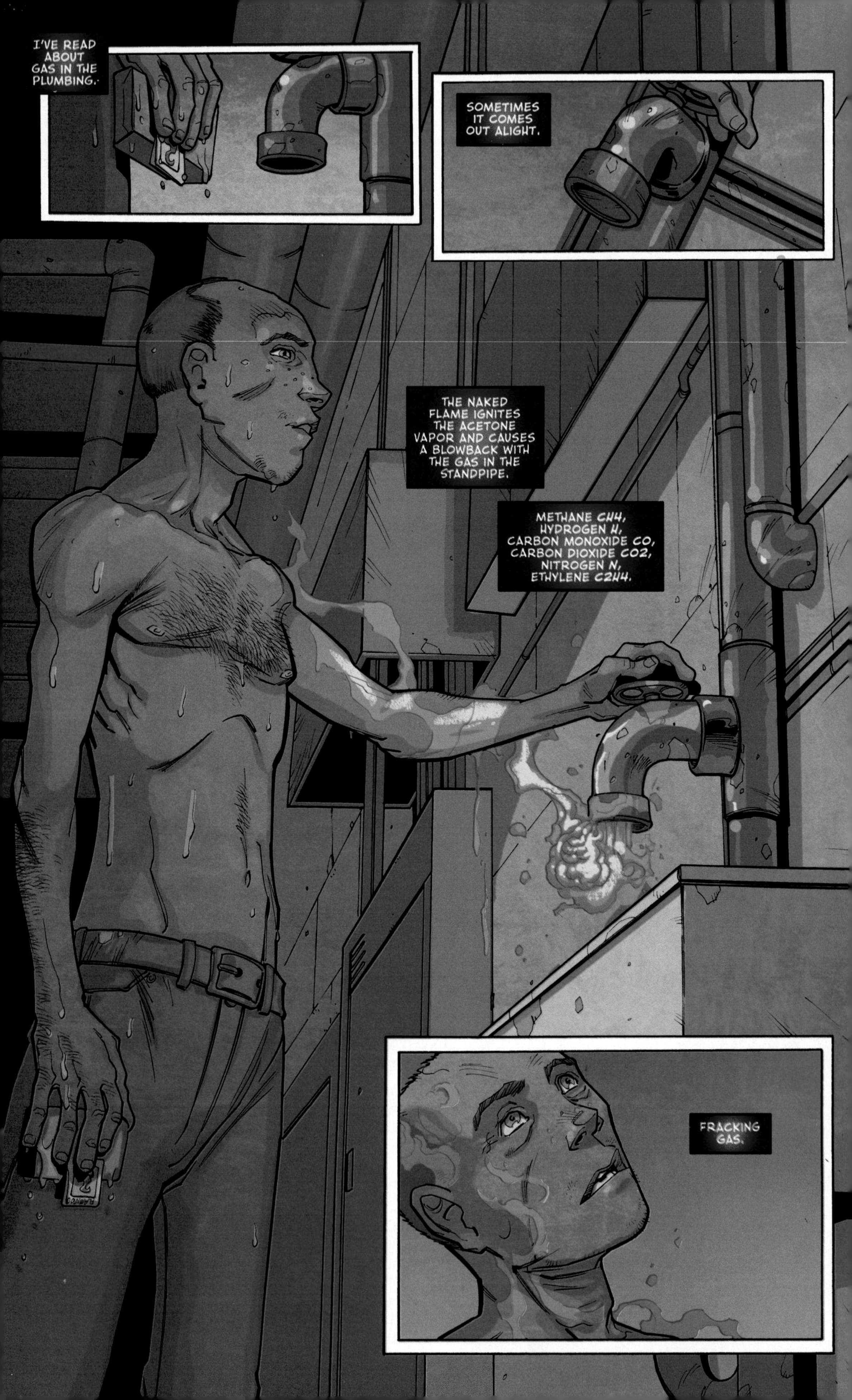
I'VE READ ABOUT GAS IN THE PLUMBING.
SOMETIMES IT COMES OUT ALIGHT.
THE NAKED FLAME IGNITES THE ACETONE VAPOR AND CAUSES A BLOWBACK WITH THE GAS IN THE STANDPIPE.
METHANE CH4, HYDROGEN H, CARBON MONOXIDE CO, CARBON DIOXIDE CO2, NITROGEN N, ETHYLENE C2H4.
FRACKING GAS.

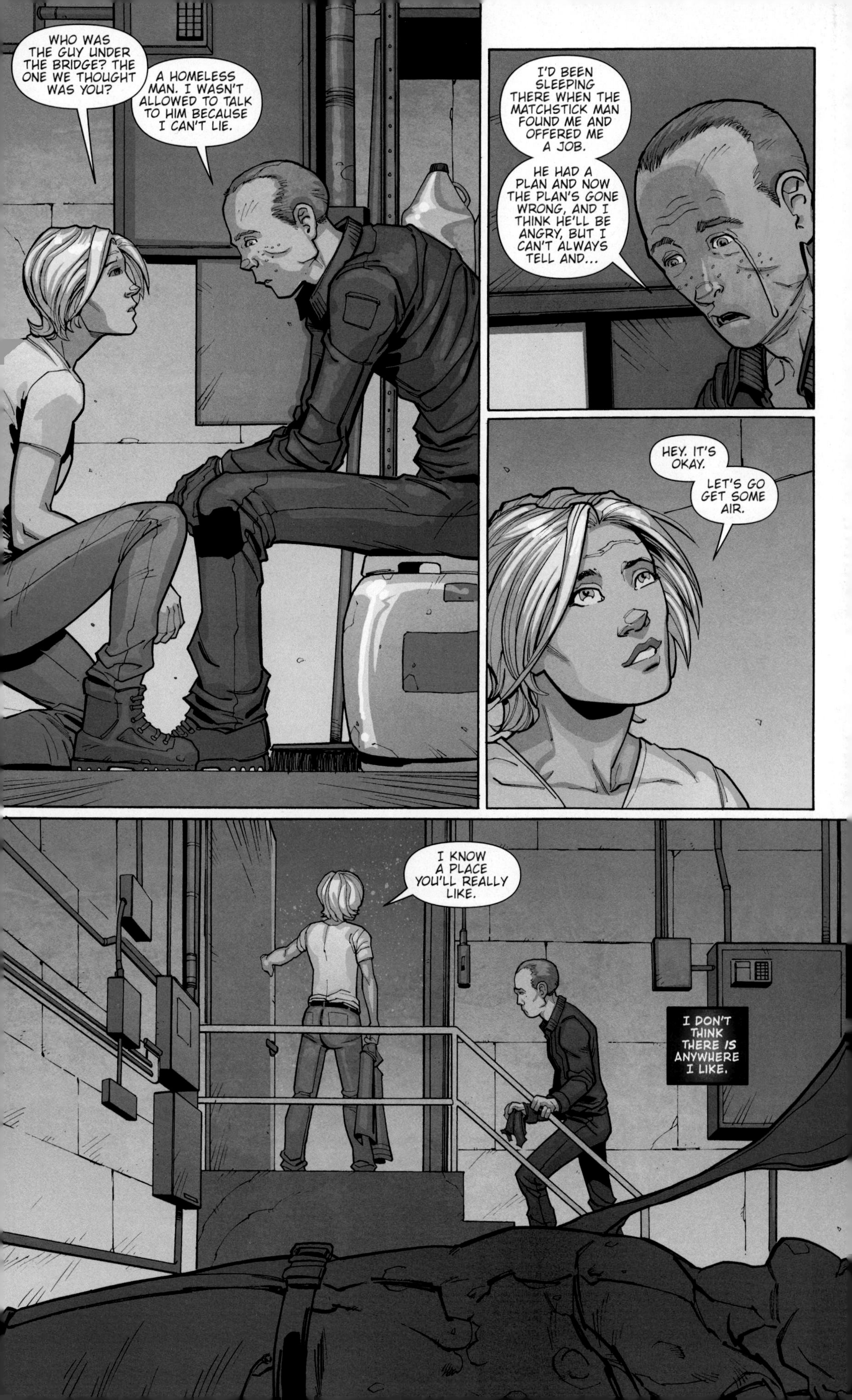
WHO WAS THE GUY UNDER THE BRIDGE? THE ONE WE THOUGHT WAS YOU?
A HOMELESS MAN. I WASN'T ALLOWED TO TALK TO HIM BECAUSE I CAN'T LIE.
I'D BEEN SLEEPING THERE WHEN THE MATCHSTICK MAN FOUND ME AND OFFERED ME A JOB.
HE HAD A PLAN AND NOW THE PLAN'S GONE WRONG, AND I THINK HE'LL BE ANGRY, BUT I CAN'T ALWAYS TELL AND...
HEY. IT'S OKAY.
LET'S GO GET SOME AIR.
I KNOW A PLACE YOU'LL REALLY LIKE.
I DON'T THINK THERE IS ANYWHERE I LIKE.

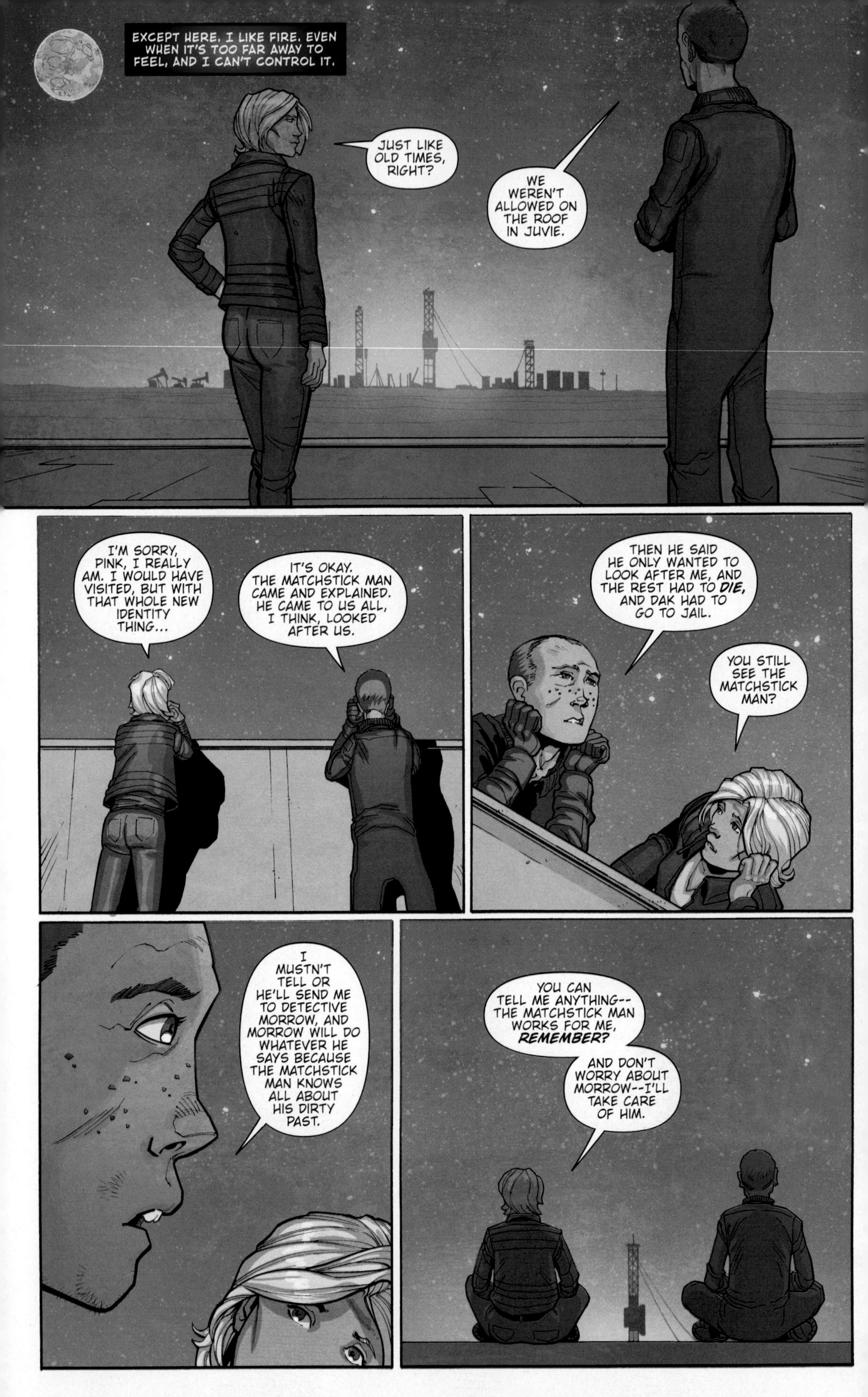
EXCEPT HERE. I LIKE FIRE. EVEN WHEN IT'S TOO FAR AWAY TO FEEL, AND I CAN'T CONTROL IT.
JUST LIKE OLD TIMES, RIGHT?
WE WEREN'T ALLOWED ON THE ROOF IN JUVIE.
I'M SORRY, PINK, I REALLY AM. I WOULD HAVE VISITED, BUT WITH THAT WHOLE NEW IDENTITY THING...
IT'S OKAY. THE MATCHSTICK MAN CAME AND EXPLAINED. HE CAME TO US ALL, I THINK, LOOKED AFTER US.
THEN HE SAID HE ONLY WANTED TO LOOK AFTER ME, AND THE REST HAD TO ***DIE,*** AND DAK HAD TO GO TO JAIL.
YOU STILL SEE THE MATCHSTICK MAN?
I MUSTN'T TELL OR HE'LL SEND ME TO DETECTIVE MORROW, AND MORROW WILL DO WHATEVER HE SAYS BECAUSE THE MATCHSTICK MAN KNOWS ALL ABOUT HIS DIRTY PAST.
YOU CAN TELL ME ANYTHING-- THE MATCHSTICK MAN WORKS FOR ME, ***REMEMBER?***
AND DON'T WORRY ABOUT MORROW--I'LL TAKE CARE OF HIM.

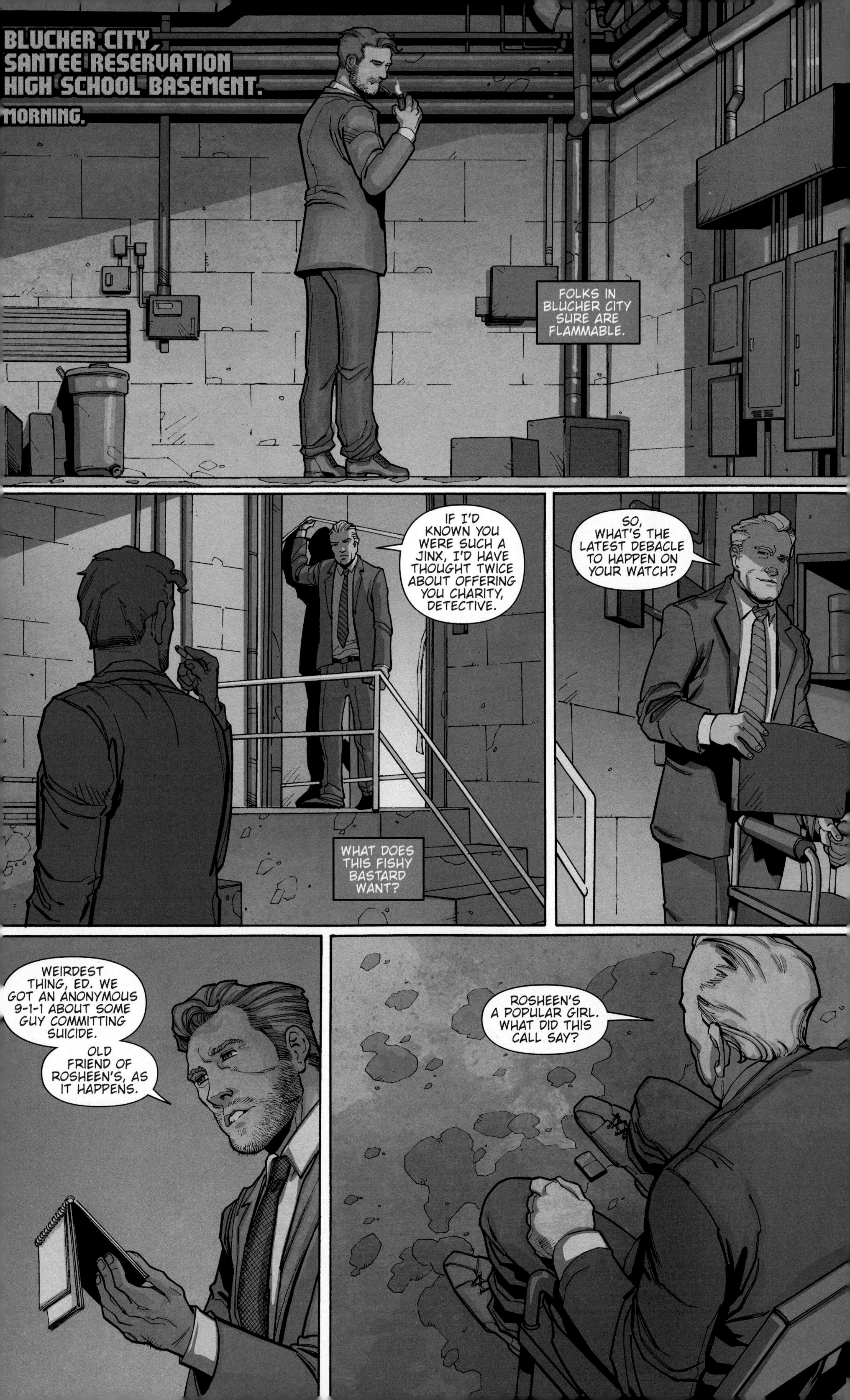
BLUCHER CITY, SANTEE RESERVATION HIGH SCHOOL BASEMENT.
MORNING.
FOLKS IN BLUCHER CITY SURE ARE FLAMMABLE.
IF I'D KNOWN YOU WERE SUCH A JINX, I'D HAVE THOUGHT TWICE ABOUT OFFERING YOU CHARITY, DETECTIVE.
WHAT DOES THIS FISHY BASTARD WANT?
SO, WHAT'S THE LATEST DEBACLE TO HAPPEN ON YOUR WATCH?
WEIRDEST THING, ED. WE GOT AN ANONYMOUS 9-1-1 ABOUT SOME GUY COMMITTING SUICIDE.
OLD FRIEND OF ROSHEEN'S, AS IT HAPPENS.
ROSHEEN'S A POPULAR GIRL. WHAT DID THIS CALL SAY?

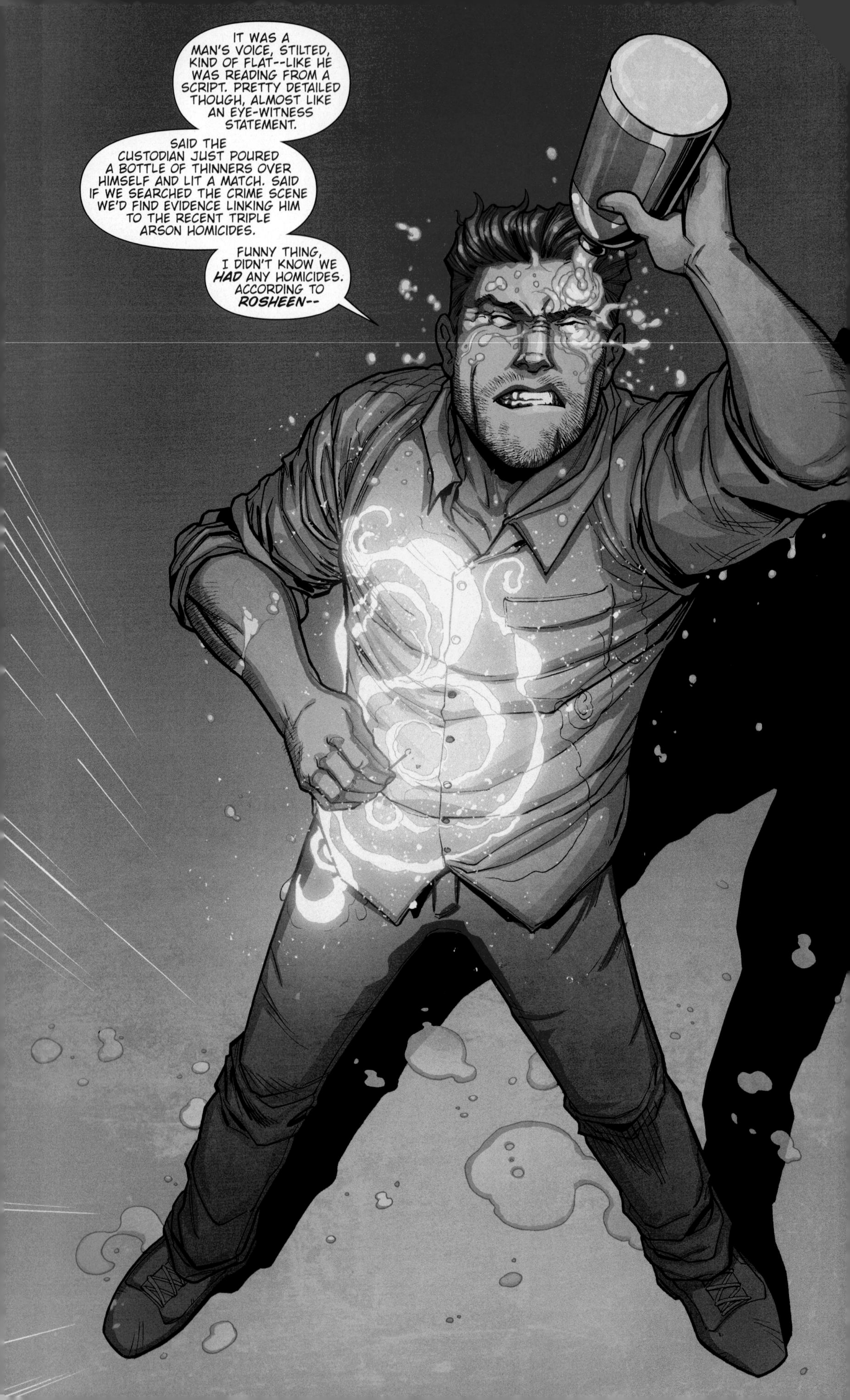
IT WAS A MAN'S VOICE, STILTED, KIND OF FLAT--LIKE HE WAS READING FROM A SCRIPT. PRETTY DETAILED THOUGH, ALMOST LIKE AN EYE-WITNESS STATEMENT.
SAID THE CUSTODIAN JUST POURED A BOTTLE OF THINNERS OVER HIMSELF AND LIT A MATCH. SAID IF WE SEARCHED THE CRIME SCENE WE'D FIND EVIDENCE LINKING HIM TO THE RECENT TRIPLE ARSON HOMICIDES.
FUNNY THING, I DIDN'T KNOW WE *HAD* ANY HOMICIDES. ACCORDING TO *ROSHEEN--*

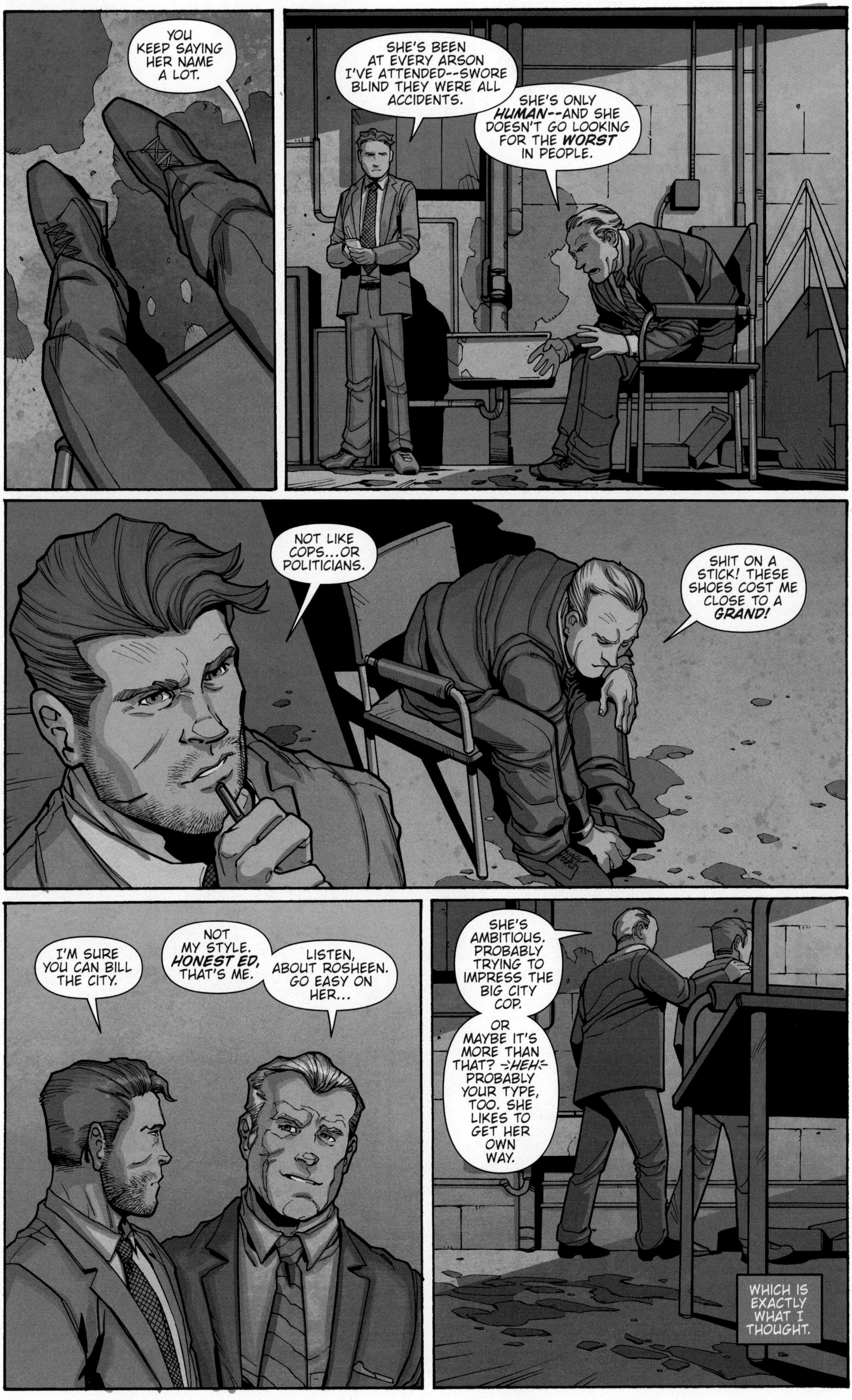

YOU KEEP SAYING HER NAME A LOT.
SHE'S BEEN AT EVERY ARSON I'VE ATTENDED--SWORE BLIND THEY WERE ALL ACCIDENTS.
SHE'S ONLY HUMAN--AND SHE DOESN'T GO LOOKING FOR THE WORST IN PEOPLE.
NOT LIKE COPS...OR POLITICIANS.
SHIT ON A STICK! THESE SHOES COST ME CLOSE TO A GRAND!
I'M SURE YOU CAN BILL THE CITY.
NOT MY STYLE. HONEST ED, THAT'S ME.
LISTEN, ABOUT ROSHEEN. GO EASY ON HER...
SHE'S AMBITIOUS. PROBABLY TRYING TO IMPRESS THE BIG CITY COP.
OR MAYBE IT'S MORE THAN THAT? -HEH- PROBABLY YOUR TYPE, TOO. SHE LIKES TO GET HER OWN WAY.
WHICH IS EXACTLY WHAT I THOUGHT.

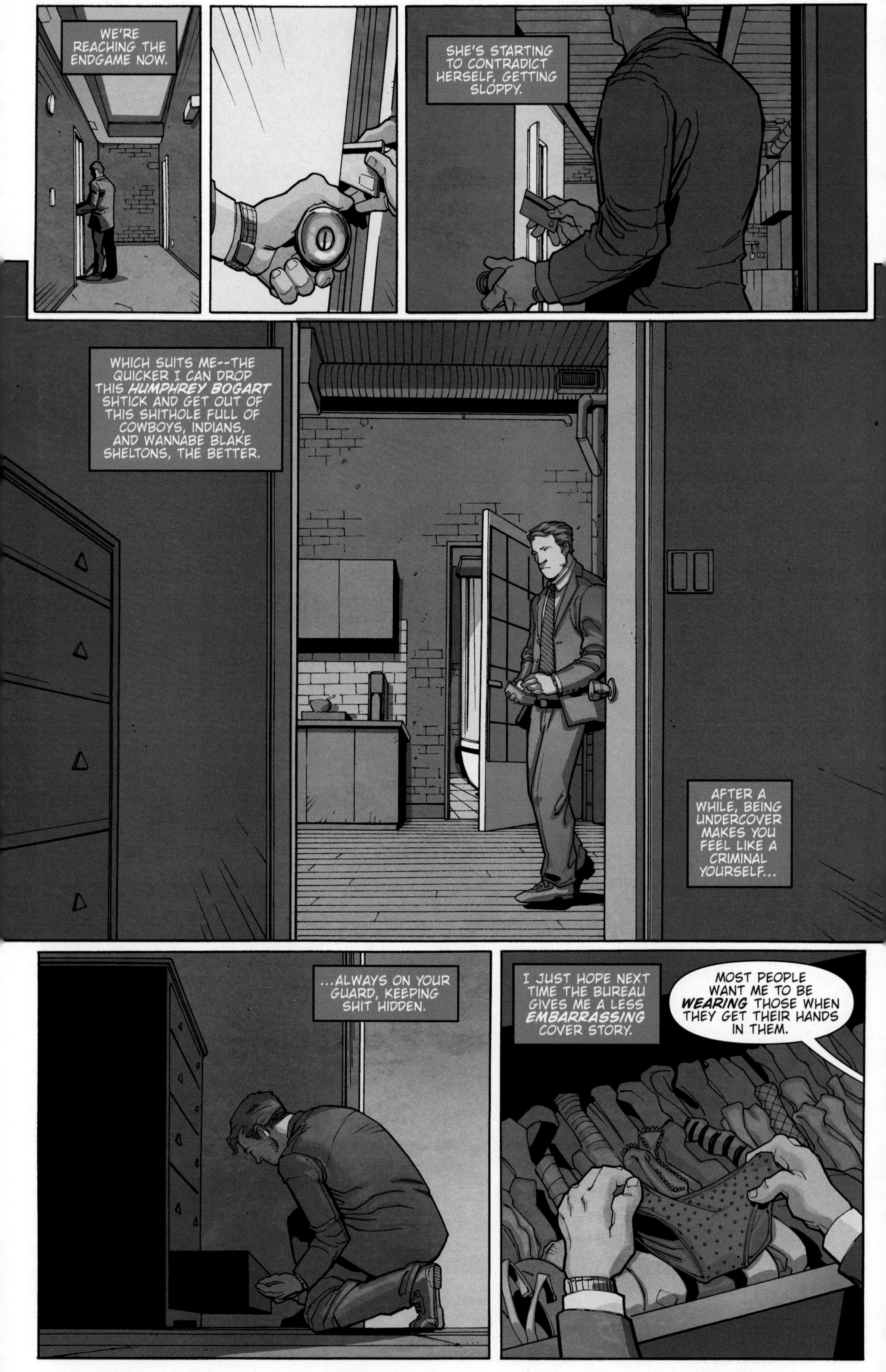
WE'RE REACHING THE ENDGAME NOW.
SHE'S STARTING TO CONTRADICT HERSELF, GETTING SLOPPY.
WHICH SUITS ME--THE QUICKER I CAN DROP THIS HUMPHREY BOGART SHTICK AND GET OUT OF THIS SHITHOLE FULL OF COWBOYS, INDIANS, AND WANNABE BLAKE SHELTONS, THE BETTER.
AFTER A WHILE, BEING UNDERCOVER MAKES YOU FEEL LIKE A CRIMINAL YOURSELF...
...ALWAYS ON YOUR GUARD, KEEPING SHIT HIDDEN.
I JUST HOPE NEXT TIME THE BUREAU GIVES ME A LESS EMBARRASSING COVER STORY.
MOST PEOPLE WANT ME TO BE WEARING THOSE WHEN THEY GET THEIR HANDS IN THEM.

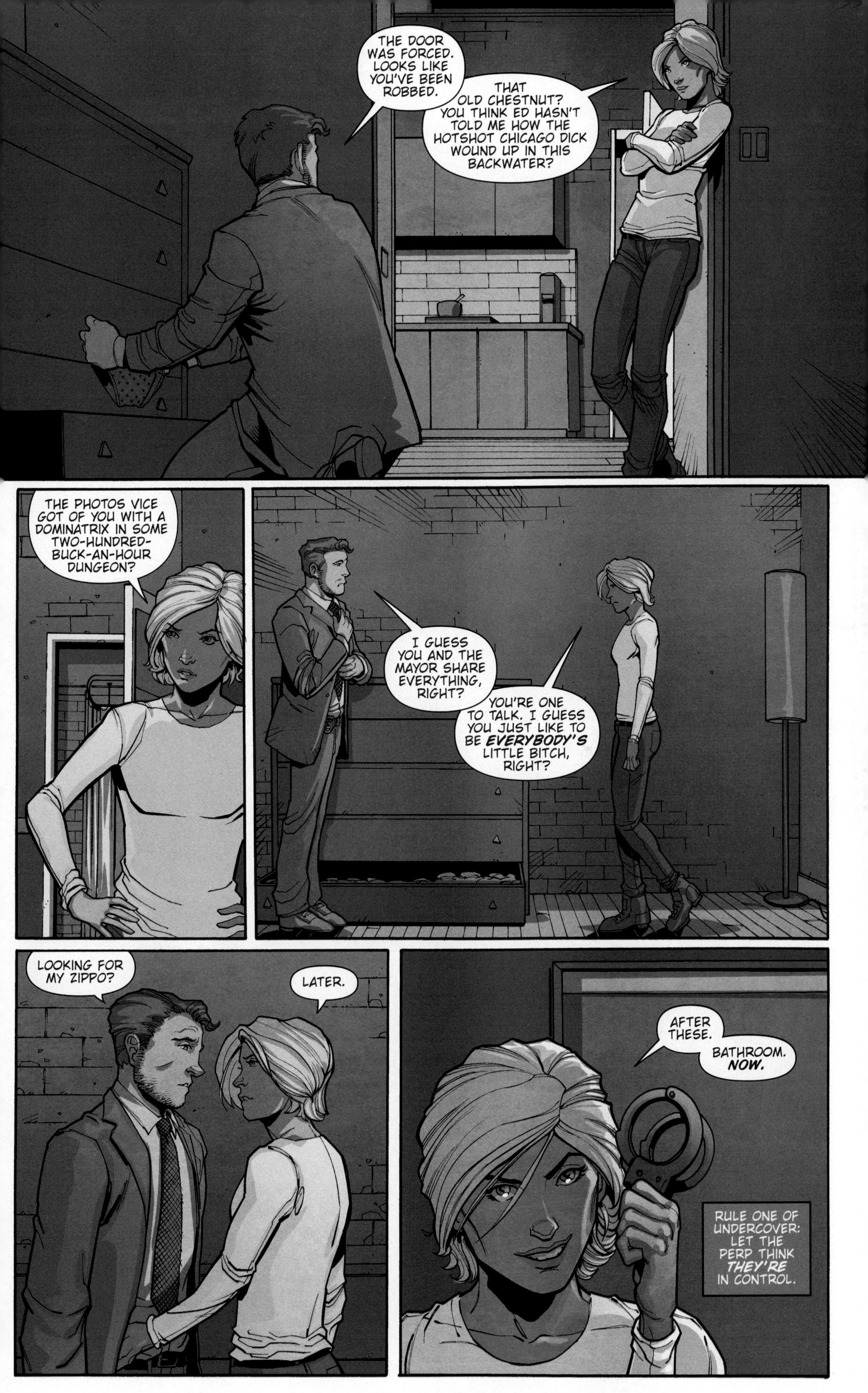
THE DOOR WAS FORCED. LOOKS LIKE YOU'VE BEEN ROBBED.
THAT OLD CHESTNUT? YOU THINK ED HASN'T TOLD ME HOW THE HOTSHOT CHICAGO DICK WOUND UP IN THIS BACKWATER?
THE PHOTOS VICE GOT OF YOU WITH A DOMINATRIX IN SOME TWO-HUNDRED-BUCK-AN-HOUR DUNGEON?
I GUESS YOU AND THE MAYOR SHARE EVERYTHING, RIGHT?
YOU'RE ONE TO TALK. I GUESS YOU JUST LIKE TO BE EVERYBODY'S LITTLE BITCH, RIGHT?
LOOKING FOR MY ZIPPO?
LATER.
AFTER THESE.
BATHROOM. NOW.
RULE ONE OF UNDERCOVER: LET THE PERP THINK THEY'RE IN CONTROL.

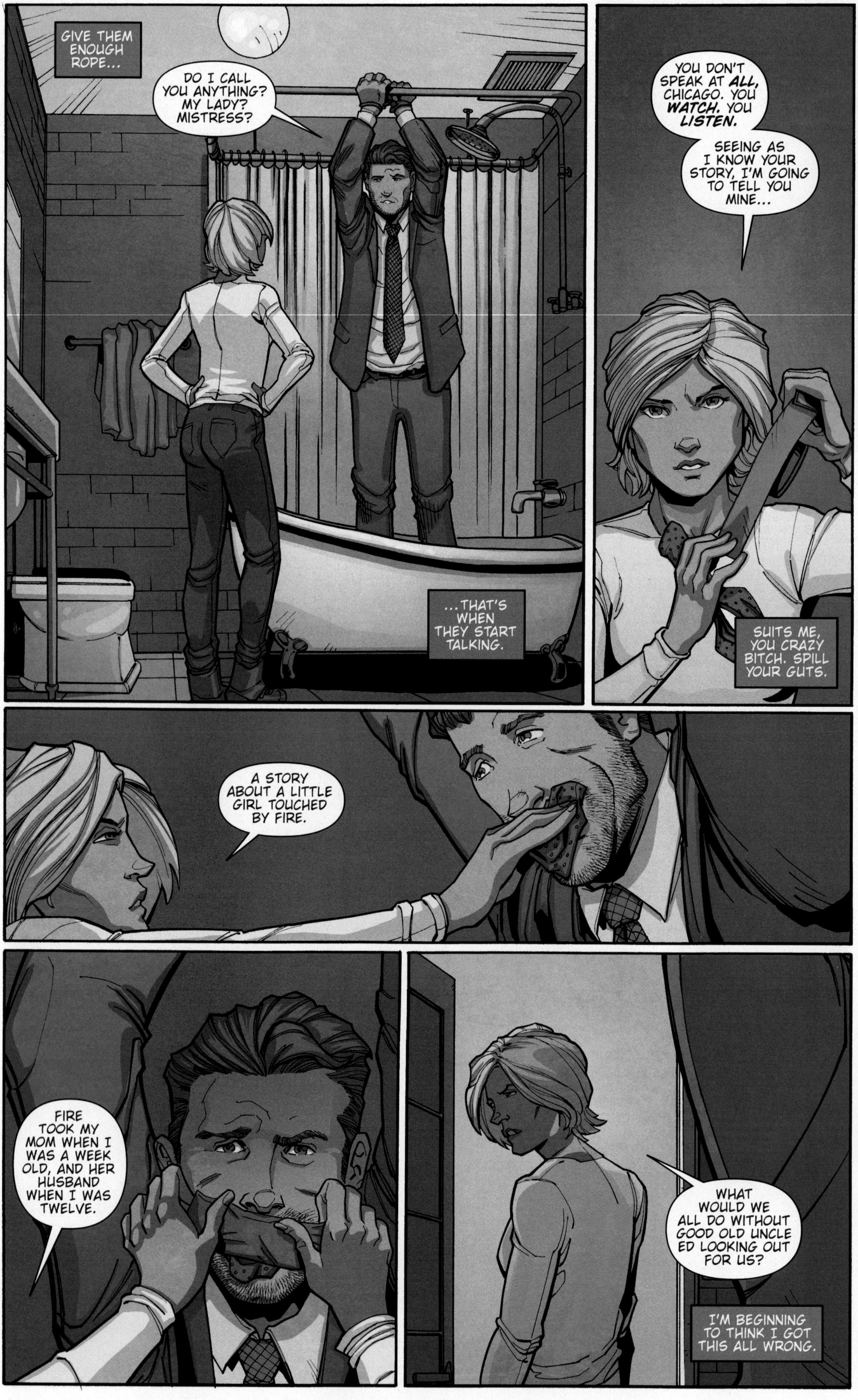
GIVE THEM ENOUGH ROPE...
DO I CALL YOU ANYTHING? MY LADY? MISTRESS?
...THAT'S WHEN THEY START TALKING.
YOU DON'T SPEAK AT **ALL,** CHICAGO. YOU **WATCH.** YOU **LISTEN.**
SEEING AS I KNOW YOUR STORY, I'M GOING TO TELL YOU MINE...
SUITS ME, YOU CRAZY BITCH. SPILL YOUR GUTS.
A STORY ABOUT A LITTLE GIRL TOUCHED BY FIRE.
FIRE TOOK MY MOM WHEN I WAS A WEEK OLD, AND HER HUSBAND WHEN I WAS TWELVE.
WHAT WOULD WE ALL DO WITHOUT GOOD OLD UNCLE ED LOOKING OUT FOR US?
I'M BEGINNING TO THINK I GOT THIS ALL WRONG.

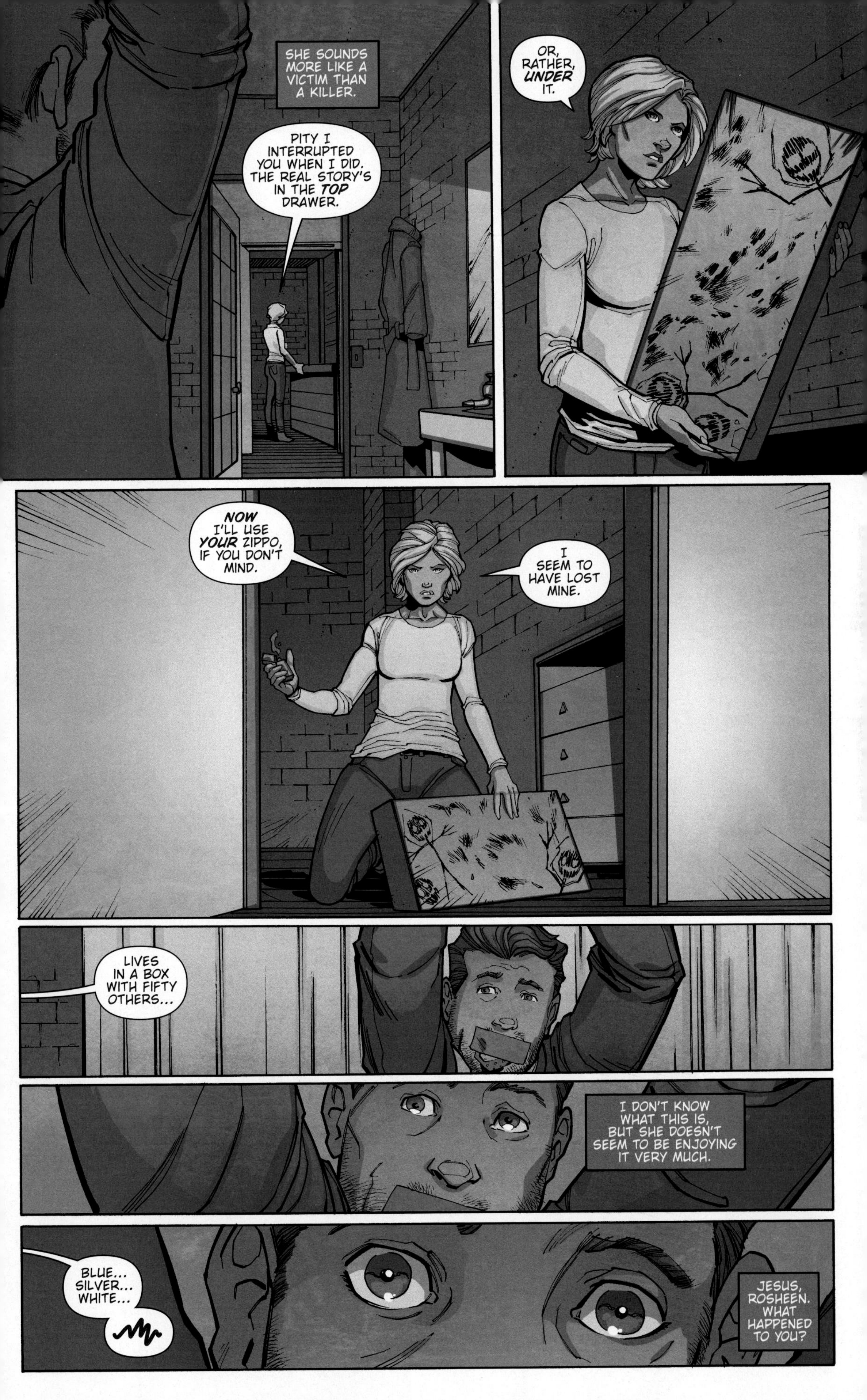
SHE SOUNDS MORE LIKE A VICTIM THAN A KILLER.
PITY I INTERRUPTED YOU WHEN I DID. THE REAL STORY'S IN THE *TOP* DRAWER.
OR, RATHER, *UNDER* IT.
NOW I'LL USE *YOUR* ZIPPO, IF YOU DON'T MIND.
I SEEM TO HAVE LOST MINE.
LIVES IN A BOX WITH FIFTY OTHERS...
I DON'T KNOW WHAT THIS IS, BUT SHE DOESN'T SEEM TO BE ENJOYING IT VERY MUCH.
BLUE... SILVER... WHITE...
JESUS, ROSHEEN. WHAT HAPPENED TO YOU?

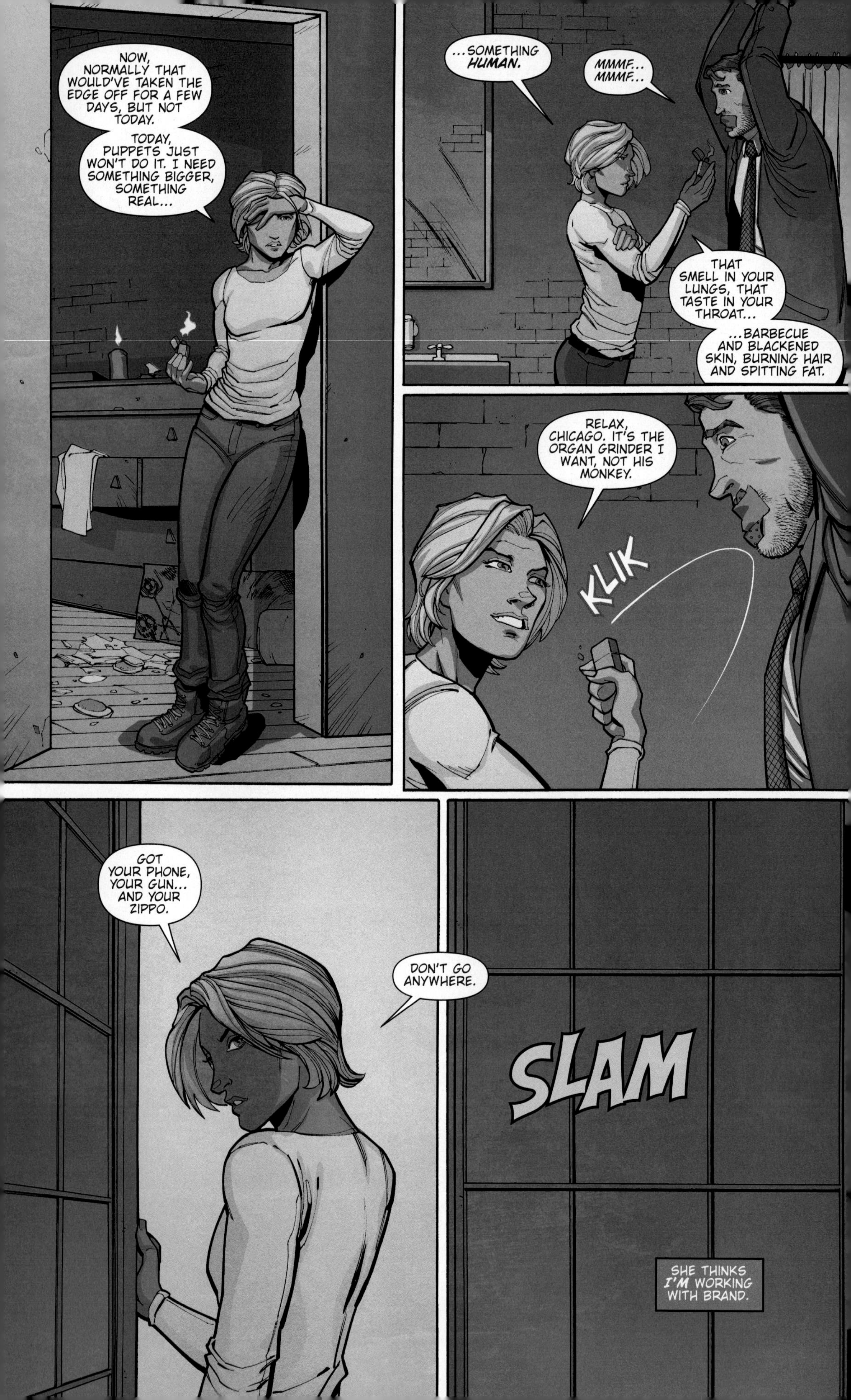
NOW, NORMALLY THAT WOULD'VE TAKEN THE EDGE OFF FOR A FEW DAYS, BUT NOT TODAY.
TODAY, PUPPETS JUST WON'T DO IT. I NEED SOMETHING BIGGER, SOMETHING REAL...
...SOMETHING **HUMAN.**
MMMF... MMMF...
THAT SMELL IN YOUR LUNGS, THAT TASTE IN YOUR THROAT...
...BARBECUE AND BLACKENED SKIN, BURNING HAIR AND SPITTING FAT.
RELAX, CHICAGO. IT'S THE ORGAN GRINDER I WANT, NOT HIS MONKEY.
KLIK
GOT YOUR PHONE, YOUR GUN... AND YOUR ZIPPO.
DON'T GO ANYWHERE.
SLAM
SHE THINKS ***I'M*** WORKING WITH BRAND.

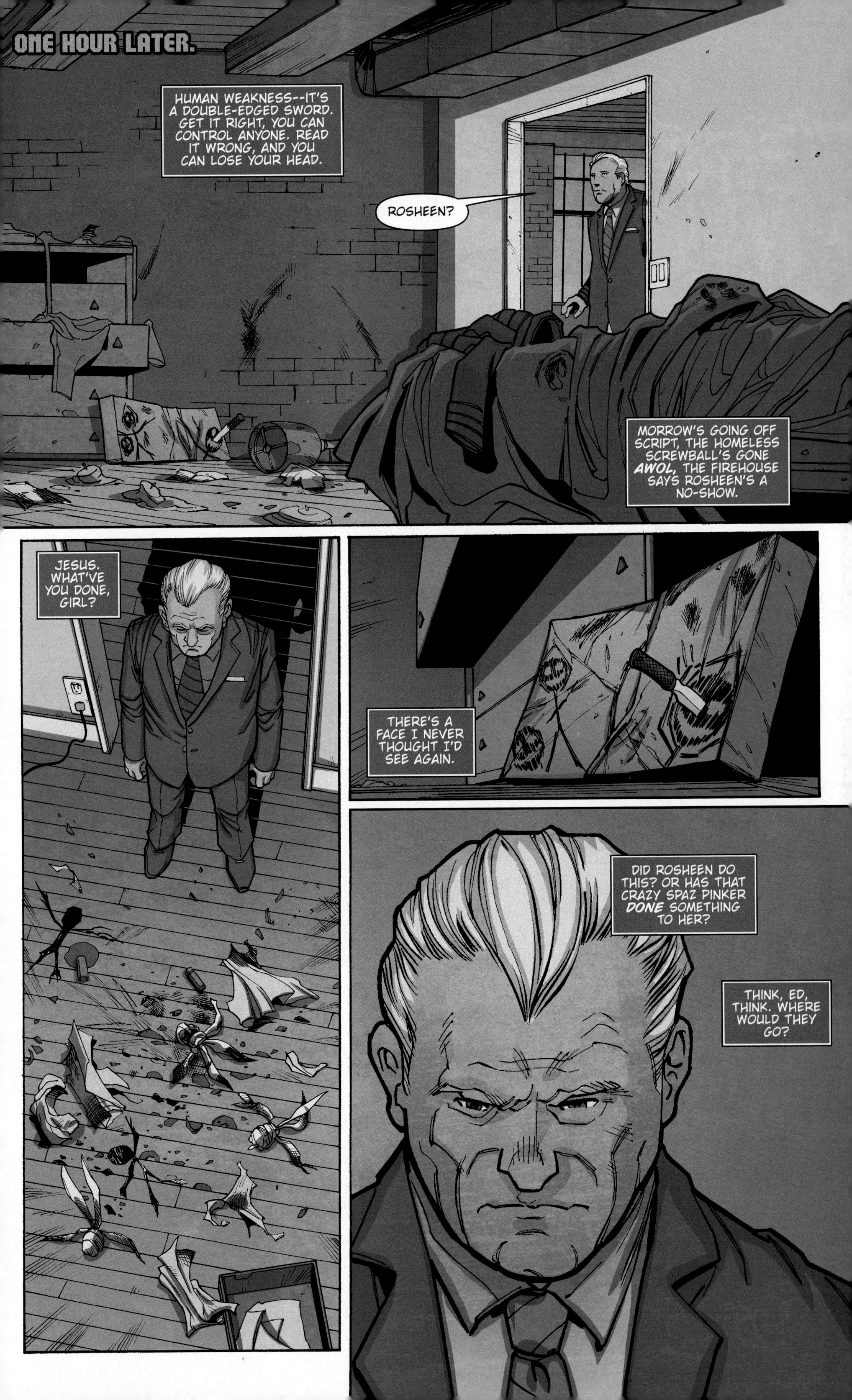
ONE HOUR LATER.
HUMAN WEAKNESS--IT'S A DOUBLE-EDGED SWORD. GET IT RIGHT, YOU CAN CONTROL ANYONE. READ IT WRONG, AND YOU CAN LOSE YOUR HEAD.
ROSHEEN?
MORROW'S GOING OFF SCRIPT, THE HOMELESS SCREWBALL'S GONE AWOL, THE FIREHOUSE SAYS ROSHEEN'S A NO-SHOW.
JESUS. WHAT'VE YOU DONE, GIRL?
THERE'S A FACE I NEVER THOUGHT I'D SEE AGAIN.
DID ROSHEEN DO THIS? OR HAS THAT CRAZY SPAZ PINKER DONE SOMETHING TO HER?
THINK, ED, THINK. WHERE WOULD THEY GO?

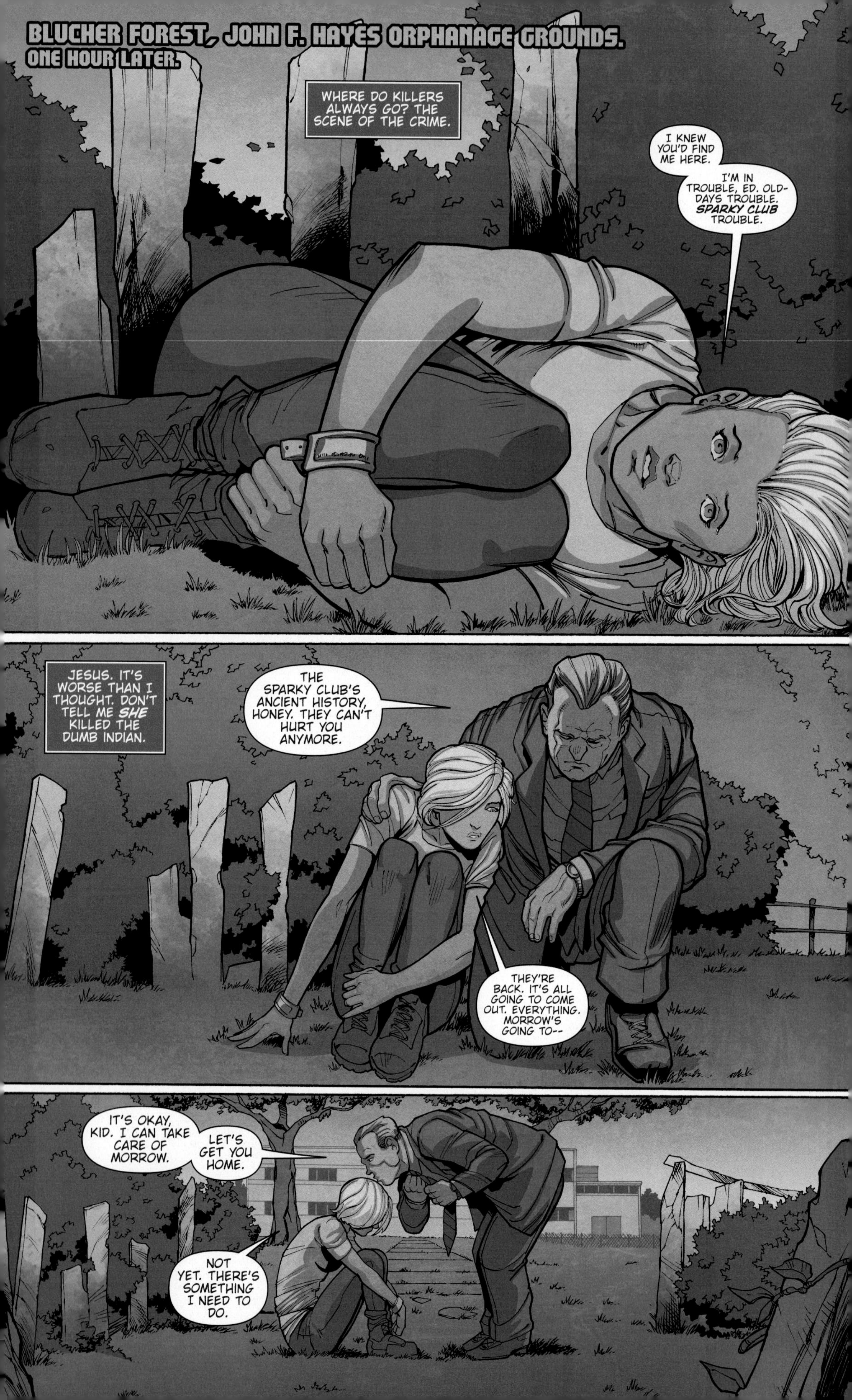
BLUCHER FOREST, JOHN F. HAYES ORPHANAGE GROUNDS.
ONE HOUR LATER.
WHERE DO KILLERS ALWAYS GO? THE SCENE OF THE CRIME.
I KNEW YOU'D FIND ME HERE.
I'M IN TROUBLE, ED. OLD-DAYS TROUBLE. SPARKY CLUB TROUBLE.
JESUS. IT'S WORSE THAN I THOUGHT. DON'T TELL ME SHE KILLED THE DUMB INDIAN.
THE SPARKY CLUB'S ANCIENT HISTORY, HONEY. THEY CAN'T HURT YOU ANYMORE.
THEY'RE BACK. IT'S ALL GOING TO COME OUT. EVERYTHING. MORROW'S GOING TO--
IT'S OKAY, KID. I CAN TAKE CARE OF MORROW.
LET'S GET YOU HOME.
NOT YET. THERE'S SOMETHING I NEED TO DO.

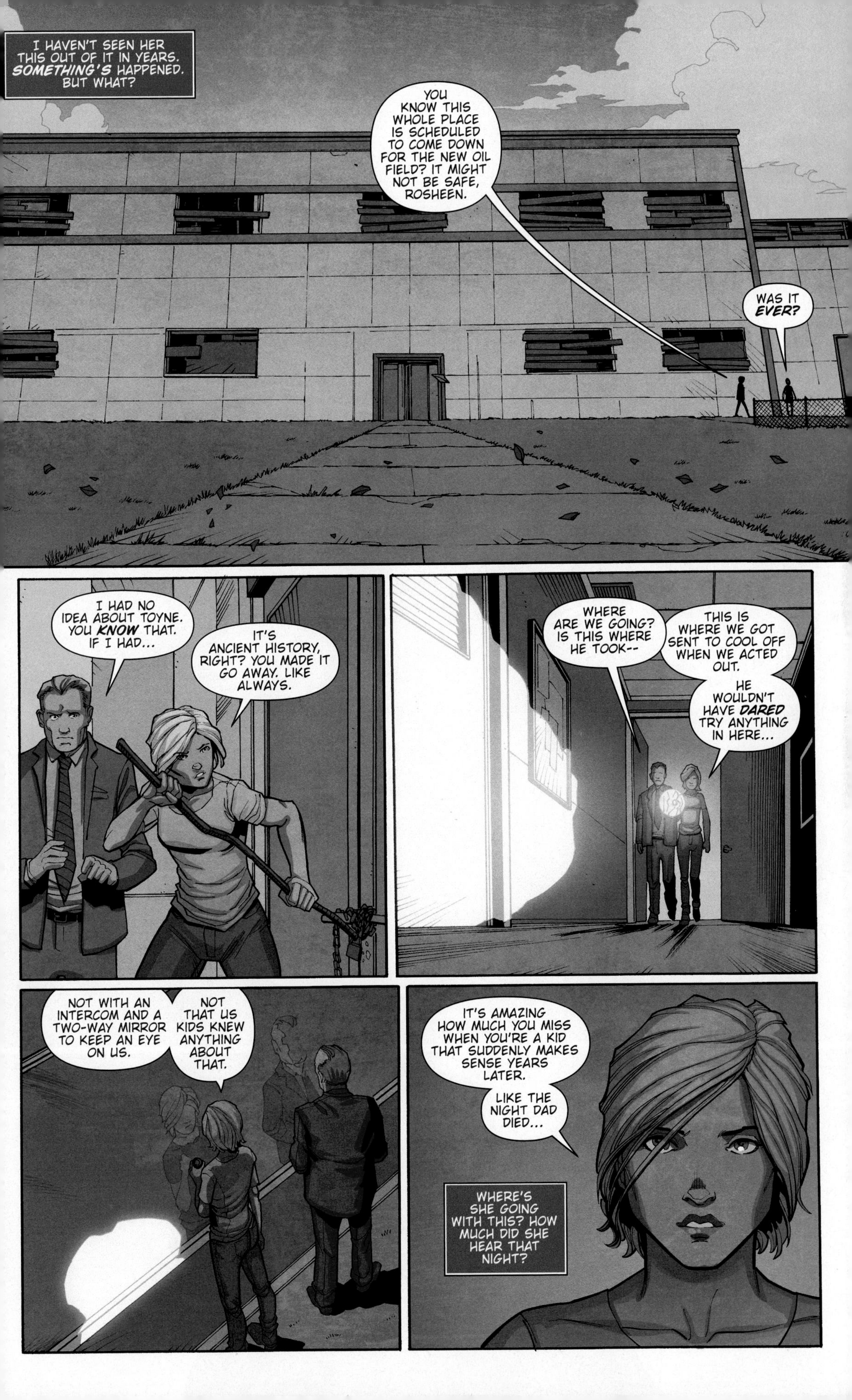
I HAVEN'T SEEN HER THIS OUT OF IT IN YEARS. SOMETHING'S HAPPENED. BUT WHAT?
YOU KNOW THIS WHOLE PLACE IS SCHEDULED TO COME DOWN FOR THE NEW OIL FIELD? IT MIGHT NOT BE SAFE, ROSHEEN.
WAS IT EVER?
I HAD NO IDEA ABOUT TOYNE. YOU KNOW THAT. IF I HAD...
IT'S ANCIENT HISTORY, RIGHT? YOU MADE IT GO AWAY. LIKE ALWAYS.
WHERE ARE WE GOING? IS THIS WHERE HE TOOK--
THIS IS WHERE WE GOT SENT TO COOL OFF WHEN WE ACTED OUT.
HE WOULDN'T HAVE DARED TRY ANYTHING IN HERE...
NOT WITH AN INTERCOM AND A TWO-WAY MIRROR TO KEEP AN EYE ON US.
NOT THAT US KIDS KNEW ANYTHING ABOUT THAT.
IT'S AMAZING HOW MUCH YOU MISS WHEN YOU'RE A KID THAT SUDDENLY MAKES SENSE YEARS LATER.
LIKE THE NIGHT DAD DIED...
WHERE'S SHE GOING WITH THIS? HOW MUCH DID SHE HEAR THAT NIGHT?

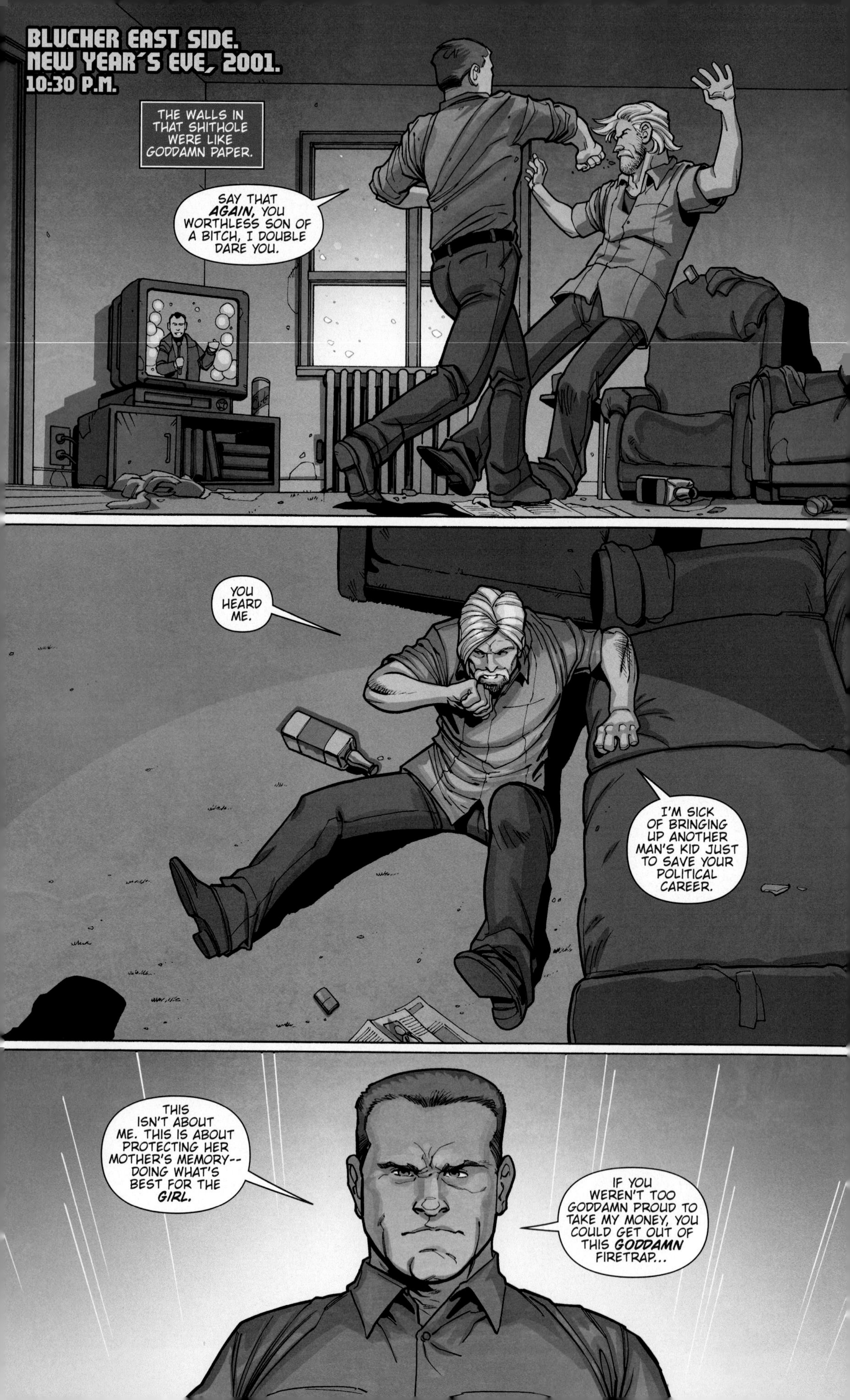

BLUCHER EAST SIDE. NEW YEAR'S EVE, 2001. 10:30 P.M.
THE WALLS IN THAT SHITHOLE WERE LIKE GODDAMN PAPER.
SAY THAT AGAIN, YOU WORTHLESS SON OF A BITCH, I DOUBLE DARE YOU.
YOU HEARD ME.
I'M SICK OF BRINGING UP ANOTHER MAN'S KID JUST TO SAVE YOUR POLITICAL CAREER.
THIS ISN'T ABOUT ME. THIS IS ABOUT PROTECTING HER MOTHER'S MEMORY-- DOING WHAT'S BEST FOR THE GIRL.
IF YOU WEREN'T TOO GODDAMN PROUD TO TAKE MY MONEY, YOU COULD GET OUT OF THIS GODDAMN FIRETRAP...

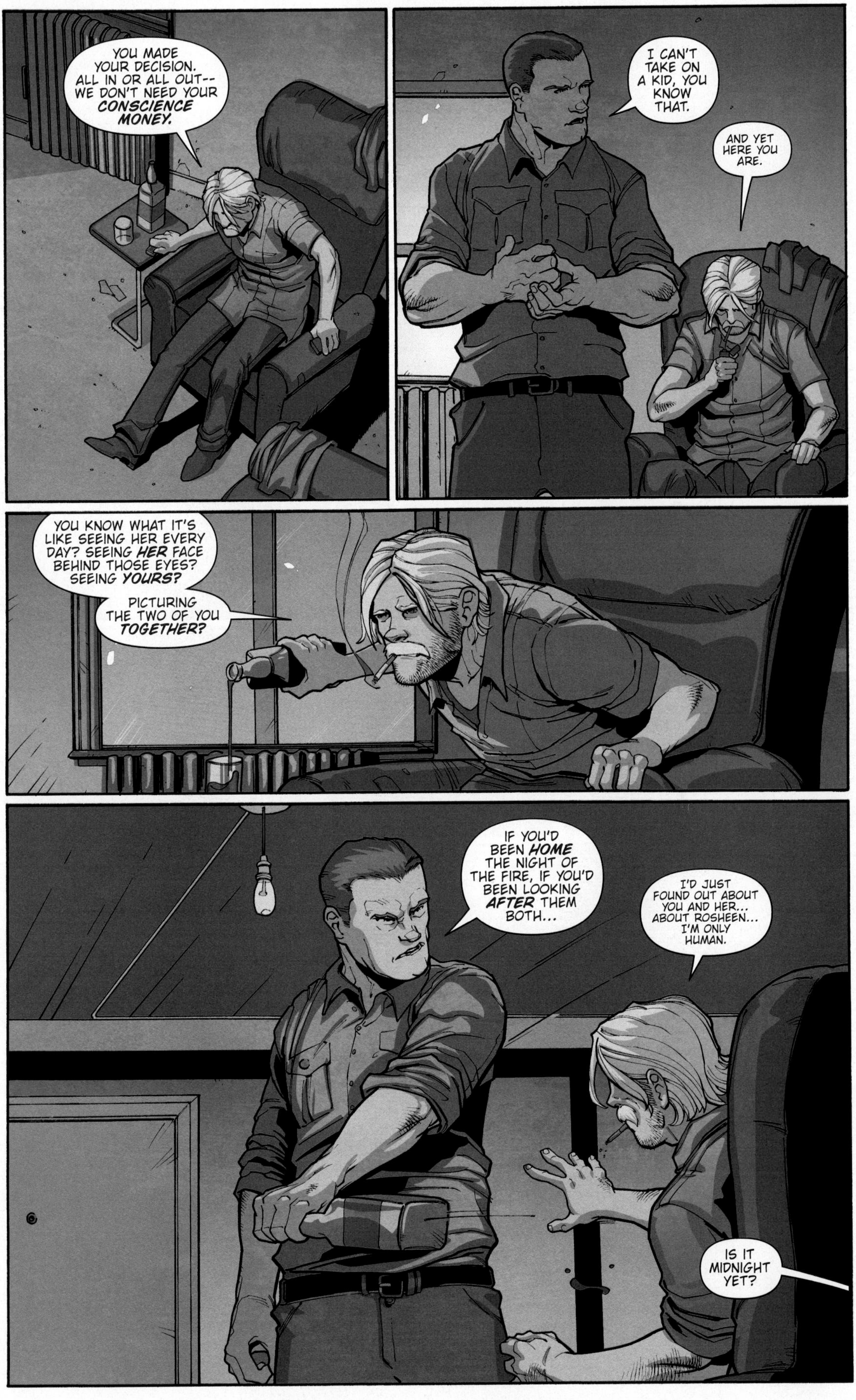
YOU MADE YOUR DECISION. ALL IN OR ALL OUT-- WE DON'T NEED YOUR CONSCIENCE MONEY.
I CAN'T TAKE ON A KID, YOU KNOW THAT.
AND YET HERE YOU ARE.
YOU KNOW WHAT IT'S LIKE SEEING HER EVERY DAY? SEEING HER FACE BEHIND THOSE EYES? SEEING YOURS?
PICTURING THE TWO OF YOU TOGETHER?
IF YOU'D BEEN HOME THE NIGHT OF THE FIRE, IF YOU'D BEEN LOOKING AFTER THEM BOTH...
I'D JUST FOUND OUT ABOUT YOU AND HER... ABOUT ROSHEEN... I'M ONLY HUMAN.
IS IT MIDNIGHT YET?

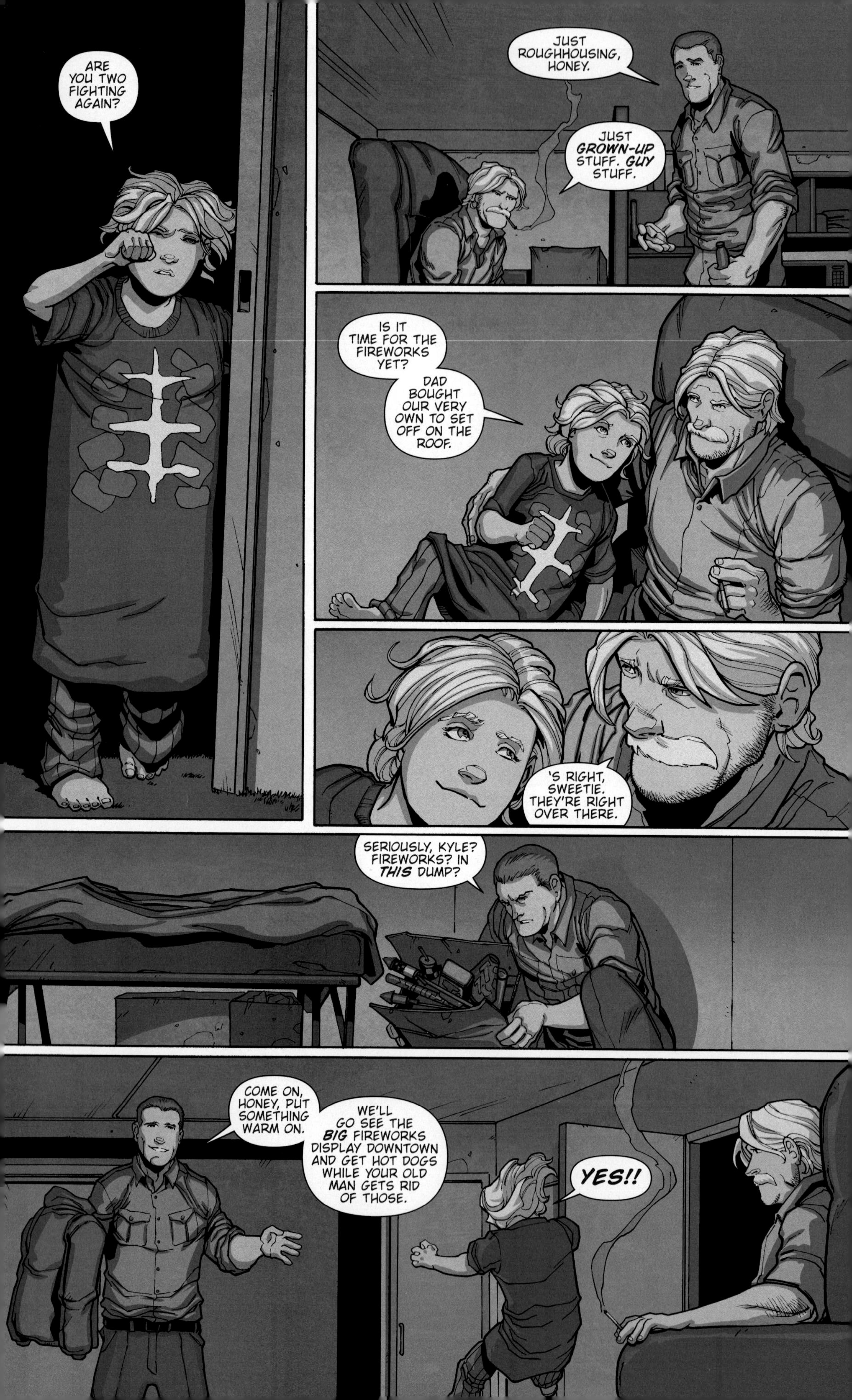

ARE YOU TWO FIGHTING AGAIN?
JUST ROUGHHOUSING, HONEY.
JUST GROWN-UP STUFF. GUY STUFF.
IS IT TIME FOR THE FIREWORKS YET?
DAD BOUGHT OUR VERY OWN TO SET OFF ON THE ROOF.
'S RIGHT, SWEETIE. THEY'RE RIGHT OVER THERE.
SERIOUSLY, KYLE? FIREWORKS? IN THIS DUMP?
COME ON, HONEY, PUT SOMETHING WARM ON.
WE'LL GO SEE THE BIG FIREWORKS DISPLAY DOWNTOWN AND GET HOT DOGS WHILE YOUR OLD MAN GETS RID OF THOSE.
YES!!

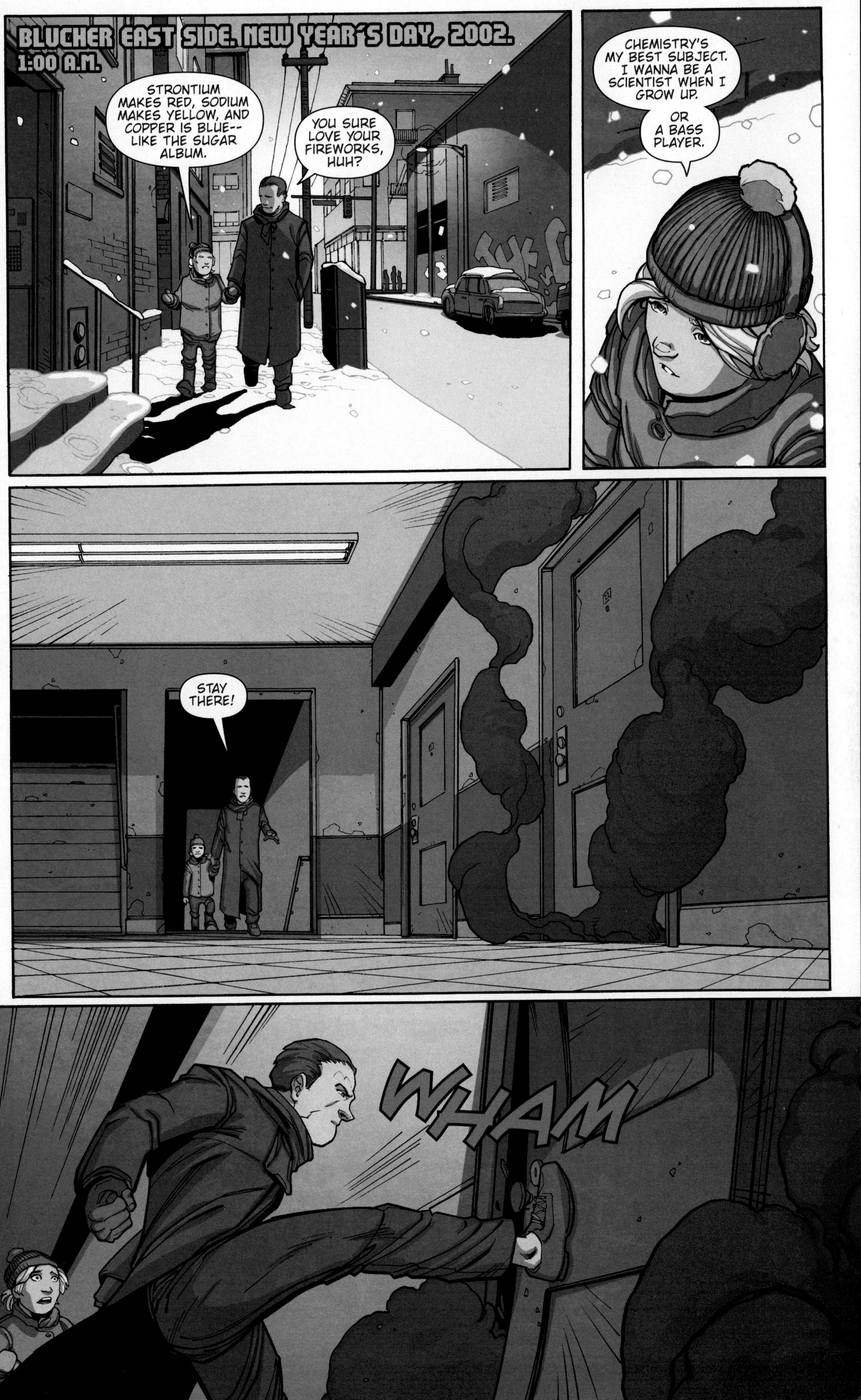
BLUCHER EAST SIDE. NEW YEAR'S DAY, 2002.
1:00 A.M.
STRONTIUM MAKES RED, SODIUM MAKES YELLOW, AND COPPER IS BLUE-- LIKE THE SUGAR ALBUM.
YOU SURE LOVE YOUR FIREWORKS, HUH?
CHEMISTRY'S MY BEST SUBJECT. I WANNA BE A SCIENTIST WHEN I GROW UP.
OR A BASS PLAYER.
STAY THERE!
WHAM

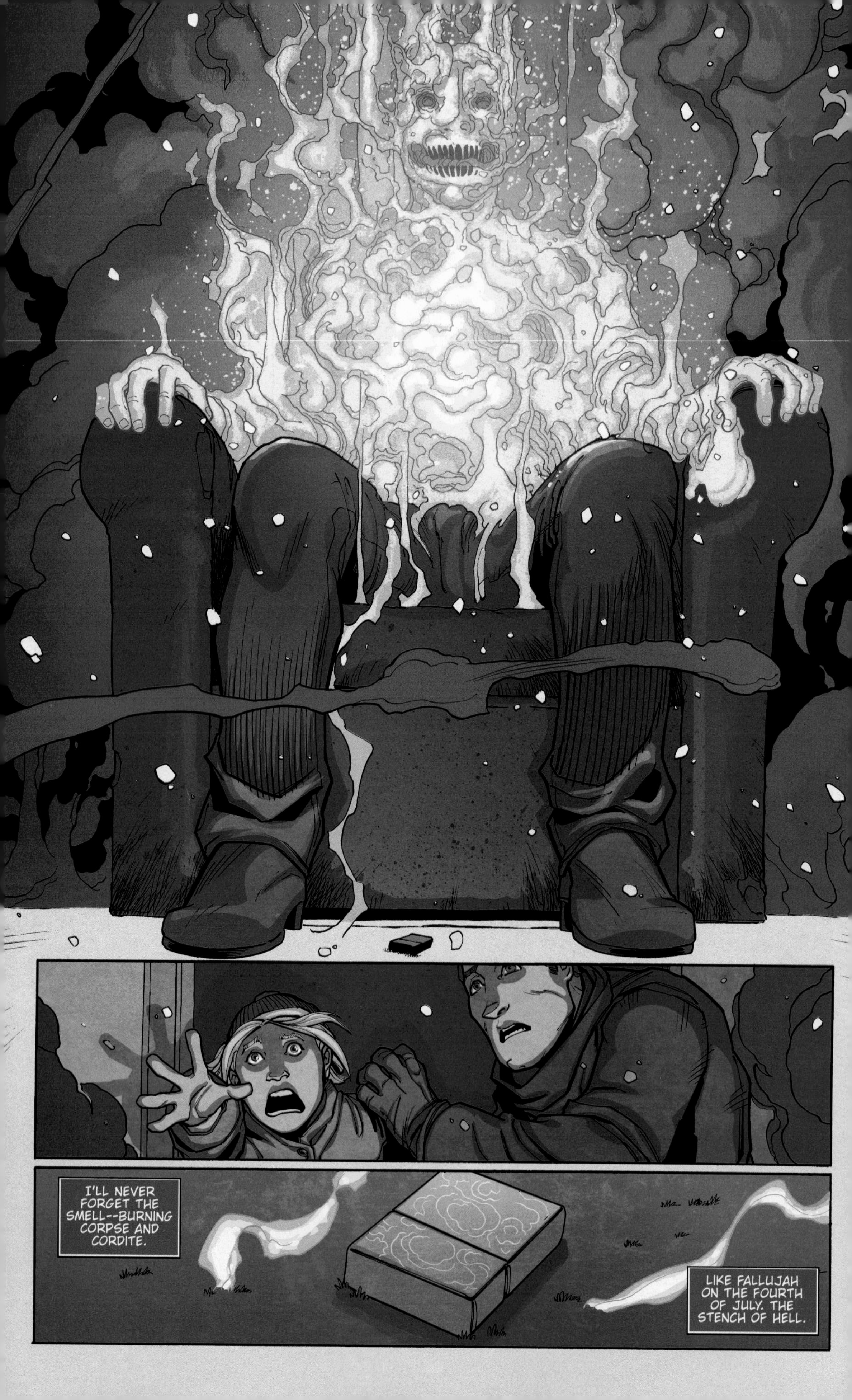
I'LL NEVER FORGET THE SMELL--BURNING CORPSE AND CORDITE.
LIKE FALLUJAH ON THE FOURTH OF JULY. THE STENCH OF HELL.

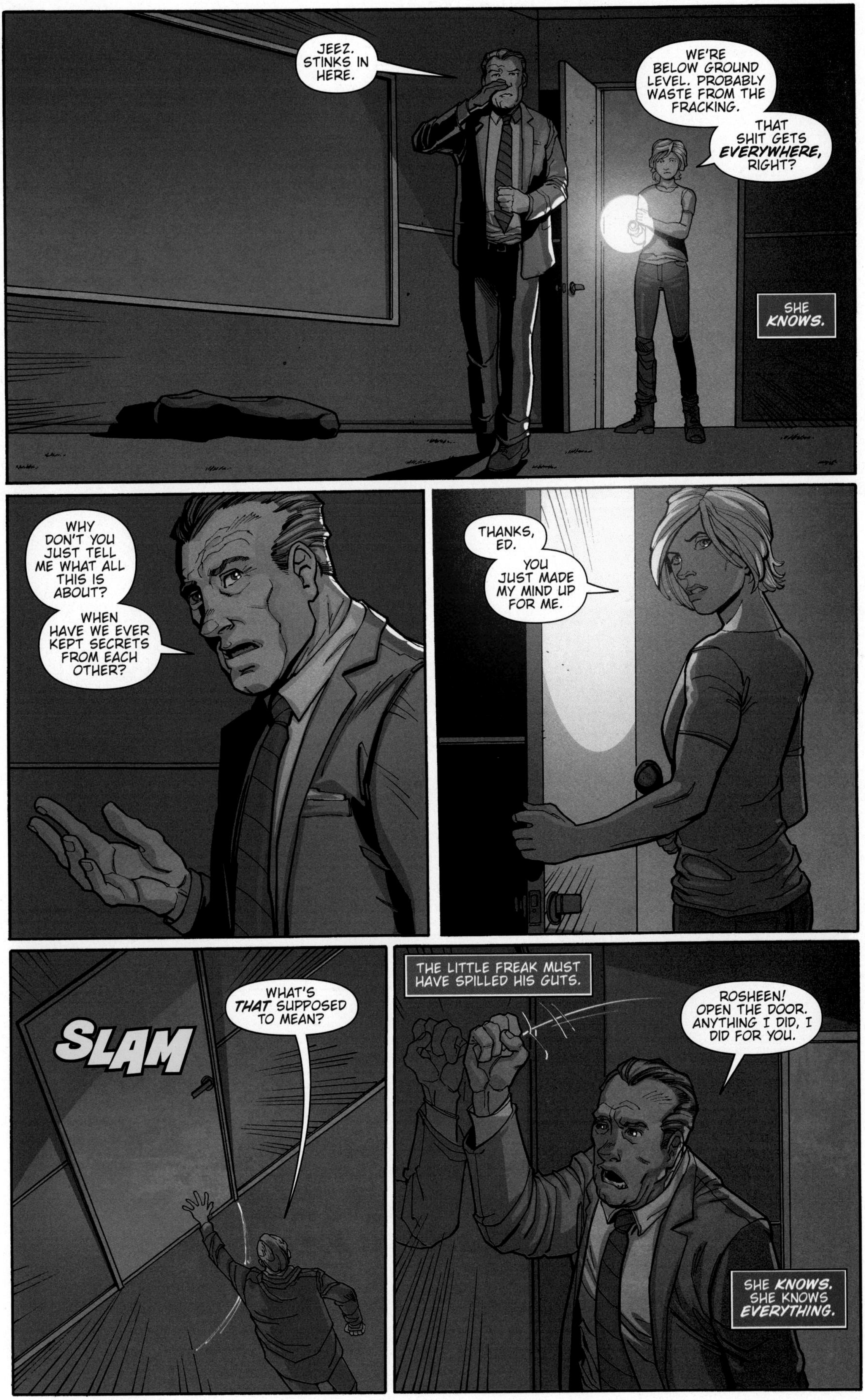
JEEZ. STINKS IN HERE.
WE'RE BELOW GROUND LEVEL. PROBABLY WASTE FROM THE FRACKING.
THAT SHIT GETS EVERYWHERE, RIGHT?
SHE KNOWS.
WHY DON'T YOU JUST TELL ME WHAT ALL THIS IS ABOUT?
WHEN HAVE WE EVER KEPT SECRETS FROM EACH OTHER?
THANKS, ED.
YOU JUST MADE MY MIND UP FOR ME.
SLAM
WHAT'S THAT SUPPOSED TO MEAN?
THE LITTLE FREAK MUST HAVE SPILLED HIS GUTS.
ROSHEEN! OPEN THE DOOR. ANYTHING I DID, I DID FOR YOU.
SHE KNOWS. SHE KNOWS EVERYTHING.

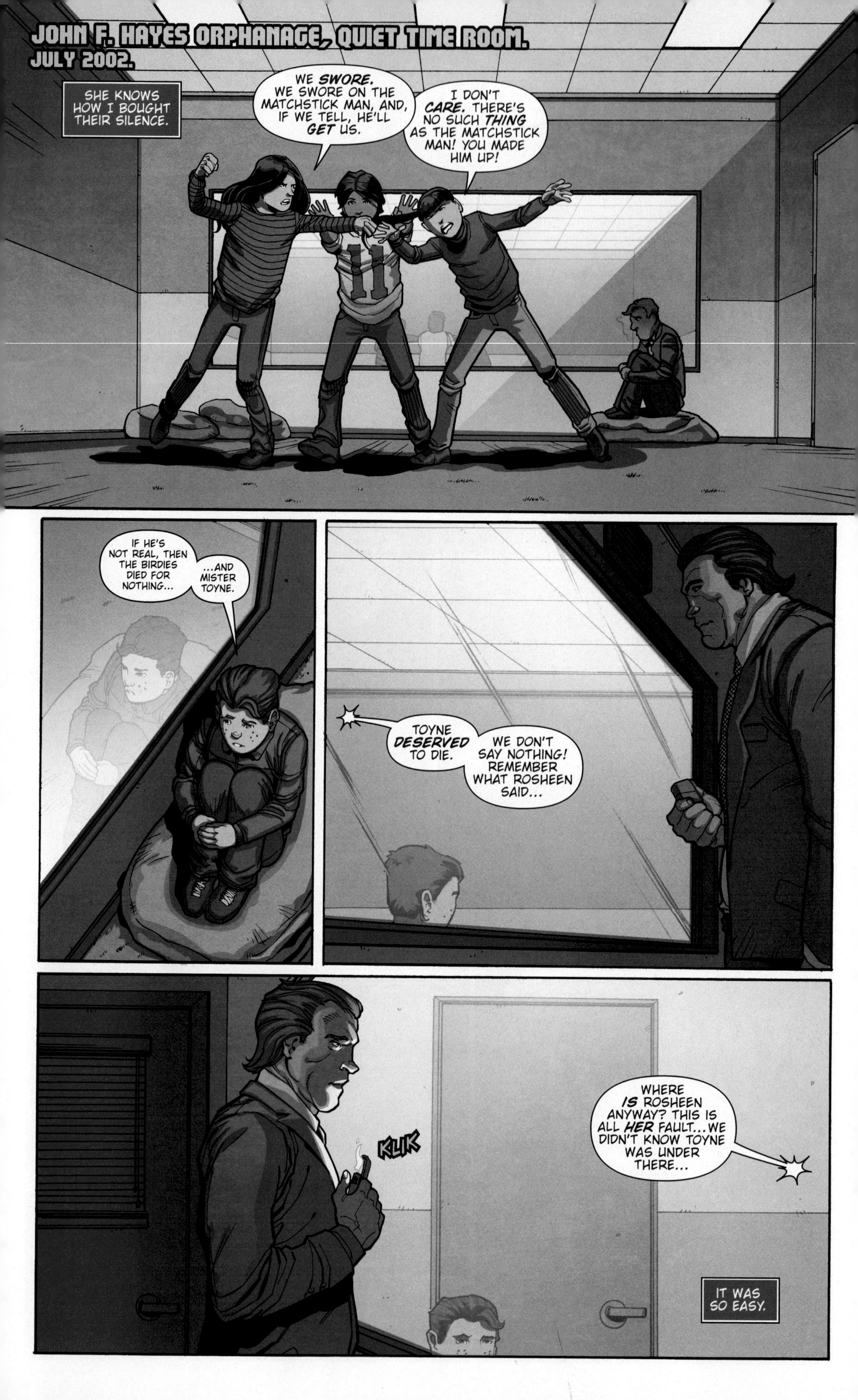
JOHN F. HAYES ORPHANAGE, QUIET TIME ROOM.
JULY 2002.
SHE KNOWS HOW I BOUGHT THEIR SILENCE.
WE SWORE. WE SWORE ON THE MATCHSTICK MAN, AND, IF WE TELL, HE'LL GET US.
I DON'T CARE. THERE'S NO SUCH THING AS THE MATCHSTICK MAN! YOU MADE HIM UP!
IF HE'S NOT REAL, THEN THE BIRDIES DIED FOR NOTHING...
...AND MISTER TOYNE.
TOYNE DESERVED TO DIE.
WE DON'T SAY NOTHING! REMEMBER WHAT ROSHEEN SAID...
KLIK
WHERE IS ROSHEEN ANYWAY? THIS IS ALL HER FAULT...WE DIDN'T KNOW TOYNE WAS UNDER THERE...
IT WAS SO EASY.

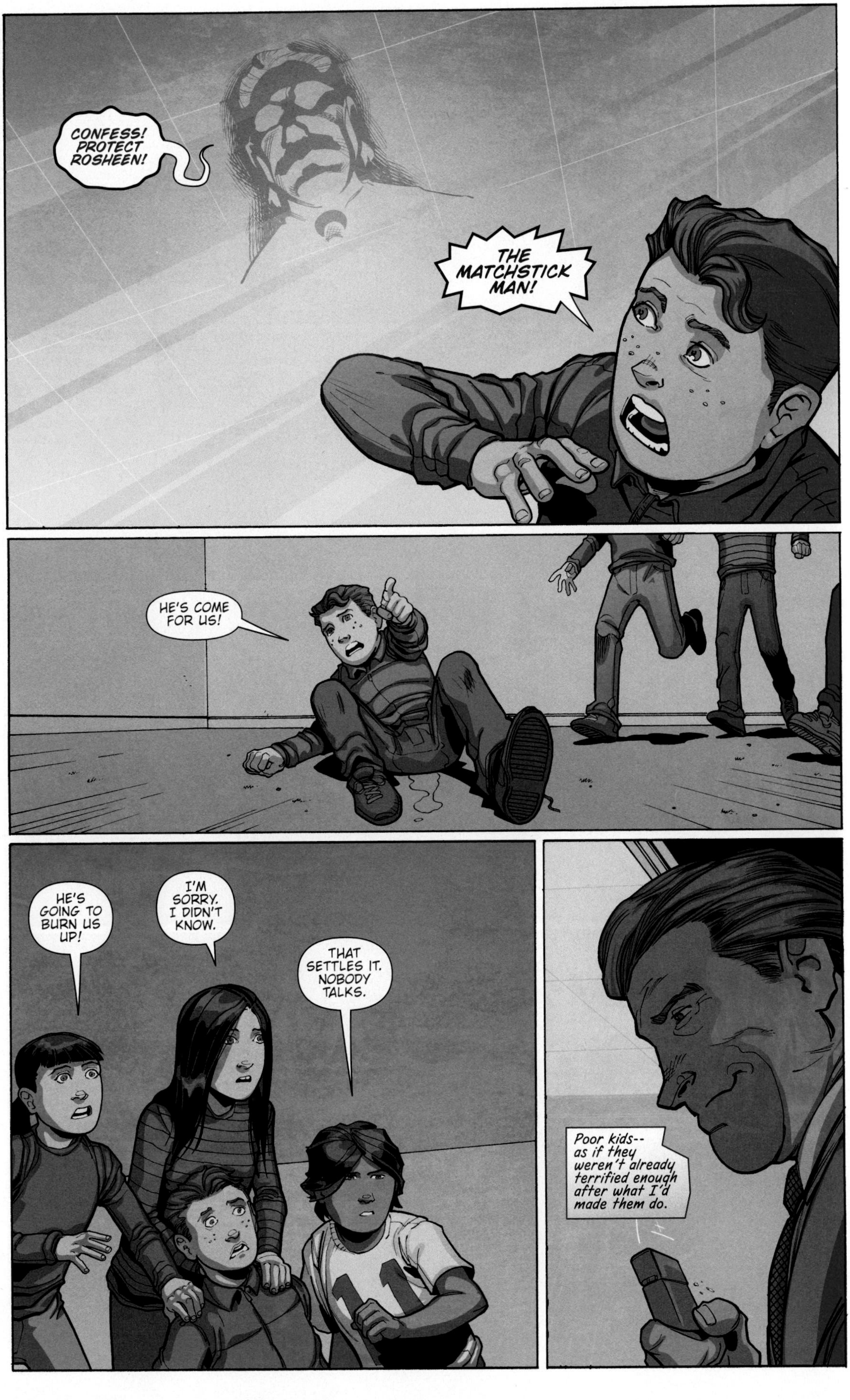
CONFESS! PROTECT ROSHEEN!
THE MATCHSTICK MAN!
HE'S COME FOR US!
HE'S GOING TO BURN US UP!
I'M SORRY. I DIDN'T KNOW.
THAT SETTLES IT. NOBODY TALKS.
Poor kids-- as if they weren't already terrified enough after what I'd made them do.

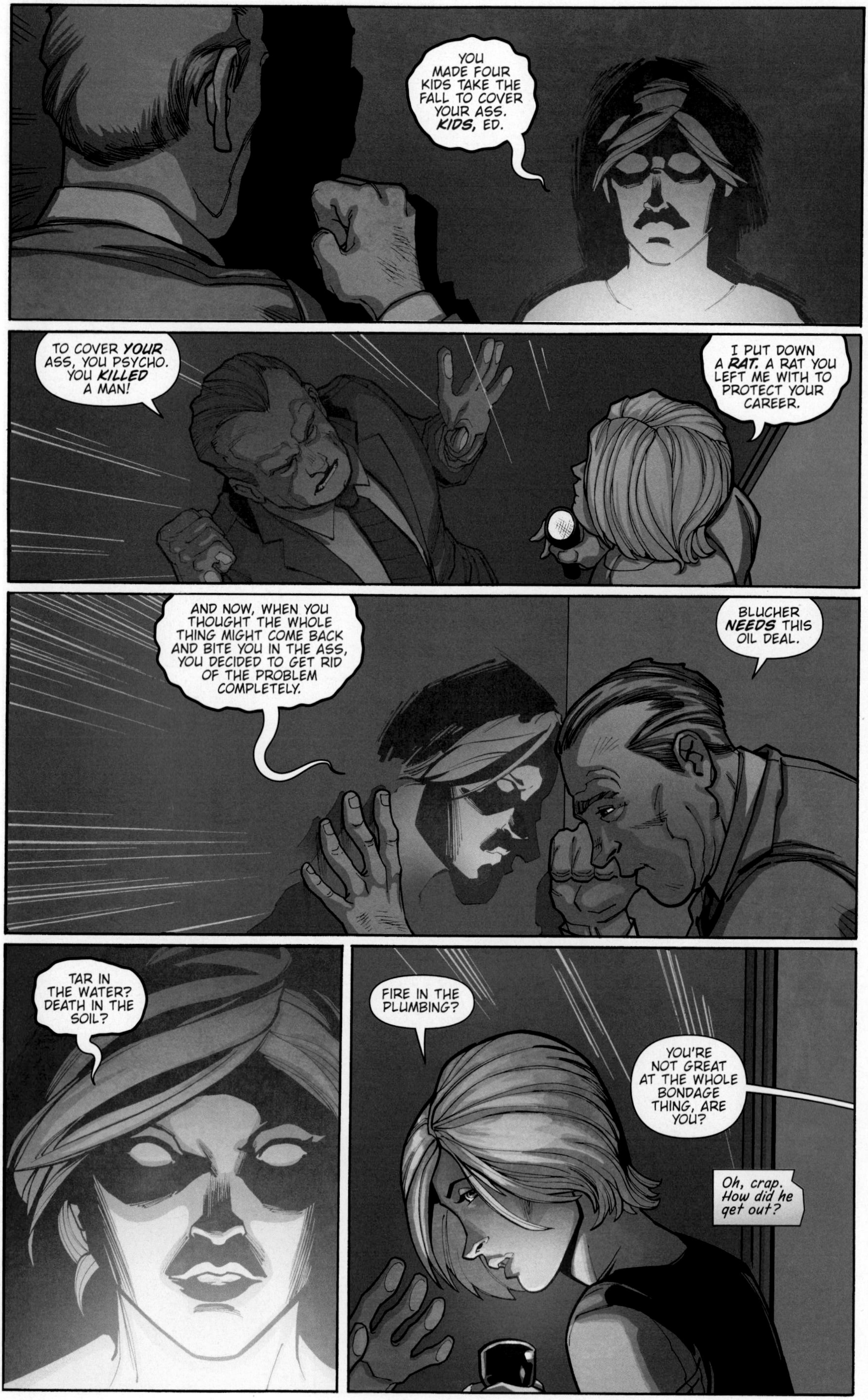
YOU MADE FOUR KIDS TAKE THE FALL TO COVER YOUR ASS. KIDS, ED.
TO COVER YOUR ASS, YOU PSYCHO. YOU KILLED A MAN!
I PUT DOWN A RAT. A RAT YOU LEFT ME WITH TO PROTECT YOUR CAREER.
AND NOW, WHEN YOU THOUGHT THE WHOLE THING MIGHT COME BACK AND BITE YOU IN THE ASS, YOU DECIDED TO GET RID OF THE PROBLEM COMPLETELY.
BLUCHER NEEDS THIS OIL DEAL.
TAR IN THE WATER? DEATH IN THE SOIL?
FIRE IN THE PLUMBING?
YOU'RE NOT GREAT AT THE WHOLE BONDAGE THING, ARE YOU?
Oh, crap. How did he get out?

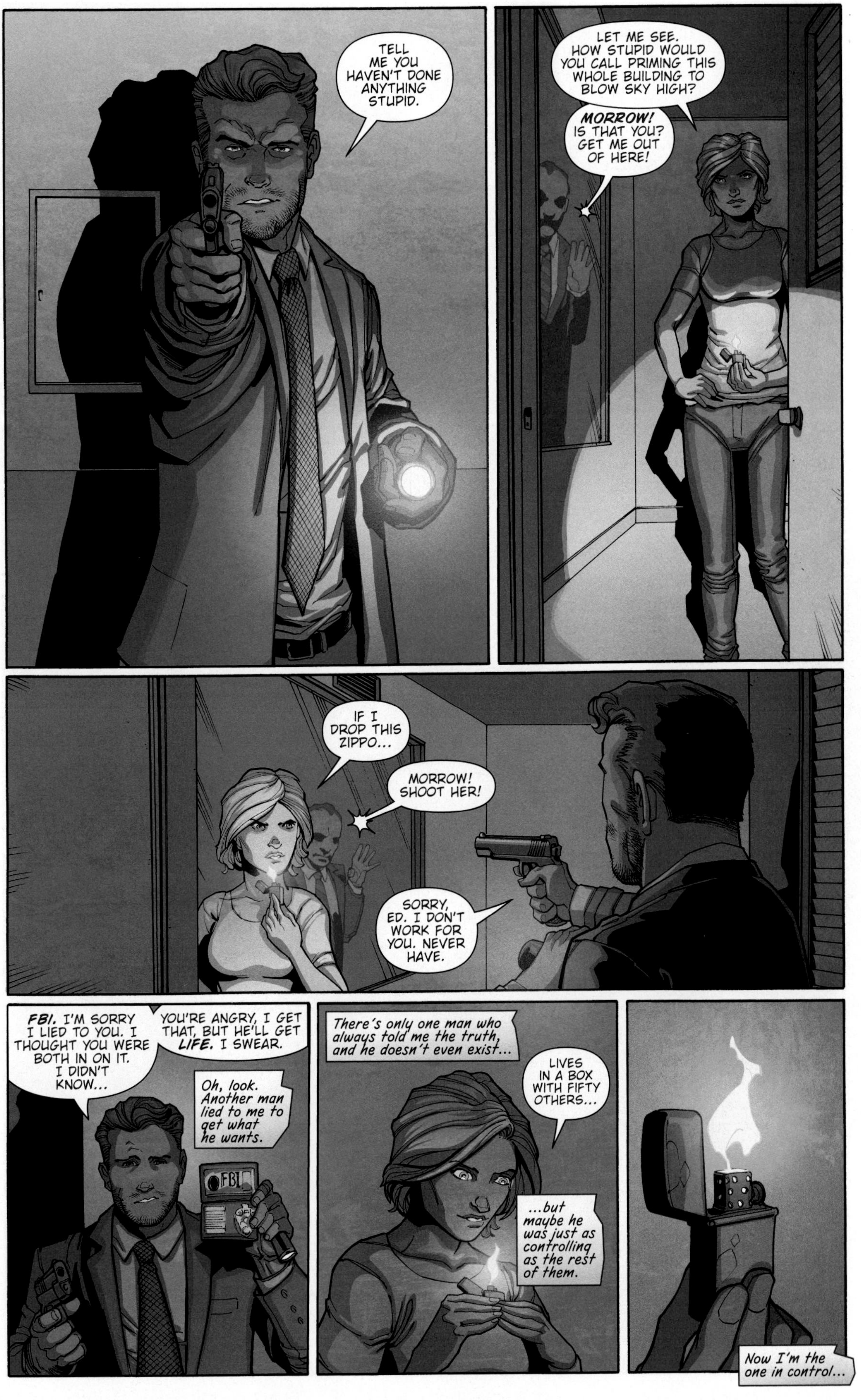

TELL ME YOU HAVEN'T DONE ANYTHING STUPID.
LET ME SEE. HOW STUPID WOULD YOU CALL PRIMING THIS WHOLE BUILDING TO BLOW SKY HIGH?
MORROW! IS THAT YOU? GET ME OUT OF HERE!
IF I DROP THIS ZIPPO...
MORROW! SHOOT HER!
SORRY, ED. I DON'T WORK FOR YOU. NEVER HAVE.
FBI. I'M SORRY I LIED TO YOU. I THOUGHT YOU WERE BOTH IN ON IT. I DIDN'T KNOW...
YOU'RE ANGRY, I GET THAT, BUT HE'LL GET LIFE. I SWEAR.
Oh, look. Another man lied to me to get what he wants.
FBI
There's only one man who always told me the truth, and he doesn't even exist...
LIVES IN A BOX WITH FIFTY OTHERS...
...but maybe he was just as controlling as the rest of them.
Now I'm the one in control...

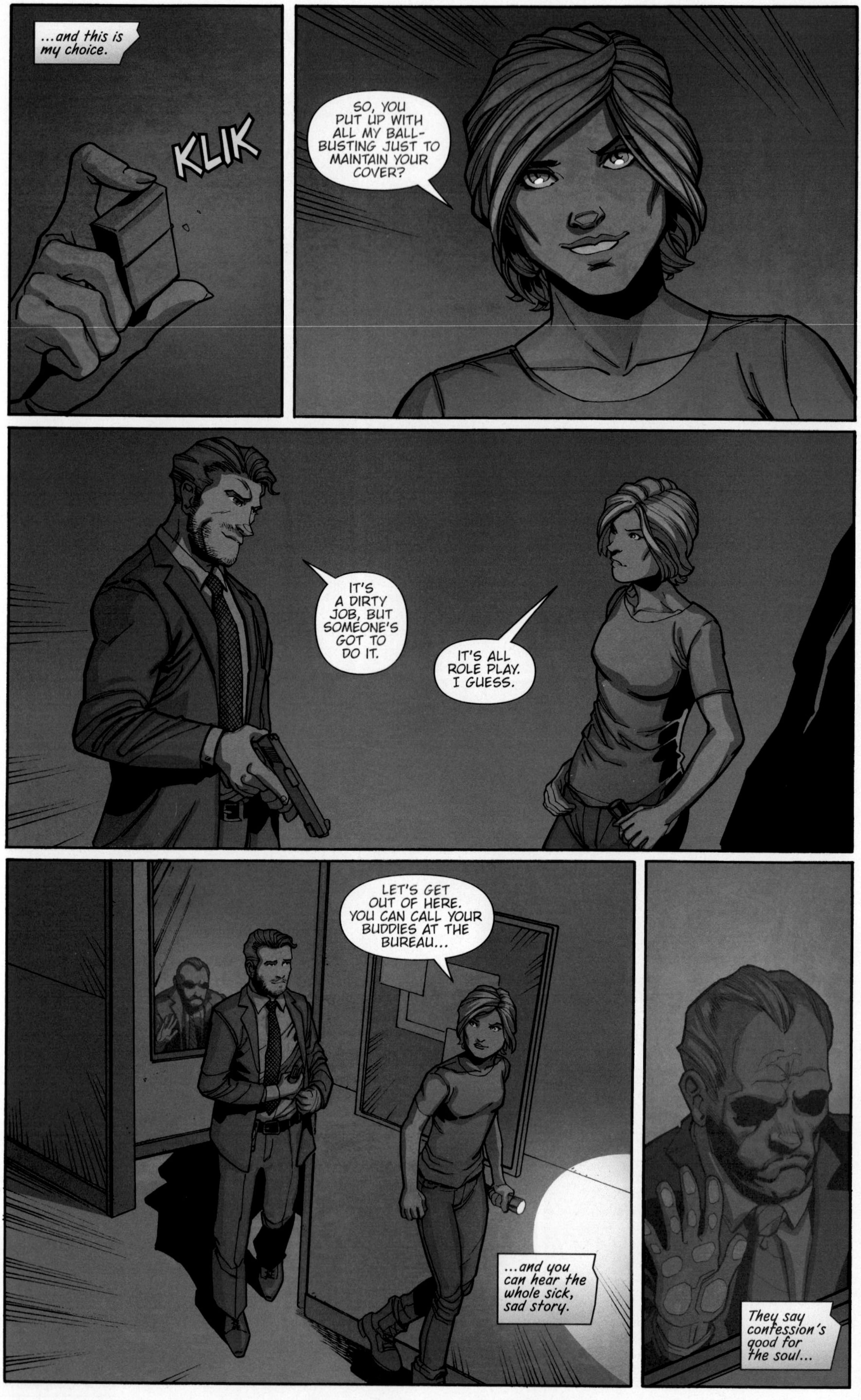
...and this is my choice.
KLIK
SO, YOU PUT UP WITH ALL MY BALL-BUSTING JUST TO MAINTAIN YOUR COVER?
IT'S A DIRTY JOB, BUT SOMEONE'S GOT TO DO IT.
IT'S ALL ROLE PLAY. I GUESS.
LET'S GET OUT OF HERE. YOU CAN CALL YOUR BUDDIES AT THE BUREAU...
...and you can hear the whole sick, sad story.
They say confession's good for the soul...

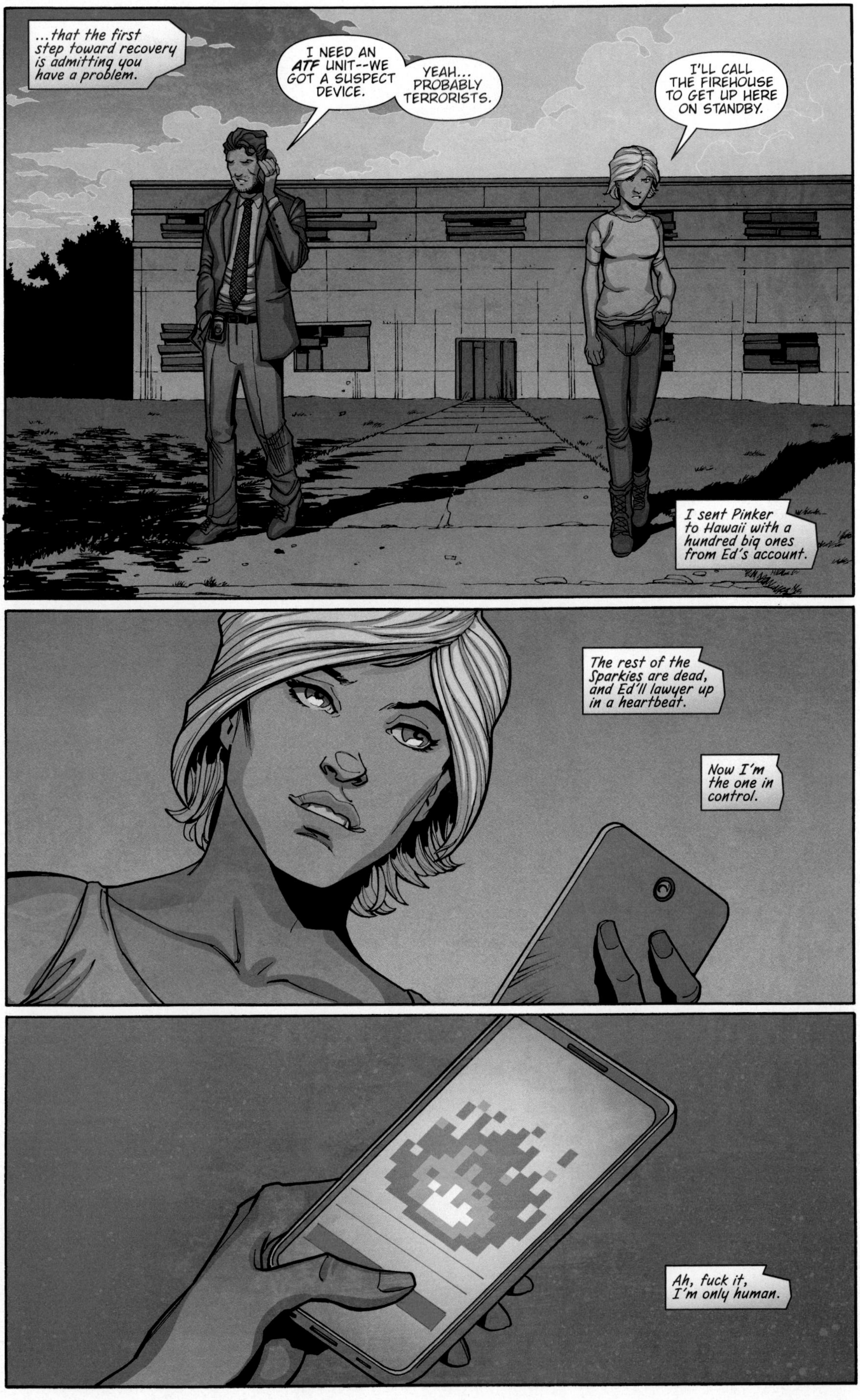
...that the first step toward recovery is admitting you have a problem.
I NEED AN ATF UNIT--WE GOT A SUSPECT DEVICE.
YEAH... PROBABLY TERRORISTS.
I'LL CALL THE FIREHOUSE TO GET UP HERE ON STANDBY.
I sent Pinker to Hawaii with a hundred big ones from Ed's account.
The rest of the Sparkies are dead, and Ed'll lawyer up in a heartbeat.
Now I'm the one in control.
Ah, fuck it, I'm only human.

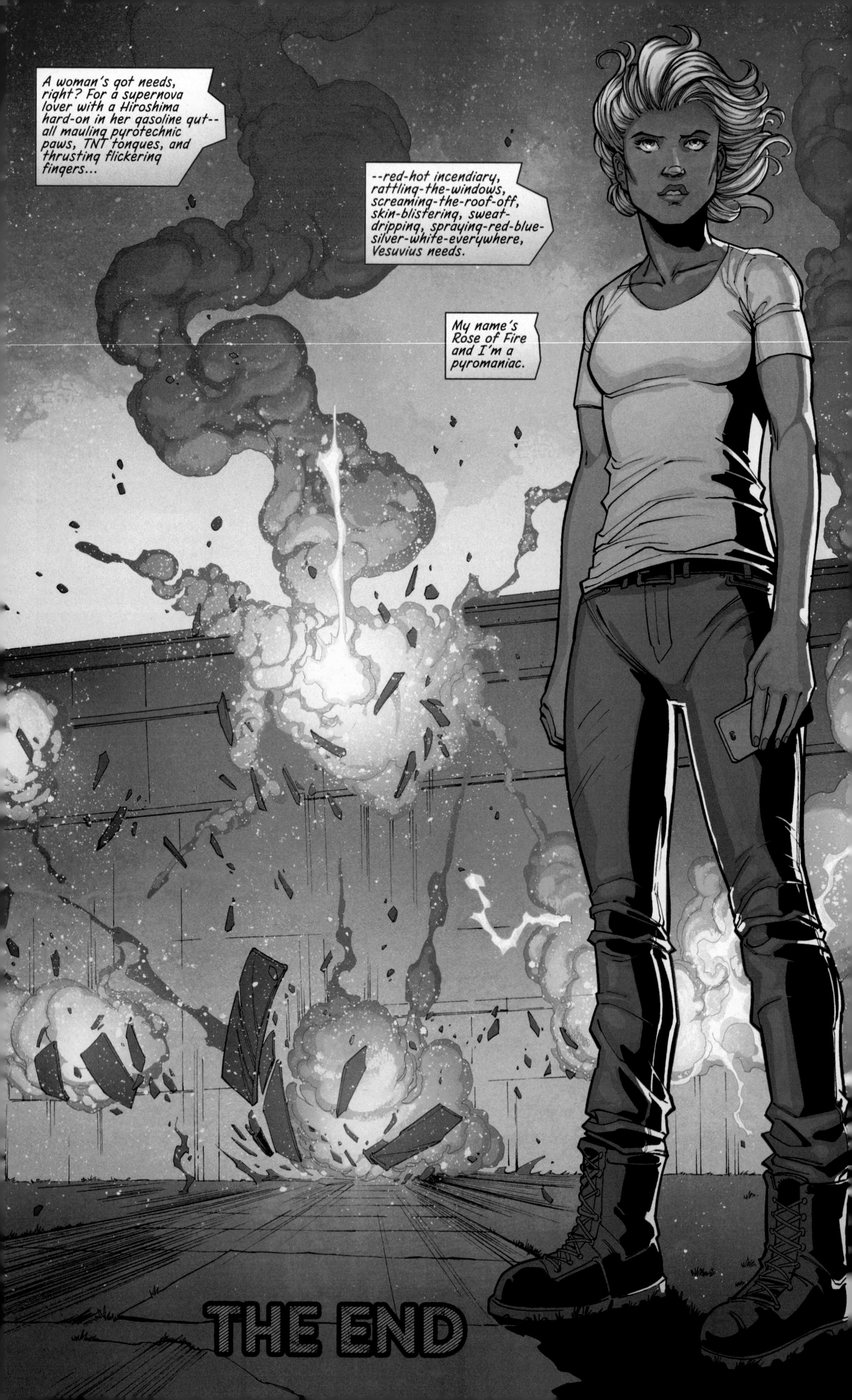
A woman's got needs, right? For a supernova lover with a Hiroshima hard-on in her gasoline gut--all mauling pyrotechnic paws, TNT tongues, and thrusting flickering fingers...
--red-hot incendiary, rattling-the-windows, screaming-the-roof-off, skin-blistering, sweat-dripping, spraying-red-blue-silver-white-everywhere, Vesuvius needs.
My name's Rose of Fire and I'm a pyromaniac.
THE END

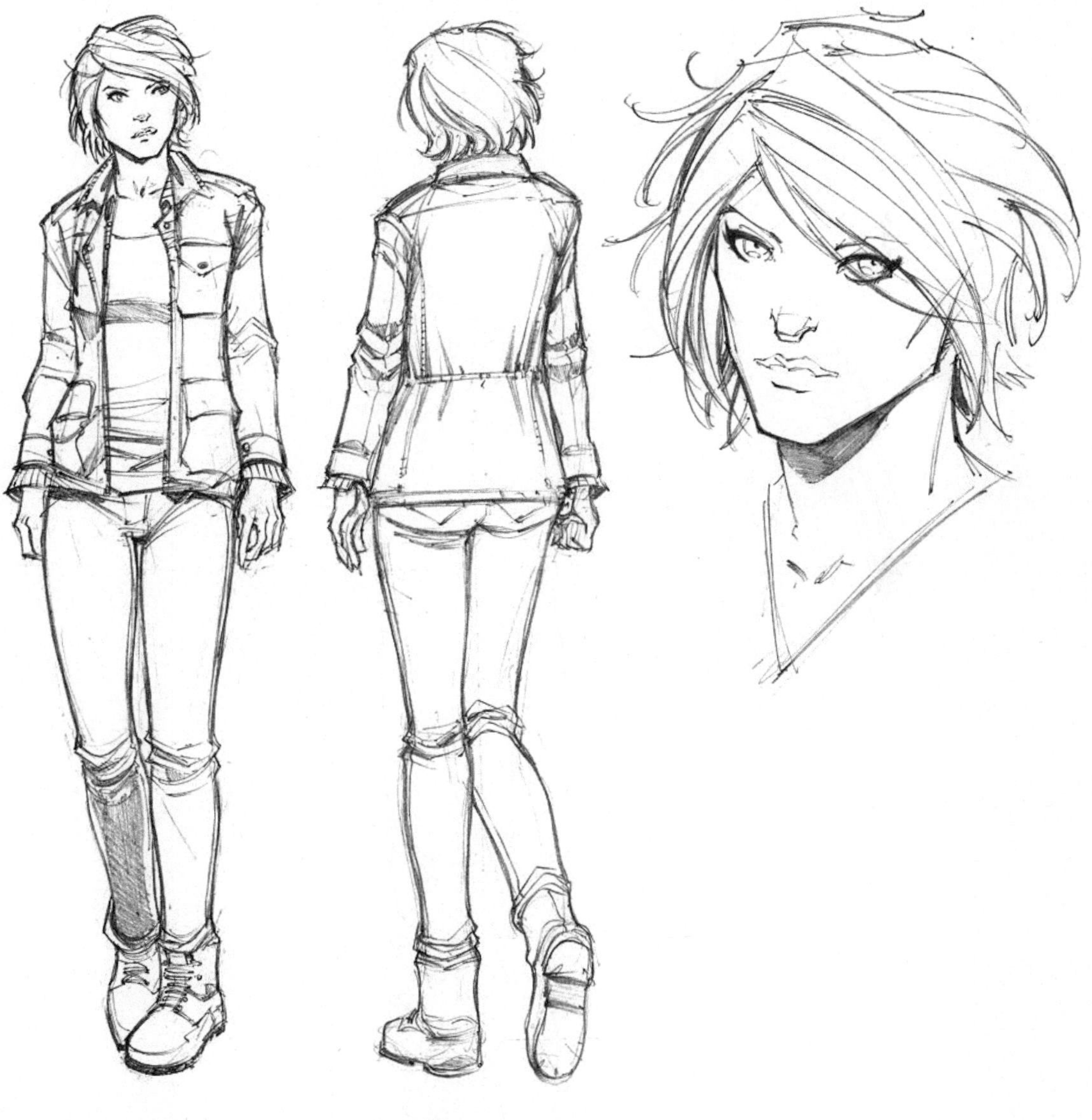

Character designs by
MAX DUNBAR

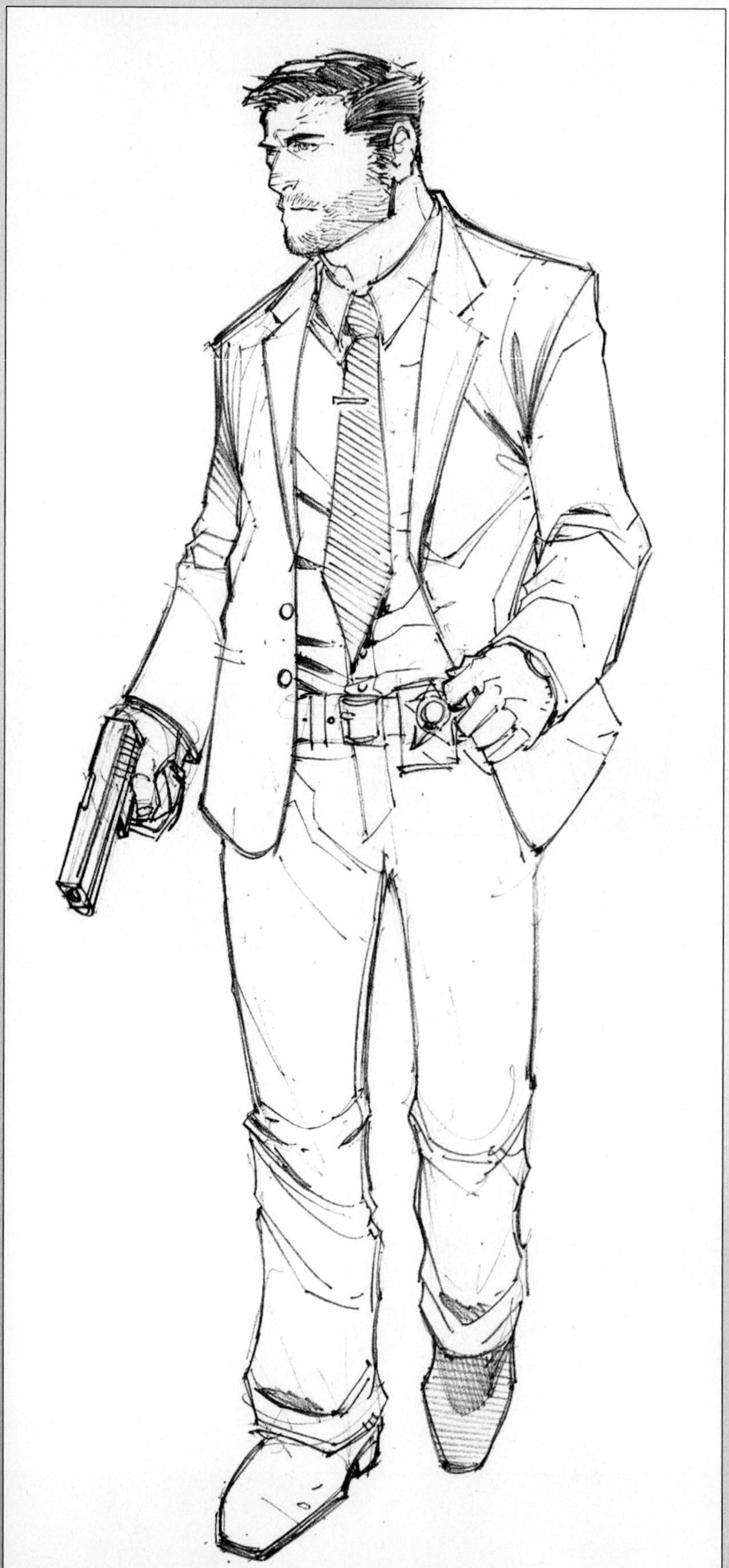

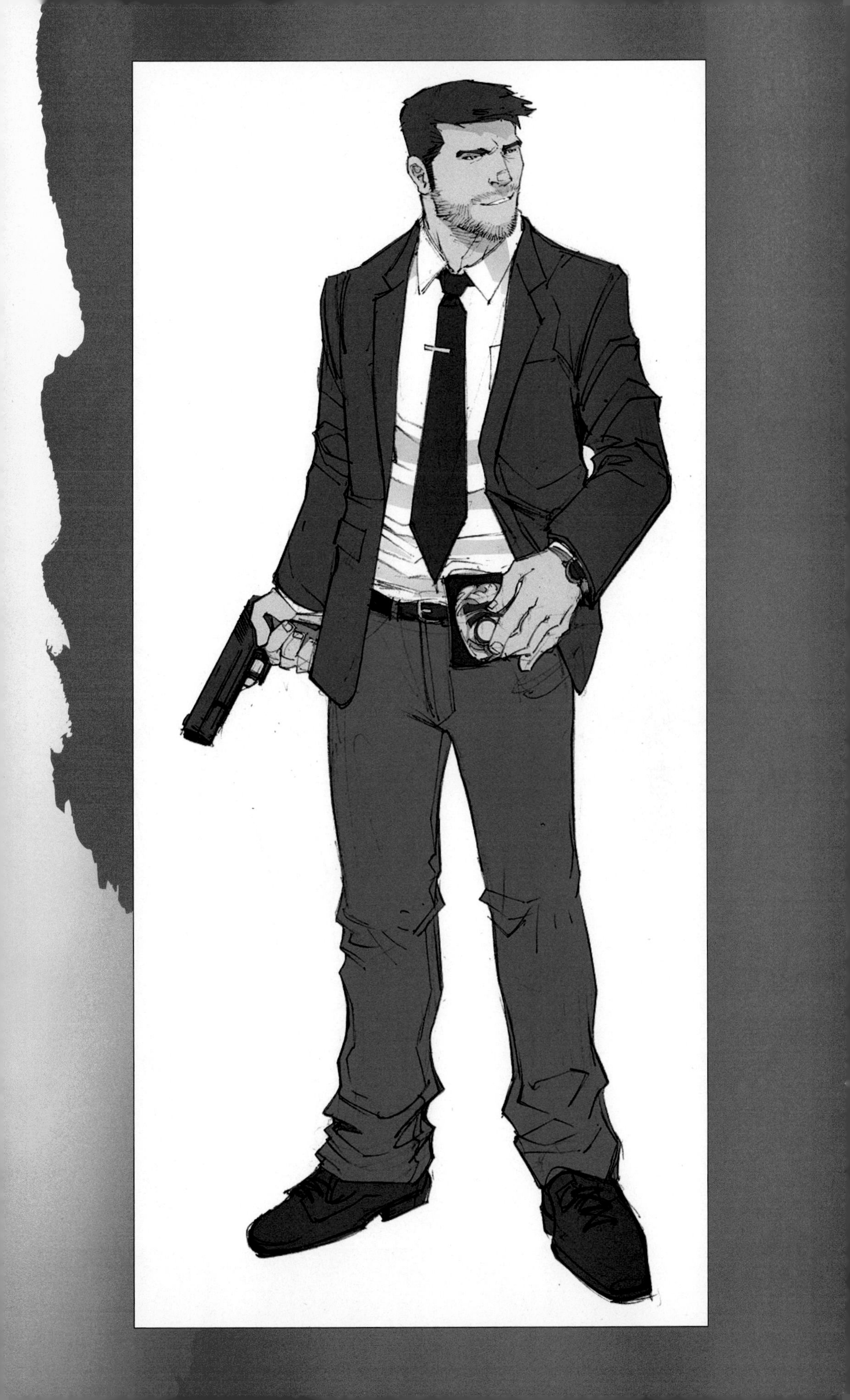

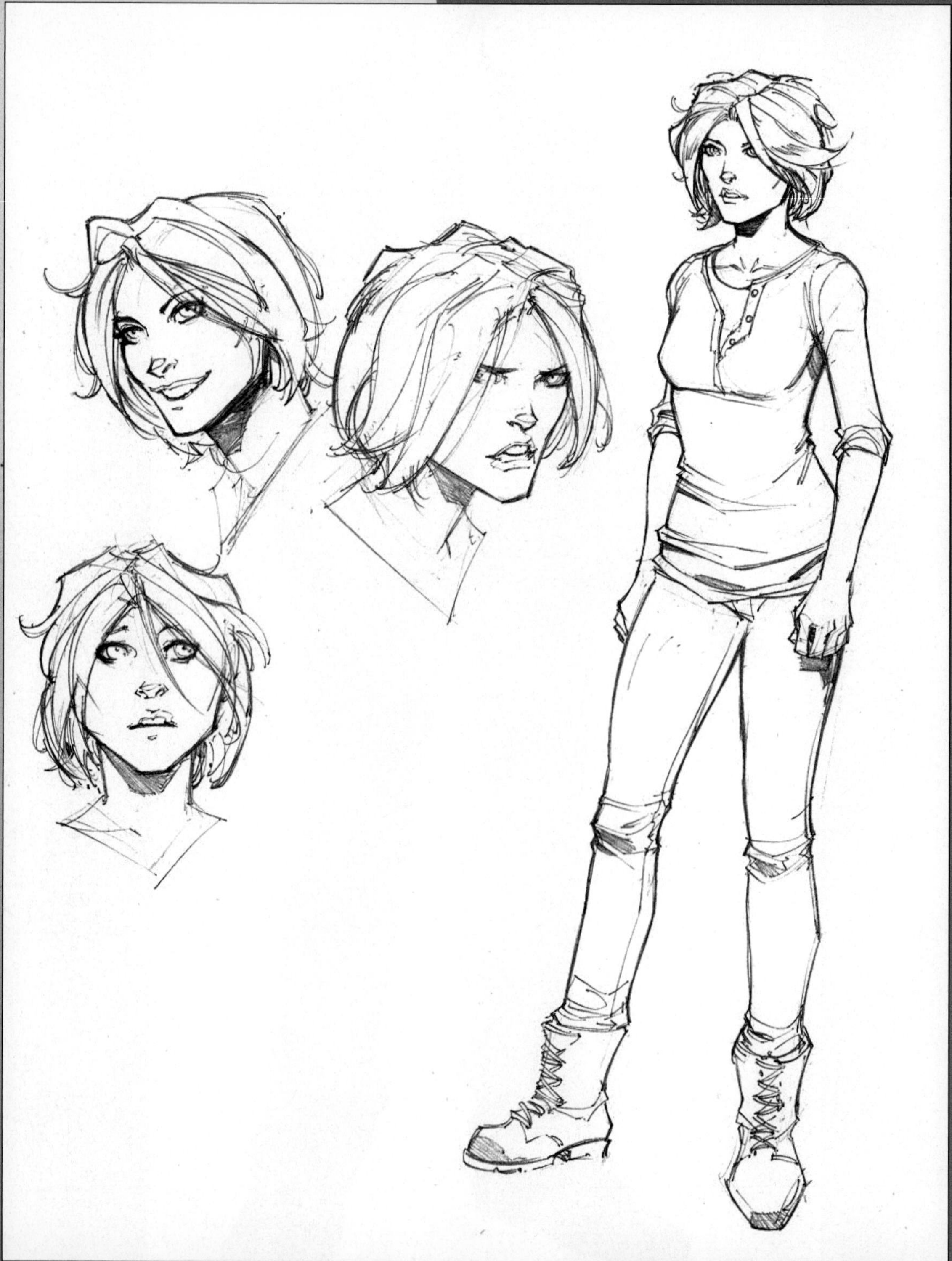

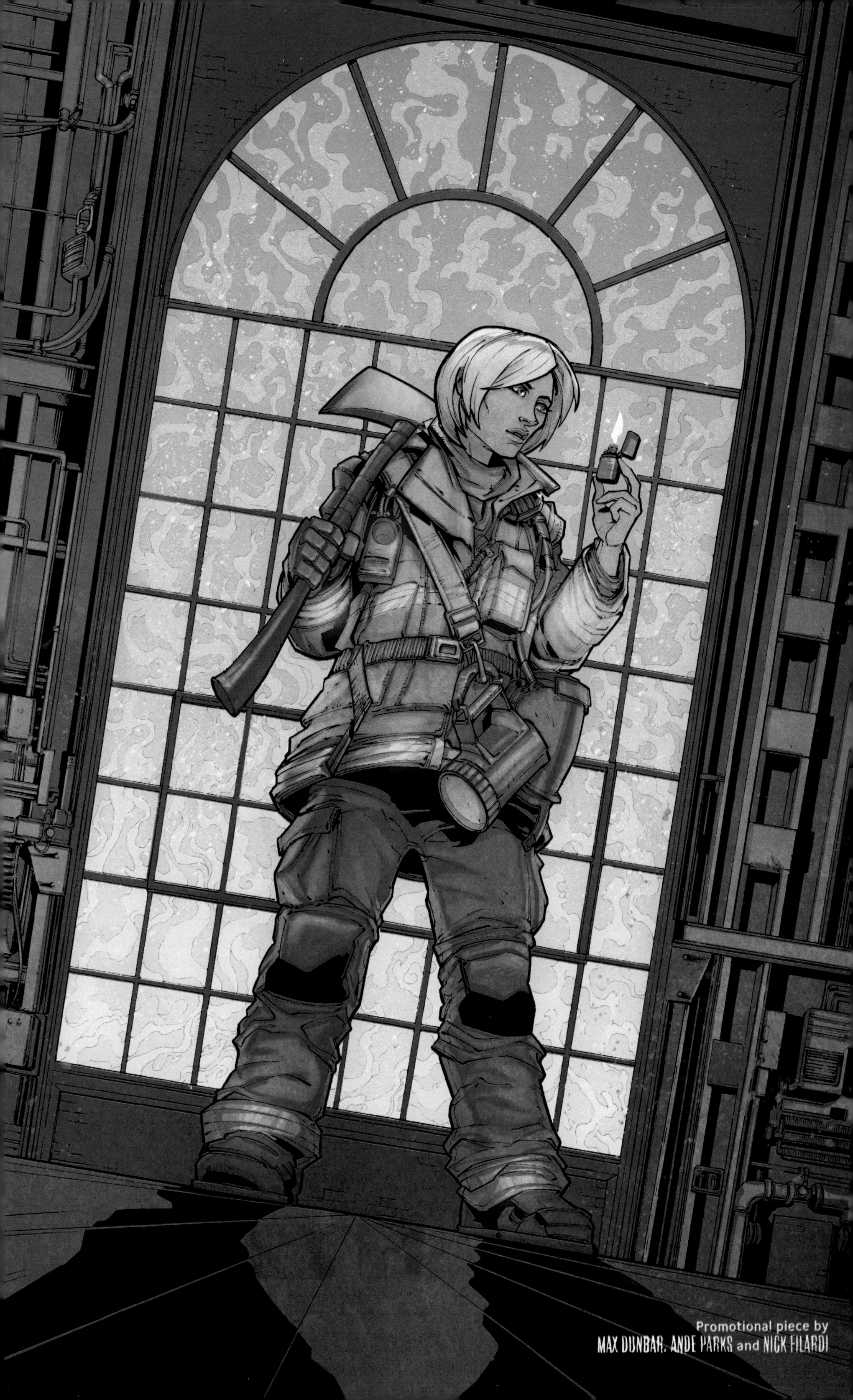

Promotional piece by
MAX DUNBAR, ANDE PARKS and NICK FILARDI